The FPGA Programming Handbook

Handbook

Second Edition

An essential guide to FPGA design for transforming ideas into hardware using SystemVerilog and VHDL

Frank Bruno

Guy Eschemann

The FPGA Programming Handbook

Second Edition

Copyright © 2024 Packt Publishing

Senior Publishing Product Manager: Rahul Nair

Acquisition Editor – Peer Reviews: Gaurav Gavas

Project Editor: Parvathy Nair

Content Development Editor: Shikha Parashar

Copy Editor: Safis Editing

Technical Editor: Karan Sonawane

Proofreader: Safis Editing

Indexer: Manju Arasan

Presentation Designer: Ganesh Bhadwalkar

Developer Relations Marketing Executive: Maran Fernandes

First published: March 2021

Second edition: April 2024

Production reference: 1220424

Published by Packt Publishing Ltd.

Grosvenor House

11 St Paul's Square

Birmingham

B3 1RB, UK.

ISBN: 978-1-80512-559-4

www.packt.com

In loving memory of Guy Eschemann, whose expertise and dedication significantly enriched this book. He generously served as both a technical reviewer and co-author, offering invaluable insights that guided us throughout the writing journey. His contributions will forever be cherished and reflected within these pages.

Contributors

About the authors

Frank Bruno is an experienced high-performance design engineer specializing in FPGAs and ASICs. He has over thirty years of experience working for companies such as SpaceX, GM Cruise, Belvedere Trading, and Allston Trading. He is currently working as an FPGA engineer for Belvedere Trading and is available for FPGA consulting. He is the author of *FPGA Programming for Beginners*, Packt 2022. In his limited spare time, he contributes to retro computing projects such as MiSTer and MiSTeX.

I'd like to thank my family for giving me the time to work on the book, my parents for being there to support my dreams of being an engineer, and Guy Eschemann for stepping up and helping with the VHDL portion of the book. I'd also like to thank my cats, my constant companions and adventure partners, for sitting by my side and making sure I took breaks from working.

Guy Eschemann was an electrical engineer with over twenty years of experience in designing FPGA-based embedded systems for automotive, industrial, medical, aerospace, military and telecom applications. He was working as an FPGA engineer at plc2 Design GmbH, and ran airhdl.com, a popular, web-based AXI4 register generator as a side business.

About the reviewers

Dr. Yang Yang Lee, graduated with a Bachelor (Hons) in Mechatronic Engineering and an MSc and PhD in Electrical and Electronic Engineering from the University of Science Malaysia and has over 10 years of experience in embedded systems. Research focuses on AI algorithms, AI hardware acceleration architecture, and FPGA hardware-software co-design. Other research interests include data analytics, embedded systems, machine vision and automation.

Join our community on Discord

Join our community's Discord space for discussions with the authors and other readers:

https://packt.link/embedded

Table of Contents

Chapter 3: Combinational Logic   59

Chapter 4: Counting Button Presses 105

Preface

Prepare yourself for some fun. I have been designing ASICs and FPGAs for over 30 years and every day brings new challenges and excitement as I push technology to develop new applications. Over the course of my career, I've developed ASICs that powered military aircrafts, graphics that ran on high-end workstations and mainstream PCs, technology to power the next generation of software-defined radios, supplied space-based internet to the globe, and worked on self-driving cars and high-frequency automated trading systems. I believe in paying it forward and I want to give some of my experience back to you.

Who this book is for

This book is for someone interested in learning about FPGA technology and how you might use it in your own projects. We assume that you know nothing about digital logic and start by introducing basic gates and their functions, and then eventually develop full systems. A little programming or hardware knowledge is helpful but not necessary. If you can install software, plug in a USB cable, and follow the projects you will learn a lot.

What this book covers

Chapter 1, Introduction to FPGA Architectures, explains what an ASIC and an FPGA are and gives some background on Boolean logic that will be the building blocks for your designs.

Chapter 2, FPGA Programming Languages and Tools, introduces **Hardware Description Language (HDL)** and Vivado/ Vitis. A sample design is introduced to showcase the flow and demonstrate the development of a testbench for verification.

Chapter 3, Combinational Logic, looks at writing a complete SystemVerilog module from scratch to perform some basic operations to show how to use combinational logic in your own designs. We'll also introduce testbenches and how to write one that self-checks.

Chapter 4, Counting Button Presses, builds upon the previous chapter's combination logic, adding storage—sequential elements. We'll learn about the capabilities of the Artix-7 and other FPGA devices to store data and design a simple project to count button presses. We'll also take a look at using clocks and synchronization, one of the few things that can break a design completely if not done correctly.

Chapter 5, Let's Build a Calculator, looks at how to create more complex design. Inevitably, you need to keep track of the design state. In this chapter, we'll learn about state machines and use a classic staple of engineering, the traffic light controller. We'll also enhance our calculator and show how we can design a divider using a state-based design.

Chapter 6, FPGA Resources and How to Use Them, takes a step back after having quickly dived into FPGA designs, examining some of the FPGA resources in more detail. To use these resources, we'll introduce some of the board resources, the PDM microphone and i2c temperature sensor attached to the FPGA and use them in projects.

Chapter 7, Math, Parallelism, and Pipelined Design, takes a deeper dive into fixed-point and floating-point numbers. We'll also look at pipelined designs and parallelism for performance.

Chapter 8, Introduction to AXI, covers how Xilinx has adopted the AXI standard to interface its IP and has developed a tool, IP integrator, to easily connect the IP graphically. In this chapter, we'll look at AXI by taking our temperature sensor and using the IP integrator to integrate the design.

Chapter 9, Lots of Data? MIG and DDR2, looks at how the Artix-7 provides a good amount of memory, but what happens if we need access to megabytes or gigabytes of temporary storage? Our board has DDR2 on it and in anticipation of implementing a display controller, we'll look at the Xilinx Memory Interface Generator to implement the DDR2 interface and test it in simulation and on the board.

Chapter 10, A Better Way to Display – VGA, looks at implementing a VGA and an easy way to display text. We've used LEDs and a seven-segment display to output information from our projects. This does limit us to what can be shown; for example, we can't display our captured audio data and text.

Chapter 11, Bringing It All Together, covers adding to our inputs. We've covered the output with VGA, but we'll add to our inputs by interfacing to the keyboard using PS/2. We'll take our temperature sensor and PDM microphone and create a project that uses the VGA to display this data.

Chapter 12, Using the PMOD Connectors – SPI and UART, will explore the PMOD connectors on the Nexys A7 board. By the end of this chapter, we will have created AXI reusable components for a **Universal Asynchronous Receiver-Transmitter (UART)** and a **Serial Peripheral Interface (SPI)** bus.

Chapter 13, Embedded Microcontrollers Using the Xilinx MicroBlaze, will introduce the Xilinx Microblaze processor, how to implement one using Vivado and how to develop software for it using Vitis.

Chapter 14, Advanced Topics, wraps things up by looking at some SystemVerilog concepts that I skipped over but you may still find them useful. We'll look at some of the more advanced verification constructs and finally look at some other gotchas and how to avoid them.

To get the most out of this book

Software/hardware covered in the book	OS requirements
Xilinx Vivado 2022.2	Windows 10/11 or Linux (RHEL 7 or 8, CentOS 7/8, SUSE LE 12.4, 15.2, Ubuntu 16.04, 18.04, 20,04, 22.04)
Nexys A7 100T Board	Windows 10/11 or Linux (RHEL 7 or 8, CentOS 7/8, SUSE LE 12.4, 15.2, Ubuntu 16.04, 18.04, 20,04, 22.04)

If you are using the digital version of this book, we advise you to type the code yourself or access the code via the GitHub repository (link available in the next section). Doing so will help you avoid any potential errors related to the copying and pasting of code.

Download the example code files

The code bundle for the book is also hosted on GitHub at https://github.com/PacktPublishing/The-FPGA-Programming-Handbook-Second-Edition. In case there's an update to the code, it will be updated on the existing GitHub repository.

We also have other code bundles from our rich catalog of books and videos available at https://github.com/PacktPublishing/. Check them out!

Download the color images

We also provide a PDF file that has color images of the screenshots/diagrams used in this book. You can download it here: https://packt.link/gbp/9781805125594

Conventions used

There are a number of text conventions used throughout this book.

`Code in text`: Indicates code words in text, database table names, folder names, filenames, file extensions, pathnames, dummy URLs, user input, and Twitter handles. Here is an example: "`adt7420_i2c_bd.v` provides the Verilog wrapper."

A block of code is set as follows:

```
always @(posedge CK) begin
  stage  = D;
  Q      = stage;
end
```

When we wish to draw your attention to a particular part of a code block, the relevant lines or items are set in bold:

```
module dff (input wire D, CK, output logic Q);
  initial Q = 1;
  always_ff @(posedge CK) Q <= D;
endmodule
```

Any command-line input or output is written as follows:

```
'timescale 1ps/100fs
```

Bold: Indicates a new term, an important word, or words that you see onscreen. For example, words in menus or dialog boxes appear in the text like this. Here is an example: "In the block design, right-click and select **Add Module**."

 Warnings or important notes appear like this.

 Tips and tricks appear like this.

Get in touch

Feedback from our readers is always welcome.

General feedback: If you have questions about any aspect of this book, mention the book title in the subject of your message and email us at customercare@packtpub.com.

Errata: Although we have taken every care to ensure the accuracy of our content, mistakes do happen. If you have found a mistake in this book, we would be grateful if you would report this to us. Please visit www.packtpub.com/support/errata, selecting your book, clicking on the Errata Submission Form link, and entering the details.

Piracy: If you come across any illegal copies of our works in any form on the Internet, we would be grateful if you would provide us with the location address or website name. Please contact us at copyright@packt.com with a link to the material.

If you are interested in becoming an author: If there is a topic that you have expertise in and you are interested in either writing or contributing to a book, please visit authors.packtpub.com.

Share your thoughts

Once you've read *The FPGA Programming Handbook - Second Edition*, we'd love to hear your thoughts! Scan the QR code below to go straight to the Amazon review page for this book and share your feedback.

https://packt.link/r/1805125591

Your review is important to us and the tech community and will help us make sure we're delivering excellent quality content.

Download a free PDF copy of this book

Thanks for purchasing this book!

Do you like to read on the go but are unable to carry your print books everywhere?

Is your eBook purchase not compatible with the device of your choice?

Don't worry, now with every Packt book you get a DRM-free PDF version of that book at no cost.

Read anywhere, any place, on any device. Search, copy, and paste code from your favorite technical books directly into your application.

The perks don't stop there, you can get exclusive access to discounts, newsletters, and great free content in your inbox daily.

Follow these simple steps to get the benefits:

1. Scan the QR code or visit the link below:

https://packt.link/free-ebook/9781805125594

2. Submit your proof of purchase.
3. That's it! We'll send your free PDF and other benefits to your email directly.

1

Introduction to FPGA Architectures

Whether you want to accelerate mathematically complex operations such as machine learning or artificial intelligence, or simply want to do some projects for fun, such as retro computing or reproducing obsolete video game machines (`https://github.com/MiSTer-devel/Main_MiSTer/wiki`), this book will jumpstart your journey. There couldn't be a better time to get into this field than the present, even if only as a hobby. Development boards are cheap and plentiful, and vendors have started making their tools available for free because of their low-cost, smaller parts.

In this book, we are going to build some example designs to introduce you to FPGA development, culminating in a CPU-based project that can drive a **Video Graphics Array (VGA)** monitor. Along the way, we'll interface with **Double Data Rate (DDR)** memory, temperature sensors, microphones, speakers, and serial ports, often referred to as **Universal Asynchronous Receivers/Transmitters (UARTs)**.

In the this chapter, we will be exploring **Field Programmable Gate Arrays (FPGAs)** and the underlying technology that creates them. This underlying technology allows companies such as AMD (formerly Xilinx) to produce a reprogrammable chip from an **Application-Specific Integrated Circuit (ASIC)** process. By the end of this chapter, you should have a good understanding of an FPGA and its components, having covered the following topics:

- What is an ASIC?
- Introducing FPGAs
- Evaluation boards

Technical requirements

This chapter is an optional overview chapter and doesn't have any technical requirements. We will look at the underlying FPGA and ASIC technology and primitive logic gates in this chapter. If you are already comfortable with this information, please feel free to use this as a reference and jump ahead to *Chapter 2, FPGA Programming Languages and Tools*.

What is an ASIC?

ASICs are the fundamental building blocks of modern electronics – your laptop or PC, TV, cell phone, digital watch, almost everything you use on a day-to-day basis. It is also the fundamental building block upon which the FPGA we will be looking at is built. In short, an ASIC is a custom-built chip designed using the same language and methods we will be introducing in this book.

 Note: This section is for reference and an introduction to basic digital electronics. ASICs and FPGAs are both developed using similar **Hardware Descriptive Language (HDL)** coding methods. This opens up additional career opportunities for someone with this knowledge.

FPGAs came about as the technology to create ASICs followed Moore's law (*Gordon E. Moore, Cramming More Components Onto Integrated Circuits, Electronics, Volume 38, Number 8,* https://archive.computerhistory.org/resources/access/text/2017/03/102770822-05-01-acc.pdf) – the idea that the number of transistors on a chip doubles every 2 years. This has both allowed for very cheap electronics, in the case of mass-produced items containing ASICs, and led to the proliferation of lower-cost FPGAs.

The first commercial FPGA was introduced by Xilinx in 1985, the XC2064. This part is only slightly larger than the **Combination Logic Block (CLB)**s we'll look at later, but at the time, it was revolutionary. Prior to this, the only programmable logic was based on **Erasable Programmable Memory (EPROM)** arrays to implement small logic functions, sometimes with storage elements included on the chip. This was long before HDL languages were used to program the devices and they were often configured with a much simpler syntaxed language.

FPGAs are an ASIC at heart. Xilinx has used an ASIC process to create a reconfigurable chip. However, we must consider the trade-offs in choosing an FPGA or ASIC.

Why an ASIC or FPGA?

ASICs can be an inexpensive part when manufactured in high volumes. You can buy a disposable calculator, a flash drive for pennies/cents per gigabyte, or an inexpensive cell phone; they are all powered by at least one ASIC. ASICs are also sometimes a necessity when speed is of the utmost importance, or the amount of logic that is needed is very large. However, in these cases, they are typically only used when cost is not a factor.

We can break down the costs of developing a product based on an ASIC or FPGA into **Non-Recurring Engineering** (**NRE**), the one-time cost to develop a chip, and the piece price for every chip, excluding NRE. Ed Sperling stated the following in *CEO Outlook: It Gets Much Harder From Here, Semiconductor Engineering, June 3, 2019*, https://semiengineering.com/ceo-outlook-the-easy-stuff-is-over/: "*The NRE for a 7nm chip is $25 million to $30 million, including mask set and labor.*"

These costs are a necessity to build a chip and the main reason why ASICs, especially very advanced ones, are very expensive to produce. They include more than just the mask sets, the blueprint for the ASIC, if you will, that is used to deposit the materials on the silicon wafers that build the chip. These costs also include the salaries for teams of design, implementation, and verification engineers that can number into the hundreds. Re-spins, or bug fixes, are usually factored into ASIC costs because large, complex devices struggle with first-time success.

Compare this to an FPGA, where complex chips can be developed by a single person or small teams. Most of the NRE has been shouldered by the FPGA vendor in the design of the FPGA chips, which are known good quantities. The little NRE expense left is for tools and engineering. Re-spins are free, except for time, since the chip can be reprogrammed using flash memory, without million-dollar mask sets.

The trade-off is the per-part cost. High-volume ASICs with low complexity, like the one inside a pocket calculator or a digital watch, can cost pennies. CPUs can run into the hundreds or thousands of dollars. Compare that to FPGAs where even the most inexpensive Spartan-7 starts at a few dollars, and the largest and fastest can stretch into tens of thousands of dollars.

Another factor is tool costs. As we will see in *Chapter 2, FPGA Programming Languages and Tools*, AMD provides the Xilinx Vivado tool suite for free for the smaller parts. Other FPGA vendors, such as Intel (formerly Altera), also offer free versions for lower-end parts. This speeds up adoption, where the barrier to entry is now a computer and a development board. Even the cost of developing more expensive parts is only a few thousand dollars if you need to purchase a professional copy of Vivado for AMD or Quartus for Intel. In contrast, ASIC tools can run into millions of dollars and require years of training since the risk of failure is extremely high. As we will see in our projects, we'll make mistakes, sometimes to demonstrate a concept, but the cost to fix it will only be a few minutes, mostly spent on understanding why it actually failed.

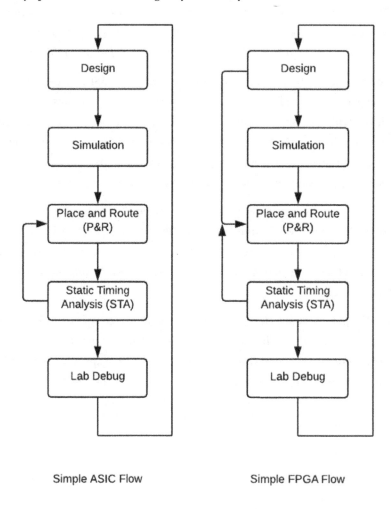

Figure 1.1: Simple ASIC versus FPGA flow

The flow for an ASIC or FPGA is essentially the same as shown above in *Figure 1.1*. ASIC flows tend to be more linear in that you have one chance to make a working part. With an FPGA, things such as simulation can become an option, although strongly suggested for complex designs. One difference is that the lab debug stage can also act as a form of simulation by using **ChipScope**, or similar on-chip debugging techniques, to monitor internal signals for debugging. The main difference is that each iteration through the steps costs only time in an FPGA flow. In this situation, any changes to a fabricated ASIC design would require some number of new mask sets, the costs of which could run into the millions of dollars.

We summarize the choice between an ASIC and FPGA in *Table 1.1* below:

FPGA	ASIC
Mostly reprogrammable	Limited or no programmability
Very high piece price	Extremely low to high piece price, usually based on volumes
Very low NRE	Very high NRE
Low tool cost	Very high tool cost
Easy to debug in lab/high visibility into design	Usually limited ability to view internal states

Table 1.1: FPGA versus ASIC summary

We've briefly looked at what an ASIC is and why we might choose an ASIC or an FPGA for a given application. Now, let's look at how an FPGA is created using an ASIC process.

How does a company create a programmable device using an ASIC process?

The basis of any ASIC technology is the transistor, with the largest devices made up of billions of transistors. Multiple ASIC processes have been developed over the years, and they all rely on transistors, which can be on or off, represented as 1s and 0s. These can be thought of as Booleans, true or false values.

The basis of Boolean algebra was developed by George Bool in 1847. The fundamentals of Boolean algebra make up the basis of the logic gates upon which all digital logic is formed. The code that we will be writing is at a high level of abstraction from the actual hardware implementation and the tools will convert our design into a physical implementation. It is important to understand the basics and will give us a good springboard for a first project. Thousands of engineers have struggled to build efficient logic by hand in the past using individual ICs on a breadboard. I want to get you past that with a minimum of fuss since modern tools are very good at what they do.

An FPGA company, such as AMD or Intel, develops an FPGA by creating configurable structures that can be loaded at the initialization of the device or modified during runtime. The same techniques we will talk about here are used to design blocks that are then synthesized directly into transistors rather than mapped to lookup tables and routing resources. The interesting thing about the fact that the same design techniques are used for FPGAs and ASICs is that many ASICs are prototyped on FPGAs to minimize logic errors and re-spins.

We'll need to know a little **Hardware Description Language (HDL)** such as **Very High Speed Integrated Circuit HDL (VHDL)** or **SystemVerilog** to go through this section.

Introduction to HDLs

We'll need to define some terminology for discussing HDLs.

Logical versus bitwise operations

Logical functions operate on Boolean values. A Boolean is an object that can hold one of two values: true or false for VHDL, and 1 or 0 for SystemVerilog/Verilog. SystemVerilog/Verilog has no concept of true and false. Note that this can be viewed as an advantage of SystemVerilog as it behaves like hardware in that there is no difference between a 1 and true or 0 and false when you implement hardware. VHDL proponents view the strong typing of VHDL as an important feature since it clarifies intent by forcing the correct types to be used.

A bitwise function operates on a 1 or 0 (or as we will discuss later in the book, other values representing unknown, tri-state or different drive strengths). Both VHDL and SystemVerilog/Verilog have objects that hold these values and are operated on in a bitwise function. We will dive deeper into this in *Chapter 3*, *Combinational Logic*, but we'll be using if statements in some of the examples below to demonstrate the logic gates.

Bitwise functions also have the ability to act as reduction operators in SystemVerilog/Verilog and there are similar functions in VHDL. These will be discussed in *Chapter 2*, *FPGA Programming Languages and Tools*.

 In this section, we are primarily discussing logical functions. In SystemVerilog and Verilog, logical and bitwise functions can be intermixed as they are weakly typed languages. VHDL is strongly typed and you will run into problems mixing them up. This will be discussed further in *Chapter 3*.

Armed with this knowledge, let's dip our toes into some HDL code.

Creating gates using HDL

In this section, we'll take a look at some basic HDL code that will allow us to demonstrate the gates that underlie all digital designs. We need a way of inferring these operations and we'll start by looking at signal assignments.

Assign statement (SystemVerilog/Verilog)

We can use an `assign` statement to take whatever value is on the **right-hand side** (**RHS**) of the equal sign to the **left-hand side** (**LHS**). Its usage is as follows:

```
assign out = in;
```

`in` can be another signal, function, or operation on multiple signals. `out` can be any valid signal declared prior to the `assign` statement. The above code simply acts like a wire.

Assign statement equivalent (VHDL)

In VHDL, a signal can be assigned as follows:

```
output <= input;
```

Similar to SystemVerilog/Verilog, whatever is on the RHS will be assigned to the LHS.

 in and out are reserved words used for port directions in VHDL. input and output are reserved words used for port direction in SystemVerilog, hence the signal name changes between language examples.

Single line comments

SystemVerilog and VHDL both provide a method for creating a comment on a single line. The comment runs from the comment character, which is // for SystemVerilog or – for VHDL, until the end of the line:

```
// Everything here is a comment. (SystemVerilog)
-- Everything here is a comment. (VHDL)
```

Multiline comments

Both SystemVerilog and Verilog share the same type of multiline comments, based upon the C style of comment. Block comments have also been supported in VHDL since 2008:

```
/*
   I can span    Multiple    Lines
*/
```

Prior to VHDL-2008, VHDL only supported single line comments (–).

if statement

Both SystemVerilog/Verilog and VHDL provide a way of testing conditions via the `if` statement. The basic syntax is as follows:

```
if (condition) …; // SystemVerilog/ Verilog
if condition then ... end if; // VHDL
```

The `if` statement will be used throughout the book and there are some nuances that we will discuss in more detail in *Chapter 3, Combinational Logic*.

With the terminology out of the way, let's look at Boolean logic gates used Boolean operations.

Fundamental logic gates

There are four basic logic gates. These gates are necessary for anything from simple control logic to complex arithemetic and processing algorithms. AI is all the rage at the time of authoring this book and the heart of every AI system boils down to these simple structures.

We typically write the truth tables for the gates to understand their functionality. A truth table shows us what the output is for every set of inputs to a circuit. Refer to the following example involving a NOT gate.

Logical NOT

The output of the NOT gate produces the opposite value of a signal going in. It's often called an inverter since it inverts the value. The function in SystemVerilog can be written as follows:

```
assign out = !in; // logical NOT Boolean operator
```

In VHDL, we would write:

```
out <= not in; // Boolean operator
```

The associated truth table is as follows:

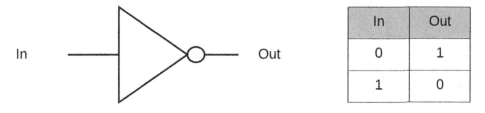

In	Out
0	1
1	0

Graphical Representation   Truth Table

Figure 1.2: NOT gate representation

The NOT gate is one of the most common operators we will be using:

```
if (!empty) ... // SystemVerilog/Verilog
if not empty then .- -- VHDL
```

Often, we need to test a signal before performing an operation. For example, if we are using a **First In, First Out (FIFO)** storage to smooth out sporadic data or for crossing clock domains, we'll need to test whether there is data available before *popping* it out for use. FIFOs have flags used for flow control, the two most common being full and empty. We can do this by testing the empty flag, as shown here.

We will go into greater depth in later chapters on how to design a FIFO as well as use one.

Logical AND

Often, we will want to test whether one or more conditions are active at the same time. To do this, we will be using the **AND** gate. An AND gate tests two or more inputs to determine if all of them are set. If any input is a 0, the AND gate will return a 0. If all of them are set, it will return a 1.

The function in SystemVerilog/Verilog can be written as follows:

```
assign out = in1 && in0; // Logical AND Boolean operator
```

The function in VHDL can be written as follows:

```
out <= in1 and in0; -- Logical AND Boolean operator
```

The associated truth table is as follows:

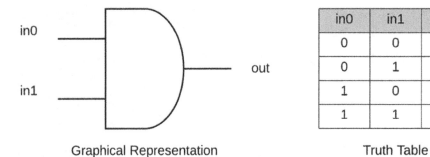

in0	in1	out
0	0	0
0	1	0
1	0	0
1	1	1

Graphical Representation   Truth Table

Figure 1.3: AND gate representation

Continuing our FIFO example, you might be popping from one FIFO and pushing into another:

```
if (!src_fifo_empty && !dst_fifo_full) ... // SV/ Verilog
if (not src_fifo_empty) and (not dst_fifo_full) then .- -- VHDL
```

In this case, you want to make sure that both the source FIFO has data (i.e., is not empty) and that the destination is not full. We can accomplish this by testing it via the if statement.

Logical OR

Another common occurrence is to check whether any one signal out of a group is set to perform an operation. An **OR** gate tests two or more inputs to determine if any of them are set to a 1. If any input is a 1, then the output will be a 1. If all inputs are 0, then the output is a 0.

The function in **SystemVerilog/Verilog** can be written as follows:

```
assign out = in1 || in0; // logical Boolean operator
```

The function in **VHDL** can be written as follows:

```
out <= in1 or in0; // logical Boolean operator
```

The associated truth table is as follows:

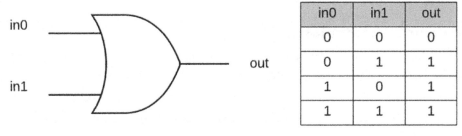

in0	in1	out
0	0	0
0	1	1
1	0	1
1	1	1

Graphical Representation   Truth Table

Figure 1.4: OR gate representation

Next, we will look at the exclusive OR function.

XOR

The **exclusive OR (XOR)** function checks whether either one of two inputs is set, but not both. XOR functions test whether an odd number of inputs are set to a 1 if you have more than two inputs.

The function in **SystemVerilog/Verilog** can be written as follows:

```
assign out = in1 ^ in0; // XOR Boolean operator
```

The function in **VHDL** can be written as follows:

```
out <= in1 xor in0; -- XOR Boolean operator
```

The associated truth table is as follows:

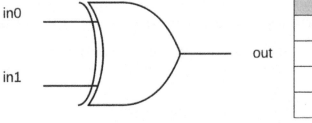

in0	in1	out
0	0	0
0	1	1
1	0	1
1	1	0

Graphical Representation   Truth Table

Figure 1.5: XOR gate representation

This function is used in building adders, parity, and error-checking and correcting code. In the next section, we'll look at how an adder is built using the preceding gates.

More complex operations

We've seen the basic building blocks in the previous sections that make up every digital design. Here, we'll look at an example of how we can put together multiple logic gates to perform work. For this, we will introduce the concept of a full adder. A full adder takes three inputs, **A**, **B**, and **carry in** (**Cin**), and produces two outputs, **Sum** and **Carry out** (**Cout**). Let's look at the truth table of a full adder.

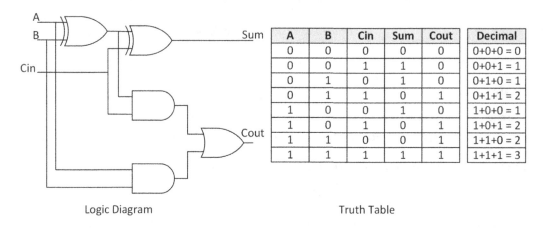

A	B	Cin	Sum	Cout	Decimal
0	0	0	0	0	0+0+0 = 0
0	0	1	1	0	0+0+1 = 1
0	1	0	1	0	0+1+0 = 1
0	1	1	0	1	0+1+1 = 2
1	0	0	1	0	1+0+0 = 1
1	0	1	0	1	1+0+1 = 2
1	1	0	0	1	1+1+0 = 2
1	1	1	1	1	1+1+1 = 3

Logic Diagram   Truth Table

Figure 1.6: Full adder

Algebraically, a full adder represents A + B + Cin. Each input is a single bit, so the output could be 0, 1, or 2 in decimal. Since we can only represent 0 and 1 in a single bit, if the addition produces a result of 2, that represents a carry out. The carry out would propagate into the next bit. This cascading of full adders is called a ripple carry adder, since they carry ripples from one cell to the next.

The **SystemVerilog/ Verilog** for the full adder written as Boolean logic would be as follows:

```
assign Sum = A ^ B ^ Cin;
assign Cout = A & B | (A ^ B) & Cin;
```

You'll notice that we are using the bitwise operators for AND (&) and OR (|) since we are operating on bits. These are equivalent to the logical operators AND (&&) and OR (||). This is true for SystemVerilog/Verilog, but not in VHDL.

The **VHDL** code for the full adder written as Boolean logic would be as follows:

```
Sum <= A xor B xor Cin;
Cout <= (A and B) or ((A xor B) and Cin);
```

From this straightforward yet important example, you can see how real-world functionality can be built from these basic building blocks. All the circuits in an ASIC or FPGA are built this way, but luckily, you don't need to dive into this level of detail unless you want to thanks to the proliferation of HDLs such as **SystemVerilog/Verilog** and **VHDL**.

With this basic understanding of gates and logic under our belts, we can look at FPGAs.

Introducing FPGAs

A gate array in ASIC terms is a sea of gates with some number of mask steps that can be configured for a given application. This allows for a more inexpensive product since the company designing the ASIC only needs to pay for the masks necessary for configuring. The FPGA takes this one step further by providing the programmability of the fabric as part of the device. This results in an increased cost as you are paying for the interconnect you are not using and the storage devices necessary to configure the FPGA fabric but allows for cost reductions as these parts become standard devices that can be mass produced.

If we look at the functions in the previous section through the adder example, we can see one commonality; they can all be produced using a truth table. This becomes key in FPGA development. We can regard these truth tables as **Read-Only Memory (ROM)** representations of the functions. In fact, we can regard them as **Programmable ROMs (PROMs)** in the case of building up our FPGA.

If you look at the truth table for the full adder, you can see that there are three inputs and two outputs. If we look at the inputs as an address, then we could use storage to look up the data stored at that location and use it as an output. A ROM can be very tiny since it is hardcoded to look up certain values. A PROM uses some storage elements that can be changed to implement new functions, which is closer to what we will use in the FPGA.

Let's take the example of the fundamental logic functions. We can reproduce any of them by utilizing a two-input lookup table, which could look something like this:

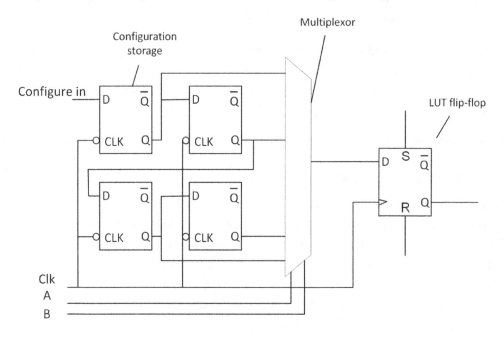

Figure 1.7: Two-input LUT examples

In *Figure 1.7*, we can see an oversimplified example with four storage elements, in this case, flip-flops (configuration storage), but in the case of an actual FPGA, we would more likely have a much simpler structure utilizing far fewer transistors. We will discuss storage elements in *Chapter 4, Counting Button Presses*. The storage elements are connected to one another such that their configuration can be loaded. By attaching other **Lookup Tables (LUTs)** to the chain, multiple LUTs can be configured at startup or, in the case of partial reconfiguration, during normal operation.

We have a component called a MUX, or multiplexor, that acts as the address lookup by selecting the storage element pointed to by the address made up of inputs A and B. This gives us the value at that location. If you look back at our two input gates, you should be able to see that we can map any two-input gate to this structure. By adding a flip-flop, we can see the final structure of the LUT takes shape.

The power of the simplicity of the structure is the ability to replicate this design many times over. In the case of modern FPGAs, they are built of many tiles or columns of logic such as this, allowing a much simpler piece to be designed, implemented, verified, and then replicated to produce the large gate count devices available. This allows for a range of lower-cost devices with fewer columns of resources to larger devices with many more, some even using **Stacked Silicon Interconnects (SSIs)**, which allows multiple ASIC dies to be attached via an interconnect substrate.

In 1985, Xilinx introduced the XC2064, which was what we would consider the first FPGA utilizing an array of 64 three-input LUTs with one flip-flop. The breakthrough with this design was that it was modular and had good interconnect resources. This entire part would be approximately equivalent to one **CLB** in the Artix-7 we will be targeting.

The combinational logic blocks would be useless if we didn't have a way for them to communicate with each other. This is where programmable interconnect gets involved. The FPGA fabric consists of LUTs with associated flip-flops making up slices and, ultimately, CLBs. These blocks are all connected using a rich topology of routing channels, allowing for almost limitless configuration. FPGAs also contain many other resources that we will explore over the course of this book, block RAMs, **Serial-Deserial (SERDES)** cores, **Digital Signal Processing (DSP)** elements, and many types of programmable **Input/Output (I/O)**.

We've seen the theory of a simple device, but this isn't really that useful today. Next, we will look at the FPGAs, which, although a few years old, are still great devices to choose for hobbyists and low-cost designs.

Exploring the Xilinx Artix-7 and 7 series devices

The FPGA we will be looking at in this book is an Artix-7 device. These devices have the highest performance per watt of the Xilinx 7 series devices. For a reasonable price, they feature a large amount of relatively high-performance logic to implement your designs. The FPGA components we will introduce here are common in the Artix (low-end), Kintex (mid-range), and Virtex (high-end) parts in the 7 series.

Combinational logic blocks

ASICs are made up of logic gates based upon libraries provided by ASIC foundries, such as Taiwan Semiconductor Manufacturing Company and Tower Semiconductor. These libraries can contain everything from AND, OR, and NOT gates to more complicated math cells and storage elements. When developing an FPGA, you will be targeting the same Boolean logic equations as you would in an ASIC. We will be using a very similar flow. However, the synthesis process will target the CLBs of the FPGA:

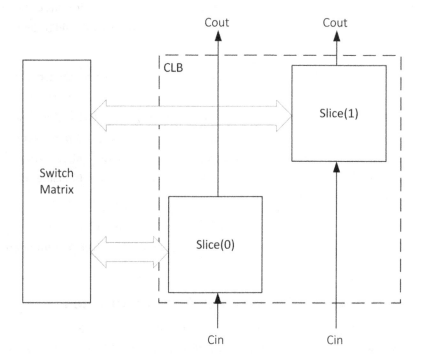

Figure 1.8: CLB internals

A CLB consists of a pair of slices, each of which contains four six-input **LUT**s and their eight flip-flops. Vivado (or optionally a third-party synthesis tool such as Synopsys Synplify) compiles the **SystemVerilog/Verilog** or **VHDL** code and maps it to these CLB elements. To fully explore the details of the CLB, I would suggest reading the Xilinx UG474, 7 Series FPGAs CLB user guide (https://www.xilinx.com/support/documentation/user_guides/ug474_7Series_CLB.pdf). At a high level, each LUT allows a degree of flexibility such that any Boolean function with six inputs can be implemented or two arbitrarily defined five-input functions if they share common inputs. There is also dedicated high speed carry logic for arithmetic functions, which will be discussed in later chapters.

The slices come in two formats, **SLICEL (L = logic)**, which can only implement logic functions and storage elements, and **SLICEM (M = memory)**, which additionally can be reconfigured for use as a small memory element (distributed RAM) or a shift register. There are approximately three times the number of SLICELs as SLICEMs. The following table, for the one suggested development board for this book, shows the breakdown:

Board	Device	Slices	SLICEL	SLICEM	6-Input LUTs	Distributed RAM (Kb)	Shift Register (Kb)	Flip-Flops
Nexys A7	7A100T	15,850	11,100	4,750	63,400	1,188	594	126,800

Table 1.2: Nexys A7 FPGA resources

Although it is possible to instantiate and force the functionality of lower-level components, such as slices or LUTs, this is beyond the scope of this book, and a feature not widely used. We will be targeting CLB usage through the synthesis of the HDL that we write.

Storage

Aside from the SLICEMs that make up the CLBs that can be used as memories or shift registers, FPGAs contain **Block RAMs (BRAMs)** that are larger storage elements. The 7 series parts all have a 36 Kb BRAM that can be split into two 18 Kb BRAMs. The recommended development board, the Nexys A7 with the 100T part has 135 BRAMs, 36Kb each.

 In normal computer parlance, Kb is kilobits, while KB is kilobytes – lowercase b for bits, and uppercase B for bytes.

BRAMs can be configured as follows:

- True dual port memories – Two read/write ports.
- Simple dual port memories – 1 read/1 write. In this case, a 36-Kb BRAM can be up to 72 bits wide and an 18-Kb BRAM up to 36 bits wide.
- A single port.

The contents of BRAMs can be loaded at initialization and configured via a file or initial block in the code. This can be useful for implementing ROMs or start-up conditions.

BRAMs in 7 series devices also contain logic to implement FIFOs. This saves CLB resources and reduces synthesis overhead and potential timing problems in a design. We will go over FIFOs in a later chapter.

All 36-Kb BRAMs have dedicated **Error Correction Code** (**ECC**) functions. As this is something more related to high-reliability applications, such as medical-, automotive-, or space-based, we will not go into detail on it in this book.

Clocking

7 series devices implement a rich clocking methodology, which can be explored in detail in the UG472 7 series FPGAs clocking resources user guide (`https://www.xilinx.com/support/documentation/user_guides/ug472_7Series_Clocking.pdf`). For most purposes, our discussion in the **Phase Locked Loop** (**PLL**) section will give you everything you need to know; however, the referenced document will delve into far more detail.

I/Os

For the most part, we will limit ourselves to the I/Os supported by the two targeted development boards. In general, the 7 series devices handle a variety of interfaces from 3.3v CMOS/TTL to LVDS and memory interface types. The boards we are using will dictate the I/Os defined in our project files. For more information on all the supported types, you can reference the UG471 7 Series FPGAs **SelectIO** resources user guide.

DSP48E1 – Xilinx DSP core in 7 series devices

FPGAs have a large footprint in DSP applications that use a lot of multipliers and, more specifically, **Multiply Accumulate** (**MAC**) functions. One of the first innovations in FPGAs was to include hard multipliers, which were quickly replaced by DSP blocks that could implement MAC functions. *Figure 1.9* shows the implementation of the DSP48E1 implemented in the Artix-7.

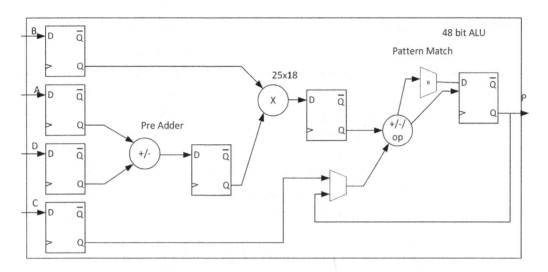

Figure 1.9: Xilinx UG479 7 series DSP48E1

One of the most expensive operations in an FPGA is arithmetic. In an ASIC, the largest and slowest operation is typically a multiplication operation, and the smaller or faster operation is an add operation. For this reason, for many years, FPGA manufacturers have been implementing hard arithmetic cores in their fabric. This makes the opposite true in an FPGA, where the slower operation is typically an adder, especially as the widths get larger. The reason for this is that the multiply has been hardened into a complex, pipelined operation. We will explore the DSP operator more in later chapters. The UG479 7 Series **DSP48E1** user guide (https://www.xilinx.com/support/documentation/user_guides/ug479_7Series_DSP48E1.pdf) is a good reference if you are interested in delving into the details.

ASMBL architecture

The 7 series devices are the fourth generation where Xilinx has used the **Advanced Silicon Modular Block (ASMBL)** architecture for implementation purposes. The idea behind this is to enable FPGA platforms to be optimized for different target applications. Looking at the 7 series families, we can see how different configurations of slices are brought together to achieve these goals. We can see how the pieces we covered in this chapter are arranged as columns to give us the resources we will be using for our example projects ahead. *Figure 1.10* below shows the internal configuration of the FPGA, which is built by implementing vertical columns of different element types. From the point of view of the FGPA vendor, this simplifies the design and testing of new devices by simply adding more columns, or expanding columns vertically to make larger devices.

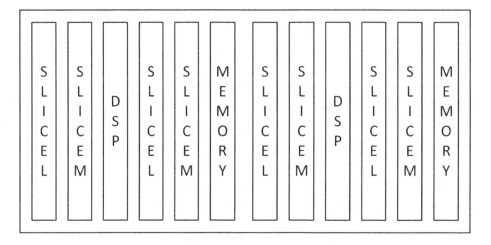

Figure 1.10: Example FPGA internal layout based upon ASMBL

Now that we have looked at what makes up the Artix-7 and other 7 series devices, we need to get the Xilinx tools installed so that we can get to our first project.

We've looked at FPGAs and the specific FPGA we will target in the book. Now let's look at the evaluation board that we will target in the book.

Evaluation boards

There is no shortage of FPGA evaluation boards available for us to purchase. One company that makes very affordable boards is Digilent. There are several nice features that its boards tend to include, but one of the best is that they have a built-in USB-to-UART controller that Xilinx Vivado recognizes as a programming cable. This makes configuring the device painless. The recommended boards also have the added advantage of being powered over this same USB cable.

The Nexys A7 is the recommended board for this book. It has all the devices we'll target over the course of the book.

Nexys A7 100T (or 50T)

Figure 1.11 below is a picture of the Nexys A7 board. There are two variants of the board at the time of writing, the 100T variant and the 50T variant. The difference is only the size of the device installed on the board.

Figure 1.11: Digilent Nexys A7 board

The board features are as follows:

- Artix-7 XC7A100T or 50T
- 450+ MHz operation
- 128 MB DDR2
- Serial flash

- Built-in USB UART for downloading images and ChipScope debugging
- MicroSD card reader
- 10/100 Ethernet PHY
- PWM audio output/microphone input
- Temperature sensor
- 3-axis accelerometer
- 16 switches
- 16 LEDs
- 5 push buttons
- Two 3-color LEDs
- Two 4-digit 7-segment displays
- USB host device support
- Five PMOD (one XADC)

Let's take a look at the breakdown of the two devices that the Nexys board can be ordered with:

Device	XC7A100T-1CSG324C	XC7A50T-1CSG324C
Logic slices	15,850	8,150
BRAM (Kbits)	4,860	2,700
Clock management tiles	6	5
DSP	240	120

Table 1.3: Breakdown of the devices

One benefit of choosing the XC7A100T is the additional RAM. Especially at the start, you may find yourself relying on chip debugging using ChipScope, and the additional RAM will allow for additional storage for wider busses or longer capture times. We'll discuss ChipScope in the later chapters.

Summary

In this chapter, we've learned the basics of ASICs and FPGAs, how they are built, and when they make monetary sense. We've looked at the basic building blocks and gates, and learned how larger components are built from these fundamental cells. We've also identified other FPGA components, namely, DSP, BRAM, and PLLs, which we will use throughout the book.

The next chapter will discuss **SystemVerilog/Verilog** and **VHDL**, detailing some of the commonalities and differences and why you might pick one over the other. We'll load up Vivado, develop our first application, and run it.

Questions

1. When might you use an FPGA?

   a. You are prototyping an application that may eventually be an ASIC.

   b. You will only have very small volumes.

   c. You need something that you can easily change the algorithms on in the future.

   d. All of the above.

2. When would you use an ASIC?

   a. You are developing a very specialized application, with just a small number to be built and the budget is tight.

   b. You've been asked to design a calculator that will be mass produced and that requires a custom processor.

   c. You need something extremely low power and cost is not a consideration.

   d. You are developing an imaging satellite and want the ability to update the algorithms over the lifetime of the satellite.

   e. a, b, and c.

3. We have seen a full adder in the chapter. A half adder is a circuit that can add two inputs; in other words, no carry in. Can you complete the truth table for the sum and carry for a half adder?

A	B	Sum	Carry
0	0		
0	1		
1	0		
1	1		

Answers

1. When might you use an FPGA?

   - All of the above.

2. When would you use an ASIC?

    - a, b, and c.

3. We have seen a full adder in the chapter. A half adder is a circuit that can add two inputs, in other words, no carry in. Can you complete the truth table for the sum and carry for a half adder?

A	B	Sum	Carry
0	0	0	0
0	1	1	0
1	0	1	0
1	1	1	1

Further reading

Please refer to the following links for more information:

- 7 Series FPGAs Configurable Logic Block: `https://www.xilinx.com/support/documentation/user_guides/ug474_7Series_CLB.pdf`

- 7 Series FPGAs Clocking Resources: `https://www.xilinx.com/support/documentation/user_guides/ug472_7Series_Clocking.pdf`

- 7 Series DSP48E1 Slice: `https://www.xilinx.com/support/documentation/user_guides/ug479_7Series_DSP48E1.pdf`

Join our community on Discord

Join our community's Discord space for discussions with the authors and other readers:

`https://packt.link/embedded`

2

FPGA Programming Languages and Tools

In the previous chapter, we explored what makes up an FPGA and looked at ASICs and Boolean functions, the underlying technology. We saw how these simple gates can be stitched together to create more complex functions. We explored the AMD Xilinx Artix 7 architecture and the Nexys 7 development board.

In this chapter, we are going to cover the following main topics:

- **Hardware Description Language (HDL)**
- Introducing Vitis and Vivado

Technical requirements

To follow along with the examples in this chapter, you need the following hardware and software.

Hardware

Unlike programming languages, **SystemVerilog**, **Verilog**, and **VHDL** are hardware description languages; to really see the fruits of your work in this book, you will need an FPGA board to load your designs into. For the purposes of this book, I have suggested a development board that is readily available. It is possible to target another board if you already have one. However, some of the resources may not be identical or you may need to change the constraints file (.xdc or equivalent) to access the resources that another board has.

Information on the Nexys A7

The reason that I am recommending the Nexys A7 is that it has multiple external interfaces that will be discussed in later chapters and will give you experience with interfacing with these components: `https://store.digilentinc.com/nexys-a7-fpga-trainer-board-recommended-for-ece-curriculum/`.

Although you may be able to find the older 50T board available, it is now obsolete. The 100T is the only variant still in production. 50T and 100T refer to the number of logic elements in the FPGA, 50K or 100K elements. The board also has multiple standard **Peripheral MODule (PMOD)** connectors, which can be used to add additional capability. Later in the book, we will use one as a **Univeral Asynchronous Receiver Transmitter (UART)** and another as an inertial management unit.

 Digilent offers educational pricing if you qualify.

Software

For later chapters, you'll need the following software to follow along: `https://www.xilinx.com/support/download.html`.

Code files for all the examples in this chapter can be found in this book's GitHub repository at `https://github.com/PacktPublishing/The-FPGA-Programming-Handbook-Second-Edition/tree/main/CH2`.

Hardware Description Languages (HDLs)

Prior to the development of HDLs, you would create a design using schematic capture or a very primitive language like PALASM or ABLE to implement a design. Schematic capture could be done at the transistor level for ASICs or gate-level primitives, but much of the process was manual. The very first CPUs were designed by hand on large sheets of paper. In my first VLSI class, I designed a 60 Hz notch filter by hand over very many long nights using MAGIC, a design entry package. There was no auto-routing and cell placement was manual at the transistor level. If there were lots of level changes and jogging around due to not leaving enough room for traces, everything had to be ripped up and re-placed and routed by hand.

Luckily, these days, we can do most of our designs using HDL. This textual representation is compact, relatively easy to read, and easy to simulate. However, we do have to address the fact that the industry has settled on two different languages, SystemVerilog/Verilog and VHDL.

SystemVerilog versus Verilog

There is some confusion regarding whether SystemVerilog and Verilog are two different languages. For the record, they are not. Verilog is the original language, IEEE 1364, which had three versions, 1364-1995, 1364-2001, and 1364-2005. When SystemVerilog, IEEE 1800, was introduced in 2009, it was based upon the Verilog 2005 standard. Since then, there have been two further revisions in SystemVerilog, 2009 and 2017. For this book, we'll be focusing on all the synthesizable constructs in SystemVerilog 2017. I will point out things that will need to be written differently if you stick to Verilog 2001. In fact, SystemVerilog is so well supported in FPGA tools, both paid and free, that the only time you would want to stick to Verilog 2001 is if a professor told you that you had to.

A limited subset of Verilog/SystemVerilog differences is shown below. As constructs are introduced, differences will be identified and discussed in more detail.

Verilog	SystemVerilog
`reg` type for `always` blocks	Supported but recommend against using
`wire` type for `assign` statements	Use for multiply driven events; otherwise, use bit, logic, or custom types
Limited querying functions	Querying functions for reusability: `$clog2`, `$left`, `$right`...
Limited verification support	Verification support (DPI, classes, randomization, etc.)
No custom types	Custom type support (`typedef`, `enum`)
No structures or unions	Structure and union support
Basic operators (+, -, *, /)	Complex oprators added (++, --, +=, ...)

Table 2.1: Verilog and SystemVerilog comparison

SystemVerilog versus VHDL

Depending on where you work, the project, or the area of the world you live, you might prefer or be pushed toward one language or the other. The truth is that either language is quite capable of being used for development and it's good to know both as it will open opportunities. The following table highlights the main differences between the two languages.

SystemVerilog	VHDL
Weakly typed	Strongly typed
Based loosely on C	Based on ADA
A little more compact to write	Can be more verbose
Case sensitive (and is not the same as AND)	Case insensitive (AND and "and" are the same)
Libraries are optional (packages)	Libraries are required for any real design
Many verification constructs make reusable testbenches easy to develop	Difficult to write testbenches in that they are not simply delay or file based

Table 2.2: SystemVerilog and VHDL comparison

VHDL 87, the first version of VHDL I used, was extremely verbose. It required the writing of an Entity, Architecture, and Configuration; components had to be declared before use and the strong typing required a lot of thought and work to create complicated if statements, for example. From what I see in the latest version of **VHDL**, it seems that a lot has been done to address the verboseness; component declarations are no longer required for all instances, configurations are optional, and the strong typing has been extended to make comparisons a little bit easier. We'll produce code using both languages throughout the book.

Regardless of the language you focus on, when writing code for design, it's best to make sure that the synthesis tool supports the construct. This can be a changing target as Xilinx (and other vendors) add new construct support in every release. Xilinx publishes a synthesis guide with every version that details supported constructs, so we will reference those as we build up our knowledge base throughout the book. There will be a few constructs in both languages that we don't cover during our coding, and I'll address them in *Chapter 15, Advanced Topics*.

Having introduced the two languages that we'll be covering in the book and looked at their differences, let's now look at the Xilinx tools we will need to actually build an FPGA image.

Introducing Vitis and Vivado

Once you have selected a board, the best way to get to know it is to work through an example design.

Vivado is the Xilinx tool we will be using to implement, test, download, and debug our HDL designs. It can be run as a command-line tool in non-project mode, or in project mode using the **Graphical User Interface (GUI)**. For our purposes, we will be using project mode via the GUI as this is a little easier for new users. Project mode handles the organization of the files and allows for design entry and on-the-fly error checking if you desire.

Non-project mode is more for "power users" where you would write Tcl scripts and control the flow of the tools via the command line. In this mode, you would only use the tools for timing analysis and on-chip debugging. We will go through non-project mode as an introduction in the *Appendix*.

Later in the book, we will implement MicroBlaze, an embedded CPU designed by Xilinx, in our FPGA. Vitis is the tool that we will use for writing and debugging software that we will run on the MicroBlaze.

Vivado installation

Xilinx makes Vivado and Vitis freely available for smaller devices such as the Artix 7. Licenses are required to target larger devices. It is available for either Windows or Linux. This book will show screenshots for the Linux version; however, everything is tested on both, so using either will be fine.

 The Xilinx webpack forces tool feedback information to Xilinx. The paid version allows this to be disabled.

Perform the following steps to effect installation:

1. Create an account at `https://www.xilinx.com/`.
2. Visit `https://www.xilinx.com/support/download.html`.
3. Download the Xilinx Unified Installer. For this book, we'll be using version `2022.2`.
4. On Windows, run the `.exe` file.
5. On Linux, use the following commands:

```
chmod +x Xilinx_Unified_2022.2_1014_8888_Lin64.bin; ./Xilinx_
Unified_2022.2_1014_8888_Lin64.bin
```

6. Enter your account information for the installation.
7. When prompted, install Vitis. The Vitis installation includes Vivado.
8. When prompted for the devices, you only need the 7 series. Installing other devices is optional.
9. Pick an installation location or use the default option.

Once you've completed these steps, get a cup of coffee... take a nap... write a book. It is going to take a while. Once installed, let's look at the overall design flow.

Design flow

Designing hardware, like an FPGA, can be a daunting task, so it helps to define a flow. The flow is introduced in *Figure 2.1*:

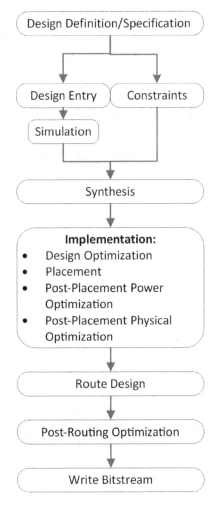

Figure 2.1: FPGA flow

Let's look at the flow in more detail in the following subsections:

Design definition/specification

In general, you would write a document that would act as a specification. In our designs, we'll have a description or register specification. An example can be found with the VGA interface that we will develop in *Chapter 10, A Better Way to Display – VGA*.

For real-world designs, you may construct a complex document with a series of shall sentences. In the case of VGA, a shall statement might be, "*The design shall support all resolutions defined by VESA.*" These types of specifications are also good for testing against as each shall statement should be a test to confirm the functionality.

A register specification for VGA can be found in *Chapter 10, A Better Way to Display – VGA.*

The next two steps of the flow are text-based.

Design entry/constraints

We will go over the actual HDL and constraints in the rest of this chapter, but you will need to choose a text editor. Since the VHDL/SystemVerilog/Verilog files as well as the XDC files are purely text-based, any text editor can be used. Some good choices are:

- Vivado design entry – error checking on the fly, project management, code highlighting, and keyword completion
- VSCode – code highlighting and keyword completion
- Emacs/VIM – code highlighting and keyword completion
- TerosHDL (https://terostechnology.github.io/terosHDLdoc/) – error checking on the fly, project management, code highlighting, and keyword completion

Once the design and constraints have been written, we can verify that our design meets our specification.

Simulation

In this book, we'll be using the Vivado simulator, XSIM. We'll be using it from within the GUI for most of the book; however, we'll also discuss how to run it from the command line. We'll discuss using the waveform viewer for debugging and verification as well as self-checking testbenches.

Typically, simulations are run on the design prior to implementation; however, it is possible to run timing simulations after the design is implemented. These will be much slower and marginally more useful since we will use static timing to verify performance and verify **clock domain crossing (CDC)**.

Once we are happy with the design, it's time to build it.

Synthesis

The first step is synthesis, where the code is translated from an HDL into an intermediate logic format and mapped to the device instances (CLB, RAM, and DSP elements). Once we have synthesized the design, we can run the implementation step.

Implementation

This step is a catch all for a few underlying steps.

Design optimization

This step can be used for area, timing, and power optimizations to improve the **Quality of Results (QOR)** of the design. This step is optional.

Placement

In the placement step, we map the synthesized and optimized design into the actual FPGA fabric. XDC constraints help guide placement. The first placement isn't always the optimal one, so we have the option of more optimizations.

Post-placement power optimization

For power-critical designs, it's possible to enable this step, which is off by default. These optimizations can lower the power requirements and thus reduce thermal requirements at the expense of design performance. The next option, which is used more frequently, is physical optimization.

Post-placement physical optimization

This step will work on improving the design to meet XDC requirements, typically area or speed. Once the design has been optimized, we can route the design.

Route design

The placement step and optimization use estimated routing delays. This step will run the autorouter to deposit actual routes on the FPGA fabric. This is an iterative set of steps to try to meet design constraints. Utilization and timing requirements determine the success of this step. As designs grow and utilization approaches 100%, it can be hard to meet constraints successfully.

There is one more step prior to writing the bitstream to help with meeting the constraints.

Post-routing optimization

Once the design has been routed, there is one more opportunity to improve results using post-routing optimization.

Write bitstream

This is the final step that generates the bit file, which can be used to program the FPGA or flash on the board. This is the file that is loaded on startup that configures the FPGA to do what we want.

Running the example

You will want to copy the files for this book from GitHub at this point or clone the repository.

Loading the design

Let's load the design into Vivado:

1. Under Windows, locate the **Vivado** installation and double-click on the Vivado icon.

2. Under Linux, the procedure is as follows:

    ```
    Source <Vivado Install>/settings.sh (or.csh)
    Vivado
    ```

3. When you run Vivado, it will create and back up `vivado.log` and `vivado.jou`. I typically run Vivado from `CH2/(SystemVerilog or VHDL)`.

4. Perform *Steps 5* and *6* the first time you run Vivado; otherwise, proceed to *Step 7*.

5. Open **Vivado Store**:

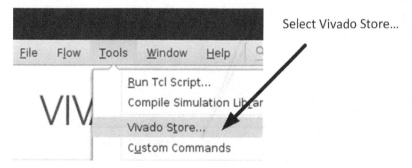

Figure 2.2: Vivado Store

 The Xilinx Vivado Store is a convenient way of adding scripts, board files, and example designs to your Vivado installation.

6. Install the board files for the example projects.

7. Select the **Boards** tab, and then navigate to the **Digilent Nexys A7-100T** or **50T**. You'll notice that there are quite a few commercial boards that easily make their files available for installation:

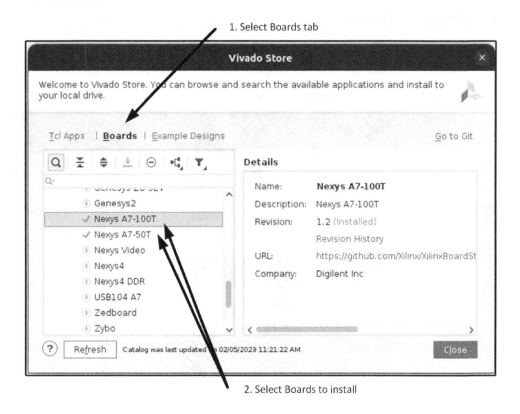

Figure 2.3: Adding the Digilent boards

8. Select the open project:

Select Project->Open...

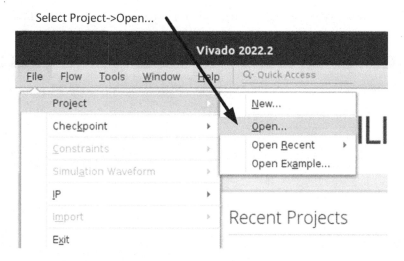

Figure 2.4: Open Project

9. Navigate to CH2/SystemVerilog/build/logic_ex.xpr or CH2/VHDL/build/logic_ex.xpr as shown in the following screenshot:

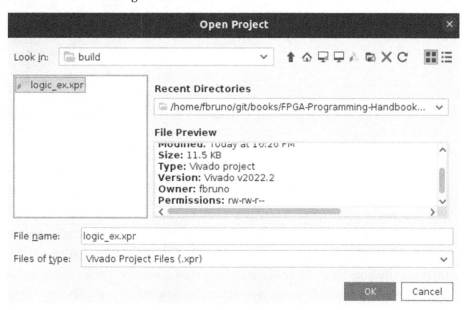

Figure 2.5: Open Project window

I've selected **SystemVerilog**, so for **VHDL**, you may see something slightly different. Once open, you'll see the following:

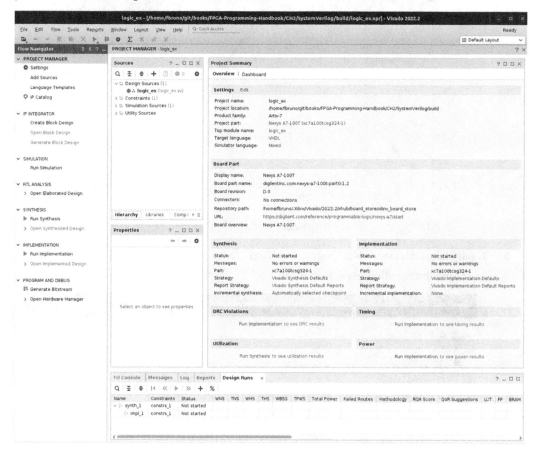

Figure 2.6: Vivado main screen for the logic_ex project

The Vivado project window gives us easy access to the design flow and all the information relating to the design. On the left-hand side, we see **Flow Navigator**. This gives us all the steps we will use to test and build our FPGA image. Currently, **PROJECT MANAGER** is highlighted. This gives us easy access to the sources in the design and the project summary. The project summary should be empty since we have loaded the project for the first time. On future loads of the project, it will display the information from the previous run.

Note

To give you a jumpstart, all the projects in this book come complete with pre-set-up project files. Please see the *Appendix* for instructions on setting up the first project in both project mode and non-project mode. This will guide you in setting up your own projects in the future.

Let's explore the sources in the design:

Figure 2.7: Design Sources

Here, we can see our design, `logic_ex.sv`. We also have a set of constraints for the Nexys A7 100T and we can see the testbench, `tb.sv`, instantiating `logic_ex.sv` under simulation sources. You can double-click on any of the files and explore them in the context-sensitive editor built into Vivado. The project is currently set up to reference the files in their current location within the directory structure, so the file can be edited with whatever your favorite editor is.

Looking at the project summary, we can see the project is currently targeting the Nexys A7-100T board.

Directory structure

With Vivado installed, we can now walk through the project to introduce you to Vivado and make sure everything is set up correctly. The directory structure I like to use looks like the following:

Figure 2.8: Directory structure

We'll have **Intellectual Property (IP)** and **Xilinx Design Constraints (XDC)** files, which are shared by both VHDL and SystemVerilog at the root of each chapter. Then we have a SystemVerilog and VHDL directory that contains the HDL files, project files, and testbenches. As we'll find out, it's easier and more accurate to use SystemVerilog to test both our VHDL and SystemVerilog designs, so some projects may have limited testing using VHDL, but the SystemVerilog test will work for both.

Inside the hdl directory within either the SystemVerilog or VHDL directory, we'll create a simple design, logic_ex, to run through Vivado. First, let's look at the SystemVerilog version:

logic_ex.sv

```
`timescale 1ns/10ps
module logic_ex
  (
    input  wire  [1:0]    SW,
    output logic [3:0]    LED
  );
  assign LED[0]  = !SW[0];
  assign LED[1]  = SW[1] && SW[0];
```

```
    assign LED[2]  = SW[1] || SW[0];
    assign LED[3]  = SW[1] ^ SW[0];
endmodule // logic_ex
```

The first line of the file defines the timescale that we will be operating at in the simulator. 1ns/10ps was standard years ago and for what we'll be doing, it will work fine. If you use high-speed transceivers, you may encounter even smaller timescales, such as 1ps/1fs.

 Each module should reside in its own file, and the file should be named the same as the module. This makes life easier when using some tools, such as commercial simulators or even custom scripting.

The syntax for defining the timescale is as follows:

```
`timescale <time unit>/<time precision>
```

time unit defines the value and unit of delays. time precision specifies the rounding precision. This value can usually be overridden in the simulator, and these settings have no effect on synthesis. When using `timescale, it is best to set it in all files:

String	Unit of time
s	Seconds
ms	Milliseconds
us	Microseconds
ns	Nanoseconds
ps	Picoseconds
fs	Femtoseconds

Table 2.3: Time units

The module defines the component that we are working with, in this case, logic_ex. In your design, you will usually have many modules, but one top-level module that is the actual name of the final implementation. In this simple example, we are developing a simple block, so logic_ex is the only module we'll have. When we look at the testbench, we'll see an example of instancing a module.

We define a port list with one input, SW, which is a 2-bit value that we will connect to the two right-most switches on the board. We also define one output named LED, which consists of four bits that represent the four LEDs above the four right-most switches:

Note on **Verilog** port lists

Throughout the book, we will be using SystemVerilog module definitions, which are the same as Verilog 2001. In Verilog 1997, the above port list would look like:

```
module logic_ex (SW, LED)
  input [1:0] SW;
  output reg [3:0] LED;
  ...
```

You can still use this style for your module, but it's not recommended as it is more verbose and doesn't add anything. You should recognize the rest of the code from the gates we introduced in *Chapter 1*.

Now let's look at the **VHDL** version:

logic_ex.vhd

```
library IEEE;
use IEEE.std_logic_1164.all;
entity logic_ex is
  port (SW : in std_logic_vector(1 downto 0),
        LED : out std_logic_vector(3 downto 0));
end entity logic_ex;
architecture rtl of logic_ex is
begin
  LED(0)  <= not SW(0);
  LED(1)  <= SW(1) and SW(0);
 --LED(1)  <= and(SW); -- VHDL 2008
  LED(2)  <= SW(1) or  SW(0);
  --LED(2)  <= or(SW); -- VHDL 2008
  LED(3)  <= SW(1) xor SW(0);
  --LED(3)  <= xor(SW); -- VHDL 2008
end architecture rtl;
```

VHDL introduces some new functions, like the reduction operators and( ), or( ), and xor( ). To do anything more advanced in VHDL, you'll need to use a library. The IEEE library contains many of the types that we'll use to build our designs as well as convenient functions such as math operations, which we will introduce in later chapters.

Tip

Although we won't be going into details on all the contents of the IEEE libraries, there are some good online resources, such as https://redirect.cs.umbc.edu/ portal/help/VHDL/stdpkg.html.

SystemVerilog includes everything that we need to create a design; however, it provides a similar capability to libraries, called a package, which we will explore in *Chapter 5, Let's Build a Calculator*. Packages provide a convenient way to group useful functions and types together for common use. An example of a SystemVerilog package from *Chapter 5* is as follows:

calculator_pkg.sv

```
package calculator_pkg;
   localparam NUM_SEGMENTS = 'NUM_SEGMENTS;
   localparam UP            = 3'd0;
   localparam DOWN          = 3'd1;
   localparam LEFT          = 3'd2;
   localparam RIGHT         = 3'd3;
   localparam CENTER        = 3'd4;

   function bit [NUM_SEGMENTS-1:0][3:0] bin_to_bcd;
     // we want to support either 4 or 8 segments
     input [31:0] bin_in;
     bit [NUM_SEGMENTS*4-1:0] shifted;
     shifted   = {30'b0, bin_in[31:30]};
     for (int i = 29; i >= 1; i--) begin
       shifted = shifted << 1 | bin_in[i];
       for (int j = 0; j < NUM_SEGMENTS; j++) begin
         if (shifted[j*4+:4] > 4) shifted[j*4+:4] += 3;
       end
     end
     shifted = shifted << 1 | bin_in[0];
     for (int i = 0; i < NUM_SEGMENTS; i++) begin
       bin_to_bcd[i] = shifted[4*i+:4];
     end
   endfunction // bin_to_bcd
endpackage // calculator_pkg
```

In the package above, we included parameter definitions and a `bin_to_bcd` function. We can then use this package in a design by adding `import calculator_pkg::*;`.

The `entity` and `architecture` together represent the unit we are developing, the `module` equivalent of SystemVerilog. The `entity` of the design contains the port list and the generic list (parameter list in SystemVerilog). The `architecture` is where the heart of the code will go. We define an architecture called `rtl` of entity `logic_ex`. The reason for keeping the entity and architecture separate is that VHDL provides the capability of binding an architecture to an entity by using the `configuration` block. As we see in the example, `logic_ex.vhd`, a configuration is not required. We'll discuss how configurations are used in *Chapter 14*.

Looking over the heart of the architecture, you'll see it is not that different from SystemVerilog. Look at the code in GitHub and you'll see that for LED 1–3, there are more ways of accomplishing the same thing using SystemVerilog.

Next, let's take a look at writing a testbench to verify our design.

Testbench

A testbench in electrical engineering terms is where you would take a circuit and verify its functionality. In terms of an HDL design, the testbench drives an HDL design and verifies that it behaves properly. In this section, we will discuss writing a testbench for our simple design.

We've seen how to write a design using SystemVerilog and VHDL. This design is so simple that we could go ahead and build it and try it on the board. The build times will be short and there are only four cases to test. However, in general, as designs get more complex, we don't want to waste time debugging on the board. This is possible and we'll see how to do this later. A better idea is to develop a self-checking testbench that we can use to verify our designs. This is a good practice and something that you should strongly consider for any design more complex than this.

The following is a SystemVerilog testbench example:

`tb.sv`

```
`timescale 1ns/ 100ps;
module tb;
  logic [1:0] SW;
  logic [3:0] LED;
  logic_ex u_logic_ex (.*);
  //logic_ex u_logic_ex (.SW, .LED);
  //logic_ex u_logic_ex (.SW(switch_sig), .LED(led_sig));
  //logic_ex u_logic_ex (.*, .LED(led_sig));
```

Here we declare a top-level module called tb. Note that the top-level testbench module should not have any ports. We also declare two logic signals that we will hook up to our device under test.

Here, we instantiate logic_ex as an instance, u_logic_ex. There are multiple ways of connecting ports. In the first example, we are using .*, which will connect all ports with the same name as a defined signal in the instantiating module.

The second example (commented out) uses the .<name> of the port you wish to connect. It requires the port name to already be defined.

Finally, if there is a signal with a different named signal, we could use the third example, which allows port renaming. It is possible to mix .* with renamed ports, as shown in the final example.

Note

When using mixed languages, as we will do later, reusing our SystemVerilog test-bench with our VHDL code, the Xilinx Xsim simulator doesn't support using .*

A testbench typically has at least two distinct parts, the stimulus generator and the stimulus checker:

```
// Stimulus
initial begin
  $printtimescale(tb); // Print the timescale
  SW = '0; // Default to all 0's for the Sw(itches)
  // Loop 4 times setting the switches to the binary value of i
  for (int i = 0; i < 4; i++) begin
    // Display what the test is doing
    $display("Setting switches to %2b", i[1:0]);
    SW = i[1:0]; // Set the switch value
    #100; // Wait 100 timeunits since we haven't introduced clocks yet
  end
  $display("PASS: logic_ex test PASSED!"); // Print test passed by default
  $stop; // End the test but stay in the simulator
end
```

The stimulus block is simple because the design we are testing is trivial. We can nest it completely in an initial block. When the simulator starts up, the initial block runs serially. First, it will print the timescale used in tb.sv. Then, SW input into the logic_ex module is set to 0. Using a '0 in the assignment to SW tells the tool to set all bits to 0. There is also an equivalent '1, which sets all bits to 1, or 'z, which would set all bits to z, or tri-state. The Verilog 1997 sizing rules say that assigning SW = 0 is equivalent to SW = 32'b0, which would result in a sizing warning. To limit warnings, using '0, '1, 'z, or proper sizing is preferable.

Note

SystemVerilog and **VHDL** are HDLs, and this is an important distinction. An HDL must be able to model parallel operations since many or all the slices in an FPGA will be running in parallel all the time. SW = '0; is a blocking assignment. In VHDL, we'll discuss how variables within a process also act as blocking assignments. So, the assignment is made before evaluating the next line of code. We will discuss blocking versus non-blocking when we discuss clocked processes.

The stimulus block then loops four times via the for loop. **SystemVerilog** has the capability of declaring the loop variable within the for loop, in this case, i. It is highly advisable to declare it this way to avoid potentially multiply driven net warnings if you are using the same signal in multiple for loops. Pre-Verilog 2001, you would need to define the loop variable external to the for loop.

Within the for loop, we print out the current setting of the switches using the system task $display. Since we want to display only the 2 bits we are incrementing without leading 0s, we specify 2%b. We then set the value of SW to the lower two bits of i. Although we don't need to, we add in a delay of 100 ns by using #100.

We are also using $stop, which will terminate the simulation run when reached.

Note

We know that the delay is in ns because of the timescale we define in the test.

We also declare a checker block. In any good testbench, the checker block should be self-checking. This means that at the end of the test, we should be able to print whether the test passed or failed, and, if it failed, why. This also means that writing a testbench can often be as involved or even more involved than writing the code for the FPGA implementation. This is beyond the scope of this book, however. All commercial simulators, including the Vivado simulator, also support the Universal Verification Methodology, which is a set of **SystemVerilog** classes and functions specifically for testing HDL designs:

```
always @(LED) begin
  if (!SW[0] !== LED[0]) begin
    $display("FAIL: NOT Gate mismatch");
    $stop;
  end
  if (&SW[1:0] !== LED[1]) begin
    $display("FAIL: AND Gate mismatch");
    $stop;
  end
  if (|SW[1:0] !== LED[2]) begin
    $display("FAIL: OR Gate mismatch");
    $stop;
  end
  if (^SW[1:0] !== LED[3]) begin
    $display("FAIL: XOR Gate mismatch");
    $stop;
  end
end
endmodule
```

Conversely to the stimulus generation, we want this block to react to events from our design. We accomplish this by using an always block, which is sensitive just to changes in the LED outputs of the design. This is a simple case where we are matching each LED to the corresponding SW values run through their respective expected logic gate. We do this by using !==, which is not equal, but takes xs into account in case there is a bug in the design. We will see more complex testbenches in later chapters.

We are also using the reduction operators, &, |, and ^, which are applied to the two bits of SW. &SW[1:0] is equivalent to SW[0] & SW[1].

Note

We are triggering our checker only on LED due to the idea of simulation ticks and how a simulator handles sensitivity lists. In the case of changing SW and monitoring the LED events, we are safe. In testing using Vivado and VHDL, the sensitivity list would trigger twice, once when SW changed and again when LED changed, which causes failures in the simulation. Usually, you will be simulating based on clocks and this wouldn't be an issue.

VHDL testbench

Now let's look at the VHDL equivalent of the testbench:

tb.vhd

```
library IEEE, STD;
use IEEE.std_logic_1164.all;
use IEEE.numeric_std.all;
```

First, we must define the libraries we need to use. We need std_logic_1164 as a base for our signals, std_logic_misc for the reduction operators, and numeric_std for the to_unsigned function.

```
entity tb is
end entity tb;
```

We define an empty entity called tb since we have no ports as this is the top level.

```
The architecture tb of tb is:

-- define the signals
signal SW: std_logic_vector(1 downto 0);
signal LED: std_logic_vector(3 downto 0);
```

We create an architecture called tb of the entity tb. The declaration portion of the architecture declares any components we'll reference in the code, in this case, logic_ex. We'll also define any signals we use here. Note that we set the default value of passed to '1', indicating the test is currently in a state of passing.

```
begin
  -- instantiate the module to be tested
  u_logic_ex: logic_ex port map (
    SW => SW,
    LED => LED);
```

We must hook up the signals to the component in the instantiation. Now let's look at the stimulus portion of the testbench.

```
-- Stimulus
-- Equivalent to the initial block in SV
initial : process
begin
  SW <= "00";
  for i in 0 to 3 loop
    SW <= std_logic_vector(to_unsigned(i, SW'length));
    report "setting SW to " & to_string(to_unsigned(i, SW'length));
    wait for 100 ns;
  end loop;
  report "PASS: logic_ex test PASSED!";
  std.env.stop;
  wait;
end process initial;
```

We can see that VHDL has a process block. This block is like the always block in SystemVerilog. It has a sensitivity list, which we leave empty, so it runs once through. When we get to the end, we check the value of passed. If it is '1', which indicates the test has passed, we'll print out the Pass message. Just like we did for SystemVerilog, we want to have a quick indication of the test passing. If the test fails, we'll see the Failed! message and we can scroll up through the log and see where the test failed.

We'll go over process blocks in more detail in a later chapter.

Now let's take a look at the checker block. This block has a sensitivity to LED. When LED changes, the process fires and we run through a series of comparisons.

```
-- Checking
  checking : process
  begin
    wait until LED'event;
    if not SW(0) /= LED(0) then
      report "FAIL: NOT Gate mismatch" severity failure;
    end if;
    if and SW /= LED(1) then
      report to_string(and SW);
      report "FAIL: AND Gate mismatch" severity failure;
    end if;
    if or SW /= LED(2) then
      report "FAIL: OR Gate mismatch" severity failure;
    end if;
    if xor SW /= LED(3) then
      report "FAIL: XOR Gate mismatch" severity failure;
    end if;
  end process checking;

end architecture tb;
```

In the above process, if any of our checks fail, we will print out a message and set the passed flag to '0', which will be checked at the end of the test.

Now let's look at running the example in Vivado to see how the Vivado simulator, xsim, is run.

Running a simulation

First, let's run the Vivado simulator to check the validity of our design.

To do this, click **Run Simulation | Run Behavioral Simulation** under **PROJECT MANAGER**.

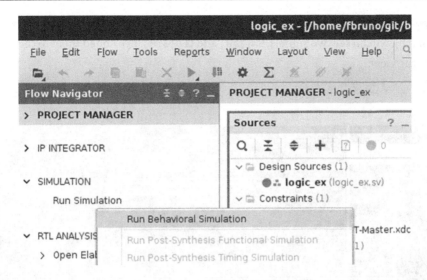

Figure 2.9: Design sources

You will see that there are some other options available that are grayed out. These options allow you to run post-synthesis or post-implementation with or without timing. Behavioral simulation is relatively quick and will accurately represent the function of your design if the code is written properly. I would recommend not running post-synthesis or post-implementation simulation unless you are debugging a board failure and need to accurately test the implemented version of the design as you'll find that the simulations will slow down dramatically.

Running the behavioral simulation will elaborate the design, the first step in the overall flow. The **Simulation** view will take over the Vivado main screen:

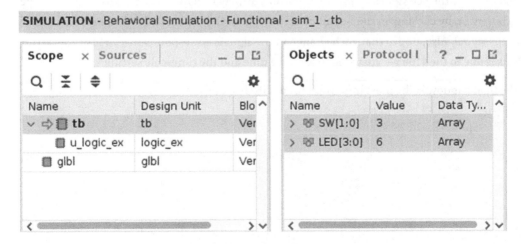

Figure 2.10: Simulation view

The **Scope** screen gives us access to the objects within a given module. In this case, within the testbench (tb), we can see two signals, SW[1:0] and LED[3:0]. I've added them to the waves and expanded the view:

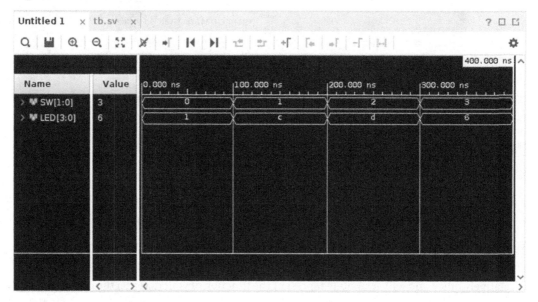

Figure 2.11: Wave view

The wave view allows us to look at the signals in the design and how they are behaving as the simulation progresses. This will be the most widely used feature of the simulator when debugging problems. We can see the SW signal incrementing due to the for loop in the testbench. Correspondingly, we see the LED values change. The current display is in hex, but it is possible to change it to binary or, by clicking on the > symbol to the right of the signal, to display the individual bits of the signal. Also, notice that each change in the signals corresponds to a 100ns time advance. This is due to the #100 we are using to advance time and the timescale setting.

The final window is the most important for a self-checking testbench:

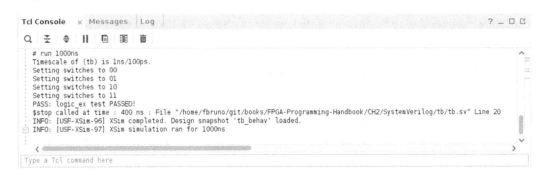

Figure 2.12: Tcl Console

The **Tool Command Language** (**TCL**) console will display all the outputs from $display, or assertions in the design. In this case, we can see the output from our $printtimescale(tb) function as 1ns/100ps. We also see the values that the switches are set to and can see the same values within the waves. Finally, we see PASS: logic_ex test PASSED!, giving us the result of the test. I would encourage you to experiment with the testbench. Change the operators or invert them to verify that the test fails if you do. This exercise will give you confidence that the testbench is functioning correctly.

The goal of verification is not to ensure the design passes; it is to try to make it fail. This is a simple case, so it is not really possible, but make sure that you test unexpected situations to make sure your design is robust.

It is advisable to adopt a convention in how you indicate tests passing and failing. This test is simple. However, a much more robust test suite for an actual design may have random stimuli and many targeted tests. Adopting a convention such as displaying the words PASS and FAIL allows for easy post-processing of test results.

Implementation

Now that we have confidence that the design works as intended, it is time to build it and test it on the board.

First, let's look at the .xdc file. **XDC** stands for **Xilinx Design Constraints**. This file holds all the constraints necessary for the physical building of the design, such as pin locations, IO standards, voltages, pblock placements of design units, and clock definitions. Click back on **Project Manager** in **Flow Navigator**, and then expand the constraints and double-click on the .xdc file.

The following lines should be uncommented out for the **Nexys A7-100T** to set the configuration voltages:

```
set_property CFGBVS VCCO [current_design]
set_property CONFIG_VOLTAGE 3.3 [current_design]
```

set_property is the tcl command that will set a given design property used by Vivado. In the preceding command, we are setting CFGBVS and CONFIG_VOLTAGE to the values required by the Artix-7 FPGA.

The following code block sets up the switch and LED locations (placed together for convenience):

```
set_property -dict { PACKAGE_PIN J15   IOSTANDARD LVCMOS33 } [get_ports {
SW[0] }]; #IO_L24N_T3_RS0_15 Sch=sw[0]
set_property -dict { PACKAGE_PIN L16   IOSTANDARD LVCMOS33 } [get_ports {
SW[1] }]; #IO_L3N_T0_DQS_EMCCLK_14 Sch=sw[1]
set_property -dict { PACKAGE_PIN H17   IOSTANDARD LVCMOS33 } [get_ports {
LED[0] }]; #IO_L18P_T2_A24_15 Sch=led[0]
set_property -dict { PACKAGE_PIN K15   IOSTANDARD LVCMOS33 } [get_ports {
LED[1] }]; #IO_L24P_T3_RS1_15 Sch=led[1]
set_property -dict { PACKAGE_PIN J13   IOSTANDARD LVCMOS33 } [get_ports {
LED[2] }]; #IO_L17N_T2_A25_15 Sch=led[2]
set_property -dict { PACKAGE_PIN N14   IOSTANDARD LVCMOS33 } [get_ports {
LED[3] }]; #IO_L8P_T1_D11_14 Sch=led[3]
```

The set_property commands create a tcl dictionary (-dict) containing PACKAGE_PIN and IOSTANDARD for each port on the design. We use the get_port Tcl command to return a port on the design. # is a comment in Tcl.

The pin locations and I/O standards are defined by the board manufacturer. They have used 3.3 V I/Os and the pins are as specified.

The XDC file for the Nexys A7 is located under CH2/XDC.

Please see https://digilent.com/reference/programmable-logic/nexys-a7/ start for documentation on the Nexys A7 100T as well as references for the XDC.

The steps to generate a bitstream are as follows:

1. **Synthesis**: Map **SystemVerilog** or **VHDL** to an intermediate logic format for optimizing.
2. **Implementation**: Place the design, optimize the place results, and route the design.

3. **Generate bitstream**: Generate the physical file to download to the board.

These can be run sequentially, one at a time. You might take this route if you need to look at the intermediate results to see how the area or timing is coming out, or if you are designing a custom board and need to do pin planning. In our case, we can click directly on **Generate Bitstream** and allow it to run all the steps automatically for us. Allow it to use the defaults. When complete, open the implemented results:

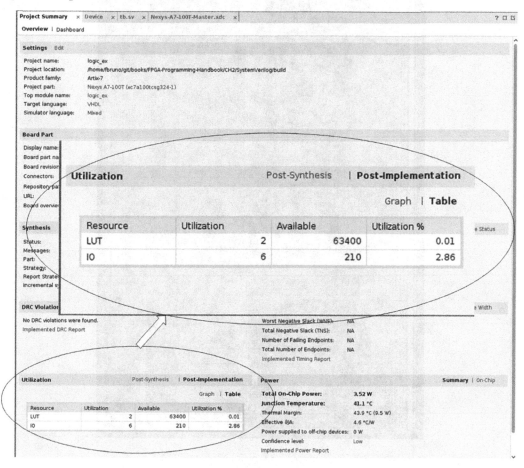

Figure 2.13: Project Summary

Here we can see the summary of our implementation. We are using 2 LUTs and 6 I/Os (SW + LED). There is no timing since this design is purely combinational logic with no storage (flip flops or RAMs); otherwise, we'd see more information regarding timing numbers.

If we click the **Device** tab, we can get a picture of how the device is being used:

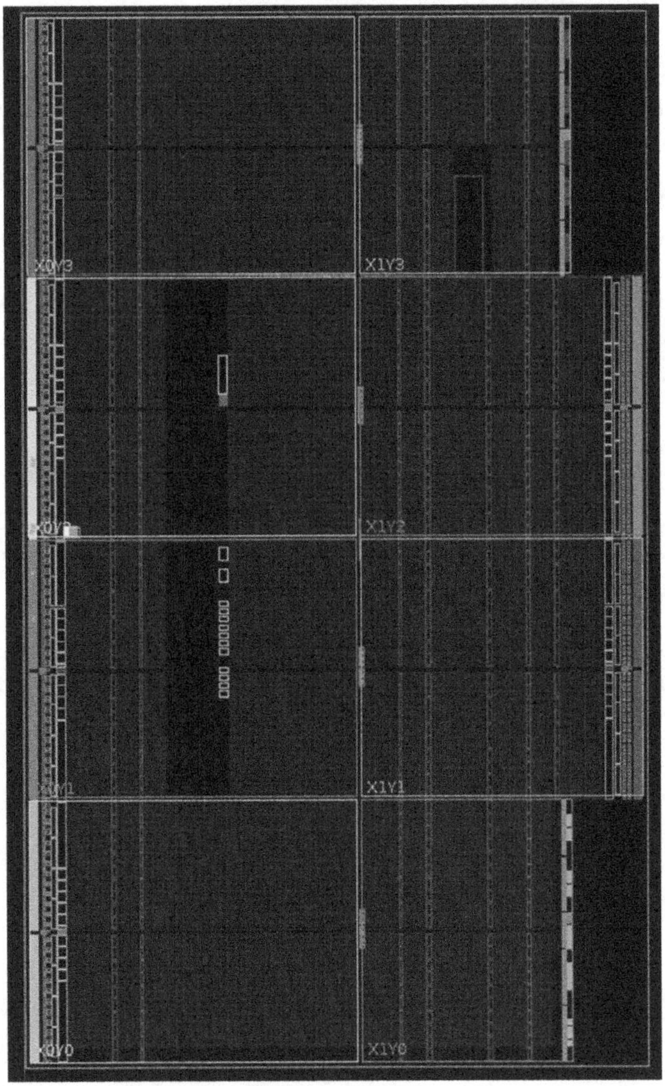

Figure 2.14: Device view

Here we can see the little white dot midway down the left-hand side. This represents where the **LookUp Tables (LUTs)**, which represent the logic in the design, are being physically placed.

Program the board

You have made it to the end of the chapter and now it's time to see the board in action. Here are the steps to do it:

1. Make sure it is plugged in and turned on.

2. Now, click on **Open hardware manager**, the last option under **Flow Navigator**. The Hardware Manager view will open in the main window.

3. Click **Open target | Autoconnect**.

4. Now, select the program device. The bitstream should be selected automatically. The lights will go out on the board for a few seconds and then, if the left two switches are down, you will be greeted with this:

Figure 2.15: Board bring-up

Flip the switches, and go through 00, 01, 10, 11, where 0 is down and 1 is up. Do the lights match the simulation? Do they match what you think they should be? Do you occasionally see one flicker as the switches are flipped? This is an actual problem with using mechanical switches that will be solved in *Chapter 3, Combinational Logic*.

Congratulations! You've completed your first project on an FPGA board. You've taken the first step on this journey and reconfigured the hardware in the FPGA to do some simple tasks. As we go through the book, the tasks will become more complex and more interesting and soon you'll be able to build upon this to create your own projects.

Summary

In this chapter, we've learned the basics of HDL design and implementation using FPGAs. We've learned how to use an FPGA board and program it. This sets us up for the rest of the book, where we will use this board and our programming skills in a variety of tasks and projects. Ultimately, these skills will be the foundation for developing your own designs, be they for work or play.

The next chapter will build upon our example design as we delve further into combinational logic design.

Questions

1. Which step in the flow is the first:

    a. Implementation

    b. Generate bitstream

    c. Synthesis

2. Match the keywords to the language:

Construct	SystemVerilog or VHDL
package	
library	
module	
entity	
architecture	
std_logic_vector	
logic	

3. Modify the code and testbench to test the following gates: NAND (not AND), NOR (not OR), and XNOR (not XOR). Hint: You can invert a unary operator by adding a ~ operator in front of it; in other words, NAND is ~&. Try it on the board.

Answers

1.   c) synthesis,

      a) implemention

      b) Generate bitstream.

2.   package - SystemVerilog

      library - VHDL

      module - SystemVerilog

      entity - VHDL

      architecture - VHDL

      std_logic_vector - VHDL

      logic - SystemVerilog

3.   This has been left for the readers

Challenge

1.   Open CH2/SystemVerilog/build/challenge.xpr or CH2/VHDL/build/challenge.xpr.

2.   Modify the lines in challenge.sv to implement a full adder:

SystemVerilog

```
assign LED[0]  = ; // Write the code for the Sum
assign LED[1]  = ; // Write the code for the Carry
```

VHDL

```
LED(0)  = ; -- Write the code for the Sum
LED(1)  = ; -- Write the code for the Carry
```

Modify tb_challenge.sv to test it:

SystemVerilog

```
if () then // Modify for checking
```

VHDL

```
if … begin -- Modify for checking
```

Hint: You may want to jump ahead in the book at *Chapter 3, Combinational Logic* to look at addition or do a quick web search.

Further reading

Please refer to the following links for more information:

- 7 Series FPGAs Configurable Logic Block: `https://www.xilinx.com/support/documentation/user_guides/ug474_7Series_CLB.pdf`

- 7 Series FPGAs Clocking Resources: `https://www.xilinx.com/support/documentation/user_guides/ug472_7Series_Clocking.pdf`

- 7 Series DSP48E1 Slice: `https://www.xilinx.com/support/documentation/user_guides/ug479_7Series_DSP48E1.pdf`

- Nexys A7 Reference Manual: `https://reference.digilentinc.com/reference/programmable-logic/nexys-a7/reference-manual`

Join our community on Discord

Join our community's Discord space for discussions with the authors and other readers:

`https://packt.link/embedded`

3

Combinational Logic

Designs are typically composed of combinational and sequential logic. In *Chapter 2, FPGA Programming Languages and Tools*, we saw how combinational logic is made up of simple gates and created a simple design to show the gate functions on the board. In contrast, it is observed that sequential logic maintains a state, usually based on a clock edge, but it can be level-based as well, as we will discuss when we learn what not to do when inferring sequential logic.

In this chapter, we are going to explore how to write a complete SystemVerilog and VHDL module from scratch that can perform some basic real-world combinational logic operations that you may use one day in your actual designs.

We are going to cover the following main topics:

- Creating FPGA designs
- Understanding the basics of HDL design
- Project 2 – Creating combinational logic

Technical requirements

The technical requirements for this chapter are the same as those for *Chapter 2, FPGA Programming Languages and Tools*.

To follow along with the examples and the project, please take a look at the code files for this chapter in the following GitHub repository: https://github.com/PacktPublishing/The-FPGA-Programming-Handbook-Second-Edition/tree/master/CH3.

Creating FPGA designs

At the heart of every design are the modules and entities that compose it. From the testbench that's used to verify the design to any instantiated components, they are all declared somewhere as a module or entity. For the example design that we'll be covering in this chapter, we'll be creating a set of underlying modules representing the functions that we can access via the buttons and switches on the evaluation board. We'll use these switches to set values, and we'll use five buttons to perform operations.

Project 1, Logic_ex, in *Chapter 2* was our first project, so we'll be starting our official project numbering here with project_2. Let's look at the parts of a SystemVerilog module declaration:

```
module project_2
#(parameter SELECTOR,
  Parameter BITS = 16)
(input wire [BITS-1:0]       SW,
 input wire                  BTNC,
 input wire                  BTNU,
 input wire                  BTNL,
 input wire                  BTNR,
 input wire                  BTND,
 output logic signed [BITS-1:0] LED);
```

We are creating a module called project_2, which will be the top level of our design. The first section within #() is the parameter list, which allows us to define parameters that we can use within the port list or module. We can also define parameters anywhere within the module, and they can also be overridden during instantiation. However, parameters must be defined prior to use.

When writing or loading VHDL files into Vivado, make sure to specify the file type is **VHDL 2008**; by default, it will not be. This can be done when reading a VHDL file from the command line:

```
read_vhdl -vhdl2008 traffic_light.vhd
```

It can also be done in the properties pane of the GUI, as shown in *Figure 3.1*:

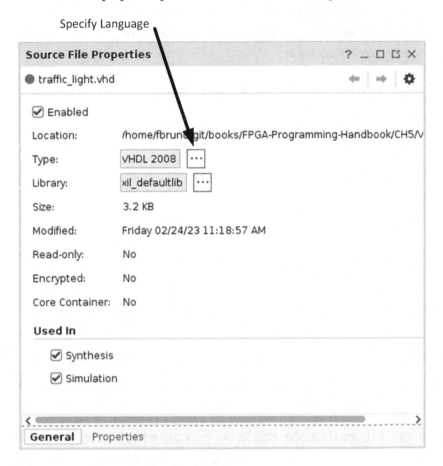

Figure 3.1: Specifying VHDL 2008

Let's look at how we can create the same design interface using a VHDL entity.

```vhdl
library IEEE;
use IEEE.std_logic_1164.all;
use IEEE.numeric_std.all;
use IEEE.math_real.all;
```

As we saw in *Chapter 2*, VHDL requires packages to be loaded for many operations and data types. Here, we are loading the std_logic_1164 package for a physical interface to our devices, numeric_std for some operations, and math_real for the log2 function that we will use for automatically sizing some of our buses:

```vhdl
entity project_2 is
  generic(
    SELECTOR : string;
    BITS     : integer := 16
  );
  port(
    SW   : in  std_logic_vector(BITS - 1 downto 0);
    BTNC : in  std_logic;
    BTNU : in  std_logic;
    BTNL : in  std_logic;
    BTNR : in  std_logic;
    BTND : in  std_logic;
    LED  : out std_logic_vector(BITS - 1 downto 0)
  );
end entity project_2;
```

The entity looks like the module of SystemVerilog. We have generics, which take the place of the parameters, and a port list.

How to create reusable code — parameters and generics

SystemVerilog provides a mechanism for configuring a design during instancing called parameters. VHDL provides a similar mechanism using generics. Both mechanisms can be used to override information in a design instantiation. The information can be used within the design to control the size of the data, as is the case with BITS, which has a default value of 16 if it's not overridden.

If BITS is not overridden, then the instance of project_2 would use 16 switches as shown below:

```vhdl
Inst1 : project_2 generic_map(SELECTOR => "UNIQUE_CASE")…
```

If our board only had 8 switches, we could instance the design as follows:

```vhdl
Inst1 : project_2 generic_map(SELECTOR => "UNIQUE_CASE", BITS => 8)…
```

Parameters and generics can also control the instantiation of logic, entities, or modules, as we'll see when we explore the `case` and `if` statements for the SystemVerilog module and VHDL architecture and the different ways we can find the leading one's value. We can also create a parameter, `SELECTOR`, which has no default. This is a good way to make sure that something is set in the instantiation since there is no default. If it is not overridden, it will result in an error.

Parameters in SystemVerilog can be integers, strings, or even types:

```
#(parameter type SW_T = logic unsigned [15:0], …
(input   SW_T      SW, …
```

Here, we created a type named `SW_T`, which defaults to `logic unsigned [15:0]` and creates a port using this type named `SW`. When the module is instantiated, a new type can be passed, thus overriding the default and allowing for greater design reuse.

It is good practice to keep parameters intended to be overridden within the parameter list and use `localparam`, which cannot be overridden, within the module itself. Parameters provide us with a great way to express design intent. When you return to a design after a long period of time, *magic numbers* such as 3.14 have much less meaning than *pi*. For instance,

```
assign a = 3.14*(r**2);
```

is less clear than reading

```
assign a = pi*(r**2);
```

Also note that parameters can be derived from other parameters. This is especially useful when defining localparams.

Generics were a little more constrained pre-VHDL-2008. Prior to VHDL-2008, generics only allowed you to create constants that could be overridden when a design was instantiated. VHDL 2008 adds the capability of declaring generic types like the parameter list of SystemVerilog allows, as well as generic subprograms that can be specified upon instantiation:

```
generic(
    BITS : integer := 16;
    type SW_T;
    function no_func(SW : std_logic_vector(BITS-1 downto 0)) return
unsigned);
```

```
port(
  SW : in SW_T; ...
  );
```

Now that we have examined the module's interface to the outside world, let's look at the data types we'll use in both languages.

Understanding the basics of HDL design

All computer programming languages need variables. A CPU with a running program can access stored values in physical memory or registers. **Hardware Description Languages (HDLs)** are a little different than the usual programming languages in that you are building hardware. There are variable equivalents in terms of storage/sequential logic, which we'll discuss in the next chapter, but we also need *wires* to move data around the hardware we're building using the FPGA routing resources, even if they are never stored:

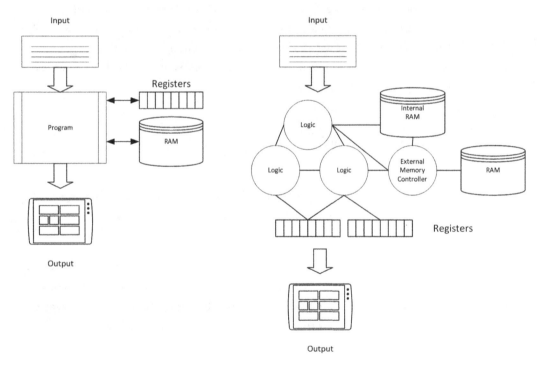

Figure 3.2: Program flow versus HDL flow

In a traditional flow, as shown on the left of *Figure 3.2*, you have a computer that has a processor and memory. The program flows linearly. Note that with modern machines, there are increasing levels of parallelism, but physical parallelism remains minimal compared to what can be possible in custom hardware such as an FPGA.

When you write HDL code, you are using data types to create hardware that will store or move data around physically to and from **Lookup Tables** (**LUTs**), DSP elements, BRAMs, IO, or other device resources. If you need a large amount of memory, you'll need to implement the external memory interface to communicate with it, which is something we will introduce in *Chapter 9, Lots of Data? MIG and DDR2*.

Introducing data types

SystemVerilog has multiple built-in types, but the most interesting ones for design are the logic and bit types:

- logic: We used this type in the previous chapter. The logic type can represent a **0, 1, x** (undefined or treated as don't care, as we'll see shortly), or **z** (tri-state or also a don't care).

- x and z are really sub bullets of logic, x is a value that represents an undefined or don't care value. When used as an undefined value in simulation, it will propagate through logic and can be used to find problems in your design. When used as a don't care value, it can allow synthesis tools to optimize designs for better area/performance. We'll see an example of optimization usage in *Chapter 12, Using the PMOD Connectors – SPI and UART*.

- z is a value used for tri-state signals. This is used to allow multiple drivers to access a shared resource. We will see how this is used in the *Handling multiple-driven nets* section. z can also be used to help logic optimization, like how x is used, which we will examine in *Chapter 10, A Better Way to Display – VGA*.

 If you've ever used verilog, you will know of the reg type. This was a confusing type to new HDL designers as they would see reg and think it was short for register. In fact, the reg type references any signal originating from an always block, even though always blocks could be used to generate combinational logic, as we'll see shortly. Although reg can still be used for backward compatibility, you would be better off using logic or bit, which can be used in both assign statements and always blocks. The logic type also allows for the propagation of x through a design. This can be helpful for debugging startup conditions.

- bit: The bit type uses less memory to store than logic, but it can only store a **0** or **1**. This allows lower memory usage and potentially faster simulation at the expense of tracking undefined values.

There are also four other lesser-used two-state types:

- byte: 8 bits
- shortint: 16 bits
- int: 32 bits
- longint: 64 bits

These types are less often used because it's usually easier to specify the exact size of signals using logic or bit.

 The differences between bit and logic are purely related to how they behave in simulation. Both types will generate the same logic and storage elements in hardware. All the other types only differ in size or default sign representation.

VHDL has a limited number of built-in data types, such as bit, boolean, and integer. You'll notice we have used a few packages in all our VHDL code so far. That is because the data types we need for logic design, such as std_logic_vector or signed and unsigned, are not part of the core language. Let's look at these packages:

- std_logic and std_logic_vector: Roughly equivalent to logic, this type is the one that is generally used. std_logic represents a single bit while std_logic_vector is used for buses. There are a few additional logic levels, such as weak pull up or pull down, but they are only useful in modeling.

 Like SystemVerilog, VHDL provides a way of setting all bits in a vector to a value:

```
my_sig <= (others => '0');
```

- boolean: VHDL, being strongly typed, has a separate boolean type. In SystemVerilog, a 0 would be false and a 1 true, but Booleans are required pre-VHDL-2008.

VHDL 2008 has relaxed some of the type checking. For instance, there is now automatic type conversion in if statements. Pre-VHDL 2008, if you wanted to check a single bit, you would have to compare it to a value so it would become a Boolean operation, rather than just simply testing the value directly.

- integer: Integers are commonly also used in VHDL. The range of the integer data type is implementation-defined, but it is guaranteed to be at least a 32-bit signed integer. Unlike SystemVerilog, integers can have a defined range allowing optimization and error checking.

 The tip box refers to the integer bullet point.

Ex: `signal my_sig : integer range 0 to 15; -- Create a 4 bit wide value`

- signed and unsigned: VHDL has dedicated types for explicitly signed and unsigned operations, unlike SystemVerilog, where signed and unsigned are operators on a data type.

With that, we've looked at the basic types. But what if we need to deal with different sizes of data or more data than the types can handle?

Creating arrays

The reason that byte, shortint, int, and longint are not used as much in SystemVerilog is because, typically, you will size your signals as needed; for example:

```
bit [7:0] my_byte; // define an 8 bit value
```

Here, my_byte is defined as a packed 8-bit value. It's possible to also create an unpacked version:

```
bit my_byte[8]; // define an 8 bit value
```

Packed versions have the advantage of slicing into arrays in SystemVerilog, while unpacked versions have the advantage of inferring memories, as we'll discuss in *Chapter 6, FPGA Resources and How to Use Them*.

Arrays can also have multiple dimensions:

```
bit [2:0][7:0] my_array[1024][768]; // define an 8 bit value
//   3    4              1     2        Array ordering
```

The ordering of the array is defined in the preceding code. The following are valid ways to access the array:

```
my_array[0][0] Returns a value of size [2:0][7:0]
my_array[1023][767][2] Returns an 8 bit value
```

Defining an array can be done using a range, such as [7:0], or the number of elements, such as [1024], which is zero-indexed and equivalent to [0:1023]; bear this in mind since it will come up if you use this style to create arrays of instances.

VHDL also provides a mechanism for creating multidimensional arrays. We can create new types based on other types:

```
type array_3d is array (natural range <>, natural range <>) of std_logic_
vector;
signal my_array : array_3d(31 downto 0, 31 downto 0)(31 downto 0);
my_array(0, 0) Returns a value of size (31 downto 0)
```

Querying arrays

SystemVerilog provides system functions for accessing array information. As we'll see in this project, this allows reusable code.

 The dimension parameter is optional and defaults to 1.

This becomes even more important when we want to implement type parameters:

`$dimensions(my_array)`	4.
`$left(my_array, [dimensions])`	[1] = 1023,[2]=767,[3]=2,[4]=7.
`$right(my_array, [dimensions])`	0 for all the dimensions.
`$high(my_array, [dimensions])`	Largest value in the dimension's range.
`$low(my_array, [dimensions])`	Smallest value in the dimension's range.
`$size(my_array, [dimensions])`	=$high(my_array, [dimensions]) - $low(my_array, [dimension]) + 1.

`$increment(my_array, [dimensions])`	Returns 1 if `$left` >= `$right`; otherwise, -1. Useful for for loops.
`$bits()`	Returns the number of bits used by a particular variable or expression. This is useful for passing size information to instantiations.
`$clog2()`	Returns the size of an array that can hold that number of items, not the value that was passed. For example, `$clog(4)` returns 2, which can store four values, 0 to 3.

Table 3.1: SystemVerilog array querying

These system functions allow us to query an array to get its parameters. VHDL has a similar set of predefined attributes that can be used to create more reusable code:

`my_array'high[(dimension)]`	Equivalent to `$high`.
`my_array'low[(dimension)]`	Equivalent to `$low`.
`my_array'left[(dimension)]`	Equivalent to `$left`.
`my_array'right[(dimension)]`	Equivalent to `$right`.
`my_array'range[(dimension)]`	Range of dimension (left to right). Used for looping.
`my_array'reverse_range[(dimension)]`	Range of dimension (right to left). Used for looping.
`my_array'length[(dimension)]`	Number of elements of array dimension.
`my_array'ascending[(dimension)]`	True if the range of array dimension is defined with to.

Table 3.2: VHDL array querying

Assigning to arrays

When we want to assign a value to a signal defined as an array, we should size it properly to avoid warnings. In the original Verilog specification and tools, if we didn't specify a size, then the size would default to 32 bits. Today, we simply want to avoid any warnings during simulation and synthesis as a standard build will already generate thousands of warnings and it becomes human nature to ignore them, which can lead to potentially missing important ones.

In SystemVerilog, there are four ways we can assign without providing a size: '1 assigns all bits to 1, '0 assigns all bits to 0, 'z assigns all bits to z, and, less useful, 'x assigns all bits to an unknown or don't care value. If we have a single packed dimension, we can use n'b to specify a binary value of n bits, n'd to specify a decimal value of n bits, or n'h to specify a hex value of n bits:

SystemVerilog

```
logic [63:0] data;
assign data = '1; // same as data = 64'hFFFFFFFFFFFFFFFF;
assign data = '0; // same as data = 64'd0;
assign data = 'z; // same as data = 64'hzzzzzzzzzzzzzzzz;
assign data = 0; // data[31:0] = 0, data[63:32] untouched (Verilog-97).
```

It's important to remember that n in these cases is the number of bits represented, not the number of digits. For example, since the character F in hex is represented by 4 bits, you would need 16 F characters to represent all ones. If you used fewer than 16 Fs, the number would be set to a smaller value. For example, 64'hFF would simply represent a value of 255 using 64 bits.

n'h represents 4-bit hex characters utilizing a total of n bits. 0-F all represent 4 bits.

n'd represents a decimal value utilizing a total of n bits. 0-9 are valid digits, but the result is limited to n bits.

n'o represents 3-bit octal values where 0-8 are valid values.

n'b represents 1-bit binary values where 0-1 represent each bit position.

VHDL

```
signal data : std_logic_vector(63 downto 0);
data <= (others => '1'); -- same as data <= 64b"11...11"
data <= (others => '0'); -- same as data <= 64b"00...00"
data <= (others => 'Z'); -- same as data <= 64b"ZZ...ZZ"
```

Now that we've seen types, arrays, array querying, and assignments, let's take a quick look at multiple driven nets.

Handling multiple-driven nets

There is one other type in SystemVerilog that deserves to be mentioned, although we will not be using it for a while. This is a wire. The wire type represents 120 different possible values, that is, the four basic values – 0, 1, x, and z – and drive strengths.

The wire type has what is known as a resolution function. Wire types are the only signals that can be connected to multiple drivers. We will see this when we introduce the **Serial Peripheral Interface (SPI)** protocol and access the DDR2 memory on the Nexys A7 board:

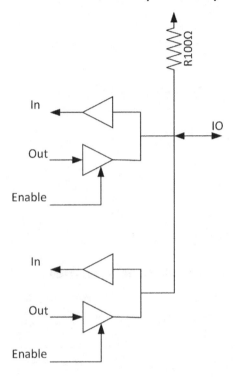

Figure 3.3: Tri-state example

FPGAs, in general, do not have internal tri-state capabilities. The preceding example shows two devices each with tri-state **Input/Output (I/O)** buffers connected:

```
logic [1:0] in;
logic [1:0] out;
logic [1:0] enable;
tri1 R_in;
assign R_in = (enable[0]) ? out[0] : 'z;
assign R_in = (enable[1]) ? out[1] : 'z;
assign in[0] = R_in;
assign in[1] = R_in;
```

The preceding code demonstrates how the two tri-state buffers are constructed. tri1 is a testbench construct where a signal is declared as a tri-state with a weak pullup to 1.

We have introduced a new operator, the conditional operator "out = a ? b : c". In this case, if a is '1' then out would be assigned the value of b, otherwise out will receive the value of c. This can be viewed as a two-input multiplexor.

If you are using std_logic and std_logic_vector, the signals have resolution functions and can be used in the same way as wires in SystemVerilog. The equivalent in VHDL would look like:

```
signal s_in   : std_logic_vector(1 downto 0);
signal s_out  : std_logic_vector(1 downto 0);
signal enable : std_logic_vector(1 downto 0);
signal r_in   : std_logic;
r_in     <= s_out(0) when enable(0) else 'Z';
r_in     <= s_out(1) when enable(1) else 'Z';
s_in(0) <= r_in;
s_in(1) <= r_in;
```

Now let's take a look at signed and unsigned numbers.

Handling signed and unsigned numbers

Verilog had just one signed signal type, integer. SystemVerilog allows us to define both unsigned and signed numbers explicitly for any built-in type:

```
bit signed [31:0] signed_vect; // Create a 32 bit signed value
bit unsigned [31:0] unsigned_vect; // create a 32 bit unsigned value
```

When performing signed arithmetic, it's important to make sure the sizing is correct. Also, when computing with signed numbers, you should make sure all the signals involved are signed so that the correct result is obtained. The table below shows an example of unsigned vs signed representation.

Value	2's complement (signed)	Signed
2'b00	0	0
2'b01	1	1
2'b10	2	-2
2'b11	3	-1

Table 3.3: Signed versus unsigned example

In *Table 3.3*, we can see an example of a signed and unsigned two-bit number. The note below describes 2's complement math.

> Digital logic, such as computer processors or FPGA implementations, use 2's complement to represent signed numbers. What this means is that to negate a number, you simply invert it and add 1. For example, to get -1 in 2's complement, assuming there are 4 bits for representation, we would take 4'b0001, invert it to get 4'b1110, and add 1, resulting in 4'b1111. Bit 3 is the sign bit, so if it's 0, the number is positive, and it's negative if it's 1. This also means that the maximum number of signed values that we can represent by using 4 bits is 4'b0111 or +7 and 4'b1000 or -8.

VHDL allows us to create signed and unsigned vectors:

```
variable a_in : signed(BITS-1 downto 0);
variable b_in : unsigned(BITS-1 downto 0);
```

Because VHDL is strongly typed, the result size must be correct to prevent errors.

Adding bits to a signal by concatenating

SystemVerilog provides a powerful concatenation function, {}. We can use it to add bits or signals to create larger vectors, or for replication. When casting an unsigned integer to a signed integer, typically, you'll want to use the concatenation operator, {}, to prepend 1'b0 to the signed bit so that the resulting signed value remains positive because the signed bit is forced to 0. The concatenation operator can be used to merge multiple signals together, such as {1'b0, unsigned_vect}. It can also be used to replicate signals. For example, {2{unsigned_vect}} would be equivalent to {unsigned_vect, unsigned_vect}.

VHDL also provides a concatenation function, &:

```
"1" & unsigned_vect
unsigned_vect & unsigned_vect
```

The only equivalent to replication, i.e., {2{unsigned_vect}} is "unsigned_vect" & "unsigned_vect".

Casting signed and unsigned numbers

You can cast an unsigned number to a signed number by using the signed' keyword, and can cast a signed number to an unsigned number by using the unsigned' keyword:

```
logic unsigned [15:0] unsigned_vect = 16'hFFFF;
logic unsigned [15:0] final_vect;
logic signed [16:0] signed_vect;
logic signed [15:0] signed_vect_small;
assign signed_vect = signed'({1'b0, unsigned_vect}); // +65535
assign signed_vect_small = signed'(unsigned_vect); // -1
assign unsigned_vect = unsigned'(signed_vect);
assign final_vect = unsigned'(signed_vect_small); // 65535
```

Here, you can see that an unsigned 16-bit number can go from 0 to 65535. A 16-bit signed number can go from -32768 to 32767, so if we assign a number larger than 32767, it would have its signed bit set in the same-sized signed number, causing it to become negative.

These are equivalent to the Verilog system functions; that is, $signed() and $unsigned(). However, it's preferable to use the casting operators.

VHDL provides similar casting functions as well as a resize function, which is important due to strict typing rules. For example, from the add_sub:

```
a_in := resize(signed(SW(BITS-1 downto BITS/2)), BITS);
```

 When casting signed to unsigned or unsigned to signed, pay attention to sizing. For example, to maintain the positive nature of unsigned, typically, you'll use the concatenation operator, {} *or* &, as in signed({1'b0, unsigned_vect}), which means the resulting signal will be 1 bit larger. When going from signed to unsigned, care must be taken to ensure that the number is positive; otherwise, the resulting assignment will not be correct. You can see an example of mismatched assignments in the preceding code, where signed_vect_small becomes -1 rather than 65535 and final_vect becomes 65535, even though signed_vect_small is -1.

Creating user-defined types

We have seen previously that to create arrays in VHDL, we could create a new type. SystemVerilog provides a similar capability.

We can create our own types using typedef. A common example that's used in SystemVerilog is to create a user-defined type for speeding up simulations. This can be done by using a define:

```
`ifdef FAST_SIM
  typedef bit bit_t
`else
  typedef logic bit_t
`endif
```

If FAST_SIM is defined, then any time we use bit_t, the simulator will use bit; otherwise, it will use logic. This will speed up simulations.

 It is a good idea to adopt a naming convention when creating types – in this case, _t. This helps you identify user-defined types and prevent confusion when using the type within your design.

Accessing signals using values with enumerated types

When it comes to readability, it's often preferable to use variables with values that make more sense and are self-documenting. We can use enumerated types in SystemVerilog to accomplish this, like so:

```
enum bit [1:0] {RED, GREEN, BLUE} color;
```

In VHDL, it would be like:

```
type color_t is (RED, GREEN, BLUE);
signal color : color_t;
```

In this case, we are creating a variable, color, made up of the values RED, GREEN, and BLUE. Simulators will display these values in their waveforms. We'll discuss enumerated types in more detail in *Chapter 4, Counting Button Presses*.

Packaging up code using functions

Often, we'll have code that we will be reusing within the same module or that's common to a group of modules. We can package this code up in a function in **SystemVerilog**:

```
function [4:0] func_addr_decode(input [31:0] addr);
  func_addr_decode = '0;
  for (int i = 0; i < 32; i++) begin
```

```
    if (addr[i]) begin
      return(i);
    end
  end
endfunction
```

We can accomplish the same thing in **VHDL**:

```
function func_addr_decoder(addr : std_logic_vector(31 downto 0)) return
integer is
  begin
    for i in addr'low to addr'high loop
      if addr(i) then
        return i;
      end if;
    end loop;
    return 0;
  end function func_addr_decoder;
```

Here, we created a function called func_addr_decode that returns a 5-bit value in SystemVerilog ($clog2 of 32) or an integer in VHDL. This address decoder function takes a 32-bit input called addr (abbreviation for address). Functions in SystemVerilog can have multiple outputs, but we will not be using this feature. To return the function's value in either language, you can use return. In SystemVerilog, you can also assign the result to the function name.

> SystemVerilog provides a convenient mechanism for getting the log base 2, or the number of bits required to index into a particular vector. This is the $clog2 function.
>
> In VHDL, we can generate the equivalent using natural(ceil(log2(real(BI TS)))). These mechanisms are particularly useful for creating reusable code.

Creating combinational logic

The first way of creating logic is via assign statements in SystemVerilog or an assignment in VHDL within the architecture, but outside of a process block (we'll refer to this as an assign for simplicity). assign statements are convenient when creating purely combinational logic with only a few terms. This is not to say the resulting logic will necessarily be small. For instance, you could create a large multiply accumulator using a single line of code, or large combinational structures by utilizing an assign statement and calling a function:

```
assign mac = (a * b) + old_mac;
assign addr_decoder = func_addr_decode(current_address);
```

In VHDL:

```
--outside of a process block
mac <= (a * b) + old_mac;
addr_decoder <= func_addr_decode(current_address);
--process block example
example : process is
```

The second way of creating logic is an `always` or `process` block allows for more complex functionality to be defined in a single process. We looked at `always` and `process` blocks in the previous chapter. There, we were using a sensitivity list in the context of a testbench. Sensitivity lists allow an `always` or `process` block to only be triggered when a signal in the list changes. Let's look back at the testbench that was provided in *Chapter 2, FPGA Programming Languages and Tools*:

```
always @(LED) begin
```

In this example, the `always` block would only be triggered when `LED` transitions from one state to another.

> Sensitivity lists are not synthesizable and are only useful in testing. `always_comb` in `SystemVerilog` or `process(all)` is recommended when describing synthesizable combinational logic in an `always` block.

When we write synthesizable code using an `always` block in `SystemVerilog`, we use the `always_comb` structure. This type of code is synthesizable and recommended for combinational logic. The reason is that `always_comb` will create a warning or error if we inadvertently create a latch. In Verilog 2001 or earlier, `always_comb` isn't available. VHDL-2008 allows us to use `process(all)` to trigger on any signal in the process block that changes but doesn't enforce combinational only logic like `always_comb`.

> A note about latches: They are a type of storage element. They are level-sensitive, meaning that they are *transparent* when the gating signal is high, but when the gating signal transitions to low, the value is held. Latches do have their uses, particularly in the ASIC world, but they should be avoided at all costs in an FPGA as they almost always lead to timing problems and random failures. We will demonstrate how a latch works and why it can be bad as part of this chapter's project.

There are a few different operations that can go within an `always`/`process` block. Since we are generating combinational logic, we must make sure that all the possible paths through any of these commands are covered. We will discuss this later.

Handling assignment operators

There are two basic types of assignments in `SystemVerilog`: blocking and non-blocking.

In VHDL, signals are non-blocking; however, local variables within a `process` can only be assigned in a blocking way, like using = in `SystemVerilog`.

Blocking versus non-blocking is a very important concern when designing hardware. Because we are writing in an HDL, we need to be able to model the hardware we are creating. All the hardware you design will be effectively running in parallel inside the FPGA. This requires a different mindset than software, which predominantly runs serially.

Creating multiple assignments using non-blocking assignments

In hardware, whenever you create multiple `always`/`process` blocks, they are all executing at the same time. Since this is effectively impossible on a normal computer running a program linearly or, at best, a few threads in parallel, we need a way to model this parallel behavior. Simulators accomplish this by using a scheduler that splits up simulation time into delta event cycles. This way, if multiple assignments are scheduled to happen, there is still a linear flow to them. This makes handling blocking and non-blocking assignments critical.

A non-blocking assignment is something that is scheduled to occur after delta events occur and when the simulator's time advances. These signals are used in sequential logic. We will discuss non-blocking in more detail in *Chapter 4, Counting Button Presses*.

Using blocking assignments

Blocking assignments occur immediately. With rare exceptions, usually only with regard to testbenches, all assignments within an `always_comb` block or a non-clocked process will be blocking.

In VHDL, only a variable assignment : = is blocking.

There are several additional blocking assignments in `SystemVerilog`:

=	Assign the RHS to the LHS.
+=	Increment by value on RHS and assign.
-=	Decrement by value on RHS and assign.
*=	Multiply by value on RHS and assign.
/=	Divide by RHS value and assign.
%=	Divide by RHS value and assign modulus.
&=	Logical and by RHS and assign.
|=	Logic or with RHS and assign.
^=	Logical XOR with RHS and assign.
<<=	Bitwise left shift and assign (equivalent to multiplying by 2^RHS).
>>=	Bitwise right shift and assign (equivalent to dividing by 2^RHS).
<<<=	Arithmetic left shift and assign (equivalent to multiplying by 2^RHS); the sign bit is preserved.
>>>=	Arithmetic right shift and assign (equivalent to dividing by 2^RHS); the sign bit is preserved.

Figure 3.4: Additional blocking assignments in SystemVerilog

In SystemVerilog, there are also some shortcuts for incrementing or decrementing signals.

Incrementing signals

Here's a list of the shortcuts for incrementing:

- Pre-increment, ++i, increments the value of i before using it

- Post-increment, i++, increments i after using it

- Pre-decrement, --i, increments the value of i before using it

- Post-decrement, i--, increments i after using it

Now that we've learned how to manipulate values, let's learn how to use these variables to make decisions.

Making decisions — if-then-else

One of the basics of any programming language is to control the flow through any operation. In the case of a HDL, this is generating the actual logic that will be implemented in the FPGA fabric. We can view an if-then-else statement as a multiplexer, the conditional expression of the if statement is the select lines. Let's take a look at it in its simplest form:

SystemVerilog

```
if (add == 1) sum = a + b;
else          sum = a - b;
```

VHDL

```
if add then
   sum := a + b;
else
   sum := a - b;
end if;
```

This will select whether b will be added or subtracted from a based on whether the add signal is high. A simplified view of what could be generated is shown in the following diagram:

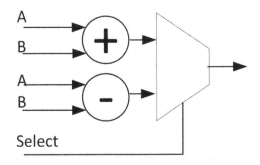

Figure 3.5: An if-then-else representation

Probably, the logic will be implemented in a much less expensive way. It's worth looking at the results of your designs as they are built to understand the kind of optimizations that occur.

Comparing values

SystemVerilog supports normal equality operations such as == and !=. These operators check if two sides of a comparison are equal or not equal, respectively. Since we are dealing with hardware and there is the possibility of us having undefined values, there is a disadvantage to these operators in that x's can cause a match, even if it's not intended, by falling through to the else clause. This is usually more of an issue in testbenches. There are versions of these operators that are resistant to x's in SystemVerilog; that is, === and !==. In a testbench, it is advised to use these operators to avoid unanticipated matches.

VHDL provides the equivalent of = and /=. Due to the strong typing of VHDL, it doesn't suffer from the same issues as SystemVerilog.

Comparing wildcard equality operators (SystemVerilog)

It is also possible to match against ranges of values. This is possible using the =?= and !?= operators. They allow us to use wildcards in the match condition. For example, say you had a 32-bit bus but needed to handle odd-aligned addressing:

```
if (address[3:0] =?= 4'b00zz)        slot = 0;
else if (address[3:0] =?= 4'b01zz) slot = 1;
```

The wildcard operators allow you to do this. The preceding examples would ignore the lower two bits.

VHDL don't care

VHDL allows "don't care" values in comparison to VHDL-2008:

```
if address(3 downto 0) ?= "00--" then
   slot := 0;
elsif address(3 downto 0) ?= "01--" then
   slot := 1;
end if;
```

Qualifying if statements with unique or priority (SystemVerilog)

Normally, when thinking of an if statement, you think of each if evaluation as a separate comparison relying on the if statements that came before it. This type of if statement is a priority, meaning that the first if that matches will evaluate to true. In the simple example shown previously, we can see that we are looking at the same address and masking out the lowest two bits. Often, during optimization, the tool will realize that the if statements cannot overlap and will optimize the logic accordingly. However, if we know this to be the case, we can use the unique keyword to tell Vivado that each if doesn't overlap with any that come before or after. This allows the tool to better optimize the resulting logic during the synthesis stage. Care must be taken, however. Let's see what would happen if we tried to do the following:

```
unique if (address[3:0] =?= 4'b00zz) slot = 0;
else    if (address[3:0] =?= 4'b01zz) slot = 1;
else    if (address[3:0] =?= 4'b1000) slot = 2;
else    if (address[3:0] =?= 4'b1zzz) slot = 3;
```

Here, we can see that the last two else if statements overlap. If we specify unique in this case, we are likely to get a mismatch between simulation and synthesis. If address[3:0] was equal to 4'b1000 during the simulation, the simulator would issue a warning that the unique condition had been violated. Synthesis would optimize incorrectly, and the logic wouldn't work as intended. We'll see this when we violate unique on a case statement, when we work on this chapter's project.

This type of if is actually a priority, and if we wanted to, we could direct the tool, like so:

```
priority if (address[3:0] =?= 4'b00zz) slot = 0;
```

Priority is not really required except to provide clarity of intent. This is because the tool will usually be able to figure out if an if can be optimized as unique. If not, it will be treated as priority by default.

Introducing the case statement (SystemVerilog)

A case statement is typically used for making a larger number of comparisons. There are three versions of the case statement you might use: case, casex, and casez. The case statement is used when wildcards are not necessary. If you want to use wildcards, as we saw previously, casez is recommended. There are two ways case statements are usually used. The first is more traditional:

```
casez (address[3:0])
  4'b00zz: slot = 0;
  4'b01zz: slot = 1;
  4'b1000: slot = 2;
  4'b1zzz: slot = 3;
endcase
```

Just like in the case of the if statement, unique or priority can be used to guide the tool. Also, we can have a default fall-through case that can be defined. This must be defined if unique is used.

unique and priority are powerful tools in that they can greatly reduce the final logic's area and timing. However, care must be taken as incorrectly specifying them can cause logic errors. Simulation will check that the conditions are not violated, but it will only detect cases that occur during simulation. They are only available in SystemVerilog.

In SystemVerilog, there is another way of writing a case statement that can be especially useful:

```
priority case (1'b1)
  address[3]: slot = 0;
  address[2]: slot = 1;
  address[1]: slot = 2;
  address[0]: slot = 3;
endcase
```

In this particular case, we have created a **leading-ones detector (LOD)**. Since we may have multiple bits set, specifying a unique modifier could cause optimization problems. If the design had one-hot encoding on address, then specifying unique would create a more optimized solution. VHDL doesn't provide a mechanism to create this kind of case statement.

There are different ways to encode data. Binary encoding can set multiple bits at the same time and is typically an incrementing value. One-hot encoding has one bit set at a time. This makes decoding simpler. There is also something we'll explore when we discuss **First-In-First-Out (FIFO)**, called gray coding, which is a manner of encoding that is impervious to synchronization problems when properly constrained.

For more simple selections, SystemVerilog supplies a simple way of handling this.

Using the conditional operator to select data

SystemVerilog provides a shortcut for conditionally selecting a result in the following form:

```
Out = (sel) ? ina : inb;
```

When sel is high, ina will be assigned to out; otherwise, inb will be assigned to out.

Writing sel ? ... is a shortcut for sel == 1'b1 ? ....

In VHDL, we have a similar function to the ? operator:

```
r_out <= ina when sel else inb;
with sel select r_out <=
  ina when '1',
  inb when '0';
```

VHDL-2008 also allows wildcards with `select`:

```
with sel select? r_out <=
  ina when "1-",
  inb when "-1";
```

Both of these operators can contain multiple when clauses.

Introducing the case statement (VHDL)

In VHDL, we have a case statement to operate on defined values:

```
case sel is
  when '0' => LED <= MULT_LED;
  when '1' => LED(natural(ceil(log2(real(BITS))))-1 downto 0) <= LO_LED;
end case;
```

We also have case? in VHDL-2008, which allows us to use wildcards:

```
case? sel is
  when "1----" => LED <= MULT_LED;
  when "01---" => LED(natural(ceil(log2(real(BITS)))) - 1 downto 0) <=
LO_LED;
  when "001--" => LED(natural(ceil(log2(real(BITS)))) - 1 downto 0) <=
NO_LED;
  when "0001-" => LED <= AD_LED;
  when "00001" => LED <= SB_LED;
  when others  => LED <= (others => '0');
end case?;
```

Note the use of others above, which is the equivalent of default in SystemVerilog.

In this section, we've looked at basic data types and arrays and how to use them. In the next section, we'll learn how to use custom data types more tailored to our designs.

Using custom data types

Both SystemVerilog and VHDL provide us with a variety of ways to create user-defined types. User-defined types can also be stored in arrays.

Creating structures

In this section, we'll look at how we can create and use structures, unions, and records.

SystemVerilog

Structures allow us to group signals that belong together. For example, if we wanted to create a 16-bit value composed of two 8-bit values, h and l, we could do something like this:

```
typedef struct packed {bit [7:0] hi; bit [7:0] lo;} reg_t;
reg_t cpu_reg;
assign cpu_reg.hi = 8'hFE;
```

Here's what the keywords signify:

- typedef signifies we are creating a user-defined type.
- struct means we are creating a structure.
- packed signifies the structure is to be packed in memory.

 Structures and unions can be packed or unpacked, but as packed tends to make more sense in the context of hardware, it's what we'll use here.

We access parts of a structure by using the created signal by appending the part of the structure – in this case, h – separated by a period.

VHDL

VHDL provides the record type, which is equivalent to the SystemVerilog structure:

```
type reg_t is record
  HI : std_logic_vector(7 downto 0);
  LO : std_logic_vector(7 downto 0);
end record reg_t;
```

Creating unions (SystemVerilog)

A union allows us to create a variable with multiple representations. This is useful if you need multiple methods for accessing the same data. For instance, as microprocessors advanced from 8 bits to 16 bits, there needed to be ways to access parts of the register for older operations:

```
union packed {bit [15:0] x; reg_t cr;} a_reg;
always_comb begin
  a_reg.x = 16'hFFFF;
  a_reg.cr.h = '0;
end
```

In the preceding example, we created a union of a 16-bit register and a structure composed of two 8-bit values. After the first blocking assignment, a_reg sets all bits to 1. After the second assignment, the upper 8 bits were set to 0, meaning a_reg is 16'h00FF.

VHDL doesn't have an equivalent to the union.

With the basics behind us, we can take a look at our project on combinational logic.

Project 2 – Creating combinational logic

In this chapter, we've discussed signal types and how to create combinational logic. This project will contain multiple components that allow us to come up with a small calculator. It will be a rather simple one and will have the following capabilities:

- Find the leading-one position of a vector's input via switches
- Add, subtract, or multiply two numbers
- Count the number of switches that have been set

The following diagram shows what the Nexys A7 board looks like:

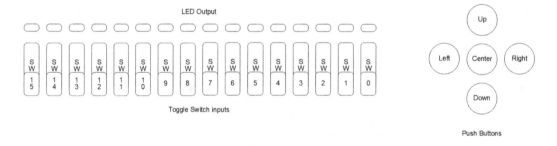

Figure 3.6: Nexys A7 board I/O

In the previous chapter's project, we learned how to use switches for input and LEDs for output. In this project, we'll be using all the switches in the preceding diagram for the number of ones calculator where we will produce a binary count from 0-16 based on the number of switches that are on. Additionally, we'll create an LOD where we'll detect the position of the left-most switch that's been set out of the 16 positions.

For the arithmetic operations, we'll divide the switches into two groups. Switches 7:0 will be for input B, while switches 15:8 will be for input A. The output will be displayed as a 2's complement number using all the 16 LEDs above the switches, as shown in the preceding diagram. This means that -1 would mean all the LEDs are lit, while 0 would mean that all the LEDs are off.

Testbench

Since we will be building up individual components, we'll want a versatile testbench that will allow us to test each component individually and then all together. We'll accomplish this by using parameters. In this testbench, there are three parameters:

- SELECTOR is used for the leading-one module to determine one of four ways of finding the leading one. It's also used to select between addition or subtraction for the add_sub module.

- UNIQUE_CASE determines whether we are going to generate unique case values or purely random numbers that can have multiple bits set. (SystemVerilog)

- TESTCASE allows us to test individual components (LEADING_ONES, NUM_ONES, ADD, SUB, and MULT) or all of them (ALL).

To change these parameters in the testbench, select **Settings | Simulation | Generics/Parameters**:

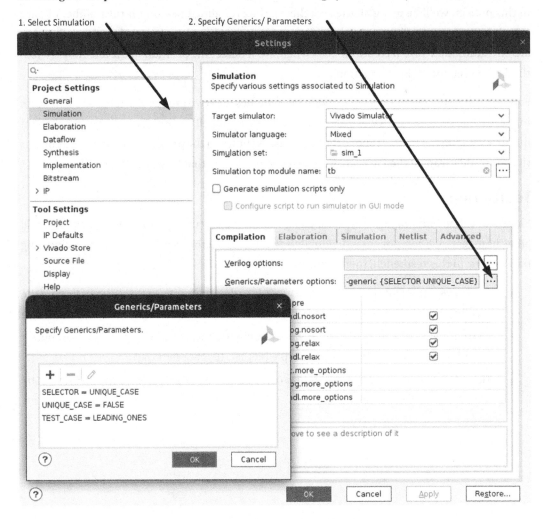

Figure 3.7: Specifying simulation parameters

Similarly, to change the parameters for the implementation, select **Settings | General | Generics/Parameters**:

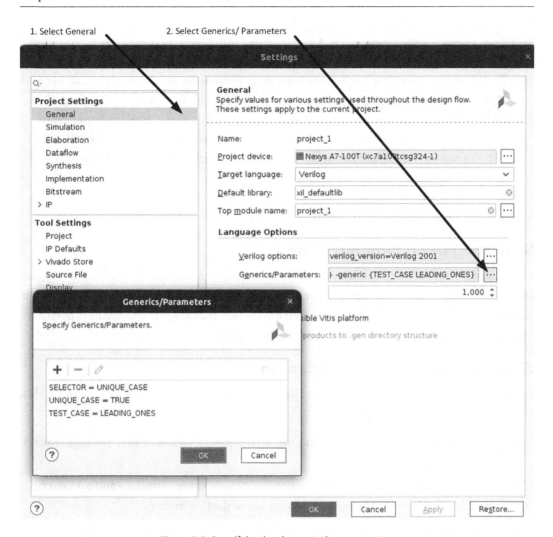

Figure 3.8: Specifying implementation parameters

There are many ways to write testbenches. In the past, I've used separate include files for individual tests and used a shell script to invoke the simulator multiple times. If you are interested in exploring this type of testbench, please check out my open source graphics accelerator GPLGPU on GitHub: https://github.com/asicguy/gplgpu. What we will be using for our project is simpler: using parameters to select test cases.

SystemVerilog and VHDL can be mixed for implementation as well as simulation. In fact, with the adoption of **Universal Verification Methodology (UVM)**, SystemVerilog has become even more popular for verification. You can use a SystemVerilog testbench for VHDL or VHDL simulation for SystemVerilog. The Vivado simulator has come a long way, but the VHDL support when it comes to testbench constructs and the issues I've seen with sensitivity lists make it unsuitable for testing. Throughout this book, I'll be primarily using SystemVerilog for simulation, but I will try to show the same concepts in VHDL.

In general, there are three ways of testing your design.

Simulating using targeted testing

This type of test is used when you have a specific test case you want to make sure is hit. Examples of this would be to see what happens when no bits are set in the LOD detector, all bits are set in the number of ones, or the largest and smallest numbers in the case of mathematical operations. This test can also be used to round out randomized testing.

Simulating using randomized testing

We use this mostly in the self-checking testbenches that we'll be creating. To accomplish this, we'll use two SystemVerilog functions:

- $random(), which returns a 32-bit random number. It returns a new random number every time it's invoked.
- $urandom_range(a,b), which returns a number inclusively between a and b. In our case, we are using $urandom_range(0,4) to set one of the four buttons.

For random numbers in VHDL, we use:

```
variable seed1, seed2 : positive;
variable rand_val: real;
seed1 := 1;
seed2 := 1;
uniform(seed1, seed2, rand_val);    -- generate random number
SW <= std_logic_vector(to_unsigned(integer(trunc(rand_val * 65636.0)),
SW'length));
```

rand_val is a real number in the open interval (0.0, 1.0). We multiply that number by 65635 to generate an integer in the range 0 to 65535.

Next, we'll learn how to simulate using constrained randomization.

Simulating using constrained randomization

SystemVerilog has a very robust set of testing capabilities built into it. You can imagine this type of testing being used if you have a CPU with several valid instructions, and you want to randomize the testbench so that it uses these instructions and makes sure they are all used at some point. This is beyond the scope of this book, but I'll provide links in the *Further reading* section to the UVM manual if this topic is of interest.

Now let's look at implementing the LOD using different methods.

Implementing an LOD using the case statement (SystemVerilog)

Our first module will be an LOD. We'll implement it in a few different ways and look at the advantages, disadvantages, and potential problems.

The first thing we need to decide is if the incoming signal is one-hot encoded. If it is one-hot encoded, we can get an optimized result by using the unique keyword:

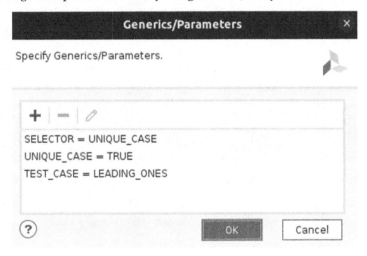

Figure 3.9: Testing the LOD using a case statement

Verify that your simulation parameters are set as shown in the preceding screenshot.

Controlling implementation using generate

Take a moment and examine the leading_ones.sv and leading_ones.vhd files. Here, you'll see how a generate statement can be used to selectively create code. The format of a generate statement is generate <condition>, as follows:

```
generate
  if (SELECTOR == "UNIQUE_CASE") begin : g_UNIQUE_CASE
```

In this case, the condition is an if statement, and it is used to selectively instantiate one of four always blocks. case statements and for loops are also valid conditions that we'll explore as we progress. This is where parameters are especially useful for controlling what gets created.

VHDL also provides a generate concept:

```
g_UNIQUE_CASE : if SELECTOR="UNIQUE_CASE" generate
```

Similarly, we can use for loops or case statements rather than if statements.

 It is a good idea to use labels inside generate blocks. The reason is that auto generated labels can change between builds if the code changes, which can cause cross module referencing to fail. Synopsys VCS and other simulators warn about this.

Notice that the case statement's default is commented out. Leave it as-is for now and run the test using the SystemVerilog code:

```
WARNING: 100000ns : none of the conditions were true for unique case from
File:/home/fbruno/git/books/Learn-FPGA-Programming/CH2/hdl/leading_ones.
sv:17
```

Why are we getting a warning? When we create a unique case, we must ensure that not only we ever match once, but we also match one. We want to make LED = 0 when no SW is set, so we uncomment the default. Now, we can run it again and the test will pass.

 Parameters can control how logic is implemented or how testbench code is executed. In the testbench, you will see if (UNIQUE_CASE == "TRUE") begin, which controls how the code is executed to limit the number of ones being set.

Now, let's allow non-unique values to see how the simulator handles them. Change UNIQUE_CASE to "FALSE":

```
Setting switches to 0011010100100100
WARNING: 0ns : Multiple conditions true
     condition at line:21 conflicts with condition at line:20
     for unique case from File:/home/fbruno/git/books/Learn-FPGA-
Programming/CH2/hdl/leading_ones.sv:17
```

This is only the first one that I saw, but you will see many. If our testbench hits cases that violate our unique assumption, we will see warnings that let us know the design may have problems.

So, let's see what happens when we take the design through to a bitstream by itself. Make sure that **Settings | General | Top Module Name** is set to leading_ones and that SELECTOR, under **Generics/Parameters**, is set to UNIQUE_CASE. Then, click on **Generate Bitstream**.

 Generics/parameters are set in two places in Vivado. General settings apply to building the design. Simulation applies only to simulation.

Take a look at the project summary. In the lower left of the window, look at the post-implementation utilization. By default, it comes up with a graph, but you can click on the table option to get hard numbers. In my build, this is what I got:

Utilization		Post-Synthesis	Post-Implementation
			Graph | **Table**
Resource	Utilization	Available	Utilization %
LUT	7	63400	0.01
IO	21	210	10.00

Figure 3.10: Post-implementation utilization

We used 7 LUTs for this implementation. But what happens when we try this on the board? Open the hardware manager and the target, and then choose **Program device**.

We are expecting one-hot encoded values, so try setting one bit at a time, starting from 0, so that only one switch is up at a time, one-hot encoded. Do you see the LEDs light up properly? You should see the binary value for the switch you have set plus one, so SW0 will show 5'b00001, SW1 will show 5'b00010, and SW15 will show 5'b10000. Now, try to set multiple switches, such as 15 and 0. What did you get? In my case, I saw 5'b10001. Now, try some others. You'll notice that some combinations still give the correct value by chance.

The reason that we see incorrect results in our implementation is that we told the compiler that the inputs would be unique. Our simulator warned us that we violated this condition and we ignored it and built anyway. This allowed the FPGA implementation to be optimized, but it will only work when one switch is flipped at a time.

Now, let's try rebuilding without the unique keyword. Set SELECTOR to "CASE" and then generate the bitstream.

By looking at the summary of this build, we can see that handling priority cost us almost 2x the number of LUTs. My build took 13. Let's try it on the board.

Try combining multiple switches. Do you always get the switch position +1 for the uppermost switch?

In this section, you saw that unique allows optimization. The unique case statement was almost half the size of the case without unique. The case statement does have the disadvantage of us having to specify all possible cases, so it's not really reusable for an arbitrary number of cases. Let's explore another, more scalable way of handling an LOD: using a for loop.

Designing a reusable LOD using a for loop

The for loop allows us to quickly create replicated logic. In the case of an LOD, it is also easy to imagine how we can do this using a for loop. There are two ways to accomplish this, both of which we'll look at in this section.

Setting SELECTOR = DOWN_FOR

The first is straightforward and follows along the lines of how the case statement accomplishes this task:

```
always_comb begin
  LED = '0;
  for (int i = $high(SW); i >= $low(SW); i--) begin
    if (SW[i]) begin
      LED = i + 1;
      break;
    end
  end
end
```

We use the $high and $low system tasks for reusability. The loop breaks when a 1 is detected for the first time. It's the same in VHDL:

```
lo := 0;
for i in SW'high downto SW'low loop
  if SW(i) then
    lo := i + 1;
    exit;
  end if;
end loop;
```

In VHDL, we can use the 'high and 'low attributes of the SW vector to iterate through its bits in a generic way. Alternatively, we could use the 'range attribute if we are sure that the vector has been defined with a descending range. The loop will exit when a 1 is detected for the first time.

 A break *or* exit in a for loop is synthesizable. The important thing to consider is whether you can unroll the loop or if there is a way to write the loop in a way that the break isn't necessary. If you can think of a relatively easy way this can be done, then you probably won't have an issue synthesizing it.

For example, we could unroll the loop by writing it as follows:

```
logic [3:0] SW;
always_comb begin
  LED = '0;
  if      (SW[3]) LED = 4;
  else if (SW[2]) LED = 3;
  else if (SW[1]) LED = 2;
  else if (SW[0]) LED = 1;
  else            LED = 0;
end
```

We can now look at another way of writing the for loop that satisfies our unrolling requirement.

Setting SELECTOR = UP_FOR

By progressing from the lowest bit to the highest bit while searching for a switch set high, we are guaranteed to find the highest bit as it will be the last 1 that's found. This is also how you know that the break can be synthesized since we have found a way to rewrite the for loop so that it's not necessary.

Counting the number of ones

Related to finding the leading one is counting the number of ones in a vector. We can do this easily using a for loop:

SystemVerilog

```
always_comb begin
  LED = '0;
  for (int i = $low(SW); i <= $high(SW); i++) begin
    LED += SW[i];
  end
end
```

VHDL

```
lo := 0;
for i in SW'low to SW'high loop
  if SW(i) then
    lo := i + 1;
  end if;
end loop;
```

Set SELECTOR to NUM_ONES and TEST_CASE to NUM_ONES and simulate to verify it works. Verify that SELECTOR is set to NUM_ONES on the **General** tab and that the top module's name is set to num_ones. Then, generate the bitstream and run it on the board.

Verify the design on the board by flipping the switches one by one in any order. You should see the LEDs light up in the pattern of a binary count; that is, 16'b0, 16'b1, 16'b10, 16'b11, and so on.

Implementing an adder/subtractor

Let's take a look at the add_sub module. There are many ways to implement an adder or subtractor in math in general. Many companies sell tools for high-performance or low gate count designs. For FPGAs, 99% of the time, you are better off letting the tools optimize your designs. Because of this, you'll see that the module itself is fairly small. We choose whether we are adding or subtracting based on the SELECTOR parameter.

Adder

For the adder:

1. Set SELECTOR to ADD and TEST_CASE to ADD.

2. Run the simulation to verify it works.

3. Verify that SELECTOR is set to ADD under the **General** tab and that the top module's name is set to add_sub.

4. Generate the bitstream and run it on the board:

Figure 3.10 shows the **Settings** window for the adder.

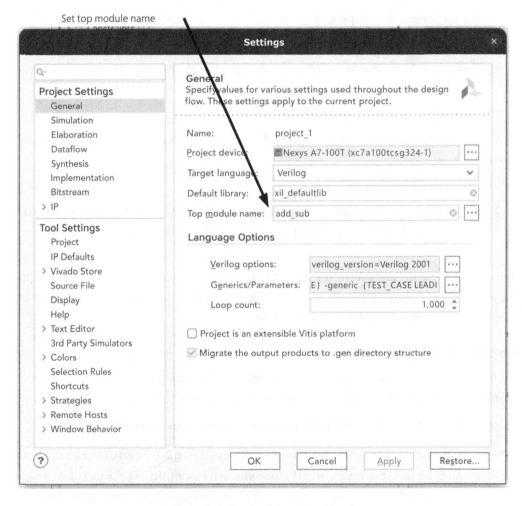

Figure 3.11: Top module set to add_sub

Once you've downloaded the bitstream on the board, try some combinations of bits on the lower 8 and upper 8 bits. In particular, if you set bit 0 and bit 8 both to 1, you should see bit 1 set on the LED; that is, a value of 16'h2. Now, try setting bit 0 and bit 15 – you should see the LEDs lit in a pattern that looks like 16'b1111111110000001.

It may look a bit weird seeing so many LEDs lit, but you'll notice that only the upper bits are lit. This is because we have specified 8'h80 + 8'h1. Since we are specifying 2's complement numbers, in decimal, this would be -128 + 1 or -127, which in hex would be 16'hFF81.

Subtractor

For the subtractor:

1. Set SELECTOR to SUB and TEST_CASE to SUB.

2. Run the simulation to verify it works.

3. Verify that SELECTOR is set to SUB under the **General** tab and that the top module's name is set to add_sub.

4. Generate the bitstream and run it on the board.

Now, we are subtracting the lower 8 bits from the upper 8 bits. Try setting bit to 0. All the LEDs should be lit, or -1.

 Remember, to get -1 in binary, we invert and add 1; for example, -16'b0000000000000001 = 16'b1111111111111110 + 1 = 16'b1111111111111111.

Note that for the adder and subtractor, no matter what you add with signed numbers, the upper 8 **most significant bits** (**MSBs**) will always be either all 0s or all 1s because we only have 8 bits from the switches for each half of the subtraction.

Implementing a Multiplier

The final module we will look at is the multiplier. HDL is the simplest out of all of them, and since the multiplier is only 8*8, by default, it is implemented in LUTs.

Set SELECTOR to MULT and TEST_CASE to MULT and run the simulation to verify it works.

This simulation is automated. However, we can also use the add_force TCL command in the simulator. An example of this is shown in the following screenshot. An add_force TCL command, or a Verilog force in the testbench will override a value on a signal in the simulator. When the simulation ended, I forced a value of 0x1234 onto the SW input of the multiplier. Since I've done this, I need to advance simulation time, which I can do with run 10ns.

The force command is good for when you are trying to isolate a particular scenario or experiment with a *what-if* scenario during a run. In general, you will not want to simulate solely this way as you'll want to have a way of reproducing your results, so putting your tests in a SystemVerilog testbench is a better long-term solution.

When you are done with a scenario, you can use the remove_forces TCL command on a signal to return control to the testbench:

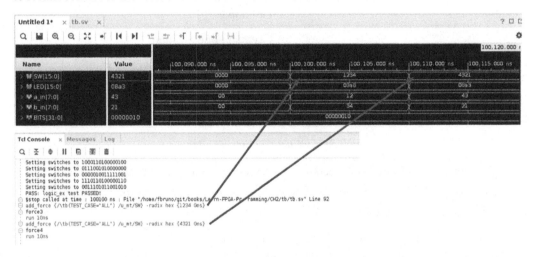

Figure 3.12: Force statement in a simulation

Verify that SELECTOR is set to MULT on the **General** tab and the top module name is set to mult then generate the bitstream and run it on the board:

Utilization			Post-Synthesis	Post-Implementation
Resource	Utilization	Available	Utilization %	
LUT	61	63400	0.10	
IO	32	210	15.24	

Figure 3.13: Multiplier utilization

The preceding snippet shows our utilization from building the multiplier.

 Adding two signed or unsigned numbers of size n will result in a value of size n+1. Multiplying two numbers of size n will result in a value of size 2*n.

Bringing it all together

Now, we'll create a simple **Arithmetic Logic Unit (ALU)** top level so that we can bring everything together. Look at project_2. There are five buttons on the board. We'll use them to control the output.

Button	Operation
Center	Multiply
Up	Leading-one position
Down	Number of switches set to one
Left	SW[15:8] + SW[7:0]
Right	SW[15:8] – SW[7:0]

Table 3.4: Calculator button operations

Instantiate the submodules. We'll need to use add_sub twice and use SELECTOR so that it's hard-coded to select the one we want. We'll still pass the selector to the leading-one calculator in case we want to play around with it:

```
leading_ones #(.SELECTOR(SELECTOR), .BITS(BITS))
  u_lo (.*, .LED(LO_LED));
add_sub      #(.SELECTOR("ADD"),    .BITS(BITS))
  u_ad (.*, .LED(AD_LED));
add_sub      #(.SELECTOR("SUB"),    .BITS(BITS))
  u_sb (.*, .LED(SB_LED));
num_ones     #(                     .BITS(BITS))
  u_no (.*, .LED(NO_LED));
mult         #(                     .BITS(BITS))
  u_mt (.*, .LED(MULT_LED));
```

 Note in the VHDL version of project_2 that VHDL doesn't support wildcard ports. This will be important in the testbench so we can reuse the SystemVerilog testbench with the VHDL design.

Now that we have overridden the names of the LED outputs of the submodules, we can mux them to the LEDs:

```
always_comb begin
  LED = '0;
```

```
  case (1'b1)
    BTNC: LED  = MULT_LED;
    BTNU: LED  = LO_LED;
    BTND: LED  = NO_LED;
    BTNL: LED  = AD_LED;
    BTNR: LED  = SB_LED;
  endcase
end
```

VHDL doesn't support the inverted case format as above, but we do have wildcard support using the *matching case statement*:

```
sel := BTNC & BTNU & BTND & BTNL & BTNR;
LED <= (others => '0');
case? sel is
  when "1----" => LED <= MULT_LED;
  when "01---" => LED(LO_LED'range) <= LO_LED;
  when "001--" => LED(NO_LED'range) <= NO_LED;
  when "0001-" => LED <= AD_LED;
  when "00001" => LED <= SB_LED;
  when others  => LED <= (others => '0');
end case?;
```

Set TEST_CASE to ALL and run the simulation to verify it works. Verify that SELECTOR is set to UNIQUE_CASE, CASE, UP_FOR, or DOWN_FOR on the **General** tab and that the top module's name is set to project_2. Then, generate the bitstream and run it on the board:

Utilization		Post-Synthesis	Post-Implementation
			Graph | **Table**
Resource	Utilization	Available	Utilization %
LUT	134	63400	0.21
IO	37	210	17.62

Figure 3.14: Complete project_2 utilization

When the image finishes downloading, the LEDs will be off. Flip some switches and select a function by pushing a button. Congratulations – your simple calculator is complete! Notice that when you release the button, the LEDs go dark. Remember that we are creating combinational logic and there is no storage. When no operator is input into the design, nothing will be displayed.

Adding a latch

Since we are not using any clocks yet, let's add a latch to demonstrate the hazards of using a latch inadvertently. In this case, the switches are static, so using a latch shouldn't cause us any problems:

SystemVerilog

```
always_latch begin
//always_comb begin
  //LED = '0;
```

Change always_comb to always_latch and comment out the LED = '0; default.

VHDL

```
btn_sel : process (all)
  -- LED <= (others => '0');
```

Comment out the LED default.

Then, rerun it. What happens when you download and try to select an operation? If your build is like mine, then this operation will not be what you expected and the LEDs will seem to behave in an almost random fashion. Latches operate in a transparent mode where data flows through them until they close. Because the latch signal has different delays to the different gating elements in the design, this can cause an almost random result. Timing closure isn't easy in this type of circuit and operation isn't guaranteed.

This is the reason that I have stressed not to use latches. If you encounter a situation where your circuit doesn't behave as intended, search the compile logs and make sure no latch is inferred.

Summary

In this chapter, we learned combinational HDL design. We looked at arrays and how we can use built-in functions to query them. We briefly looked at how data is represented in types as 0, 1, x, and z as well as multiple-driven nets. 2's complement was discussed, along with signed and unsigned calculations. Part of this discussion touched on concatenation functions. We looked at user-defined and enumerated types as well as functions for automating access to them.

We introduced the concept of functions for design reusability and non-blocking and blocking assignment types. We looked at decision-making using if-then-else, case statements, and the conditional operator. We saw how different optimizations can affect functionality and design results. We also touched on structures and unions. We then mentioned latches and the problems they cause, even when they should be safe.

The project should have given you some confidence in how to create logic and test it. In the next chapter, we'll introduce sequential logic; that is, using registers to store values and perform operations. We'll expand upon our simple calculator and see how we can improve it now that we have some storage elements.

Questions

1. A packed array in SystemVerilog is used to infer memories. True or false?

2. When can a break or exit statement be used in a for loop?

   a. Any time.

   b. If it's possible to rewrite the for loop in such a way as to not need the break.

   c. Only if you can reverse the direction of the loop; that is, go from low to high instead of high to low.

3. Size the add_unsigned, add_signed, and mult signals:

```
logic unsigned [7:0] a_unsigned;
logic unsigned [7:0] b_unsigned;
logic signed [7:0] a_signed;
logic signed [7:0] b_signed;
assign add_unsigned = a_unsigned + b_unsigned;
assign add_signed = a_signed + b_signed;
assign mult = a_unsigned * b_unsigned;
```

4. Division is a very costly operation. Look at the supported Vivado constructs in the Vivado Synthesis manual (*Further reading*). Can you easily replace the multiply operation with a division operation? What is possible without custom code?

Answers

1. True

2. b

3. Size the add_unsigned, add_signed, and mult signals:

```
logic unsigned [8:0] add_unsigned;
logic signed [8:0] add_signed;
logic unsigned [15:0] mult;
```

4. If you use fixed point notation, which we will discuss in *Chapter 7, Math, Parallelism, and Pipelined Design*, you can calculate the fractional value, i.e., 1/n, and then multiply by the calculated value.

Challenge

Look at the following add_sub module:

```
logic signed [BITS/2-1:0]        a_in;
logic signed [BITS/2-1:0]        b_in;
…
   {a_in, b_in} = SW;
```

If you were to replace a_in and b_in with a custom type that encapsulates both, would you use a structure or a union? Modify the code so that it uses your custom type, and then simulate and try it on the board.

Further reading

Please refer to the following links for more information regarding what was covered in this chapter:

1. UVM information: https://www.accellera.org/downloads/standards/uvm

2. Vivado Synthesis manual: https://www.xilinx.com/support/documentation/sw_manuals/xilinx2020_1/ug901-vivado-synthesis.pdf

3. VHDL-2008, The End of Verbosity! https://www.synthworks.com/papers/VHDL_2008_end_of_verbosity_2013.pdf

Join our community on Discord

Join our community's Discord space for discussions with the authors and other readers:

https://packt.link/embedded

4

Counting Button Presses

In *Chapter 3, Combinational Logic*, we learned the basics of **Hardware Description Language** (**HDL**) designs by creating a simple design that could detect the number of switches that are on, and the position of the highest switch. The design also featured addition, subtraction, and multiplication. We also discussed signed and unsigned numbers as well as some constructs we needed for our implementation. This was a good first step, but we lacked the ability to store values, which meant that when we released our operator button, the output would go to all 0s.

In this chapter, we'll learn how to maintain the state of a design by adding sequential elements. Limited to combinational logic with no way to store information, we can't accomplish very much. In order to have a useful CPU, you need a program counter, registers, and long-term storage. What would your cell phone be without the capability to store numbers, emails, or pictures?

To achieve this goal, we'll investigate inferring flip-flops. We'll go over non-blocking assignments in more detail. To demonstrate the use of sequential elements, we'll develop a counter that increments when a button is pressed. Sequential elements require timing constraints, so we'll look at those. We'll also look at the problems with mechanical switches and look at **clock domain crossing (CDC)** and synchronization.

In this chapter, we are going to cover the following main topics:

- What is a sequential element?
- Project 3 – Counting Button Presses
- Deep dive into Synchronization

Technical requirements

The technical requirements for this chapter are the same as those for *Chapter 2, FPGA Programming Languages and Tools*.

To follow along with the examples and the project, you can find the code files for this chapter at the following repository on GitHub: https://github.com/PacktPublishing/The-FPGA-Programming-Handbook-Second-Edition/tree/main/CH4.

What is a sequential element?

We looked at the latch in *Chapter 3, Combinational Logic*, and we saw that it's not something we really want to be using. What FPGA designers use to store information is a register, or flip-flop. Before we create our first flip-flop, we need a quick introduction to clocks.

Clocking your design

In the realm of digital logic, we usually need at least one source of timing in our design, and often several. We call this source of timing a clock, which is usually generated by an external crystal oscillator that vibrates at a certain frequency and generates a string of 0s and 1s in our design. Sometimes, we'll use the clock input directly, but if we need a specific frequency faster or slower than our input, we have other options such as **Phase-Locked Loops** (**PLLs**) and **Mixed Mode Clock Managers** (**MMCMs**), which we'll discuss in *Chapter 6, FPGA Resources and How to Use Them*.

When we draw timing diagrams, we typically draw our clocks and the inputs and outputs as square waves, as shown in *Figure 4.1*:

Figure 4.1: Simple clock

We also need to tell Vivado about the clock we have created so it can properly time our designs for implementation. Up until now, we've ignored timing since we haven't had a reference to measure time against. We'll be adding the following to our XDC file:

```
## Clock signal
set_property -dict { PACKAGE_PIN E3    IOSTANDARD LVCMOS33 } \
  [get_ports { clk }]; #IO_L12P_T1_MRCC_35 Sch=clk100mhz
create_clock -add -name clk -period 10.00 -waveform {0 5} \
  [get_ports {clk}];
```

To create a clock in a design, we use the `create_clock` **Tool Command Language (TCL)** command. We need to specify the `period` of the clock in nanoseconds and, optionally, we can specify what the waveform looks like. We apply this to a port on the design using `get_ports` and give the clock a name using `-name`. In more complex designs, it's possible to define multiple clocks on a given pin; for example, you might have a fast clock for performance and a slow clock for saving power and use a PLL to generate the clock. By applying multiple clocks, the timing analyzer can make sure that your design meets timing and has safe CDC.

> In most cases, you don't need to worry about specifying the waveform. If you have multiple clocks of the same frequency shifted in phase, then you would want to specify the waveform option to ensure the timing analysis is performed properly.

For now, we'll keep things simple and generate a single clock.

Looking at a basic register

If you were designing an **Application-Specific Integrated Circuit (ASIC)**, you'd likely have a few different register types in your library because they may be optimized for area, based on functionality, such as toggle **Flip-Flops (FFs)**, devices that toggle when the control signal is high, and they are clocked. Since Xilinx is targeting all possible design types, the registers are based on what are known as **D Flip-Flops (DFFs)**:

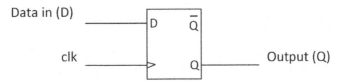

Figure 4.2: Simple DFF

The simple DFF in *Figure 4.2* accepts data in the D input and stores it every clock cycle, presenting it in the Q output. This type of storage element must be continuously fed because every change in the input is mirrored in the output.

Creating a Flip-Flops using SystemVerilog

In SystemVerilog, we can create a flip-flop in one of two ways:

```
always_ff @(edge sensitivity list)
always @(edge sensitivity list)
```

Two `SystemVerilog` keywords that convey an event occurring on the edge of a signal are posedge, the rising edge of the clock, and negedge, the falling edge. In general, we'll only be using posedge, but in some special circumstances, you may need the negedge of the clock:

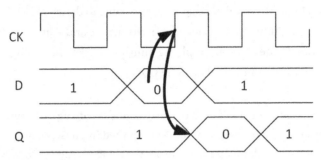

Figure 4.3: Posedge DFF timing

Figure 4.1 shows the clock edges labeled as posedge and negedge. *Figure 4.3* shows posedge flip-flop timing.

 In general, stick to one edge of the clock and use it consistently. In our designs, we'll be strictly using the positive edge. This will help prevent timing problems in your design.

Let's look at how we construct a DFF in `SystemVerilog`:

`CH4/SystemVerilog/simple_ff/hdl/simple_ff.sv`

```
module simple_ff (input wire D, CK, output logic Q);
  always_ff @(posedge CK) Q <= D;
endmodule
```

`always_ff` has the advantage of conveying design intent. Vivado accepts the construct; however, it doesn't generate an error if an FF is not inferred. Other tools will generate an error, so it's advisable to still use `always_ff` in most instances. If you'd like to try simulating this or running on the Nexys A7 board, the project is located at `https://github.com/PacktPublishing/The-FPGA-Programming-Handbook-Second-Edition/tree/main/CH4/SystemVerilog/simple_ff` or `https://github.com/PacktPublishing/The-FPGA-Programming-Handbook-Second-Edition/tree/main/CH4/VHDL/simple_ff`. Follow the procedures you learned in *Chapter 3*, *Combinational Logic*, to simulate, build, and test:

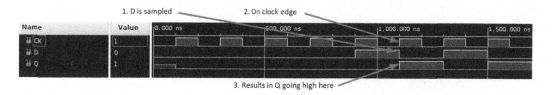

Figure 4.4: Simple FF timing

From the preceding waveform, we see that Q is changing along with every D input. It allows us to store data, but if we were just using a DFF, we would need to add recirculating logic ourselves to hold the data.

Note that **Register Trasfer Level (RTL)** simulations use ideal timing. Although you see the D input sampled and the Q output changing immediately on the rising clock edge, in actual fact, the D would have some delay and switch some time after the clock edge and the Q would also change some time after the clock edge. We are ignoring setup and hold-time requirements, which will be discussed later in this chapter.

Let's look at how we can create a flip-flop using VHDL.

Creating a flip-flop using VHDL

For SystemVerilog, there is only one way to create a flip-flop, and that is using the posedge (or negedge) event. In VHDL, we can create a flip-flop in one of two ways. The more modern way is to use the rising_edge or falling_edge functions. These functions encapsulate the older VHDL way of inferring a flip-flop, using CK'event and CK = '1'. Both are shown in the bullets below. They are equivalent in functionality:

```
{rising|falling}_edge()
CK'event and CK = '1'
```

CH4/VHDL/simple_ff/hdl/simple_ff.vhd

```
entity simple_ff is
  port(
    D  : in  std_logic;
    CK : in  std_logic;
    Q  : out std_logic
  );
end entity simple_ff;
```

```vhdl
architecture rtl of simple_ff is
  signal reg : std_logic := '0';         -- optional initial value
begin
  FF : process(CK)
  begin
    if CK'event and CK = '1' then
      reg <= D;
    end if;
    -- The following is equivalent:
    -- if rising_edge(CK) then reg <= D; end if;
  end process FF;
  Q <= reg;
end architecture rtl;
```

Both methods are equivalent from a synthesis point of view and, unlike SystemVerilog, there is no way to give a hint as to design intent. In VHDL, you can create an initial value by adding an assignment to the register signal or entity output as a default as shown here:

```vhdl
signal reg : std_logic := '0'; -- optional initial value
```

Let's take another look at SystemVerilog flip-flop generation and why you may not want to use `always_ff` in some cases.

When to use always @() for FF generation

There is a limitation of `always_ff` in that any signal generated from it cannot be driven by any other construct. FPGAs support using an initial statement to determine the FF startup value. In our `simple_ff.sv` example, the startup value for Q is not defined by the code. This can be seen in *Figure 4.4*, where the startup condition is 'x. This means that the synthesis tool can use either 0 or 1. We can, however, create an initial value for the FF:

CH4/SystemVerilog/simple_init_ff/hdl/simple_init_ff.sv

```systemverilog
module simple_init_ff (input wire D, CK, output logic Q);
  initial begin Q = 1
  end;
  always_ff @(posedge CK) Q <= D;
endmodule
```

However, if we try to run the simulator, we'll get the following in the **Messages** pane:

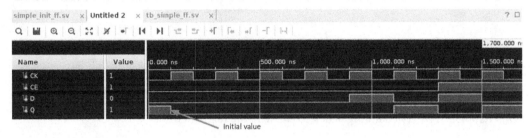

∨ 🗅 Simulation (2 errors, 1 warning)
   ∨ 🗅 sim_1 (2 errors, 1 warning)
      🔴 [VRFC 10-3818] variable 'Q' is driven by invalid combination of procedural drivers [simple_init_ff.sv:6]
      ⊙ [VRFC 10-2921] 'Q' driven by this always_ff block should not be driven by any other process [simple_init_ff.sv:10]

Figure 4.5: Simulation failure using always_ff with an initial value

The fix is to either change `always_ff` to `always` or initialize the register at its definition, and the design will work correctly. Make the change and run the simulation again:

```
simple_init_ff.sv  ×  Untitled 2  ×  tb_simple_ff.sv  ×                                    ? ☐
Q 💾 ⊕ ⊖ ⌖ ✂ ⊶ I◄ ►I ⅈ ┇┇ ⊣ I⊷ ┇ ⊣ I─┐ I⋈                                           1,700.000 n:

Name              Value    0.000 ns         500.000 ns        1,000.000 ns      1,500.000 n:
╟ CK               1
╟ CE               1
╟ D                0
╟ Q                1                                      Initial value
```

Figure 4.6: Initial value of Q

Q has an initial value of 1 in the preceding simulation; however, the first clock cycle immediately loads D, which is 0, into Q.

Using non-blocking assignments

You'll notice that for the first time in SytemVerilog, we've performed an assignment by using `<=`, or the non-blocking assignment. The reason for using a non-blocking assignment is that now that we have introduced sequential elements, we need to address the inherent parallelism in **Hardware Description Languages (HDLs)** and look at scheduling as a way of modeling it.

Up until now, everything we've done has occurred as it would in any conventional program, in a series of steps performed sequentially. Let's look at how this would work if we applied the same structure to a block of code inferring a register:

CH4/SystemVerilog/blocking/hdl/blocking.sv

```
always @(posedge CK) begin
  stage   = D;
  Q       = stage;
end
```

Now we've introduced an intermediate storage element called stage. What happens if we run a simulation on the preceding code?

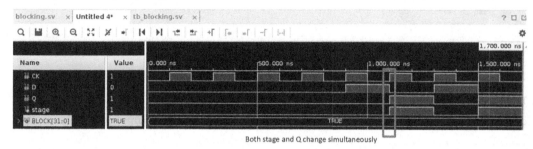

Figure 4.7: Simulation of blocking assignments in a clocked always block

The important thing to note is that stage is immediately assigned the value of D, and then Q is immediately assigned the value of stage. stage in effect becomes a wire in the final implementation.

What happens if we try changing BLOCK to FALSE in the testbench?

```
always @(posedge CK) begin
  stage  <= D;
  Q      <= stage;
end
```

If we run the simulation, we now see stage behaving as a pipeline stage, as intended:

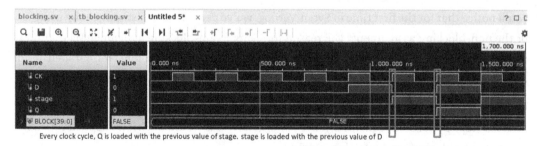

Figure 4.8: Simulation of non-blocking assignments in a clocked always block

Notice the difference. When we look at the preceding code using non-blocking assignments, it reads as follows:

- Schedule the assignment of D to the next value of stage, but the current value of stage remains the same.

- Schedule the assignment of the current value of stage to the next value of Q.

In fact, the simulator will go through the entire code of the design scheduling the assignments. These scheduled events are referred to as delta cycles. Once that has been completed, then time will advance. The assignments will then take effect and it will do it again. This is how we want our designs to behave.

Delta cycle deep dive

Because we are simulating hardware, which is inherently parallel, we need a way to model parallelism. This is accomplished via a concept known as delta cycles or events. A simulator will execute HDL code as follows:

- When the code is run, `assign` statements and `always` or `process` block ordering are not guaranteed.
- An assign statement is immediately scheduled unless a delay is applied, in which case it will be scheduled into the future based on the delay.
- Inside an `always` block or process, VHDL variables or blocking assignments will be immediately evaluated unless a delay is applied.
- Inside an `always` block or process, all VHDL signal assignments or non-blocking assignments will be scheduled for the next delta event unless a delay is applied.

The scheduling allows a serial process, like a simulator, to emulate what is happening in an inherently parallel system, your FPGA.

 Using SystemVerilog, all combinational blocks (`always_comb`) in a design should use blocking assignments. All sequential blocks (`always @(posedge)` or `always_ff`) should use non-blocking assignments. Failure to adhere to this can cause simulation/ synthesis mismatches.

The project to demonstrate blocking versus non-blocking can be found in `CH4/SystemVerilog/ blocking/build/blocking.xpr`.

 VHDL doesn't have this issue since variables have to be local to a process and are always immediate; signal assignments are "postponed."

We've learned how to create a flip-flop to register signals in our design. The next section will discuss how our registers are mapped into the Artix 7 FPGA we'll be using.

Registers in the Artix 7

We've looked at the simplest version of a register and these registers map fine into the Artix 7. However, the Artix 7 registers offer a lot more functionalities such as set/reset, latch mapping, and clock enables, which we'll examine here.

There are two FFs for every **LookUp Table (LUT)**, one dedicated FF and one that can be configured as an FF or latch. As we saw in *Chapter 3, Combinational Logic*, latches are unreliable at best, so we won't be going over them here. Also, if latches are selected, the other four FFs cannot be used, further limiting the number of resources available.

The core LUT configuration is described in *Xilinx 7 Series FPGAs Configurable Logic Block User Guide (UG474)* at https://docs.xilinx.com/v/u/en-US/ug474_7Series_CLB. The underlying LUT configuration can be complex since the basic building block is a LUT6; however, it can be split into two arbitrary LUT2s or 3s or two LUT5s if some inputs are shared. The two flip-flops per LUT facilitate these operations.

Here is an example of **Combinational Logic Block (CLB)** registers:

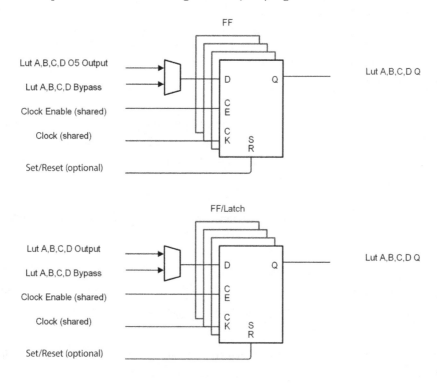

Figure 4.9: Artix 7 CLB registers

In *Figure 4.9*, we can see the two groups of FFs that exist per LUT6. The main difference between the first and second sets is that the second FF can be configured as a latch. For each group of FFs, we can see we now have a shared clock enable, a shared clock, and a shared set or reset line. The D inputs are all individually selectable from within the LUTs or the FF can be bypassed. Now let's look at how we can retain the state using clock enables.

How to retain state using clock enables

The simple DFFs we've looked at change output whenever the input changes. Clock enables allow an FF to hold onto its value whenever we are not actively changing the data. Let's look at how we can use this in practice:

SystemVerilog:

```
module dff (input wire D, CK, CE, output logic Q);
  initial Q = 1;
  always @(posedge CK) if (CE) Q <= D;
endmodule
```

VHDL:

```
entity dff is
  port(D, CK, CE : in std_logic; Q : out std_logic := '1');
end entity dff;
architecture rtl of dff is
begin
  reg : process(CK)
  begin
    if rising_edge(CK) then
      if CE then
        Q <= D;
      end if;
    end if;
  end process reg;

  -- Alternative:
  -- Q <= D when rising_edge(CK) and CE = '1';

end architecture rtl;
```

We can look at the waveforms and see how using the clock enable signal, CE, affects the Q output of the FF:

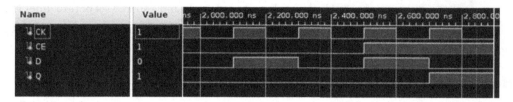

Figure 4.10: Clock enabled FF

Notice how the first time D goes high along with the CE, Q goes high also. Once CE goes low, the value of Q remains high regardless of the D input value.

Resetting the FF

We have seen how we can use an initial value to have the device come up in a known state. This works great after the initial download, but what if we need to operate in a system that gets reset on occasion? Xilinx designed the Artix 7 FPGA with a configurable set/reset system. The LUT register's **Set/Reset (SR)** input can be configured as set or reset and synchronous or asynchronous.

The first choice is whether you need to set/reset your FF asynchronously or synchronously. Synchronously means the reset signal is generated by the clock driving the FF so it will be properly timed in the design. The limitation is that a clock is required to be running when you use synchronous resets. If the clock is not guaranteed to be running, then you need an asynchronous reset. Asynchronous resets should be designed such that they will assert asynchronously and release synchronously to the FF clock. This eliminates potential timing problems in the design.

Xilinx recommends limiting resets to essential signals to speed up timing analysis and save routing resources by limiting high fanout nets:

CH4/SystemVerilog/simple_ff_async/hdl/simple_ff_async.sv, ASYNC = "TRUE"

```
always @(posedge CK, posedge SR) begin
  if (SR) Q <= '0;
  else if (CE) Q <= D;
end
```

CH4/VHDL/simple_ff_async/hdl/simple_ff_async.vhd, ASYNC = "TRUE"

```
FF : process(CK, SR)
begin
  if SR then
```

```
      reg <= '0';
   elsif rising_edge(CK) then
      reg <= D;
   end if;
 end process FF;
 Q <= reg;
```

In the preceding code, we see an example of inferring an FF with an asynchronous reset. It's a reset because Q gets a value of '0 when SR goes high. It would be a set if it went to a value of '1. Looking at the asynchronous version, we can see that posedge SR is in the sensitivity list for SystemVerilog, along with SR, plus rising_edge(SR) as an if statement in the VHDL implementation. This is what allows the reset to be effective without the clock. We can see from the waveforms that the reset immediately affects the Q output:

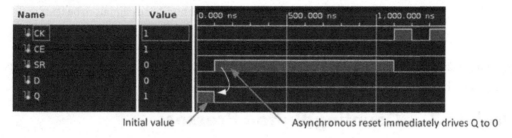

Figure 4.11: Asynchronous reset simulation

Here, we can see an example of an FF with a synchronous reset:

CH4/SystemVerilog/simple_ff_async/simple_ff_async.sv, ASYNC != "TRUE"

```
 always @(posedge CK) begin
   if (SR) Q <= '0;
   else if (CE) Q <= D;
 end
```

CH4/VHDL/simple_ff_async/hdl/simple_ff_async.vhd, ASYNC != "TRUE"

```
 FF : process (CK)
 begin
   if rising_edge(CK) then
     reg <= '0' when SR else D;
   end if;
 end process FF;
 Q <= reg;
```

We can see from the simulation waveforms that the reset is not effective until the clock starts running, unlike the asynchronous reset:

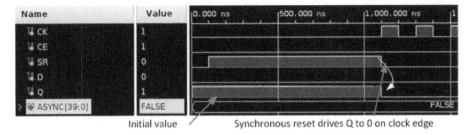

Initial value   Synchronous reset drives Q to 0 on clock edge

Figure 4.12: Synchronous reset simulation

 I would recommend synchronous resets when a reset is necessary unless you are not guaranteed to have a running clock. Limit the number of signals to be reset and the tool will take care of timing analysis.

In *Chapters 2* and *3*, we built projects 1 and 2. Now that we have the basics of registers behind us, let's tackle this chapter's project, project 3.

Project 3 – Counting Button Presses

The project in this chapter will count button presses and display the count in a human-readable form using the seven-segment display.

Introducing the seven-segment display

In the previous chapters, we displayed binary numbers by using the LEDs on the board. You might have wondered why we weren't using the row of unlit 8s. The reason is that there is timing associated with the display that we need registers to accomplish.

Let's look at how we light up the seven segments. The following diagram shows which segment is controlled by which cathode:

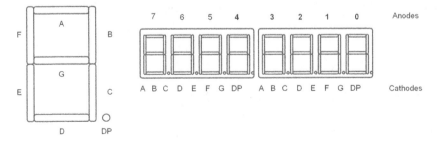

Figure 4.13: Mapping of the seven segment display

Looking at the preceding diagram, we can see there are eight signals that define whether a given LED is lit or not. To compose a numerical image, we simply need to come up with a module that takes in a **Binary-Coded Decimal (BCD)** or hexadecimal number and converts it to a format that the display can handle. We have choices of how to implement this. We can create one converter that can handle the whole display or we can have one converter for each digit. Either way, we need a design to generate our numerical representation.

> We've been using binary up until now, displaying one LED per bit. Hexadecimal numbers represent 4-bit binary numbers from 4'b0000 = 4'h0 to 4'b1111 = 4'hF. BCD numbers are a way of representing decimal numbers in computer storage by using the values 4'b0000 = 4'd0 to 4'b1001 = 4'd9; values above 9 are not used.
>
> In VHDL, the numbers would be represented in binary by using "1001", hexadecimal by using x"9", or decimal by simply using 9.

Regardless of whether we are displaying BCD or hexadecimal, we can create a module that takes in a 4-bit number and encodes the bits we want to display, in this case, onto an 8-bit cathode bus. We take the **digit point (DP)** in as a separate signal to keep it aligned with the other data:

CH4/SystemVerilog/counting_buttons/hdl/cathode_top.sv

```
always_ff @(posedge clk) begin
  cathode[7] <= digit_point;
  case (encoded)
    4'h0: cathode[6:0] <= 7'b1000000; // mapping: {G,F,E,D,C,B,A}
    4'h1: cathode[6:0] <= 7'b1111001;
    ...
    4'hE: cathode[6:0] <= 7'b0000110;
    4'hF: cathode[6:0] <= 7'b0001110;
  endcase
end
```

CH4/VHDL/counting_buttons/hdl/cathode_top.vhd

```
signal dp_reg      : std_logic                        := '0';
signal cathode_reg : std_logic_vector(6 downto 0) := (others => '0');
process(clk)
begin
  if rising_edge(clk) then
```

```
    dp_reg <= digit_point;
    case encoded is
      when x"0"   => cathode_reg <= "1000000"; -- mapping: G&F&E&D&C&B&A
      when x"1"   => cathode_reg <= "1111001";

      . . .

      when x"E"   => cathode_reg <= "0000110";
      when x"F"   => cathode_reg <= "0001110";
      when others => cathode_reg <= "0001110";
    end case;
  end if;
end process;


cathode <= dp_reg & cathode_reg;
```

If we look at *Figure 4.13*, we can see how the seven-segment displays are mapped. Each segment will light up when driven to 0. This is known as an active low signal. From the code in cathode_top, you can see, for example, that when encoded is 4'h0, segments A–F are driven low, so they will be lit, and segment G is high, so it will be off. If we look at *Figure 4.13*, you can see this would result in a 0 being displayed.

Let's now take a look at the timing we need to display on the physical display.

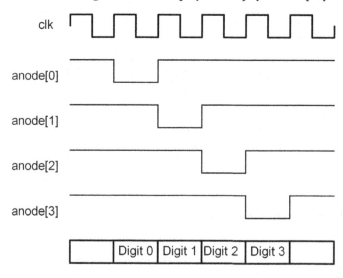

Figure 4.14: Seven-segment display timing

We need to generate the anode signal by cycling a value of 0 through all the anode positions at a refresh rate of 1/8. We'll create two counters:

CH4/SystemVerilog/counting_buttons/hdl/seven_segment.sv

```
localparam INTERVAL = int'(1000000000 / (CLK_PER *REFR_RATE));
```

CH4/VHDL/counting_buttons/hdl/seven_segment.vhd

```
constant INTERVAL : natural := 1000000000 / (CLK_PER * REFR_RATE);
```

First, we'll create a local parameter in SystemVerilog or a constant in VHDL, INTERVAL, that will be used to determine the interval in which we need to cycle through the anodes. Using parameters is a good way to generate reusable code. The calculations occur at synthesis and thus can provide an optimal implementation. Note that we can calculate parameters. In this case, we are taking $1*10^9$ nanoseconds in a second and dividing it by the clock period (100 MHz clock has a period of 10 nanoseconds, the period of the clock fed directly into the Nexys A7 100T board) multiplied by the refresh rate. Since this will return a floating point value, we cast it to an integer by using `int'()` or `integer()`:

CH4/SystemVerilog/counting_buttons/hdl/seven_segment.sv

```
initial begin
  refresh_count = '0;
  anode_count   = '0;
end
always @(posedge clk) begin
  if (refresh_count == INTERVAL) begin
    refresh_count <= '0;
    anode_count   <= anode_count + 1'b1;
  end else refresh_count <= refresh_count + 1'b1;
  anode              <= '1;
  anode[anode_count] <= '0;
  cathode            <= segments[anode_count];
end
```

CH4/VHDL/counting_buttons/hdl/seven_segment.vhd

```
signal refresh_count : integer range 0 to INTERVAL         := 0;
signal anode_count   : integer range 0 to NUM_SEGMENTS - 1 := 0;
process(clk)
begin
  if rising_edge(clk) then
```

```
      if reset then
        refresh_count <= 0;
        anode_count   <= 0;
      else
        if refresh_count = INTERVAL then
          refresh_count <= 0;
          if anode_count = NUM_SEGMENTS - 1 then
            anode_count <= 0;
          else
            anode_count <= anode_count + 1;
          end if;
        else
          refresh_count <= refresh_count + 1;
        end if;
        anode              <= (others => '1');
        anode(anode_count) <= '0';
        cathode            <= segments(anode_count);
      end if;
    end if;
end process;
```

Looking at the preceding code, we are generating two counters:

- refresh_count, which generates the timing for when we will assert each anode. The INTERVAL for this counter is set based on the refresh rate. When the refresh counter reaches the INTERVAL value, we reset it and increment our second counter.

- anode_count specifies which anode will be asserted (the signal is active low, so drive a 0) for updating the seven-segment display. In SystemVerilog, we don't set a bound for the anode_count since our board does have eight segments. We simply let it roll over naturally. If the number of displays was not a power of 2, we could bind our count the same way as we do refresh_count.

Detecting button presses

The buttons on the board are wired to deliver a 1 when pushed, meaning they are normally driving a value of 0 into the FPGA. This means that to detect a button press, we need to look for a rising edge.

Analyzing timing

Let's quickly look at clock relationships and how timing is analyzed. There are two main timing constraints between data and a clock:

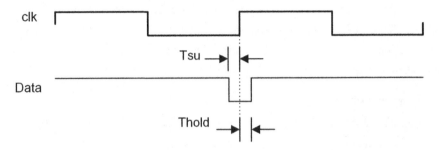

Figure 4.15: Timing constraints

These constraints must be met for a design's reliable operation. The first constraint is the setup time, or Tsu in the timing constraints diagram. This is the amount of time that the signal requires to be stable prior to the clock edge. If the signal transitions within or after the Tsu, then the device may not operate correctly. In a synchronous design, Tsu is usually only violated if the clock frequency is too fast for the longest clock to clock data paths in the design. The thing about setup time in a synchronous design is that it can be fixed by lowering the clock speed or redesigned to cut down on long timing paths, as we'll see in *Chapter 5, Let's Build a Calculator*, where we introduce a PLL to run our design at a different clock frequency.

The second constraint, hold time or Thold, is the window in which a signal must remain stable after the clock. It's normally not a problem in a single **Super Logic Region (SLR)** device such as the one we are using. However, it is often a problem when designs have multiple clocks and care is not taken to properly synchronize signals between the clocks. The issue with hold time is that there is no way to fix it by reducing clock speed—you can only prevent it. When it occurs in a synchronous design, the cause is usually locally routed clocks in designs with major routing congestion.

 Xilinx builds very large devices that consist of multiple FPGA dies bonded to a substrate. Each one of these dies is what is called an SLR. This allows for high-density devices that rival ASICs in terms of gate counts.

When we have a purely asynchronous signal, such as the center button, or port named BTNC, we cannot fix the setup and hold as easily without proper synchronization.

Looking at asynchronous issues

In the case of an asynchronous signal, the signal can change without regard to the clock edge, which could violate the Tsu and Thold of the DFF at any point of operation. This could cause setup or hold time violations, creating design instability and unpredictable behavior. To show the problem, I've added a create_clock timing constraint on the BTNC input that you can un-comment and run. The frequency doesn't matter, just that we create it so the edges will wander with its relationship to clk:

CH4/xdc/Nexys-A7-100T-Master.xdc

```
create_clock -add -name BTNC -period 99.99 [get_ports {BTNC}];
set_property CLOCK_DEDICATED_ROUTE FALSE [get_nets BTNC_IBUF]
```

We'll also need to set CLOCK_DEDICATED_ROUTE to FALSE since the BTNC, the center button, pin was not set to a dedicated clock pin. Normally, you want an external clock on your FPGA to be located on a pin that connects to the dedicated clock resources of the FPGA. CLOCK_DEDICATED_ROUTING relaxes this constraint so it can use internal routing resources. This can add clock skew, which could be a problem with related clocks, but it won't in our case. Let's look at the timing summary.

Using the asynchronous signal directly

Set the ASYNC_BUTTON parameter in counting_buttons.sv or vhd to NOCLOCK. We'll leave the clock constraints to represent an asynchronous signal coming in on the input. We'll use BTNC as an input directly to a register clocked on clk.

For this part of the demonstration, you can run it on either VHDL or SystemVerilog. You might see different numbers depending on the language or tool version, but the violation will still be present.

After building the design, look again at the clock interactions and you'll see the BTNC to the `clk` path is still unsafe:

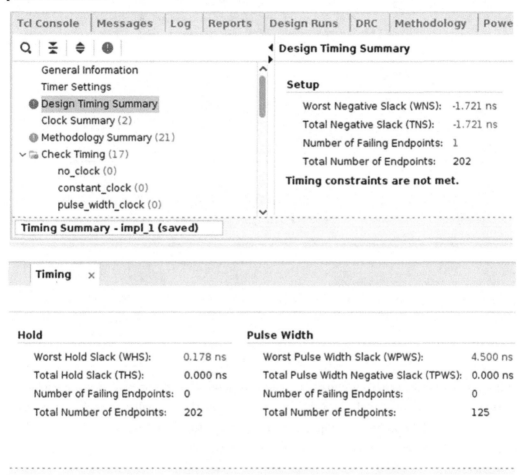

Figure 4.16: Asynchronous BTNC input

Investigating further, we see that we have a 0 ns timing requirement:

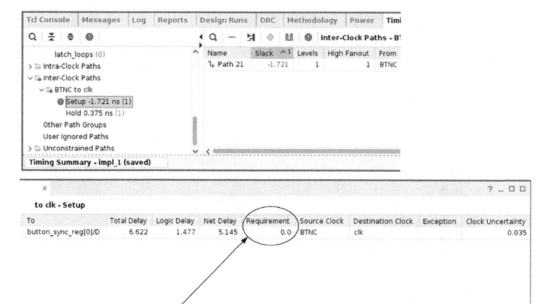

Figure 4.17: Timing requirements

This is a sign that the signals originate from asynchronous clocks. The way the timing analysis works is that when you have clocks of different frequencies, the tool will walk the edges through each other to find the worst-case alignment for timing. In this case, Vivado has found an alignment where the signal needs to meet a 0-nanosecond requirement.

You can also bring up the Clock Interaction window:

∨ **IMPLEMENTATION**

   ▶ Run Implementation

   ∨ **Open Implemented Design**

        Constraints Wizard

        Edit Timing Constraints

        ⏱ Report Timing Summary

        Report Clock Networks

        Report Clock Interaction

        📋 Report Methodology

        Report DRC

        Report Utilization

        🦋 Report Power

        🗒 Schematic

Figure 4.18: Clock interaction

The **Clock Interaction** pane shows us the paths from BTNC to clk are timed, but they are unsafe.

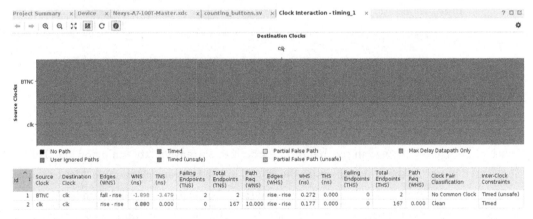

Id	Source Clock	Destination Clock	Edges (WNS)	WNS (ns)	TNS (ns)	Failing Endpoints (TNS)	Total Endpoints (TNS)	Path Req (WNS)	Edges (WHS)	WHS (ns)	THS (ns)	Failing Endpoints (THS)	Total Endpoints (THS)	Path Req (WHS)	Clock Pair Classification	Inter-Clock Constraints
1	BTNC	clk	fall - rise	-1.898	-3.479	2	2		rise - rise	0.272	0.000	0	2		No Common Clock	Timed (unsafe)
2	clk	clk	rise - rise	6.880	0.000	0	167	10.000	rise - rise	0.177	0.000	0	167	0.000	Clean	Timed

Figure 4.19: Clock Interaction report

If you try this on the board, you'll see that the seven-segment display will increment with every push of the center button. It increments in hexadecimal. You can also reset the design by using the red reset button on the board.

Problem with push buttons

The way we finally get everything to work is to properly synchronize our BTNC signal to the main clock. Because the BTNC signal is being pressed on human timescales, we can consider it a static signal except for when the button is depressed and released. When dealing with a signal like this, we can use a two-stage synchronizer plus an additional FF for edge detection:

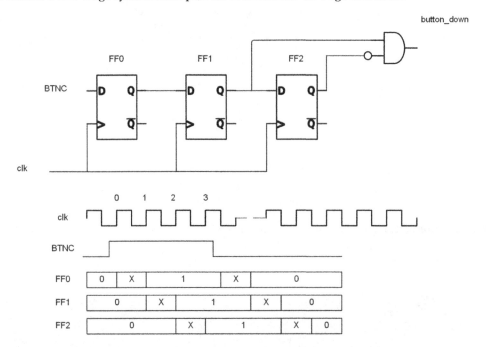

Figure 4.20: Button down synchronizer

If we look at *Figure 4.20*, we can see that on clock cycle 0, we may violate timing on FF0. This is represented by an X in the timing diagram showing that FF0 has gone metastable. Metastability is when the output Q of an FF is in an indeterminate state because setup or hold times have been violated. FF1 will recognize the output of FF0 as a 0 or a 1, but it's not guaranteed which one. This is why FF0 drives **one and only one** FF. If it were to drive two or more FFs, it is possible that each FF would see a different value. By the time FF1 has output its Q value, it is safe to use in a design on the clk clock domain, but because we cannot use FF0 and we need to detect an edge, we need FF2 to hold the old value of BTNC:

SystemVerilog:

```systemverilog
logic [2:0] button_sync;
always @(posedge clk) begin
  button_sync <= button_sync << 1 | BTNC;
  if (button_sync[2:1] == 2'b01) button_down <= '1;
  else button_down <= '0;
end
```

If you recall, `<<` is the left shift operator, so we can view `button_sync <= button_sync << 1 | BTNC` as a shift register where bit 0 is the asynchronous FF, which is why it's not used in the comparison operation.

VHDL:

```vhdl
signal button_sync : std_logic_vector(2 downto 0);
process(clk)
begin
  if rising_edge(clk) then
    button_sync <= button_sync(1 downto 0) & BTNC;
    if button_sync(2 downto 1) = "01" then
      button_down <= '1';
    else
      button_down <= '0';
    end if;
  end if;
end process;
```

In the VHDL example, we explicitly shift our value by assigning bits 1:0 to 2:1 and appending the value of BTNC to it. Just like the SystemVerilog version, bit 0 of `button_sync` can go metastable and must only drive a single flip-flop.

 Metastability is all about statistics and the mean time between failure analysis. It is still possible for FF1 or FF2 to propagate the metastability of FF0; however, it is statistically unlikely. It's important to understand this point as it's often a question asked in interviews. The tools will report the probability based on modeling and measurements. Unless you are deploying millions of units that run continuously, you will likely never hit this case.

There is still one problem we need to address: sampling mechanical switches.

Designing a safe implementation

Make sure to comment out the BTNC constraints added in the previous section and set `ASYNC_BUTTON = "SAFE"`. After running the design, open the timing summary:

Design Timing Summary

Setup		Hold		Pulse Width	
Worst Negative Slack (WNS):	6.701 ns	Worst Hold Slack (WHS):	0.158 ns	Worst Pulse Width Slack (WPWS):	4.500 ns
Total Negative Slack (TNS):	0.000 ns	Total Hold Slack (THS):	0.000 ns	Total Pulse Width Negative Slack (TPWS):	0.000 ns
Number of Failing Endpoints:	0	Number of Failing Endpoints:	0	Number of Failing Endpoints:	0
Total Number of Endpoints:	169	Total Number of Endpoints:	169	Total Number of Endpoints:	125

All user specified timing constraints are met.

Figure 4.21: Timing for properly synchronized design

If you look at the **Clock Interaction** pane, you'll see everything is safe. We can now try it on the board.

One thing you may notice is that you occasionally still see some counting weirdness. We have forgotten to take one thing into account. We are dealing with mechanical switches, which suffer from a phenomenon called bouncing, as depicted in *Figure 4.22*:

Figure 4.22: Undebounced switch

Figure 4.22 shows a condensed view of an electromechanical switch and how it will oscillate between a high and low state for some period of time before settling. What we need to do is create a circuit that waits for a period of time after it detects the switch being depressed, resetting itself if it detects a bounce:

SystemVerilog:

```
always @(posedge clk) begin
  button_down <= '0;
  button_sync <= button_sync << 1 | BTNC;
  if (button_sync[2:1] == 2'b01) counter_en <= '1;
  else if (~button_sync[1])      counter_en <= '0;
  if (counter_en) begin
    counter <= counter + 1'b1;
    if (&counter) begin
      counter_en <= '0;
```

```
                counter    <= '0;
                button_down <= '1;
            end
        end
    end
```

VHDL:

```vhdl
process (clk)
begin
  if rising_edge(clk) then
    button_down <= '0';
    button_sync <= button_sync(1 downto 0) & BTNC;
    if button_sync(2 downto 1) = "01" then
      counter_en <= '1';
    elsif button_sync(1) = '0' then
      counter_en <= '0';
      counter    <= 0;
    end if;
    if counter_en then
      if counter = 255 then
        counter_en  <= '0';
        counter     <= 0;
        button_down <= '1';
      else
        counter <= counter + 1;
      end if;
    end if;
  end if;
end process;
```

The preceding circuit starts a timer when a button push is detected, that is, the falling edge. It then waits 256 clock cycles to make sure the switch doesn't bounce, resetting the counter if it does and waiting to detect the next edge.

Try this on the board and you'll see no more weird counting issues.

The final stats for the design are 69 LUTs, 133 FFs, and a **Worst Negative Slack (WNS)** of 6.595. We have a lot of room to increase the clock speed if so desired. We were targeting a 100 MHz clock (with a 10-nanosecond period). With a WNS slack of 6.595, we could decrease our clock period to 10-6.595, which would be about a 300 MHz clock.

When analyzing timing in a design, aside from constraints, we have a few other metrics:

- **WNS**: The longest path slack in the design in nanoseconds. If a design is violating timing, it will be negative. Anything greater than or equal to 0 meets timing, a larger positive number indicates the design could run faster.

- **Total Negative Slack (TNS)**: The sum total of all violating paths in the design (0 if WNS is positive).

- **Worst Hold Slack (WHS)**: The amount of time in nanoseconds that the closest signal is to meeting the hold-time requirements for all the FFs in the design. Must be positive or 0 for a functional design. This number is usually easy to meet unless there are CDC problems or clock routing issues.

- **Total Hold Slack (THS)**: The sum total of all hold-time-violating paths in the design. Must be positive or 0 for a functional design.

Now, let's see how we can switch to decimal representation.

Switching to decimal representation

The counter up until now counts in hexadecimal. I've been working with binary/hexadecimal numbers for 30+ years, so I'm fairly used to it. However, most people are more comfortable with decimal numbers. As is usually the case, there are multiple ways of accomplishing a task. We can count in binary and convert to decimal, or simply count in decimal.

For this design, I decided to count in decimal. If we are representing decimal numbers on eight seven-segment displays, the maximum number we could represent is 99,999,999. If we counted in binary and converted, we'd get 2^32 = 4,294,967,296, and that wouldn't fit on the display (not that you would spend the rest of eternity pushing buttons to count that high):

SystemVerilog:

```
// Decimal increment function
function [NUM_SEGMENTS-1:0][3:0] dec_inc;
  input [NUM_SEGMENTS-1:0][3:0] din;
  bit [3:0]                       next_val;
  bit                             carry_in;
  carry_in = '1;
  for (int i = 0; i < NUM_SEGMENTS; i++) begin
    next_val = din[i] + carry_in;
    if (next_val > 9) begin
      dec_inc[i] = '0;
```

```
      carry_in   = '1;
    end else begin
      dec_inc[i] = next_val;
      carry_in   = '0;
    end
  end // for (int i = 0; i < NUM_SEGMENTS; i++)
endfunction // dec_inc
```

VHDL:

```
-- Decimal increment function
function dec_inc(din : in array_t(NUM_SEGMENTS-1 downto 0)(3 downto 0))
return array_t is
  variable int_val  : array_t(NUM_SEGMENTS - 1 downto 0)(3 downto 0);
  variable next_val : integer range 0 to 10;
  variable carry_in : integer range 0 to 1;
begin
  carry_in := 1;
  for i in 0 to NUM_SEGMENTS - 1 loop
    next_val := to_integer(unsigned(din(i))) + carry_in;
    if next_val = 10 then
      int_val(i) := (others => '0');
      carry_in   := 1;
    else
      int_val(i) := std_logic_vector(to_unsigned(next_val, 4));
      carry_in   := 0;
    end if;
  end loop;
  return int_val;
end function;
```

The preceding function accepts **Binary Coded Decimal (BCD)** encoded data. The for loop iterates over each digit counting up until it reaches 10, in which case, it resets that digit to 0 and feeds a carry into the next digit.

Note that the VHDL version has a hex_inc function also, shown below:

```
-- Hexadecimal increment function
function hex_inc(din : in array_t(NUM_SEGMENTS-1 downto 0)(3 downto 0))
return array_t is
```

```vhdl
    variable hex_val  : array_t(NUM_SEGMENTS - 1 downto 0)(3 downto 0);
    variable next_val : integer range 0 to 16;
    variable carry_in : integer range 0 to 1;
  begin
    carry_in := 1;
    for i in 0 to NUM_SEGMENTS - 1 loop
      next_val := to_integer(unsigned(din(i))) + carry_in;
      if next_val = 16 then
        hex_val(i) := (others => '0');
        carry_in   := 1;
      else
        hex_val(i) := std_logic_vector(to_unsigned(next_val, 4));
        carry_in   := 0;
      end if;
    end loop;
    return hex_val;
  end function;
```

SystemVerilog is more versatile in that we can simply increment the two-dimensional array and the carry will propagate correctly for how we defined it. VHDL, being strongly typed, requires us to define a way to operate on our two-dimensional array type.

Change the mode from HEX to DEC and build.

The final stats for the design are 97 LUTs, 133 FFs, and a WNS of 1.069. There is a cost for a more readable display: approximately 50% more LUTs and about 5 nanoseconds of delay; however, we still easily meet timing at 100 MHz.

Introducing the ILA

Xilinx provides a very capable on-chip debugging solution within Vivado called an **Integrated Logic Analyzer (ILA)**. An ILA gives us the ability to add a logic analyzer that we can insert into our design. The simplest way of approaching an ILA is to start by marking signals for debugging. We can do this by adding the mark_debug attribute as follows:

SystemVerilog:

```systemverilog
(* mark_debug = "true" *) logic button_down;
(* ASYNC_REG = "TRUE", mark_debug = "true" *) logic [2:0] button_sync;
```

VHDL:

```
attribute MARK_DEBUG : string;
attribute ASYNC_REG : string;
signal button_down : std_logic := '0';
attribute MARK_DEBUG of button_down : signal is "TRUE";
signal button_sync : std_logic_vector(2 downto 0);
attribute ASYNC_REG of button_sync : signal is "TRUE";
attribute MARK_DEBUG of button_sync : signal is "TRUE";
```

We apply attributes to signals by using the SystemVerilog comment style (* *) or attribute with VHDL. You can see how multiple attributes can be applied by looking at button_sync.

Both the SAFE and DEBOUNCE circuits have mark_debug already set. Pick SAFE and let's look at the steps to set up and run an ILA.

Marking signals for debugging

If you take a look at CH4/SystemVerilog/counting_buttons/hdl/counting_buttons.sv, you'll see a few signals marked for debugging. Don't worry about getting everything, but the more you can add now that are of interest, the better chance of finding them after synthesis:

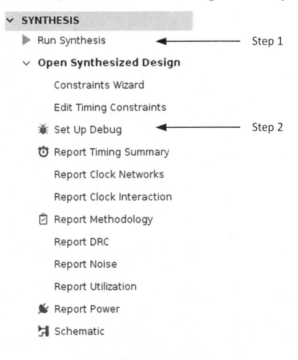

Figure 4.23: Setting up an ILA

You need to follow these steps:

1. Select **Run Synthesis** and **Open Synthesized Design**. Usually, we combine this step with generating a bitstream, but we need to run the synthesis by itself so we can set up debugging.

2. Select **Set Up Debug...**:

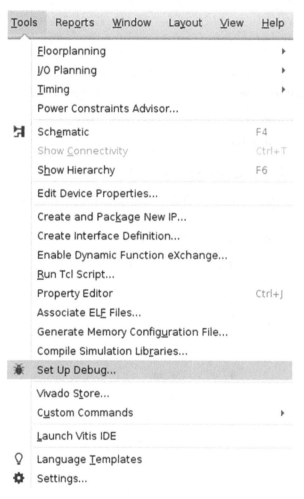

Figure 4.24: Set Up Debug...

3. A window will pop up. Select **Next**.

4. Select **Continue Debugging** (since we have already added signals via mark_debug). I've added the synchronization registers and the button-down output. If you look at the DEBOUNCE version, you'll see the counter as well.

5. Select the **Find Nets to Add...** button. Click **OK**. This will show you all the nets that you could probe in the design:

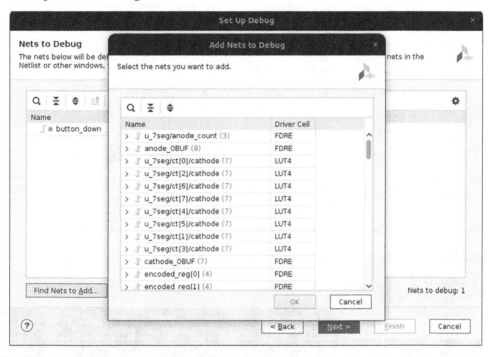

Figure 4.25: Adding nets

6. We have enough to look at, so simply hit **Cancel**.

    Feel free to add some more signals if you'd like, or experiment later. The thing to remember is that you have only the block RAM in the FPGA for internal storage of waves, so the more signals you add, potentially, the less sample depth is available. We have a large device, so there's nothing to worry about right now.

7. Back on the **Set Up Debug** screen, hit **Next**.

Leave the ILA core options at the default. A sample depth of 1024 is fine for now. Our clock speed is slow enough that we don't need pipeline stages. (Pipelining is discussed in *Chapter 7, Math, Parallelism and Pipelined Designs*.) An ILA has some advanced debugging features, but we won't get into them here.

Programming the device

As is always the case, we need to build the device so we can see our results. Select **Finish** and generate the bitstream:

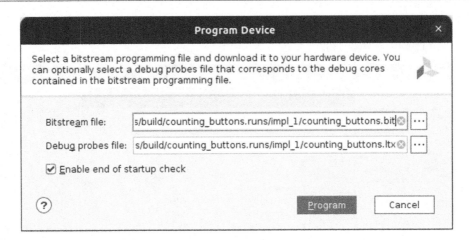

Figure 4.26: Program Device

You'll notice that the debug probes are now being set up. Select **Program**.

You'll now have the ILA view open:

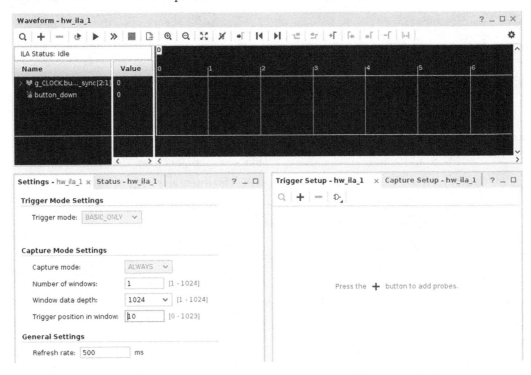

Figure 4.27: ILA view

The **Settings** pane allows you to limit the data depth. Sometimes, you may select a large storage space in a build but want to limit what you capture in a specific run, and you can do that here. The trigger position sets how many samples are captured prior to the trigger. In our case, we are looking at 10 samples prior to our trigger, and the rest are after.

In the trigger setup, we'll add something to trigger on:

Figure 4.28: Trigger Setup

I've selected to trigger whenever bit **1** of button_sync goes high:

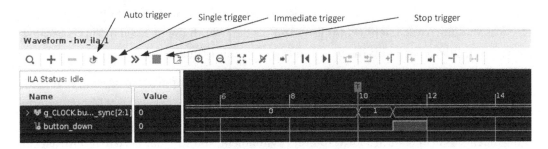

Figure 4.29: Running a trigger

We have a few choices for capturing signals in the ILA. Immediate Trigger (>>) will capture the signals in their current state. **Auto Trigger** (the right arrow with the green circle) will rearm the trigger automatically after firing. **Single Trigger** sets us up for capturing a single event. Finally, if you are unable to fire your trigger, you can stop it and set up another with the **Stop Trigger** button.

Try **Single Trigger**, then push the center button and you should see what I have in *Figure 4.29*. I was unable to capture an anomaly, but this at least shows you how to use an ILA for debugging problems on board.

What about simulation?

In this chapter, we took advantage of the capabilities of lab debugging rather than running simulations. This is not something I would normally do. However, it would take too much time and effort to write a model to test the seven-segment display and also model a bouncing switch. It's an FPGA after all, and we can program and test as many times as we want. It's not a route I usually go down, but for this project, it worked well.

Now let's turn our attention back to synchronization and look at how to handle multiple clock domains in a design.

Deep dive into synchronization

In this chapter's project, project 3, we dipped our toes into synchronizing a signal from an external source. In later designs, we'll be interfacing between multiple clock domains. For instance, in *Chapter 6, FPGA Resources and How to Use Them*, we'll be interfacing between our main logic and a DDR controller running on a different clock domain.

Why use multiple clocks?

There are several clocking considerations when architecting your FPGA design. Sometimes, you are forced to use a given clock for an interface. For example, if you are designing something that interfaces to 10G Ethernet, somewhere in your design will be a multiple of 156.25 MHz or 322.27 MHz depending on whether you are interfacing with the **Physical Coding Sublayer** (**PCS**) or **Physical Medium Attachment** (**PMA**) layer and the data width (64 or 32 bits). This is because data must be driven out at this frequency and arrive at this frequency.

At other times, you may be looking for high performance or lower power. Increasing your clock speed can increase your throughput or calculations per second if you need data fast or perform lots of operations. Running a faster clock costs more in terms of power. If you are designing something that needs to operate in a lower-power environment, you still may need to receive data at a faster rate but save power by performing operations slower.

Two-stage synchronizer

The heart of synchronization is a two-stage synchronizer. The two stages are FFs on the destination clock domain; we apply the ASYNC_REG attribute to the FFs. This attribute tells Vivado that these registers are used for synchronizing and should be placed as close together as possible in the FPGA fabric. A simple two-stage synchronizer looks like this:

SystemVerilog:

```
(* ASYNC_REG = "TRUE" *) logic [1:0] sync;
always @(posedge dst_clk) sync <= sync << 1 | async;
```

VHDL:

```
attribute ASYNC_REG : string;
signal sync : std_logic_vector(1 downto 0);
```

```
attribute ASYNC_REG of sync : signal is "TRUE";
...
process (dst_clk) begin
  if rising_edge(dst_clk) then sync <= sync(0) & async; end if;
```

This creates two flops on the dst_clk domain and tells Vivado to handle them as such.

Synchronizing control signals

Often, you may have slower speed status signals that are sent from one clock domain to another. These signals will toggle infrequently and you must handshake between both sides of the interface; for example, when using a validator the design is guaranteed to change infrequently enough that you don't need to worry about handshaking, such as a registered error signal, which must be cleared after it is set.

For this type of interface, we can use a toggle synchronizer. A toggle synchronizer toggles the signal crossing clock domains and then generates a pulse when an edge is detected on the synchronized domain. You can see why we need to make sure that we do not send toggles across faster than we can generate pulses on the receiving side. One way to prevent this is to send a similar toggle signal back as an acknowledgment. The code below shows how we can implement a toggle synchronizer:

SystemVerilog:

```
logic async_toggle;
(* ASYNC_REG = "TRUE" *) logic [2:0] sync;
logic sync_pulse;
always @(posedge src_clk)
  if (ctrl_in) async_toggle <= ~async_toggle;
always @(posedge dst_clk) sync <= sync << 1 | async_toggle;
assign sync_pulse = ^sync[2:1];
```

VHDL:

```
attribute ASYNC_REG : string;
signal async_toggle : std_logic := '0';
signal sync         : std_logic_vector(2 downto 0);
attribute ASYNC_REG of sync : signal is "TRUE";
signal sync_pulse   : std_logic;
...
process(src_clk)
begin
```

```
    if rising_edge(src_clk) then
      if ctrl_in then
        async_toggle <= not async_toggle;
      end if;
    end if;
  end process;
  process(dst_clk)
  begin
    if rising_edge(dst_clk) then
      sync <= sync(1 downto 0) & async_toggle;
    end if;
  end process;
  sync_pulse <= xor sync(2 downto 1);
```

In the following figure, you can see an illustration of a toggle synchronizer waveform:

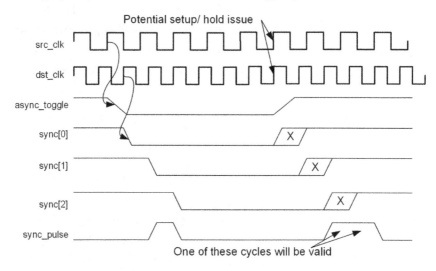

Figure 4.30: Toggle synchronizer waveform

In the figure above, we can see two clocks, src_clk, the source of the asynchronous toggle signal, and dst_clk, the destination clock that is receiving the signal. You'll note in the waveform that the rising edge of async_toggle may violate timing when sampled on src_clk, generating sync[0]. This is represented by an X. Although sync[0] may go metastable, sync[1] will statistically register a 0 or 1 and that will safely pass to sync[2]. However, since it is statistical, we don't know which of the two cycles highlighted will generate the pulse on dst_clk, but one of the two cycles will have a pulse.

Passing data

If we have data that meets the criteria of the preceding synchronizer (that is, the data will be stable for the amount of time to be captured on dst_clk), we can pass it along with the control signal. The source data is captured and held on src_clk for the time necessary for synchronizing. If the clock relationships are known, this can be done by waiting for a long enough period, or we can pass an acknowledge signal back to dst_clk when the sync pulse is received:

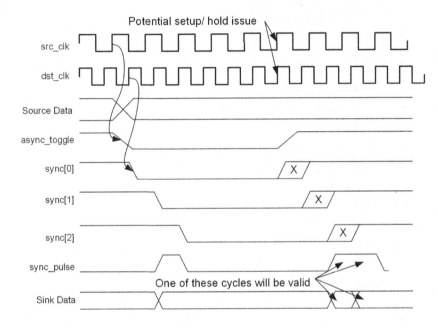

Figure 4.31: Passing data across clock domains

We do this by registering it on the same cycle we toggle the signal crossing to the synchronizer:

SystemVerilog:

```
logic async_toggle;
logic [31:0] async_data;
(* ASYNC_REG = "TRUE" *) logic [2:0] sync;
logic sync_pulse;
logic [31:0] sync_data;
always @(posedge src_clk)
  if (ctrl_in) begin
    async_toggle <= ~async_toggle;
```

```
      async_data    <= …;
    end
  always @(posedge dst_clk) begin
    sync <= sync << 1 | async_toggle;
    if (sync_pulse) sync_data <= async_data;
  end
  assign sync_pulse = ^sync[2:1];
```

VHDL:

```
  attribute ASYNC_REG : string;
  signal async_toggle : std_logic;
  signal async_data : std_logic_vector(31 downto 0);
  signal sync : std_logic_vector(2 downto 0);
  signal sync_pulse : std_logic;
  signal sync_data : std_logic_vector(31 downto 0);
  attribute ASYNC_REG of sync : signal is "TRUE";
  ...
  process(src_clk)
  begin
    if rising_edge(src_clk) then
      if ctrl_in then
        async_toggle <= not async_toggle;
        async_data    <= ...;
      end if;
    end if;
  end process;
  process(dst_clk)
  begin
    if rising_edge(dst_clk) then
      sync <= sync(1 downto 0) & async_toggle;
      if sync_pulse then
        sync_data <= async_data;
      end if;
    end if;
  end process;
  sync_pulse <= xor(sync(2 downto 1));
```

This code will safely transfer the data; however, we need to provide one constraint to Vivado:

```
set_max_delay -datapath_only \
  [2*[get_property PERIOD [get_clocks dst_clk]]] \
  -from [get_cells async_data*] -to [get_cells sync_data*]
```

This constrains the path from `async_data` to `sync_data` to be two destination clock cycles or less. The reason is that we know the two-stage synchronizer will take two or three clocks for the pulse to appear from when the toggle signal switches. We apply this constraint to all bits on the bus.

We can add an acknowledge signal if we need handshaking to let the sender know data has reached the destination. It would be synchronized the same way.

FIFOs are a third common way of synchronizing that we'll discuss in *Chapter 6, FPGA Resources and How to Use Them*. FIFOs are typically used when data is fast or comes in long bursts relative to the destination clock.

Summary

In this chapter, we introduced sequential elements, how to store data using FFs, and how to write constraints for these elements for Vivado. We've looked at synchronization and how to deal with clock domains. Along with learning how to write combinational logic, we now have the fundamentals to create just about any design. We've developed a better way of displaying information and even made a more human-readable version of it. It's important to look at what you have accomplished thus far. You've seen how to handle external inputs operating asynchronously with the system clock. You've interfaced to a more sophisticated output display. You've also debugged on the board using an ILA. This should give you the confidence to experiment a bit and the challenge will allow you to do just that.

In the next chapter, we'll build on the lessons and skills we learned in this chapter by building something more substantial: a calculator.

Questions

1. When using `SystemVerilog`, it's best to use blocking assignments in sequential blocks and non-blocking in combinational blocks.

    a. True

    b. False

2. VHDL suffers from the same potential problem as SystemVerilog regarding mixing blocking and non blocking assignments.

    a. True

    b. False

3. It is best to reset all sequential elements in a design.

    a. True

    b. False

4. What are the most common ways of synchronizing?

    a. `always @(posedge signal)` or `rising_edge(signal)`

    b. `always @(negedge signal)` or `falling_edge(signal)`

    c. FIFO or a two-stage synchronizer with or without data

    d. Synchronizers... who needs synchronizers?

5. (SystemVerilog) When would we use `always @(posedge clk)` rather than `always_ff @(posedge clk)`?

    a. When we get tired of typing

    b. When we need to use an initial statement to preload the register

    c. When we need to reset the register either synchronously or asynchronously

6. When do we need to add debouncing logic?

    a. When we cross clock domains

    b. Whenever we send data from one FF to another

    c. When we are dealing with electromechanical buttons or switches

Answers

1. b) False

2. b) False

3. b) False

4. c) FIFO or a two-stage synchronizer with or without data

5. b) When we need to use an initial statement to preload the register

6. c) When we are dealing with electromechanical buttons or switches

Challenge

In *Chapter 3*, *Combinational Logic*, we created a design that could perform some simple operations and display data in binary on the LEDs.

Modify the code to use the seven-segment display module to output the data rather than the LEDs, or in addition to the LEDs. Display in either hex or decimal. If you go the decimal route, you'll either need to use the function for adding in decimal or do a conversion before displaying it.

Run it on the board to verify its operation.

Further reading

Please refer to the following for more information:

- To read further about the design constraints that can be applied within Vivado: `https://www.xilinx.com/support/documentation-navigation/design-hubs/dh0004-vivado-applying-design-constraints-hub.html`

- More information on Vivado properties: `https://www.xilinx.com/support/documentation/sw_manuals/xilinx2020_1/ug912-vivado-properties.pdf`

Join our community on Discord

Join our community's Discord space for discussions with the authors and other readers:

`https://packt.link/embedded`

5

Let's Build a Calculator

In *Chapter 4, Counting Button Presses*, we learned how to store values using **Flip Flops (FFs)**. We learned about timing and constraints, simulation and delta cycles, and clock domain crossing. In this chapter, we are going to use our HDL knowledge of combinational logic and sequential elements to discuss state machine design. We'll look at classic state machine designs and develop a traffic light controller, a staple of **Electrical Engineering (EE)** projects.

We've built a controller for a seven-segment display that we can use to show numerical values and we know how to handle button and switch inputs safely. Now, we'll take this knowledge and show how we can define a state machine to keep track of the calculations we want to perform. We'll use this to develop our first truly useful design, a simple calculator capable of entering two 16-bit numbers and adding, subtracting, multiplying, and dividing them, placing the output on the seven-segment display.

Once you've completed this chapter, you should be able to construct simple state machines, use simple state machines to implement algorithms, and understand the basics of computer math.

In this chapter, we are going to cover the following main topics:

- What is a state machine?
- Project 4 – Building a Simple Calculator
- Project 5 – Keeping cars in line

Technical requirements

The technical requirements for this chapter are the same as those for *Chapter 2, FPGA Programming Languages and Tools*.

To follow along with the examples and the project, you can find the code files for this chapter in the following repository on GitHub: `https://github.com/PacktPublishing/The-FPGA-Programming-Handbook-Second-Edition/tree/master/CH5`.

What is a state machine?

We've seen how we can use FFs to store values. Up until now, we've only used a counter to keep track of pushbutton events or counters to cycle through a seven-segment display to our counter value. What can we use if we have something more complex such as a calculator that needs to track the accumulator or a traffic light controller that cycles through a set series of events? The answer is a state machine. In general, a state machine takes in events and, based on the events, moves through a set of states that can produce one or more outputs.

A state machine can be quite simple or extremely complex. In the previous chapter, we designed a simple circuit to control our seven-segment display. The seven-segment controller contained two counters that cycled a zero through the cathodes and presented the anode data for each digit. We could have written a state machine to handle this; however, it was easier to write it the way we did.

Before we dive into our calculator project, we need to go over the two ways of coding state machines and the two traditional state machine implementations.

Writing a purely sequential state machine

Classically, we would create a state diagram to show how our state machine will operate. In *Figure 5.1* below, you can see our simple example state machine that we will code below.

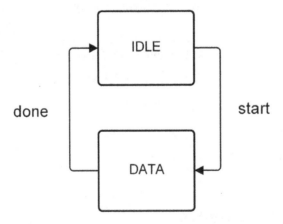

Figure 5.1: Simple state machine example

The state diagram shows we have two states, IDLE and DATA. We will go from IDLE to DATA when we receive a signal called start. We will transition back from DATA to IDLE when we receive a done signal. Now let's look at coding the state machine.

The first way of coding a state machine is to write it in a single clocked block. This kind of state machine would look something like the following.

SystemVerilog

```systemverilog
enum bit {IDLE, DATA} state;
initial state = IDLE; // Define initial state
always @(posedge clk) begin
  case (state)
    IDLE: begin
      dout_en <= '0;
      if (start) begin
        dout_en <= '1;
        state <= DATA;
      end
    end
    DATA: begin
      dout_en <= '1;
      if (done) begin
        dout_en <= '0;
        state <= IDLE;
      end
    end
  endcase
end
```

You can see from the preceding code that we are defining our states using an enum register called state. We then assign an initial value, the value that will be loaded when the FPGA starts up.

VHDL

```vhdl
type state_t is (IDLE, DATA);
signal state : state_t := IDLE;
process(clk)
begin
  if rising_edge(clk) then
```

```
    case state is
      when IDLE =>
        dout_en <= '0';
        if start then
          dout_en <= '1';
          state   <= DATA;
        end if;
      when DATA =>
        dout_en <= '1';
        if done then
          dout_en <= '0';
          state   <= IDLE;
        end if;
    end case;
  end if;
end process;
```

 Use enum types for state machine definitions in SystemVerilog or a custom type in VHDL. Good names help convey design intent and, when simulating the waves, it will display state names rather than numerical values.

The main code is in the always or process block. We use a case statement to define our state machine state operations, IDLE and DATA. There are two inputs to the state machine, start and done, and one output, dout_en, included here to show how a registered output would be described in this case. This type of code is concise and fast since there is a full clock cycle from all outputs of the state machine. It does have a potential disadvantage in that every output will be registered. In some cases, you may want an output to occur as soon as input changes and this is not possible when you write the state machine this way.

This version of the state machine simply uses a single state variable. Another way of coding a state machine is by splitting the state variable into current and next states. Let's look at this in more depth in the next section.

Splitting combination and sequential logic in a state machine

We can break up the state machine into a combinational portion based on the current state that generated the next state to be registered in **SystemVerilog**:

```systemverilog
enum bit {IDLE, DATA} current_state, next_state;
initial current_state = IDLE; // Define initial state
always @(posedge clk) current_state <= next_state;
always_comb begin
  next_state = current_state; // avoid a latch
  dout_en = '0; // avoid a latch
  case (current_state)
    IDLE: begin
      if (start) begin
        dout_en = '1;
        next_state = DATA;
      end
    end
    DATA: begin
      dout_en = '1;
      if (done) begin
        dout_en = '0;
        next_state = IDLE;
      end
    end
  endcase
end
```

We can do the same in **VHDL**:

```vhdl
type state_t is (IDLE, DATA);
signal state : state_t := IDLE;
process(clk)
begin
  if rising_edge(clk) then
    current_state <= next_state;
  end if;
end process;
process(all)
begin
  next_state <= current_state;        -- avoid a latch
  dout_en    <= '0';                  -- avoid a latch
  case current_state is
```

```
      when IDLE =>
        if start then
          dout_en    <= '1';
          next_state <= DATA;
        end if;
      when DATA =>
        dout_en <= '1';
        if done then
          dout_en    <= '0';
          next_state <= IDLE;
        end if;
    end case;
  end process;
```

Looking at the preceding code, we can see there are a lot of similarities. There are some functional differences in that dout_en is combinationally generated. To make this equivalent, we would need to register dout_en.

Either way is acceptable for constructing a state machine. In fact, both have advantages and I tend to mix up their usage depending on the situation. Before we discuss the two classic state machine types, let's define what we want to accomplish in this project.

Designing a calculator interface

Let's look again at what we have available for inputs and outputs. The *Nexys A7* has an array of 16 LEDs, 16 switches, and a 5-pushbutton array:

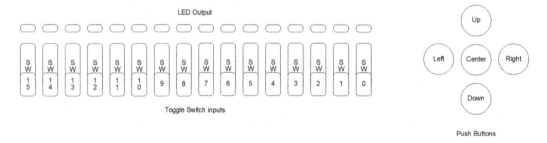

Figure 5.2: FPGA board buttons and switches

We can use the switches to input a 16-bit value in either hex or **Binary Coded Decimal** (BCD). We have 5 buttons available. *Table 5.1* below shows how the functions are mapped to the physical inputs on the board.

Button	Function
Left	A + B
Right	A − B
Up	A * B
Center	=
Down	Clear (Output = 0)

Table 5.1: Calculator functions mapped to the Nexys A7 board

Using the seven-segment displays, we can handle the result output and, using an LED, we can show the sign bit.

With our **input/output (I/O)** designed, we can focus on a state machine:

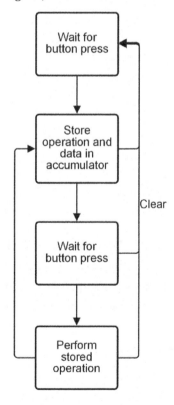

Figure 5.3: Ideal calculator state machine

Now, let's discuss the two classic state machine types, Moore and Mealy, and how we could implement the calculator using either one.

Designing a Moore state machine

In 1956, Edward F. Moore presented the concept of a state machine whose outputs are governed strictly by the state of the machine in his paper "*Gedanken-experiments on Sequential Machines.*"

What this means in practice is that the current state generates the outputs. The inputs only govern the next state logic. In general, this type of state machine can reach high clock speeds since the outputs have a full clock cycle to affect the design. These state machines can be large since decision logic doesn't affect the outputs directly, but rather leads to new states, increasing the state space.

You can find the following code in:

CH5/SystemVerilog/hdl/calculator_moore.sv

```
typedef enum bit [2:0]
            {
             IDLE,
             WAIT4BUTTON,
             ADD,
             SUB,
             MULT,
             RESET_S,
             } state_t;
```

CH5/VHDL/hdl/calculator_moore.vhd

```
type state_t is (IDLE, WAIT4BUTTON, ADD, SUB, MULT, RESET_S);
signal state : state_t := IDLE;
```

Looking at the Moore version of the calculator, we can see individual states for each operation. As we stated previously, we have a full clock cycle for each operation. This could be an advantage if we were pushing speed in our technology, but, as we saw previously in *Chapter 4, Counting Button Presses*, when we looked at the timing reports for the incrementer, the add operation has plenty of time:

CH5/SystemVerilog/hdl/calculator_moore.sv

```
IDLE: begin
  last_op     <= buttons; // operation to perform
  accumulator <= switch;
  if (start) state <= WAIT4BUTTON;
end
WAIT4BUTTON: begin
```

```verilog
      case (1'b1)
        last_op[UP]:     state <= MULT;
        last_op[DOWN]:   state <= RESET_S;
        last_op[LEFT]:   state <= ADD;
        last_op[RIGHT]:  state <= SUB;
        default:         state <= IDLE;
      endcase // case (1'b1)
  end
MULT: begin
  accumulator <= accumulator * switch;
  state       <= IDLE;
end
```

CH5/VHDL/hdl/calculator_moore.vhd

```vhdl
when IDLE =>
  -- Wait for data to be operated on to be entered. Then the user presses
  -- The operation, add, sub, multiply, clear or equal
  last_op <= buttons;         -- operation to perform
  if start then
    state <= WAIT4BUTTON;
  end if;
when WAIT4BUTTON =>
  -- Wait for second data to be entered, then user presses next operation.
  -- In this case, if we get an =, we perform the operation and we're
  -- done. The user can also put in another operation to perform with
  -- a new value on the accumulator.
  if last_op(UP) then
    state <= MULT;
  elsif last_op(DOWN) then
    state <= RESET_S;
  elsif last_op(LEFT) then
    state <= ADD;
  elsif last_op(RIGHT) then
    state <= SUB;
  else
    state <= IDLE;
  end if;
when MULT =>
```

```
product    := accumulator * unsigned(switch);
-- Note that even though the output is > 32 bits we will overflow
-- if larger.
accumulator <= product(accumulator'range);
state      <= IDLE;
```

We won't go through the entire state machine here. Please take a few minutes and peruse the following link: https://github.com/PacktPublishing/The-FPGA-Programming-Handbook-Second-Edition/blob/main/CH5/SystemVerilog/hdl/calculator_moore.sv or https://github.com/PacktPublishing/The-FPGA-Programming-Handbook-Second-Edition/blob/main/CH5/VHDL/hdl/calculator_moore.vhd.

Once a button has been pushed, the switch values and the operation are loaded into the accumulator register and the last_op register. When the next button is pushed, we execute the previous operation on the accumulator and the second switch values. This behaves like a pocket calculator, where you would push X + Y = and the result would appear on the screen. Also, you can chain operations, X + Y - Z =, for example.

If you look at the state machine design, you'll see that inputs only affect the next state values and that operations on data take a state.

Let's examine how this would look in a Mealy state machine design.

Implementing a Mealy state machine

In 1955, George H. Mealy introduced the concept of a state machine whose outputs are determined by the current state and inputs. We can refer to the implementation of our calculator state machine.

You can find the following Mealy state machine code in the CH5/SystemVerilog/hdl/calculator_mealy.sv folder:

```
typedef enum bit {IDLE, WAIT4BUTTON} state_t;
```

or CH5/VHDL/hdl/calculator_mealy.vhd:

```
type state_t is (IDLE, WAIT4BUTTON);
signal state : state_t := IDLE;
```

From the state definitions, you can see that the state space is greatly reduced. We've reduced five states to two. How are we able to accomplish this?

We no longer have the limitation of using an input to only change states. Now we can use the inputs to affect the operations directly. In the Moore state machine, we had states dedicated to our operations. Now we simply stay in the WAIT4BUTTON state.

SystemVerilog

```systemverilog
case (state)
  IDLE: begin
    last_op      <= buttons; // operation to perform
    if (start) state <= WAIT4BUTTON;
  end
  WAIT4BUTTON: begin
      case (1'b1)
        last_op[UP]:    accumulator <= accumulator * switch;
        last_op[DOWN]:  accumulator <= '0;
        last_op[LEFT]:  accumulator <= accumulator + switch;
        last_op[RIGHT]: accumulator <= accumulator - switch;
      endcase // case (1'b1)
  end
endcase // case (state)
```

VHDL

```vhdl
case state is
  when IDLE =>
    -- Wait for data to be operated on to be entered. Then the user
presses
    -- The operation, add, sub, multiply, clear or equal
    last_op <= buttons;           -- operation to perform
    if start then
      state <= WAIT4BUTTON;
    end if;
  when WAIT4BUTTON =>
    -- Wait for second data to be entered, then user presses next
operation.
```

```
  -- In this case, if we get an =, we perform the operation and we're
  -- done. The user can also put in another operation to perform with
  -- a new value on the accumulator.
  state <= IDLE;
  if last_op(UP) then
    product    := unsigned(accumulator) * unsigned(switch);
    -- Note that even though the output is > 32 bits we will overflow
    -- if larger.
    accumulator <= product(accumulator'range);
  elsif last_op(DOWN) then
    accumulator <= (others => '0');
  elsif last_op(LEFT) then
    accumulator <= accumulator + unsigned(switch);
  elsif last_op(RIGHT) then
    accumulator <= accumulator - unsigned(switch);
  end if;
end case;
```

Knowing about Mealy and Moore state machine design is mostly academic. If you decide to pursue a career in FPGAs, you'll probably be asked what the difference is in an interview – mostly because, when applying for a first job in a field, there's not much beyond academics that we engineers know to ask.

Table 5.2 shows the fundamental differences between Mealy and Moore state machines.

Moore state machine	Mealy state machine
Inputs can only affect the next state logic	Inputs can affect the next state logic as well as outputs
Generally more states than Mealy	Can have fewer states than Moore
Timing is usually easier to meet; optimal for Fmax	Fewer registers, timing can be more difficult to meet, Fmax can be reduced
More registers can result in more LUT/ FFs	Fewer registers can lead to fewer LUT/ FFs

Table 5.2: Moore vs Mealy comparison

What you will need going forward is some practical advice.

Practical state machine design

The reality of state machine design is that you should not worry about the formality of the code and whether it is Mealy or Moore. Use what you are comfortable with and fit the solution you are working towards. In practice, I tend to use a mix of styles based on the task I'm working on. In some cases, it might be a Moore type, or it may be a hybrid type using a split current state/ next state design.

With the basics of state machine design under our belt, let's look at a practical project whose heart is a state machine.

Project 4 – Building a Simple Calculator

Now that we've gone over state machine basics and shown the core of our calculator, we need to look at how we'll actually implement the calculator. The first issue that will come up is how we store our data in the design. Previously, we used **Binary Coded Decimal (BCD)** when we were incrementing our values. There was a simple solution presented for the BCD incrementor.

If we wanted to keep the internal data as BCD, we would need to develop a custom BCD adder in the hardware, subtractor, and multiplier. This is a more complicated option than a simple incrementor. Alternatively, we can explore the possibility of keeping our internal representation as binary data, but convert it to decimal to display it. This has the added advantage that we can use the SystemVerilog add, subtract, and multiply operators as is on binary representation and then create a conversion function.

The project files can be found in the following locations:

        CH5/SystemVerilog/build/calculator/calculator.xpr

        CH5/VHDL/build/calculator/calculator.xpr

Before we go down that route, let's consider packages.

Packaging for reuse

SystemVerilog and VHDL both provide the capability to create packages to encapsulate code that we want to reuse among multiple modules. It also provides a convenient way of reusing code for multiple applications.

You can find the following code in the CH4/SystemVerilog/hdl/calculator_pkg.sv folder:

```
`ifndef NUM_SEGMENTS
`define NUM_SEGMENTS 8
`endif
`ifndef _CALCULATOR_PKG
`define _CALCULATOR_PKG
package calculator_pkg;
  localparam NUM_SEGMENTS = `NUM_SEGMENTS;
  localparam UP           = 3'd0;
  localparam DOWN         = 3'd1;
```

When we create a package, it is structured like an empty SystemVerilog module – package <package name>;.

A package can contain parameters, functions, tasks, and user-defined types. In our case, we define localparams to make identifying the buttons easier and a function to convert the binary representation to BCD:

```
  function bit [NUM_SEGMENTS-1:0][3:0] bin_to_bcd;
    // we want to support either 4 or 8 segments
    input [31:0] bin_in;
    bit [NUM_SEGMENTS*4-1:0] shifted;
    shifted    = {30'b0, bin_in[31:30]};
    for (int i = 29; i >= 1; i--) begin
      shifted = shifted << 1 | bin_in[i];
      for (int j = 0; j < NUM_SEGMENTS; j++) begin
        if (shifted[j*4+:4] > 4) shifted[j*4+:4] += 3;
      end
    end
    shifted = shifted << 1 | bin_in[0];
    for (int i = 0; i < NUM_SEGMENTS; i++) begin
      bin_to_bcd[i] = shifted[4*i+:4];
    end
  endfunction // bin_to_bcd
endpackage // calculator_pkg
`endif
```

You can see that there is some complexity to the conversion function. It's this type of thing that worries me when designing. There are multiple for loops with an interdependency that need to be unrolled to create the logic that will perform the actual task in the FPGA. This can lead to many logic levels, which makes it difficult to meet our WNS timing constraints, as we will see. Even at 100 MHz, this will be a challenge.

 for loops are not inherently bad. If you need to replicate logic or are cognizant of it being generated, they can greatly reduce a design's complexity.

Here is the equivalent package in VHDL:

CH5VHDL/hdl/calculator_pkg.vhd

```
LIBRARY IEEE;
USE IEEE.std_logic_1164.all;
USE IEEE.numeric_std.all;

PACKAGE calculator_pkg IS
  constant NUM_SEGMENTS : integer := 8;
  constant UP           : natural := 0;
  constant DOWN         : natural := 1;
  ...
  constant CENTER       : natural := 4;
```

You'll see here that we need to include the packages necessary for the package. NUM_SEGMENTS is defined as a constant. We declare the signature of the bin_to_bcd function in the declarative part of the package:

```
function bin_to_bcd(bin_in : in std_logic_vector(31 downto 0)) return
array_t;
```

The body of that function is declared in the package body:

```
package body calculator_pkg is
  function bin_to_bcd(bin_in : in std_logic_vector(31 downto 0)) return
array_t is
    variable shifted : std_logic_vector(NUM_SEGMENTS *4 - 1 downto 0);
    variable bin2bcd : array_t(NUM_SEGMEN-S - 1 downto 0)(3 downto 0);
    variable digit   : unsigned(3 downto 0);
```

```
  begin
    shifted              := (others '>''0');
    shifted(1 downto 0) := bin_in(31 downto 30);
    for i in 29 downto 1 loop
      shifted := shifted(30 downto 0) & bin_in(i);
      for j in 0 to NUM_SEGMEN-S - 1 loop
        digit := unsigned(shifted(j * 4 + 3 downto j * 4));
        if digit > 4 then
          shifted(j * 4 + 3 downto j * 4) := std_logic_vector(digit + 3);
        end if;
      end loop;
    end loop;
    shifted              := shifted(30 downto 0) & bin_in(0);
    for i in 0 to NUM_SEGMEN-S - 1 loop
      bin2bcd(i) := shifted(4 * i + 3 downto 4 * i);
    end loop;
    return bin2bcd;
  end function bin_to_bcd;
```

TIP (for SystemVerilog)

If you are using SystemVerilog and non-project flow, rather than project flow, like we are, you should add the following:

`` `ifndef _CALCULATOR_PKG ``

`` `define _CALCULATOR_PKG ``

This will prevent the package from being redefined, which can cause warnings or errors in Vivado or other tools.

There is one major limitation with SystemVerilog packages. You can't pass in parameters. This is why you see that I had to define NUM_SEGMENTS within the package itself.

We can get around this by using `` `define ``:

```
`ifndef NUM_SEGMENTS
`define NUM_SEGMENTS 8
`endif
```

Then we can assign the definition to localparam:

```
localparam NUM_SEGMENTS = `NUM_SEGMENTS;
```

Within non-project mode, you can override the parameters within your TCL scripts. Within project mode, you can override the defines from within the PROJECT MANAGER settings. Now you'll need to do it within multiple areas as we have done before for synthesis and simulation.

Coding the top level

Take a look at the top-level calculator module.

You can find the following code in the CH5/SystemVerilog/hdl/calculator_top.sv folder:

```
`ifndef NUM_SEGMENTS
`define NUM_SEGMENTS 8
`endif
module calculator_top
  #(
    parameter BITS         = 32,
    parameter NUM_SEGMENTS = `NUM_SEGMENTS,
    parameter SM_TYPE      "= "MEALY" // MEALY or MOORE
    parameter USE_PLL      = "TRUE"
    )(
    input wire                        clk,
    input wire [15:0]                 SW,
    input wire [4:0]                  buttons,
    input wire                        CPU_RESETN,
    output logic [NUM_SEGMENTS-1:0]   anode,
    output logic [7:0]                cathode
    );
```

CH5/VHDL/hdl/calculator_top.vhd for **VHDL**:

```
entity calculator_top is
  generic(
    BITS         : integer := 32;
    NUM_SEGMENTS : integer := 8;
    SM_TYPE      : string  "= "MEALY";   -- MEALY or MOORE
    USE_PLL      : string  "= "TRUE"
```

```
  );
  port(
    clk         : in  std_logic;
    CPU_RESETN  : in  std_logic;
    SW          : in  std_logic_vector(15 downto 0);
    buttons     : in  std_logic_vector(4 downto 0);
    anode       : out std_logic_vector(NUM_SEGMENTS - 1 downto 0);
    cathode     : out std_logic_vector(7 downto 0)
  );
end entity calculator_top;
```

We can select the internal data storage size by setting the BITS parameter. We can also set the number of segments (as we discussed in the *Packages* section) and the state machine type.

We will use the seven_segment controller that we developed in *Chapter 4, Counting Button Presses*, as well as the button debouncing machine:

SystemVerilog:

```
generate
  if (USE_PLL = "TRUE") begin : g_USE_PLL
    logic int_reset;
    (* ASYNC_REG = "TRUE" *) logic [1:0] reset_sync = '1;
    sys_pll u_sys_pll
      (
        .clk_in1  (clk),
        .clk_out1 (clk_50)
        .locked   (int_reset)
        );
```

```
          always_ff @(posedge clk_50) begin
            reset_sync <= {reset_sync[0], ~(int_reset & CPU_RESETN)};
          end
          assign reset = reset_sync[1];


        end else  begin : g_NO_PLL
          assign clk_50 = clk;
        assign reset = '0; // No reset necessary unless using external reset
    or PLL
        end
      endgenerate
```

VHDL:

```
    g_USE_PLL : if USE_PLL = "TRUE" generate
      u_sys_ ll : sys_pll
        port map(
          clk_in1  => clk,
          clk_out1 => clk_50,
          locked   => int_reset
        );
      ...
    else generate
      clk_50 <= clk;
      reset  <= '0'; -- No reset necessary unless using external reset or PLL
      ...
```

You'll notice that there is a **Phase Locked Loop (PLL)** in the design and I've created an internal clock, clk_50. The next section will cover PLL generation. For our first run, we'll be using USE_PLL = "FALSE":

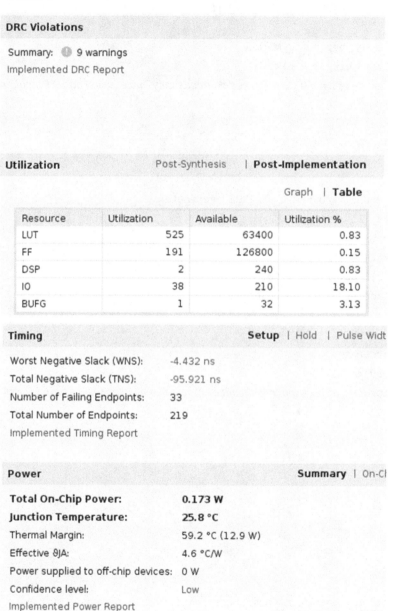

Figure 5.4: Mealy calculator design, 100 MHz

From this run, we can see that the design doesn't meet the timing requirements at 100 MHz. We can look at the failing paths in the timing analyzer and note that the binary to BCD converter doesn't meet the timing requirements:

Tcl Console	Messages	Log	Report

Q ⋢ ⬍ ❶

    Clock Summary (1)
    Methodology Summary (66)
> 🖿 Check Timing (36)
∨ 🖿 Intra-Clock Paths
  ∨ 🖿 sys_clk_pin
    ❶ Setup -4.432 ns (10)
    Hold 0.131 ns (10)
    Pulse Width 4.500 ns (30)
  Inter-Clock Paths

Timing Summary - impl_1 (saved)

Design Runs	DRC	Methodology	Power	**Timing**	×

Q — ⬚ ◈ ⫼ ❶ Intra-Clock Paths - sys_clk_pin - Setup

Name	Slack ^1	Levels	High Fanout	From	To	Total Delay	Logic Delay	Net Delay	Requirement
⌁ Path 1	-4.432	14	17	g_MEALY.u_sm...or_reg[30]/C	encoded_reg[6][2]/D	14.389	2.192	12.197	10.0
⌁ Path 2	-4.414	14	17	g_MEALY.u_sm...or_reg[30]/C	encoded_reg[7][0]/D	14.415	2.218	12.197	10.0
⌁ Path 3	-4.398	14	17	g_MEALY.u_sm...or_reg[30]/C	encoded_reg[6][1]/D	14.353	2.192	12.161	10.0
⌁ Path 4	-4.384	14	17	g_MEALY.u_sm...or_reg[30]/C	encoded_reg[6][3]/D	14.383	2.222	12.161	10.0
⌁ Path 5	-4.377	14	17	g_MEALY.u_sm...or_reg[30]/C	encoded_reg[7][2]/D	14.378	2.192	12.186	10.0
⌁ Path 6	-4.356	14	17	g_MEALY.u_sm...or_reg[30]/C	encoded_reg[7][3]/D	14.310	2.192	12.118	10.0
⌁ Path 7	-4.314	14	17	g_MEALY.u_sm...or_reg[30]/C	encoded_reg[7][1]/D	14.271	2.192	12.079	10.0

Figure 5.5: Mealy timing

The Moore state machine has more time to perform operations, but it likely won't do much for our violating paths as these are through the BCD converter. Try running it again with SM_TYPE set to MOORE. You'll see that the results are very similar – there are a few more storage elements in the Moore design and slightly better timing.

Changing frequencies by using a PLL or MMCM

The Artix 7 has **Clock Management Tiles (CMTs)** that are the core of the clocking resources in the devices we are using. The Nexys A7 100T has 6 CMTs and the Nexys A7 50T has 5 CMTs.

A CMT contains one **Phase Locked Loop (PLL)** and one **Mixed Mode Clock Manager (MMCM)**. PLLs and MMCMs can be used for frequency synthesis, that is, creating a faster or slower clock from an incoming clock:

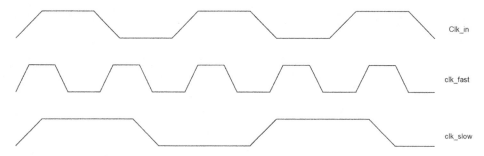

Figure 5.6: PLL/MMCM clock synthesis

You can see from the preceding diagram that we can take a clock input. For our boards, this is a 100 MHz clock and can generate a faster or slower clock based on our needs. There are other uses for the CMT that we won't get into in this book because of the limited interfaces our boards have.

Let's build our PLL to reduce our internal clock to 50 MHz so we can meet the timing in our design. This will be our introduction to the IP catalog. Xilinx and its partners provide IP for their FPGA devices, some of which are free while others can be licensed. I'd encourage you to look over what's available, especially the free options. Let's see how to do this:

1.   Select **IP Catalog**:

Figure 5.7: IP Catalog

2. Next, we'll look at **Clocking Wizard**:

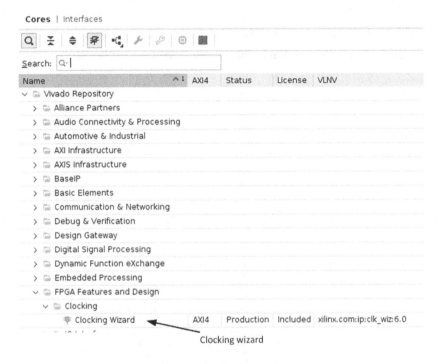

Figure 5.8: Clocking Wizard

3. The first step to creating an IP from the wizard is to customize it. Select the **IP Location** button and make sure to specify CH5/IP. Then, change the component name to sys_pll. Make sure CLK_IN1 is set to sys clock:

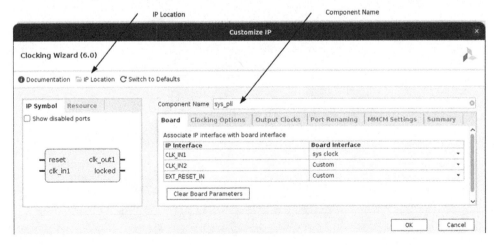

Figure 5.9: Customize IP

4. Select output clocks and set `clk_out1` to 50 MHz. Since this is an even division of 100 MHz, it will be able to do it exactly. In some cases, it will do its best, but the frequency will be off a little. Make sure to deselect `reset` and `locked` as we don't need those outputs:

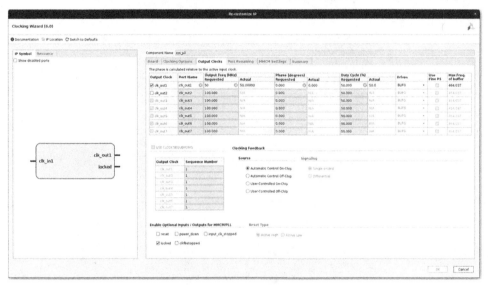

Figure 5.10: Output clocks

5. We have already built the FPGA, so you can cancel it. If you want to build it, then click OK and it will ask you to add it to the project and generate the output products.

6. Now, set the USE_PLL parameter in PROJECT MANAGER | Settings | General to TRUE, as we have done previously.

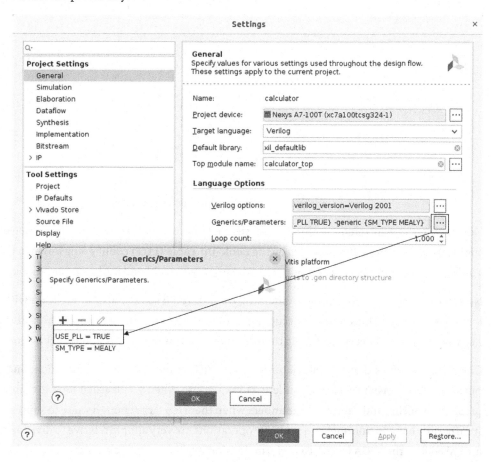

Figure 5.11: Output clocks

7. Now, set PLL to TRUE and perform the following build:

DRC Violations			
Summary: 9 warnings			
Implemented DRC Report			

Timing		Setup | Hold | Pulse Width
Worst Negative Slack (WNS):	2.322 ns	
Total Negative Slack (TNS):	0 ns	
Number of Failing Endpoints:	0	
Total Number of Endpoints:	219	
Implemented Timing Report		

Utilization — Post-Synthesis | **Post-Implementation**

Graph | Table

Resource	Utilization	Available	Utilization %
LUT	486	63400	0.77
FF	191	126800	0.15
DSP	2	240	0.83
IO	38	210	18.10
BUFG	2	32	6.25
MMCM	1	6	16.67

Power		Summary | On-Chip
Total On-Chip Power:	**0.238 W**	
Junction Temperature:	**26.1 °C**	
Thermal Margin:	58.9 °C (12.8 W)	
Effective θJA:	4.6 °C/W	
Power supplied to off-chip devices:	0 W	
Confidence level:	Low	
Implemented Power Report		

Figure 5.12: Mealy state machine at 50 MHz

Now that we have lowered the clock speed, the tool doesn't work as hard to meet unreasonable timing. You can see the effects of this by the **Look-Up Table (LUT)** count going down in this run. Timing is met comfortably. Try it out on the board. Try the add and multiply operations.

Now, try reloading it and subtract something from 0. You'll see the display all lit up with what looks like random values. What is occurring is underflow. We didn't add support for displaying negative numbers. This is something to think about for this chapter's challenge question.

One thing to note is that our calculator is simple. It supports addition, subtraction, and multiplication. Why wasn't division included? Think back to when you learned long division. It's a process of shifting and subtracting numbers when there is a large enough value to subtract from. It turns out that add/subtract and multiply operations are very simple relative to division and so are baked into the FPGA fabric. To perform division, we'll need to look at how this can be done.

Investigating the divider

Computer division is just like the long division you learned in school – an iterative process of shift and subtraction and addition in the case of non-restoring division.

There are two classic algorithms for integer division: restoring and non-restoring. The difference between the two methods is that when you perform the test subtraction at every pass, you either restore if using restoring division or keep the result negative if using non-restoring division. Non-restoring division has a correction step at the end.

Let's now explore how to implement a non-restoring divider for our calculator.

Building a non-restoring divider state machine

The first step is to create a state diagram for our proposed state machine. We can find the non-restoring algorithm defined in many places on the internet. I've created a proposed state diagram here:

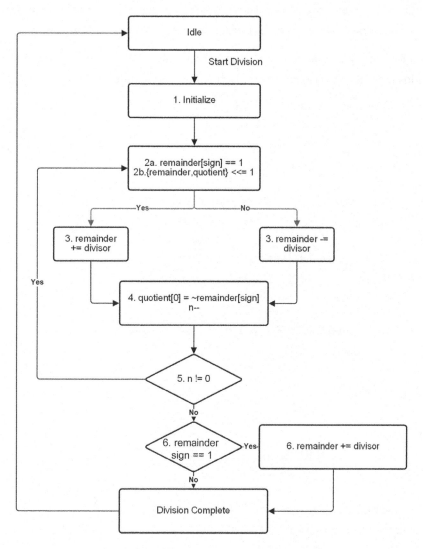

Figure 5.13: Non-restoring division algorithm

From the preceding state machine diagram, we can see that this is one of the more involved state machine designs we have approached yet. We have multiple tests and branch conditions.

As in many state machines, we begin idle. When we are instructed to divide, we initialize our internal variables. Then, enter the main loop in *Step 2*. We test the remainder sign and then shift our remainder and quotient. If the remainder is negative, we add the divisor, otherwise we subtract it. Then we feed the inverted remainder sign back into the quotient lowest bit and subtract our counter. If the counter is not zero, we return to *Step 2*, otherwise we test the remainder sign one last time and if it is negative, we add the divisor in again, otherwise we are done.

Let's take a look at the divider source code and, hopefully, it will be clear. You can find the following code in the CH5/SystemVerilog/hdl/divider_nr.sv folder:

```systemverilog
module divider_nr #(parameter BITS        = 16)
  (
   input wire                      clk,
   input wire                      reset,
   input wire                      start,
   input wire unsigned [BITS-1:0]  dividend,
   input wire unsigned [BITS-1:0]  divisor,
   output logic                    done,
   output logic unsigned [BITS-1:0] quotient,
   output logic unsigned [BITS-1:0] remainder
   );
```

And the VHDL version in the CH5/VHDL/hdl/divider_nr.sv folder:

```vhdl
entity divider_nr is
  generic(
    BITS : integer := 16
  );
  port(
    clk      : in  std_logic;
    reset    : in  std_logic;
    start    : in  std_logic;
    dividend : in  unsigned(BITS - 1 downto 0);
    divisor  : in  unsigned(BITS - 1 downto 0);
    done     : out std_logic;
    quotient : out unsigned(BITS - 1 downto 0);
    remainder : out unsigned(BITS - 1 downto 0)
  );
end entity divider_nr;
```

The first thing to note is that we've added two signals to control the state machine execution, start and done. We have a couple of options when handling division. We can either always take the number of clock cycles equal to the number of bits of the dividend, or we can adjust the dividend to remove leading 0s as these will always result in those bits being 0 on the quotient. Since we already developed a leading 1s detector, I chose to use this to speed up the division operation when we can. For our current application, this is not important. However, I tend to design for performance, so I wanted to reuse the module.

When we receive a start signal, the divider will begin operation:

SystemVerilog

```systemverilog
always @(posedge clk) begin
  done <= '0;
  case (state)
    IDLE: begin
      if (start) state <= INIT;
    end
    INIT: begin
      state          <= LEFT_SHIFT;
      quotient       <= dividend << (BITS - num_bits_w);
      int_remainder <= '0;
      num_bits       <= num_bits_w;
    end
```

VHDL

```vhdl
fsm : process(clk)
begin
  if rising_edge(clk) then
    if reset then
      done  <= '0';
      state <= IDLE;
    else
      done <= '0';
      case state is
        when IDLE =>
          if start then
            state <= INIT;
```

```
              end if;
         when INIT =>
             state          <= LEFT_SHIFT;
             quotient       <= shift_left(dividend, BITS - to_
   integer(unsigned(num_bits_w)));
             int_remainder <= (others => '0');
             num_bits       <= to_integer(unsigned(num_bits_w));
```

Note that done has a default value of '0', so it will only go high for as long as we assert it. When we enter the INIT state, we'll left-shift the dividend to remove leading 0s and set num_bits to know how long the divider will run for. We also define an intermediate remainder result of 0:

SystemVerilog

```
    leading_ones
      #(
        .SELECTOR   ("DOWN_FOR"),
        .BITS       (BITS)
        )
    u_leading_ones
      (
        .SW        (dividend),
        .LED       (num_bits_w)
        );
```

VHDL

```
    u_leading_ones : entity work.leading_ones
      generic map(
        SELECTOR => "DOWN_FOR",
        BITS     => BITS
      )
      port map(
        SW  => std_logic_vector(dividend),
        LED => num_bits_w
        );
```

Currently, leading_ones is built as a module for the board, and we are using the port names that the boards provided. To make this truly portable, we would rename the ports to be something more in line with our leading one detectors. For example, vector_in instead of SW and ones_position instead of LED:

SystemVerilog

```
LEFT_SHIFT: begin
  {int_remainder, quotient} <= {int_remainder, quotient} << 1;
  if (int_remainder[$left(int_remainder)])
    state   <= ADJ_REMAINDER0;
  else
    state   <= ADJ_REMAINDER1;
end
```

VHDL

```
when LEFT_SHIFT =>
  int_remainder <= int_remainder(BITS - 1 downto 0) & quotient(BITS - 1);
  quotient      <= quotient(BITS - 2 downto 0) & '0';
  if int_remainder(int_remainder'high) then
    state <= ADJ_REMAINDER0;
  else
    state <= ADJ_REMAINDER1;
  end if;
```

The number of bits is returned from the leading_ones function we developed. LEFT_SHIFT represents states 2a and 2b in our state diagram. Left-shift our intermediate results.

In SystemVerilog, when we do the comparison on the sign bit, int_remainder[$left(int_ remainder)], remember that $left will return the uppermost bit or the sign bit of our internal remainder. Also recall that since we are using non-blocking, we can shift and test the previous value in the same clock cycle.

The VHDL code checks int_remainder(int_remainder'high) to find out whether the most significant bit of int_remainder is set.

 if (A) is a shortcut for if (A!=0).

We have two states for updating the internal remainder, AJD_REMAINDER[2]. These two states represent the third steps in the state diagram:

SystemVerilog

```
UPDATE_QUOTIENT: begin
  state        <= TEST_N;
  quotient[0] <= ~int_remainder[$left(int_remainder)];
  num_bits     <= num_bits - 1'b1;
end
TEST_N: begin
  if (|num_bits)
    state <= LEFT_SHIFT;
  else
    state <= TEST_REMAINDER1;
end
```

VHDL

```
when UPDATE_QUOTIENT =>
  state        <= TEST_N;
  quotient(0) <= not int_remainder(int_remainder'high);
  num_bits     <= num_bits - 1;
when TEST_N =>
  if num_bits > 0 then
    state <= LEFT_SHIFT;
  else
    state <= TEST_REMAINDER1;
  end if;
```

We then update the quotient least significant bit, adjust the number of bits processed, and then test whether we have completed shifting:

SystemVerilog

```
TEST_REMAINDER1: begin
  if (int_remainder[$left(int_remainder)])
    state    <= ADJ_REMAINDER2;
  else
    state    <= DIV_DONE;
end
```

```
ADJ_REMAINDER2: begin
  state       <= DIV_DONE;
  int_remainder <= int_remainder + divisor;
end
DIV_DONE: begin
  done <= '1;
  state    <= IDLE;
end
```

VHDL

```
when TEST_REMAINDER1 =>
  if int_remainder(int_remainder'high) then
    state <= ADJ_REMAINDER2;
  else
    state <= DIV_DONE;
  end if;
when ADJ_REMAINDER2 =>
  state         <= DIV_DONE;
  int_remainder <= int_remainder + signed('0' & divisor);
when DIV_DONE =>
  done  <= '1';
  state <= IDLE;
when others =>
  state <= IDLE;
```

If we have completed shifting, we then test and update the intermediate remainder if appropriate. Finally, we assert the done signal to signify that the result is ready.

With the design complete, let's try it in a simulation.

Simulating the divider

I've created a divider testbench in SystemVerilog. This will allow us to verify our division algorithm prior to implementation.

You can find the following code in the CH5tb/tb_divider_nr.sv folder:

```
for (int i = 0; i < 100; i++) begin
  dividend <= $random;
  divisor  <= $random;
```

```
    start    <= '1;
    @(posedge clk);
    start    <= '0;
    while (!done) @(posedge clk);
    repeat (5) @(posedge clk);
  end
```

The heart of the code creates a random dividend and divisor. We start and then wait until done goes high before injecting the next values:

```
always @(posedge clk) begin
  if (done &&
      (quotient != dividend/divisor) &&
      (remainder != dividend%divisor)) begin
    $display("failure!");
    $display("quotient:   %d", quotient);
    $display("remainder:  %d", remainder);
    $display("expected Q: %d", dividend/divisor);
    $display("expected R: %d", dividend%divisor);
    $stop;
  end
end
```

The testing logic checks the quotient and remainder against the values returned by the System-Verilog division operator (/) and the modulo operator (%).

 SystemVerilog has a division operator. However, it is only synthesizable if it is a power of 2 or returns a fixed value. There is also a modulo operator (%), which will return the remainder of a value divided by another value. This is only synthesizable if it returns a fixed value or the right-hand side is a power of 2. VHDL operates similarly.

Sizing the intermediate remainder

Note that I've declared the intermediate remainder result as 1 bit larger than our actual remainder:

```
logic signed [BITS:0] int_remainder; // SystemVerilog
signal int_remainder : std_logic_vector(BITS downto 0); -- VHDL
```

I'm not ashamed to admit that I struggled to verify the design. I had initially declared the internal remainder as BITS-1:0. What I had neglected to consider was that we are dealing with unsigned numbers up to 64,535. Since we are adding or subtracting the divisor from int_remainder, we have a 16-bit unsigned value +/- a 16-bit unsigned value. This means we need a 17-bit internal 2's complement remainder to preserve the sign bit.

We've now finished our simple calculator. We've made it complete by creating a complex division function. Now, let's move on to another staple from the engineering curriculum – the traffic light controller.

Project 5 – Keeping cars in line

A classic design challenge for budding engineers is designing a traffic light controller. The Xilinx project can be found in CH5/SystemVerilog/build/traffic_light/traffic_light.xpr or CH5/VHDL/build/traffic_light/traffic_light.xpr.

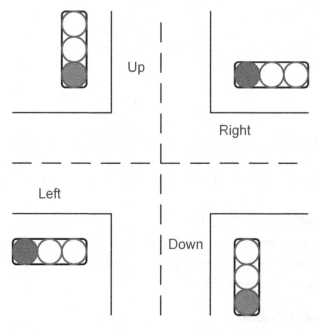

Figure 5.14: Traffic light controller intersection

The preceding diagram shows the basic scenario. We have an intersection with four traffic lights and four sensors labeled up, down, left, and right.

The ground rules are as follows:

- When a light is green, it will stay green for a minimum of 10 seconds.
- When a car goes through a green light, it is ignored.
- When a car waits at the red light, it signals the green to switch after it has been green for 10 seconds.

The light will stay yellow for 1 second when transitioning from green to red.

We've defined the problem. The first step, as always, is to create our state diagram.

Creating the state diagram

Oftentimes, I'll dive right in and code, so a state diagram can be a good way of documenting intent and finding potential problems ahead of time:

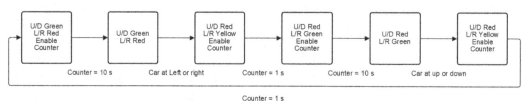

Figure 5.15: Traffic light controller state diagram

The state machine looks relatively straightforward. It has a linear flow, with only two inputs and counters that hold state for a minimum amount of time. We know how to run our traffic lights, but how can we use our board to display the state of our traffic lights?

Displaying our traffic lights

Luckily, our boards have three colored LEDs on them. With the tricolor LEDs, we can display just about any color on the spectrum by using **Pulse Width Modulation (PWM)**. There are three outputs for each LED: red, green, and blue.

Pulse width modulation

In digital logic, we convey information at its most basic level as strings of ones and zeros. When we lit LEDs before, we applied a '1' for the LED to be lit and a '0' for it to be off. With these tricolor LEDs, we have control over three outputs, one each for red, green, and blue. If we set any of these to a '1' by itself, we will get that color lit at 100% brightness. PWM works by using the on/off timer to control the average voltage through the LED to control the brightness. As we'll see, we will use a counter and comparator to create the PWM signal.

It is recommended that we apply a signal with a duty cycle of less than 100% to keep the LED from being blinding. In the case of the traffic light controller, I have it set at 50%:

SystemVerilog

```
always @(posedge clk) begin
  if (pwm_count == COUNT_500US - 1) begin
    pwm_count    <= '0;
    light_count <= ~light_count;
  end else begin
    pwm_count    <= pwm_count + 1;
  end
  R            <= '0;
  G            <= '0;
  B            <= '0;
  if (light_count) begin
```

VHDL

```
process(clk)
  variable pwm_count : natural range 0 to COUNT_500US - 1 := 0;
begin
  if rising_edge(clk) then
    if pwm_count = COUNT_500US - 1 then
      pwm_count    := 0;
      light_count <= not light_count;
    else
      pwm_count := pwm_count + 1;
    end if;
    R <= (others => '0');
    G <= (others => '0');
    B <= (others => '0');
    if light_count then
```

By creating a single-bit signal, called `light_count`, and using the `if` statement, I make sure the LED is only lit 50% of the time, with a PWM base frequency of 1 kHz.

You might notice one potential problem with the tricolor LED. We have red and green for our traffic light, but not yellow. If you remember color theory, you know we can mix red and green to make yellow:

SystemVerilog

```
GREEN: begin
  G[0] <= '1;
end
YELLOW: begin
  R[0] <= '1;
  G[0] <= '1;
end
RED: begin
  R[0] <= '1;
end
```

VHDL

```
when GREEN =>
  G(0) <= '1';
when YELLOW =>
  R(0) <= '1';
  G(0) <= '1';
when RED =>
  R(0) <= '1';
when others =>
```

It's not really practical to create a state space large enough to implement the 1-second or 10-second delay. We'll need to find a way to implement the delay circuit. One method is to create a counter and reference it within our state machine.

Implementing delays with a counter

The last element we need is a counter. If you take a look at our state diagram in *Figure 4.13*, you'll see we are only ever counting 1 second or 10 seconds. We could make two separate counters, but what I did was create one counter large enough to count to 10 seconds and reuse it for both:

SystemVerilog

```
localparam COUNT_1S  = int'(100000000 / CLK_PER);
localparam COUNT_10S = 10 * int'(100000000 / CLK_PER);
localparam COUNT_500US = int'(COUNT_1S / 2000); // 500 us x 2 gives a 1
kHz PWM base frequency
bit [$clog2(COUNT_10S)-1:0]        counter;
```

VHDL

```vhdl
constant COUNT_1S  : integer := 1000000000 / CLK_PER;
constant COUNT_10S : integer := 10 * COUNT_1S;
constant COUNT_500US : integer := COUNT_1S / 2000; -- 500 us x 2 gives a 1
kHz PWM base frequency
signal counter : integer range 0 to COUNT_10S;
```

We've sized the counter to 10 seconds, and we have two parameters (constants) defined for terminal counts. When we want to count, we simply enable the counter via enable_count and test for the terminal value using the if statement. When the counter is not in use, we reset it to 0:

SystemVerilog

```systemverilog
always @(posedge clk) begin
  lr_reg          <= lr_reg << 1 | SW[0];
  ud_reg          <= ud_reg << 1 | SW[1];
  enable_count    <= '0;
  if (enable_count) begin
    counter <= counter + 1'b1;
  end else begin
    counter <= '0;
  end
  case (state)
    INIT_UD_GREEN: begin
      up_down       <= GREEN;
      left_right    <= RED;
      enable_count <= '1;
      if (counter == COUNT_10S) state <= UD_GREEN_LR_RED;
    end
```

VHDL

```vhdl
process(clk)
begin
  if rising_edge(clk) then
    lr_reg        <= lr_reg(1 downto 0) & SW(0);
    ud_reg        <= ud_reg(1 downto 0) & SW(1);
    enable_count <= '0';
```

```
    if enable_count then
      if counter < COUNT_10S then
        counter <= counter + 1;
      end if;
    else
      counter <= 0;
    end if;

    case state is
      when INIT_UD_GREEN =>
        up_down      <= GREEN;
        left_right   <= RED;
        enable_count <= '1';
        if counter = COUNT_10S then
          state <= UD_GREEN_LR_RED;
        end if;
```

Look over the state machine and see that its flow matches the state diagram. Run it on the board.

Now you should have a functional traffic light controller. Play with the switches and verify that the lights will stay in a given state until a car is detected. Verify the lights cycle correctly. It's a lot simpler to design a traffic light controller nowadays. I had to do it on a breadboard with discrete parts when I went through university.

Summary

In this chapter, we've seen how we can use our knowledge of both SystemVerilog and VHDL sequential and combinational elements to develop and implement state machines. We've looked at two classical state machine designs, Mealy and Moore, and then implemented a simple calculator using this knowledge. We also touched on some basic math as well as exploring how to develop an integer divider using HDLs.

We looked at design reuse by implementing a package for our calculator and also reusing the leading ones detector we developed previously.

We saw at a high level how we can control our clock speed using a PLL so the design will run on the board.

With this knowledge, you can now look at expanding the calculator. We are currently only handling unsigned numbers. However, it wouldn't be that hard to make it handle signed numbers. We also took a look at how we can use PWM to light an RGB LED and we created a traffic light controller to take advantage of those resources.

In the next chapter, we are going to take a look at some of the board resources. We'll learn how to capture audio data and play it back. We'll learn about the temperature sensor, make a thermostat, and display the temperature on our trusty seven-segment display. We'll also learn about data processing and smooth out our sensor to make it a little less jumpy.

Questions

1. In the SystemVerilog divider module, we perform a shift of the intermediate results. Why did we use the following:

    ```
    {int_remainder, quotient} <= {int_remainder, quotient} << 1;
    ```

    Rather than this?

    ```
    {int_remainder, quotient} <<= 1;
    ```

    a. It better conveys design intent.
    b. <<= is a blocking assignment and we are using it in a clocked block, which violates the principles we laid out regarding safe design practices.
    c. When we use a concatenation function, {}, we cannot use <<=.

2. Which of the following are synthesizable HDL? (Multiple correct answers)

    ```
    logic [15:0] A, B; // SystemVerilog

    signal A, B : std_logic_vector(15 downto 0);
    ```

    a. A / B
    b. A / 4
    c. A % B
    d. 5 % 4

3. Experiment with the colors in the traffic light controller design. Can you come up with different colors by expanding the counter size and enabling the RGB outputs at different times? The color space is practically unlimited.

4. Our calculator doesn't currently implement the divide function. Can you modify it to support division? You can use the CPU reset button or remap the buttons.

Answers

1. b) <<= is a blocking assignment and we are using it in a clocked block, which violates the principles we laid out regarding safe design practices.

2. Both b) A/4 & d) 5 % 4

3. This has been left for the readers to do.

4. This has been left for the readers to do.

Challenge

Our simple calculator currently only handles unsigned numbers. In the case of addition, subtraction, and multiplication, the binary representation is already in 2's complement representation. Remember that to take the two's complement of a number, you invert and add one. Can you modify the design to handle negative number representation? You might want to use one of the LEDs to represent the sign of the result.

Extra challenge

It is harder to handle negative numbers from the divider. Can you modify the non-restoring divider to make it also handle negative numbers?

Further reading

Please refer to the following links for more information regarding what was covered in this chapter:

- https://reference.digilentinc.com/reference/programmable-logic/nexys-a7/reference-manual
- https://www.xilinx.com/support/documentation/user_guides/ug472_7Series_Clocking.pdf

Join our community on Discord

Join our community's Discord space for discussions with the authors and other readers:

https://packt.link/embedded

6

FPGA Resources and How to Use Them

In the previous chapter, we discussed state machines. We looked at how we can use state machines to design a simple calculator and looked at some more complex operations, such as division. This allowed us to see a practical example of complex state machine design. We briefly discussed packaging for reuse and demonstrated this with a simple traffic light controller.

In this chapter, we are going to look at some of the underlying FPGA resources in more detail. You've been briefly introduced to some of these, such as **Random Access Memory (RAM)** and **Digital Signal Processing (DSP)** blocks, while others have been glossed over, such as **Phase Locked Loops (PLLs)**, where we used one to fix a timing problem in our calculator design. We'll build upon our previous experience by incorporating these new resources.

By the completion of this chapter, you'll have a good idea of how to interface with external components. We've previously seen in *Chapter 5*, *Let's Build a Calculator*, how to use **pulse-width modulation (PWM)**. In this chapter, we'll see how to use pulse data modulation in conjunction with the microphone on the board. You'll see a simple serial bus in action, I2C, as well as how to implement storage in the form of **first in, first out (FIFO)** storage.

In this chapter, we are going to cover the following main topics:

- What is a digital microphone?
- Project 6 – Listening and learning
- Project 7 – Using the temperature sensor

Technical requirements

The technical requirements for this chapter are the same as those for *Chapter 2, FPGA Programming Languages and Tools*.

To follow along with the examples and the project, you can find the code files for this chapter at the following repository on GitHub: https://github.com/PacktPublishing/The-FPGA-Programming-Handbook-Second-Edition/tree/master/CH6.

What is a digital microphone?

A digital microphone needs to receive analog audio data and convert it to digital data, which is usable for digital electronics. Let's look at how we can accomplish this using **Pulse-Density Modulation (PDM)**.

What is PDM?

A PDM signal is captured by a 1-bit **analog-to-digital converter (ADC)** that receives an analog waveform and encodes its output as a string of digital pulses, as shown in *Figure 6.1*. When the pulses are denser over a period of time, they represent larger values. In *Figure 6.1*, we see a signal from the testbench as a sine wave. The following signal shows an example of what a PDM form of that waveform might look like:

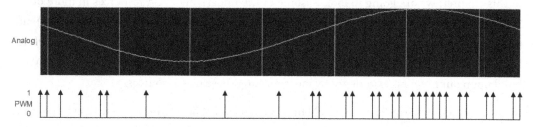

Figure 6.1: PDM waveform example

The advantage of this type of signal is that we only need a single wire to transmit the information since audio is limited to about 24 kHz and our clock rate will be orders of magnitude above this.

With the basics of digital microphones and PDM, let's now look at a practical project.

Project 6 – Listening and learning

The Nexys A7 board has a digital microphone on board that we can use to capture ambient noise, speech, and such from the environment the board is in. We'll be utilizing this microphone to capture sound. In order to do that, we'll need to explore the format of the data and how to sample it.

It's also possible to play it back.

Let's take a look at interfacing with the microphone. The project is located at CH6/SystemVerilog/ build/pdm_audio/pdm_audio.xpr or CH6/VHDL/build/pdm_audio/pdm_audio.xpr.

You can find the following code in the CH6/SystemVerilog/hdl/pdm_top.sv folder:

```systemverilog
module pdm_top
  #(
    parameter RAM_SIZE     = 16384,
    parameter CLK_FREQ = 100,
    parameter SAMPLE_COUNT = 128
  )
  (
  input wire   clk, // 100Mhz clock
  // Microphone interface
  output logic m_clk,
  output logic m_lr_sel,
  input wire   m_data,
  // Tricolor LED
  output logic R,
  output logic G,
  output logic B,
  // LED Array
  output logic [15:0] LED
  );
```

Or in the CH6/VHDL/hdl/pdm_top.vhd folder:

```vhdl
entity pdm_top is
  generic(
    RAM_SIZE : integer := 16384;          -- bytes
    CLK_FREQ : integer := 100;            -- MHz
    SAMPLE_COUNT : natural := 128);
  port(
    clk     : in  std_logic;
    -- Microphone interface
    m_clk   : out std_logic;
    m_lr_sel : out std_logic;
    m_data  : in  std_logic;
```

```
    -- Tricolor LED
    R, G, B  : out std_logic;
    -- Pushbutton interface
    BTNU      : in  std_logic;
    BTNC      : in  std_logic;
    -- LED Array
    LED       : out std_logic_vector(15 downto 0) := (others => '0');
    -- PDM output
    AUD_PWM  : out std_logic;
    AUD_SD   : out std_logic);
end entity pdm_top;
```

We can see here that we are using the 100 MHz clock as we will need a clock source to communicate with the microphone. There are two outputs for the microphone and the data back (m_data). The two outputs are a clock at the frequency of the data * the number of sampling cycles; in this case, 12.5 kHz * 200 samples = 2.5 MHz. The last signal, m_lr_sel, selects whether data is presented on the rising or falling edge of the clock. This is so two devices could share the same data bus to give a left and right channel, as shown in *Figure 6.2*:

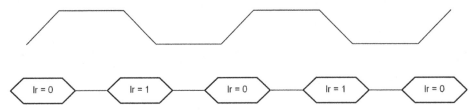

Figure 6.2: Microphone timing – left/right channel

I've also brought out one of our tricolor LEDs to display the amplitude information as feedback. This can be useful for debugging as simply snapping your fingers will give you visual feedback if the microphone is sampling and outputting the data that the FPGA is receiving.

The clock to the microphone needs to be between 1 and 3.3 MHz. Following the design guidance from the Nexys A7 manual, I've constructed a circuit to generate timing for the device.

You can find the following code in the CH6/SystemVeriloghdl/pdm_inputs.sv folder:

SystemVerilog

```systemverilog
module pdm_inputs
  #(
    parameter              CLK_FREQ     = 100,    // Mhz
    parameter              SAMPLE_RATE = 2500000 // Hz
    localparam             SAMPLE_COUNT = 128,      // Number of samples
    localparam             SAMPLE_BITS  = $clog2(SAMPLE_COUNT+1) // bits needed
for sample counter
  )
  (
    input wire             clk, // 100Mhz
    // Microphone interface
    output logic           m_clk,
    output logic           m_clk_en,
    input wire             m_data,
    // Amplitude outputs
    output logic [SAMPLE_BITS-1 :0] amplitude,
    output logic           amplitude_valid
    );
```

VHDL in the CH6/VHDL/hdl/pdm_inputs.vhd folder:

```vhdl
entity pdm_inputs is
  generic(
    CLK_FREQ     : natural := 100;        -- MHz
    MCLK_FREQ    : natural := 2500000;   -- Hz
    SAMPLE_COUNT : natural := 128
  );
  port(
    clk             : in  std_logic;
    -- Microphone interface
    m_clk           : out std_logic := '0';
    m_clk_en        : out std_logic := '0';
    m_data          : in  std_logic;
    -- Amplitude outputs
    amplitude       : out std_logic_vector(clog2(SAMPLE_COUNT + 1) - 1
downto 0);
    amplitude_valid : out std_logic := '0'
  );
end entity pdm_inputs;
```

The `pdm_inputs` module generates the clock to the microphone and receives the data back:

SystemVerilog

```
localparam CLK_COUNT = int'((CLK_FREQ*1000000)/(MCLK_FREQ*2));
...
    if (clk_counter == CLK_COUNT - 1) begin
      clk_counter <= '0;
      m_clk      <= ~m_clk;
      m_clk_en   <= ~m_clk;
    end else begin
      clk_counter <= clk_counter + 1;
    end
```

VHDL

```
constant CLK_COUNT : integer := (CLK_FREQ * 1000000) / (MCLK_FREQ * 2);
...
if clk_counter = CLK_COUNT - 1 then
  clk_counter <= 0;
  m_clk      <= not m_clk;
  m_clk_en   <= not m_clk;
else
  clk_counter <= clk_counter + 1;
end if;
```

In terms of generating a new clock, we have a couple of choices. The best option is to use a PLL or **Mixed-Mode Clock Manager** (**MMCM**) to generate a precise clock that we can use. In the case of such a slow clock, this is not possible. What we can do, since we have a high-speed clock running at 100 MHz, is we can create a counter that counts to a value representing half the clock period of our generated clock, and then we can create a clean clock from a flip flop. We don't want to see this clock directly in our design, so we create a `m_clk_en` pulse that lets us know when we can capture data on the rising edge of this clock.

To quantize the PDM data, we need to create a set of overlapping windows as shown in *Figure 6.3*. The overlapping windows allow us to sub-sample the results to increase the resolution of our samples, doubling our sampling frequency:

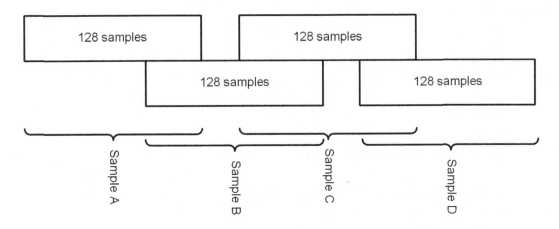

Figure 6.3: Sampling

We have a routine that collects 12.5 kHz samples interleaved to create a 25 kHz output:

SystemVerilog

```
if (m_clk_en) begin
  if (counter < WINDOW_SIZE-1) counter <= counter + 1'b1;
  else                         counter <= '0;

  if (counter == TERMINAL_COUNT0) begin
    amplitude        <= sample_counter[0];
    amplitude_valid  <= '1;
    sample_counter[0] <= '0;
  end else if (counter < TERMINAL_COUNT0) begin
    sample_counter[0] <= sample_counter[0] + m_data;
  end
  if (counter == TERMINAL_COUNT1) begin
    amplitude        <= sample_counter[1];
    amplitude_valid  <= '1;
    sample_counter[1] <= '0;
  end else if (counter < TERMINAL_COUNT1 || counter >= COUNTER1_OFFSET)
begin
    sample_counter[1] <= sample_counter[1] + m_data;
  end
end
```

VHDL

```vhdl
if m_clk_en then
  if counter < WINDOW_SIZE - 1 then
    counter <= counter + 1;
  else
    counter <= 0;
  end if;
  if counter = TERMINAL_COUNT0 then
    amplitude          <= std_logic_vector(to_unsigned(sample_counter(0),
amplitude'length));
    amplitude_valid    <= '1';
    sample_counter(0) <= 0;
  elsif counter < TERMINAL_COUNT0 then
    if m_data then
      sample_counter(0) <= sample_counter(0) + 1;
    end if;
  end if;
  if counter = TERMINAL_COUNT1 then
    amplitude          <= std_logic_vector(to_unsigned(sample_counter(1),
amplitude'length));
    amplitude_valid    <= '1';
    sample_counter(1) <= 0;
  elsif (counter < TERMINAL_COUNT1) or (counter >= COUNTER1_OFFSET) then
    if m_data then
      sample_counter(1) <= sample_counter(1) + 1;
    end if;
  end if;
end if;
```

The sampling logic operates on the rising edge of the 2.5 MHz clock generated by the microphone. We accomplish this by using `m_clk_en` to limit when the logic operates. The timers are set up according to the Nexys A7 documentation: `https://reference.digilentinc.com/reference/programmable-logic/nexys-a7/reference-manual`.

Now, the coding is complete. In this case, it's easy to simulate. We can create a testbench that feeds in a sine wave and see how our design reacts. The testbench has been constructed using both VHDL and SystemVerilog.

Simulating the microphone

I've created a testbench that we can use to verify our core. Let's verify our code and make sure we can capture the data.

You can find the following code in the CH6/SystemVerilog/tb/tb_pdm_top.sv folder:

```
`timescale 1ns/10ps
module tb_pdm_top;
```

Or, you can find the following code in the CH6/VHDL/tb/tb_pdm_top.vhd folder:

```
entity tb_pdm_top is
end entity tb_pdm_top;
```

The testbench is made up of a sine wave generator and a PDM encoder. If you run the testbench, you can see by the waves that the pdm_inputs module tracks the data from the sine wave generator:

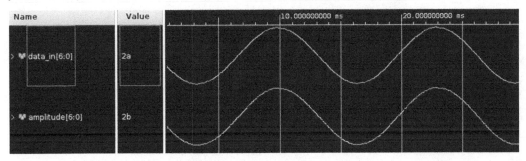

Figure 6.4: Sine wave data versus amplitude data

I've also added the amplitude signals into the chipscope so we can see the results on the board. Build the design and run it. We can use an online tone generator, such as the one at https://www.szynalski.com/tone-generator/, as a sine wave to generate a test tone using a computer:

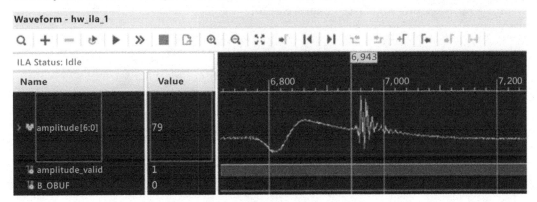

Figure 6.5: Chipscope wave capture

In *Figure 6.5*, we can see a capture of my voice in the microphone. I found that you need to be very close to the microphone to capture anything of use.

One setting in the chipscope that is very helpful for a very slow clock speed is to enable capture control:

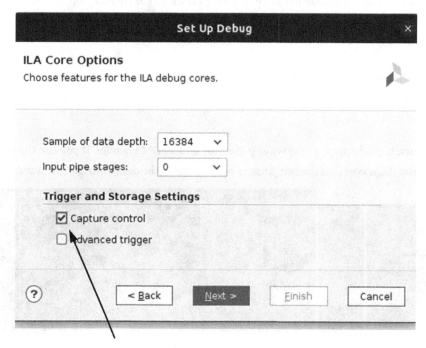

Figure 6.6: Capture control

When **Capture control** is enabled, you can access another pane in the **Integrated logic analyzer (ILA)**, which allows you to limit when data is captured to your buffer:

Figure 6.7: Capture settings

amplitude_valid is set at a rate of 25 kHz. Capture Setup allows us to capture only what we really want to capture to extract the valid amplitude information. Looking at the preceding waveform in *Figure 6.5*, the center point is at ~7'd64, which corresponds to 0.

We've shown that we can receive the PDM data and generate amplitude values at 25 kHz, but we aren't doing anything with it yet. Let's add some storage.

Introducing storage

Now that we have managed to capture some audio data, we need to do something with it. Currently, the data register is constantly overwritten every 25 kHz. There's a lot we can do with audio data, but initially, we need to store it away. What we can do is create RAM and when we push a button, start capturing the data, lighting an LED when complete.

Inferring, instantiating, or using the IP catalog to generate RAM

We have a number of choices in creating RAM. The most flexible method of creating RAM is to infer it. This has the advantage of having cross-platform support by most FPGA vendors as well as devices. Xilinx has provided several templates you can use that will aid you in getting started:

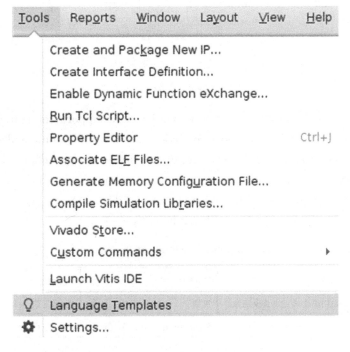

Figure 6.8: Language Templates

If you select **Tools | Language Templates**, you can access a variety of code samples that can help jump-start your design. Before we get into coding our RAM, let's look at the basic types.

Basic RAM types

There are three basic RAM types:

- **Single port (SP)**
- **Simple dual port (SDP)**
- **True dual port (TDP)**

Often, we'll look at schematics to see what the ports of a core look like. In this case, we can show you how RAM would connect to a design, as shown in *Figure 6.9*:

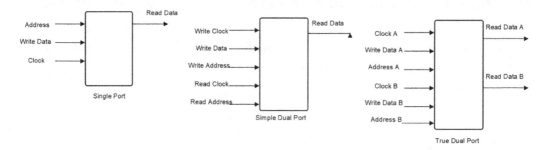

Figure 6.9: RAM types

Internally, RAM blocks in the Artix 7 are fairly complex. RAM supports configurable data widths from 1 bit to 64 bits, byte enables, and error correction codes. I would recommend reading through the 7-series memory resource guide (reference in the *Further reading* section) in order to get an idea of what RAM is capable of. I've found ways around seemingly insurmountable engineering problems, such as how to effectively implement a 64 KB deep RAM, by realizing that different configurations of RAM can solve the problem inherently.

Table 6.1 shows the three types of RAM we'll be looking at.

RAM Type	Port A	Port B	Clocks
SP	Read and Write Address	N/A	Single Clock
SDP	Write to Write Address	Read from Read Address	Single Clock
TDP	Write to Write Address	Read from Read Address	Independent Read/Write Clock

Table 6.1: RAM summary

Single Port RAM

Single Port RAM is the simplest type. This RAM has one address port, meaning that it can read from and write to memory at a single memory location on a clock cycle. *Figure 6.10* shows an example of reading and writing an SP RAM configured for write before read. We can see that DOUT0 comes out one cycle after location A0 and DIN1 comes out one cycle after writing DIN1 to location A1.

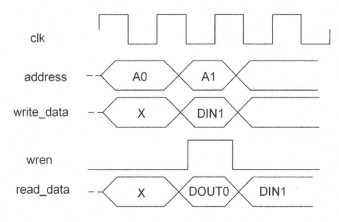

Figure 6.10: SP RAM access with write before read

Figure 6.11 shows read before write operation on an SP RAM.

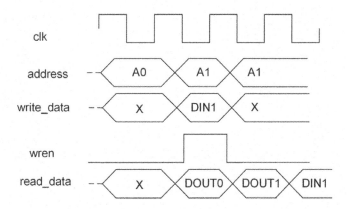

Figure 6.11: SP RAM access with read before write

This type of RAM is simple to infer. The following code shows how to infer a read-before-write version of RAM:

SystemVerilog

```systemverilog
localparam MEM_DEPTH = 256;
localparam MEM_WIDTH = 8;
logic [MEM_WIDTH-1:0]         memory[MEM_DEPTH];
logic [$clog2(MEM_DEPTH)-1:0] address;
logic [MEM_WIDTH-1:0]         write_data, read_data;
logic                         wren;
initial memory = '{default: '0};
always @(posedge clk) begin
  if (wren) memory[address] <= write_data;
  read_data <= memory[address];
end
```

VHDL

```vhdl
constant MEM_DEPTH           : natural := 256;
constant MEM_WIDTH           : natural := 8;
type array_2d is array (natural range <>) of std_logic_vector(MEM_WIDTH -
1 downto 0);
signal memory                : array_2d(0 to MEM_DEPTH - 1) := (others =>
(others => '0'));
signal address               : natural range 0 to MEM_DEPTH - 1;
signal write_data, read_data : std_logic_vector(MEM_WIDTH - 1 downto 0);
signal wren                  : std_logic;

process(clk)
begin
  if rising_edge(clk) then
    if wren then
      memory(address) <= write_data;
    end if;
    read_data <= memory(address);
  end if;
end process;
```

The preceding code shows how you can infer an SP RAM. We define a MEM_WIDTH parameter of 8 bits (or one byte) and a MEM_DEPTH parameter of 256 bytes. We can see the memory array is written when the wren is high. RAM is read every cycle based on the input address. The initial statement is optional. Block RAM and SLICEM memory can have an initial value, whereas UltraRAM cannot.

A few important points to consider are the following:

- The storage must be declared as unpacked in SystemVerilog:

  ```
  logic [MEM_WIDTH-1:0]            memory[MEM_DEPTH];
  ```

- You can initialize the memory types with the exception of UltraRAM, which the Artix 7 doesn't have. To keep things portable, you shouldn't initialize very large RAM blocks.

- Block RAM must have synchronous read data. Distributed RAM (remember those SLICEMs?) can have asynchronous read ports. Having an asynchronous read port cuts into your timing budget significantly resulting in worse timing values.

Tip:

Using the '{} representation in SystemVerilog makes it easier to initialize sparsely populated unpacked arrays. You can initialize individual locations by using their address and the defaults for all others. For example, `{0: 8'hFF, 7'h40, default: '0}; would initialize location 0 to 0xFF, 1 to 0x40, and the rest to 0.

Similarly, in **VHDL**:

```
my_array <= (0 => to_unsigned(16#FF#,MEM_WIDTH),
             1 => to_unsigned(16#40#,MEM_WIDTH),
         others => to_unsigned(16#00#,MEM_WIDTH));
```

We can specify the value in hex by using 16#nn# and use others to fill locations we don't specify.

SP memories can only read from, or write to, a single location at a time. SDP memories are a little more flexible in that you have independent control of the read and write addresses, so it's possible to read from a different location than where you are writing from. This is particularly useful when building FIFOs.

Simple Dual Port RAM

Simple Dual Port (SDP) RAM consists of two clocks, a read and write clock. It is a subset of the True Dual Port RAM where you have one write port and one read port both utilizing the same or different clocks. These types of RAM are often used for elasticity, in the case of a FIFO, or when data needs to be written from different addresses from where writes are currently occurring. These types of RAM are also easy to code up:

SystemVerilog

```systemverilog
localparam MEM_DEPTH = 256;
localparam MEM_WIDTH = 8;
logic [MEM_WIDTH-1:0]        memory[MEM_DEPTH];
logic [$clog2(MEM_DEPTH)-1:0] wr_address, rd_address;
logic [MEM_WIDTH-1:0]        write_data, read_data;
logic                        wren;
initial memory = '{default: '0};
always @(posedge wr_clk)
  if (wren) memory[wr_address] <= write_data;
always @(posedge rd_clk) read_data <= memory[rd_address];
```

VHDL

```vhdl
constant MEM_DEPTH : natural := 256;
constant MEM_WIDTH : natural := 8;
type array_2d is array (natural range <>) of std_logic_vector(MEM_WIDTH -
1 downto 0);
signal memory                : array_2d(0 to MEM_DEPTH - 1) := (others =>
(others => '0'));
signal wraddress, rdaddress  : natural range 0 to MEM_DEPTH - 1;
signal write_data, read_data : std_logic_vector(MEM_WIDTH - 1 downto 0);
signal wren                  : std_logic;
...
process(wrclk)
begin
  if rising_edge(wrclk) then
    if wren then
      memory(wraddress) <= write_data;
    end if;
  end if;
end process;
process(rdclk)
begin
  if rising_edge(rdclk) then
    read_data <= memory(rdaddress);
  end if;
end process;
```

SDP RAM looks very much like SP RAM, the main difference being the separation of the write and read addresses. Note that wr_clk and rd_clk can be the same clock or different. The underlying resource is the same.

The first two memory types are the ones you'll use the most. However, there is one other type that is less frequently used.

True Dual Port RAM

A **True Dual Port (TDP) RAM** allows full read/write access from both ports. There are some restrictions in terms of what happens if there are address collisions on a read or write. We saw this previously when we discussed read before write or write before read. I usually will use the option of xilinx xpm_memory if I am using a TDP RAM; however, a TDP RAM too can be inferred:

SystemVerilog

```
localparam MEM_DEPTH = 256;
localparam MEM_WIDTH = 8;
logic [MEM_WIDTH-1:0]          memory[MEM_DEPTH];
logic [$clog2(MEM_DEPTH)-1:0] address_a, address_b;
logic [MEM_WIDTH-1:0]          write_data_a, read_data_a;
logic [MEM_WIDTH-1:0]          write_data_b, read_data_b;
logic                          wren_a, wren_b;
initial memory = '{default: '0};
always @(posedge clk_a) begin
  if (wren_a) memory[address_a] <= write_data_a;
  read_data_a <= memory[address_a];
end
always @(posedge clk_b) begin
  if (wren_b) memory[address_b] <= write_data_b;
  read_data_b <= memory[address_b];
end
```

VHDL

```
constant MEM_DEPTH             : natural                := 256;
constant MEM_WIDTH             : natural                := 8;
type array_2d is array (natural range <>) of std_logic_vector(MEM_WIDTH -
1 downto 0);
shared variable memory         : array_2d(0 to MEM_DEPTH - 1) := (others
=> (others => '0'));
```

```
signal address_a, address_b        : natural range 0 to MEM_DEPTH - 1;
signal write_data_a, read_data_a : std_logic_vector(MEM_WIDTH - 1 downto
0);
signal write_data_b, read_data_b : std_logic_vector(MEM_WIDTH - 1 downto
0);
signal wren_a, wren_b              : std_logic;
...
process(clk_a)
begin
  if rising_edge(clk_a) then
    if wren_a then
      memory(address_a) := write_data_a;
    end if;
    read_data_a <= memory(address_a);
  end if;
end process;

process(clk_b)
begin
  if rising_edge(clk_b) then
    if wren_b then
      memory(address_b) := write_data_b;
    end if;
    read_data_b <= memory(address_b);
  end if;
end process;
```

From the preceding code, you'll notice it looks very much like two SP memories. The difference is that both always blocks reference the same storage, providing dual ports in the memory. In VHDL, we have to use a *shared variable* to be able to write to the memory from two different processes.

We've seen how to infer all three memory types. Xilinx provides macros for common functions such as **clock domain crossing (CDC)**, FIFOs, and RAM as part of their **Xilinx Parameterized Macro (XPM)** functions.

Vivado will map your inferred memory based on size. You can force a particular implementation by using the `ram_style` attribute, for example:

SystemVerilog

```
(* ram_style = "block" *) logic [7:0] memory[256]; // Block
RAM
(* ram_style = "distributed" *) logic [7:0] memory[256]; //
SLICEM based memory
(* ram_style = "registers" *) logic [7:0] memory[256]; //
Use FFs
VHDL
attribute RAM_STYLE : string;
attribute RAM_STYLE of memory : signal is "block"; -- block
RAM
attribute RAM_STYLE of memory : signal is "distributed"; --
SliceM
attribute RAM_STYLE of memory : signal is "registers"; --
FFs M
```

Now, let's look at the Xilinx macros provided.

Using xpm_cdc for clock domain crossing

Xilinx provides macros for handling CDC. They can be found in <vivado install>/data/ip/ xpm/xpm_cdc. This module contains a variety of functions related to CDC. For simple synchronization, as we discussed in *Chapter 4, Counting Button Presses*, I would recommend simply using the async_reg attribute and good coding practice. For more complex CDC, the XPM provides:

- xpm_cdc_single: Single-bit synchronizer
- xpm_cdc_gray: Binary Bus Synchronizer
- xpm_cdc_handshake: Handshake CDC
- xpm_cdc_pulse: Pulse synchronized from one domain to another
- xpm_cdc_array_single: Single-bit array synchronizer

- `xpm_cdc_sync_rst`: Synchronous reset synchronizer
- `xpm_cdc_async_rst`: Asynchronous reset synchronizer
- `xpm_cdc_low_latency_handshake`: Low latency data CDC

Similarly, we have XPM macros available for FIFOs, which we will discuss in the upcoming section on FIFOs in Project 7.

Instantiating memories using xpm_memory

The XPM functions are all located in `<vivado install>/data/ip/xpm`. We want to look at xpm_memory. There are six variants within the file:

- `xpm_memory_dpdistram`: DP distributed RAM
- `xpm_memory_dprom`: DP ROM
- `xpm_memory_sdpram`: SDP RAM
- `xpm_memory_spram`: SP RAM
- `xpm_memory_sprom`: SP ROM
- `xpm_memory_tdpram`: TDP RAM

If you need a TDP RAM, I would explore this file and use xpm_memory_tdpram to instantiate it.

 When using XPM macros in VHDL, you need to include the following library and components before the entity using them:

```
Library xpm;
use xpm.vcomponents.all;
```

XPM macros are instantiated like any other module in a design. An example of using xpm_memory_tdpram would be:

SystemVerilog

```
xpm_memory_tdpram # (
  <module parameter overrides>
) tdpram (
  <module ports> );
```

VHDL

```vhdl
tdpram: xpm_memory_tdpram
  generic map()
  port map();
```

Now we can look at Vivado language templates.

Vivado language templates

Vivado provides a convenient way to generate XPM components as well as many other FPGA constructs in VHDL, Verilog, and SystemVerilog. This is the **Language Templates** menu option, which can be found under the **Tools** menu option as we discussed briefly earlier.

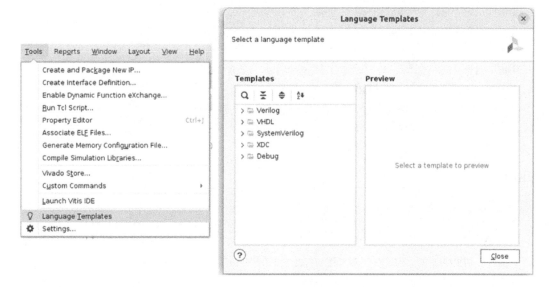

Figure 6.12: RAM types

It's worth the time to explore the available templates or remember to check the language templates if you are stuck when trying to implement something. Now, we can look at how to use the IP catalog.

Using the IP catalog to create memory

The last option is to use the IP catalog to create a specific memory function. I would not recommend this option as it limits your ability to target newer FPGA families or other vendors' FPGAs without regenerating the components.

In the previous section, we saw how to infer or instantiate memory. We have choices to make in the next section, where we'll capture the audio data.

Capturing audio data

Now that we know how to build RAM, we can infer one to capture some audio data. This allows for post-processing or playback. Without storage, we would be limited to pass-through operations or real-time processing only.

SystemVerilog

```systemverilog
// Capture RAM
logic [6:0]                amplitude_store[RAM_SIZE];
logic [$clog2(RAM_SIZE)-1:0] ram_wraddr;
logic [$clog2(RAM_SIZE)-1:0] ram_rdaddr;
logic                      ram_we;
logic [6:0]                ram_dout;
always @(posedge clk) begin
  if (ram_we) amplitude_store[ram_wraddr] <= amplitude;
  ram_dout <= amplitude_store[ram_rdaddr];
end
```

VHDL

```vhdl
-- Capture RAM
type array_2d is array (natural range <>) of std_logic_vector(SAMPLE_BITS
- 1 downto 0);
signal amplitude_store : array_2d(0 to RAM_SIZE - 1); -- capture RAM
signal ram_wraddr      : unsigned(RAM_ADDR_BITS - 1 downto 0) := (others
=> '0');
signal ram_rdaddr      : unsigned(RAM_ADDR_BITS - 1 downto 0) := (others
=> '0');
signal ram_we          : std_logic                             := '0';
signal ram_dout        : std_logic_vector(SAMPLE_BITS - 1 downto 0);
...
ram : process(clk)
begin
  if rising_edge(clk) then
    if ram_we then
      amplitude_store(to_integer(ram_wraddr)) <= amplitude;
    end if;
```

```
        ram_dout <= amplitude_store(to_integer(ram_rdaddr));
    end if;
end process;
```

We can utilize one of the push buttons to initiate the capture:

SystemVerilog

```
// Capture the Audio data
always @(posedge clk) begin
  button_csync <= button_csync << 1 | BTNC;
  ram_we       <= '0;
  for (int i = 0; i < 16; i++)
    if (clr_led[i]) LED[i] <= '0;
  if (button_csync[2:1] == 2'b01) begin
    start_capture <= '1;
    LED           <= '0;
  end else if (start_capture && amplitude_valid) begin
    LED[ram_wraddr[$clog2(RAM_SIZE)-1:$clog2(RAM_SIZE)-4]] <= '1;
    ram_we                      <= '1;
    ram_wraddr                  <= ram_wraddr + 1'b1;
    if (&ram_wraddr) begin
      start_capture <= '0;
      LED[15]       <= '1;
    end
  end
end // always @ (posedge clk)
```

VHDL

```
-- Capture the audio data
capture : process(clk)
  variable led_index : integer range 0 to LED'high;
begin
  if rising_edge(clk) then
    button_csync <= button_csync(1 downto 0) & BTNC;
    ram_we       <= '0';

    -- Clear LEDs (during playback)
    for i in LED'range loop
```

```
    if clr_led(i) then
      LED(i) <= '0';
    end if;
  end loop;

  -- Generate RAM write address
  if ram_we then
    if ram_wraddr = RAM_SIZE - 1 then
      ram_wraddr <= (others => '0');
    else
      ram_wraddr <= ram_wraddr + 1;
    end if;
  end if;

  if button_csync(2 downto 1) = "01" then
    ram_wraddr     <= (others => '0');
    start_capture <= '1';
    LED            <= (others => '0');
  elsif start_capture and amplitude_valid then
    -- Turn ON the LED corresponding to the current write address
region:
    -- 0x0000 - 0x03FF -> LED 0
    -- 0x0400 - 0x07FF -> LED 1
    -- ...
    -- 0x3C00 - 0x3FFF -> LED 15
    led_index      := to_integer(ram_wraddr(ram_wraddr'high downto ram_
wraddr'high - 3));
    LED(led_index) <= '1';
    ram_we         <= '1';
    if ram_wraddr = RAM_SIZE - 1 then
      start_capture <= '0';
    end if;
  end if;
  end if;
end process;
```

The preceding code synchronizes the center button press and then starts a counter to capture
RAM_SIZE samples. It's good to give feedback to the user, so we'll use the upper bits of the address
to light the LEDs one at a time.

Once we capture the audio data, we need to do something with it to show our mastery of memory creation. Luckily, the Nexys A7 board does offer audio out:

SystemVerilog

```systemverilog
// Playback the audio
always @(posedge clk) begin
  button_usync <= button_usync << 1 | BTNU;
  m_clk_en_del <= m_clk_en;
  clr_led      <= '0;
  if (button_usync[2:1] == 2'b01) begin
    start_playback <= '1;
    ram_rdaddr     <= '0;
  end else if (start_playback && m_clk_en_del) begin
    clr_led[clr_addr] <= '1;
    AUD_PWM_en <= '1;
    if (amplitude_valid) begin
      ram_rdaddr <= ram_rdaddr + 1'b1;
      amp_counter <= 7'd1;
      amp_capture <= ram_dout;
      if (ram_dout != 0) AUD_PWM_en <= '0; // Activate pull up
    end else begin
      amp_counter <= amp_counter + 1'b1;
      if (amp_capture < amp_counter) AUD_PWM_en <= '0; // Activate pull up
    end
    if (&ram_rdaddr) start_playback <= '0;
  end
end
assign AUD_PWM = AUD_PWM_en ? '0 : 'z;
```

VHDL

```vhdl
pwm : process(clk) is
begin
  if rising_edge(clk) then

    clr_led    <= (others => '0');
    start_sync <= start_sync(start_sync'high - 1 downto 0) & start_
playback;
```

```vhdl
      sample_valid <= '0';
      if clk_counter = CLK_COUNT - 1 then
        sample_valid <= '1';
        clk_counter  <= 0;
      else
        clk_counter <= clk_counter + 1;
      end if;

      if start_sync(2 downto 1) = "01" then -- Rising edge on start_playback
        playback       <= '1';
        ram_rdaddr     <= (others => '0');
        sample_counter <= 0;
        amp_capture    <= (others => '0');
      elsif playback and sample_valid then
        clr_led(to_integer(clr_addr)) <= '1';
        AUD_PWM_en                    <= '1';
        if sample_counter <= unsigned(amp_capture) then
          AUD_PWM_en <= '0';                  -- Activate pull up
        end if;
        if sample_counter = SAMPLE_COUNT - 1 then
          -- We've generated a single audio sample
          sample_counter <= 0;
          if ram_rdaddr = RAM_SIZE - 1 then
            playback   <= '0';
            ram_rdaddr <= (others => '0');
          end if;
        else
          sample_counter <= sample_counter + 1;
          if sample_counter = 0 then
            ram_rdaddr <= ram_rdaddr + 1; -- We are capturing the previous
sample
            if unsigned(ram_sample) > 0 then
              AUD_PWM_en <= '0';          -- Activate pull up
            end if;
            amp_capture <= ram_sample;
          end if;
```

```
      end if;
    end if;
  end if;
end process;
```

Again, we'll need to capture the button press and look for an edge. We have similar code to walk through the memory to output the data. We also turn off the LEDs one by one to show our activity:

1. There's one thing to note about driving the speaker. The output is an open drain output. This means that in order to drive a signal to the circuit driving, we will drive the signal low for a 0, but when we want the output to be a '1', we'll tristate it and a pull-up resistor on the board will take it to the correct level. The way we build a tristate signal is as follows:

    - Define the output as a wire (SystemVerilog):

      ```
      output wire          AUD_PWM
      ```

    - Define the internal control signal:

      ```
      logic                AUD_PWM_en; // SystemVerilog
      signal AUD_PWM_en : std_logic; -- VHDL
      ```

    - Infer the tristate output:

      ```
      assign AUD_PWM = AUD_PWM_en ? '0 : 'z; // SystemVerilog
      AUD_PWM <= '0' when AUD_PWM_en else 'Z'; -- VHDL
      ```

When AUD_PWM_en is driven high, the output will be 0. When it's low, the output will be tristated.

Now that we can drive our headphone jack, we need to look at the output format. Much like our input uses PDM, the output uses PWM. In PDM, we received a string of ones and zeros that we could count over a period of time to determine the amplitude of a signal.

Now that we've got the amplitude, we need to turn it into a PWM signal. Luckily, that is a fairly easy process. We can accomplish this by creating a 7-bit counter, comparing the count value to the amplitude over that period, and sending a 1 out as long as it's less.

Now, it's time to build and try it on the board. Press the *center* button. The lights should turn on one by one. When complete, press the *up* button and the lights will go off one by one. If you plug in headphones, you should hear some noise. I tapped the microphone and heard the taps when played back.

In Project 6, we learned how to capture PDM data and store it in RAM. We also learned how to play the data back using PWM through the audio port. It's just an introduction and gives you an opportunity to improve upon it. With an FPGA with hundreds of DSP blocks and RAM, you could add audio effects, play sounds backward, amplify, filter, and so on.

Now, let's turn our attention to another board component, the temperature sensor.

Project 7 – Using the temperature sensor

The Nexys A7 board has an Analog Device ADT7420 temperature sensor. This chip uses an industry-standard I2C interface to communicate. This two-wire interface is used primarily for slower-speed devices. It has the advantage of allowing multiple chips to be connected through the same interface and be addressed individually. In our case, we will be using it to simply read the current temperature from the device and display the value on the seven-segment display.

Our first step will be to design an I2C interface. In *Chapter 8, Introduction to AXI*, we'll be looking at designing a general-purpose I2C interface, but for now, we'll use the fact that the ADT7420 comes up in a mode where we can get temperature data by reading two I2C memory locations. First, let's look at the timing diagram for the I2C bus and the read cycle we'll be using:

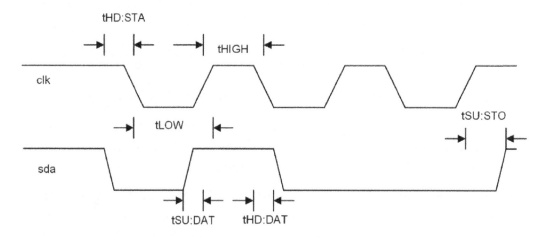

Figure 6.13: I2C timing

We can see from the timing diagram in *Figure 6.13* that we have setup and hold times, which we have seen before relative to our own designs. We also have minimum clock widths we need to maintain. We can define parameters to handle these.

You can find the following code in the `CH6/SystemVerilog/hdl/i2c_temp.sv` folder:

```
localparam TIME_1SEC   = int'(INTERVAL/CLK_PER); // Clock ticks in 1 sec
localparam TIME_THDSTA = int'(600/CLK_PER);
localparam TIME_TSUSTA = int'(600/CLK_PER);
localparam TIME_THIGH  = int'(600/CLK_PER);
localparam TIME_TLOW   = int'(1300/CLK_PER);
localparam TIME_TSUDAT = int'(20/CLK_PER);
localparam TIME_TSUSTO = int'(600/CLK_PER);
localparam TIME_THDDAT = int'(30/CLK_PER);
```

Or, you can find the following code in the `CH6/VHDL/hdl/i2c_temp.vhd` folder:

```
constant TIME_1SEC   : integer        := INTERVAL / CLK_PER; -- Clock
ticks in 1 sec
constant TIME_THDSTA : integer        := 600 / CLK_PER;
constant TIME_TSUSTA : integer        := 600 / CLK_PER;
constant TIME_THIGH  : integer        := 600 / CLK_PER;
constant TIME_TLOW   : integer        := 1300 / CLK_PER;
constant TIME_TSUSTO : integer        := 600 / CLK_PER;
constant TIME_THDDAT : integer        := 30 / CLK_PER;
```

1. I would encourage you to look at the state machine in the `i2c_temp` module in System-Verilog or VHDL. The state machine controls the access to the temperature sensor on the Nexys A7 board. It's fairly straightforward:

2. Wait for 1 second.

3. Send the start pattern on the **Serial Data (SDA)**/**Serial Clock (SCL)** wires. This sends out the read command consisting of the 8-bit device address, the read bit plus the register address to the temperature sensor, and then reads back the 2 8-bit registers that contain the current temperature in Celsius.

4. Iterate until we have transmitted and received the data back.

5. Stop the transfer and go back to *Step 1*.

To access the temperature sensor, we've defined three buses:

1. Send the predefined start, device address, read bit, and stop signals.

2. Force the bus to tristate during the ACK cycles and data cycles.

3. Capture the data from the SDA bus.

The state machine provides us with access to the temperature sensor itself and returns the data. Now, we'll need to find a way to display the data so a human can understand it.

Processing and displaying the data

We need to determine how best to display the temperature. The ADT7420 returns the data as a 16-bit fixed point value:

```
[15:7] Integer
[6:3] fraction * 0.0625
[2:0] Don't Care
```

Fixed point values are a user-defined type as there is no standard for representation. We'll often refer to fixed point numbers as integer fractions. The ADT7420 outputs its temperature values as a 9.4 representation. We will discuss fixed-point math in more detail in the next section.

We can use our bin_to_bcd function on the integer portion to generate our seven-segment display data, but what can we do to calculate the fractional portion? We only have 16 values, so we could create a lookup table and simply look up the lower 4 digits. This is effectively creating ROM that can be indexed. ROM is created much like RAM:

SystemVerilog

```
logic [15:0] fraction_table[16];
initial begin
  for (int i = 0; i < 16; i++) fraction_table[i] = i*625;
end
```

VHDL

```
type slv16_array_t is array (0 to 15) of std_logic_vector(15 downto 0);
constant FRACTION_TABLE : slv16_array_t := (
  0  => std_logic_vector(to_unsigned(0 * 625, 16)),
  1  => std_logic_vector(to_unsigned(1 * 625, 16)),
  ...
  15 => std_logic_vector(to_unsigned(15 * 625, 16)));
```

In the preceding VHDL code, we have written out the sixteen array entries. While this may be acceptable for small, simple array constants, it is quite verbose and not very flexible. A better way to do this would be to initialize the constant with the return value of a function that computes the array elements:

VHDL

```
constant FRACTION_TABLE : slv16_array_t := init_fraction_table();
```

We can then convert the temperature based on the output of the temperature sensor chip:

SystemVerilog

```
// convert temperature from
  always @(posedge clk) begin
    digit_point  <= 8'b00010000;
    if (smooth_convert) begin
      if (smooth_data < 0) begin
        // negative values saturate at 0
        encoded_int  <= '0;
        fraction     <= '0;
      end else begin
        encoded_int  <= bin_to_bcd(smooth_data[15:7]); // Decimal portion
        fraction     <= bin_to_bcd(fraction_table[smooth_data[6:3]]);
      end
    end
  end // always @ (posedge clk)

  assign encoded = {encoded_int[3:0], fraction[3:0]};
```

VHDL

```
-- Convert temperature from binary to BCD
process(clk)
  variable sd_int : integer range 0 to 15;
begin
  if rising_edge(clk) then
    if smooth_convert then
      encoded_int  <= bin_to_bcd(23d"0" & smooth_data(15 downto 7)); --
integer portion
      sd_int       := to_integer(unsigned(smooth_data(6 downto 3)));
      encoded_frac <= bin_to_bcd(16d"0" & FRACTION_TABLE(sd_int)); --
```

```
fractional portion
    digit_point  <= "00010000";
  end if;
 end if;
end process;
```

One disadvantage of converting the temperature every second and having fractional precision is that the display will change quite a bit depending on your environment. We can apply what is essentially a filter to the data so that we take the average temperature over a period of time.

Now that we have learned how to handle the data, let's learn more about how we can filter and improve the quality of that data by applying a smoothing function.

Smoothing out the data (oversampling)

In base 10, it's very inexpensive to divide by a multiple of 10. Every multiple of 10 is simply a shift to the right of 1 digit:

```
12345 / 10  = 1234.5 Truncated = 1234, Rounded = 1235
12345 / 100 = 123.45 Truncated = 123,  Rounded = 123
```

Similarly, in binary, every shift to the right is a division by 2:

```
10110 >> 1 = 1011.0 Truncated = 1011, Rounded = 1011
10110 >> 2 = 101.10 Truncated = 101,  Rounded = 110
```

How does this help us with filtering? If we want to filter over a period of 2, 4, 8, 16, 32... 2^n samples, the division operation is virtually free since it is simply a shift and possible rounding.

We can create a simple filter by summing our temperature data over a period of time:

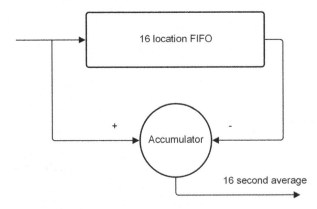

Figure 6.14: Simple moving average filter

The way we create a moving average filter is to keep a running average over a period of time. In the preceding case, I picked 16 cycles, although any power of 2 is a good choice. A non-power of two is an option, but until we discuss how to improve this filter in *Chapter 7, Math, Parallelism, and Pipelined Design*, I wouldn't consider it.

The way the filter works is that we add incoming data to an accumulator and subtract the input from 16 previous clock cycles. The accumulator then contains the sum of the incoming data over the last 16 cycles. If we divide this by 16 (right shift by 4 bits), we have an average over the last 16 cycles.

A deeper dive into FIFOs

The heart of a FIFO is RAM, a read and a write pointer, and flag generation logic. In a synchronous FIFO, it is very easy to implement:

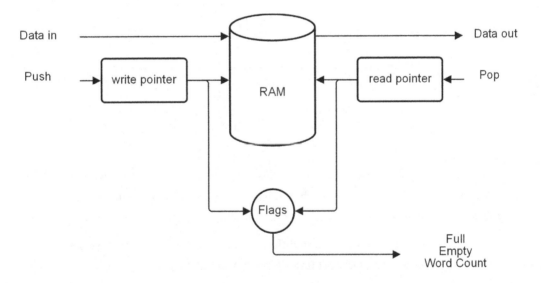

Figure 6.15: Synchronous FIFO

The write pointer increments on every push and the read pointer increments on every pop.

Generating the flags boils down to comparing the read and write pointers against one another. When we are dealing with a synchronous FIFO, these comparisons are easy since everything is generated by the same clock and is properly timed. What about an asynchronous FIFO, that is, a FIFO with separate read and write clocks?

Remember our discussions on synchronization and multi-bit buses. What happens if we try to compare a read-and-write address on different clocks?

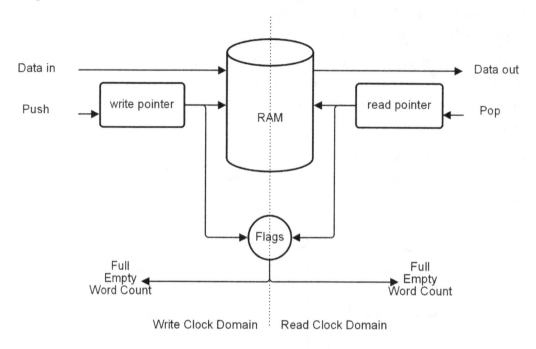

Figure 6.16: Asynchronous FIFO (non-functional)

The difference between a synchronous FIFO and an asynchronous FIFO is shown by the dotted line down the middle of *Figure 6.16*. Each half is an independent clock domain. In *Figure 6.15*, everything is on a single clock domain.

Let's consider a read and write pointer on different clock domains. Assume the clocks have no relationship and that the depth of the FIFO is 16 with 4-bit addresses:

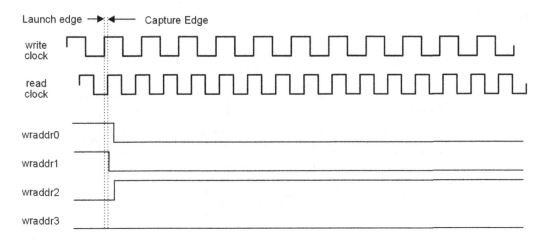

Figure 6.17: FIFO addressing

Looking at the preceding diagram, you can see that when the counter has multiple bits changing at the same time and the clocks are asynchronous, we really can't determine what the captured address will be.

We can fix this issue by Gray coding the address pointers.

Using Gray coding for passing counter values

Binary counts increment by adding a 1 to the lowest bit. This results in a count such as the following:

```
00 - 01 - 10 - 11
```

Gray coding only allows one bit to change at a time, such as the following sequence:

```
00 - 01 - 11 - 10
```

 Gray-coded counters have a limited range as they must always only have one-bit change at a time. A power of 2 is always safe to implement, but other combinations, such as $2^n + 2^m$, also work.

Let's look at a FIFO using a Gray code:

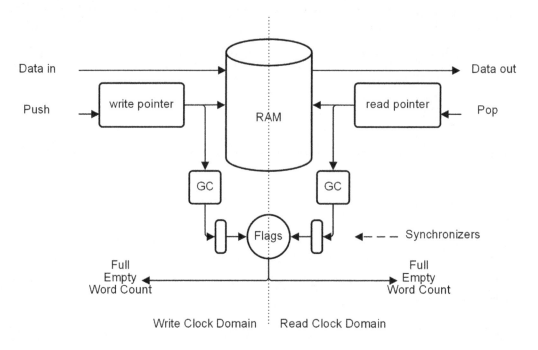

Figure 6.18: Asynchronous FIFO with Gray coding

By adding a Gray code module and synchronizers across each clock domain, we can compare the gray-coded values against each other or convert them back to binary on the destination clock.

Since Gray code only allows one bit to change at a time, we are guaranteed to either capture the old value or the new one and not capture a transitional value that would cause a FIFO empty, full, or word count error.

Constraints

This is a case where we will want to utilize the set_max_delay constraint between the write pointer and the first register in the synchronizer:

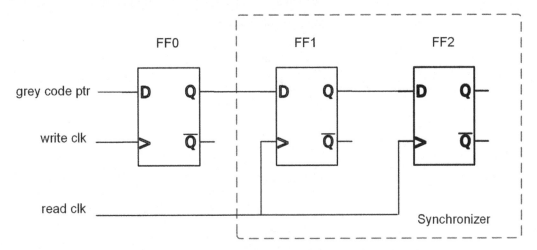

Figure 6.19: Using set_max_delay

Looking at one side of the Gray code and synchronizer logic (there is a similar circuit on the read side), we can see where we need to apply the set max_delay timing constraint:

```
Set_max_delay -datapath_only <delay> -from [get_pins FF0/Q] -to [get_pins
FF1/D] -datapath_only
```

To be absolutely safe, the delay should be set to the destination clock period or less. It can be up to 2 destination clocks, but to be safe, use between 1 and 1.5 times the destination clock period.

Generating our FIFO

We will be using a synchronous FIFO, but understanding how an asynchronous FIFO works is of critical importance if you decide to pursue a career utilizing FPGAs. You will almost certainly be asked an interview question regarding this.

We have the advantage that Xilinx has created a macro for us to use, xpm_fifo_(sync | async). You can view the instantiation in i2c_temp.sv. You'll see that there are a lot of ports that we are not using (I've left them disconnected in the VHDL version). We'll simply be pushing data into the FIFO on every convert signal and we have a small state machine that generates our data to be converted to send to our seven-segment display interface:

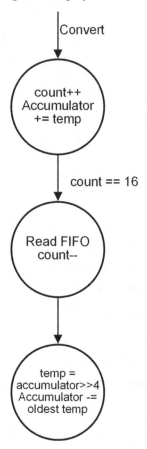

Figure 6.20: Simple temperature filter state machine

We can look at the state machine and see that it's very straightforward. We create an elastic buffer using the FIFO to hold 16 samples. As each new sample comes in, we build up our accumulator value. When we hit 16 samples, we divide the accumulator by 16 and that gives us the average temperature over the previous 16 seconds:

SystemVerilog

```
localparam SMOOTHING_SHIFT = $clog2(SMOOTHING);
...
always @(posedge clk) begin
  rden           <= '0;
  rden_del       <= rden;
  smooth_convert <= '0;
  if (convert) begin
    smooth_count                <= smooth_count + 1'b1;
    accumulator                 <= accumulator + unsigned'({temp_data[15:3],
3'b0}));
  end else if (smooth_count == SMOOTHING+1) begin
    rden                        <= '1;
    smooth_count                <= smooth_count - 1'b1;
    accumulator                 <= accumulator - signed'(dout);
  end else if (rden) begin
    smooth_data                 <= accumulator >>> SMOOTHING_SHIFT;
    smooth_convert              <= '1;
  end
end
```

VHDL

```
smooth : process(clk)
  constant SMOOTHING_SHIFT : natural := natural(log2(real(SMOOTHING))); --
number of bits to shift to implement division by SMOOTHING factor
begin
  if rising_edge(clk) then
    rden          <= '0';
    smooth_convert <= '0';
    if convert then
      smooth_count <= smooth_count + 1;
      accumulator  <= accumulator + (unsigned(temp_data(temp_data'high
downto 3)) & 3d"0");
    elsif smooth_count = SMOOTHING + 1 then
      rden          <= '1';
      smooth_count <= smooth_count - 1;
      accumulator  <= accumulator - unsigned(dout);
```

```
    elsif rden then
      smooth_convert <= '1';
      smooth_data    <= std_logic_vector(shift_right(accumulator,
SMOOTHING_SHIFT)(smooth_data'range));
    end if;
  end if;
end process;
```

Take a look at the preceding code and see whether you can pick out the state progression. It's not written as we have written it before, but you should be able to make out the flow. Once you've had a chance to look over the code, build it and try it out on the board.

One thing that may be a surprise is that the output stays 0 for a long period of time, 16 seconds to be precise. This is because we are waiting to fill the FIFO. What would happen if we output the accumulator/16 every cycle? Think about it for a minute or change the code and see.

If we always output accumulator/16, we would end up with a temperature creeping up from 1/16 of the current temperature to the average current temperature of the room. For something non-critical such as this, either method would be acceptable, but what if we didn't want to do this and we always wanted the current value? For that, you'll need to wait until *Chapter 7, Math, Parallelism, and Pipelined Design*, where we discuss fixed point representation.

Summary

In this chapter, we've explored how to do some simple communication with the outside world. We've gathered microphone data, stored it, and played it back. With our interface to the ADT7420, we've also explored the I2C bus, a common way of communicating with slower devices. We captured temperature data and showed how we could display a fixed-point number on the seven-segment display. We introduced FIFOs and discussed how we can filter the data to remove the noisiness of the temperature data varying.

I2C interfaces are used to communicate with many low-speed devices such as A/Ds and D/As and are very important for a lot of FPGA designs. You should feel comfortable that you can do it at this point, and we will explore how to make a more generic version of the interface in a later chapter. If you are interested in audio data, you should have some confidence in capturing, manipulating, and generating audio.

In the next chapter, we are going to look at some mathematical operations. We'll explore how we can smoothly bring up our temperature sensor with fixed-point math. We'll take a look at floating point numbers and operations we can perform on the audio data.

Questions

1. What are the advantages of an I2C bus?

    a. We can move large amounts of data quickly.

    b. We only need two wires to communicate.

    c. Multiple devices can be connected using only two wires.

    d. All of the above.

    e. Only (b) and (c).

2. What would be the preferred order of preference when you require a type of memory?

    a. Use the IP catalog, infer, and then use xpm_memory.

    b. Use xpm_memory, use the IP catalog, and then infer.

    c. Infer, use xpm_memory, and then use the IP catalog.

    d. Use the IP catalog, use xpm_memory, and then infer.

3. The following code infers a:

    ```
    assign data = (data_en) ? 'z : '0; // SystemVerilog
    data <= 'Z' when data_en else '0'; -- VHDL
    ```

    a. multiplier.

    b. register.

    c. tristate IO.

4. Gray coding is used in FIFOs.

    a. Always.

    b. To pass counter information across clock domains in an asynchronous FIFO.

    c. Only in synchronous FIFOs.

5. The following code creates what kind of memory?

    *   **SystemVerilog**

        ```
        always @(posedge clk) begin
          if (wren) store[addr] <= din;
          dout <= store[addr];
        end
        ```

- **VHDL**

```
process (clk) begin
  if rising_edge(clk) then
    if wren then store(addr) <= din; end if;
    dout <= store(addr);
  end if;
end process;
```

a. Simple dual port

b. True dual port

c. Single port

d. ROM

Answers

1. e. Only (b) and (c).

2. c. Infer, use xpm_memory, and then use the IP catalog.

3. c. tristate IO.

4. b. To pass counter information across clock domains in an asynchronous FIFO.

5. a. Simple dual port

Further reading

Please refer to the following links for more information regarding what was covered in this chapter:

- https://reference.digilentinc.com/reference/programmable-logic/nexys-a7/reference-manual

- **Temperature sensor specification:** https://www.analog.com/media/en/technical-documentation/data-sheets/adt7420.pdf

- **Deeper dive into FIFOs:** http://www.sunburst-design.com/papers/CummingsSNUG2002SJ_FIFO2.pdf

- https://www.xilinx.com/support/documentation/user_guides/ug473_7Series_Memory_Resources.pdf

Join our community on Discord

Join our community's Discord space for discussions with the authors and other readers:

`https://packt.link/embedded`

7

Math, Parallelism, and Pipelined Design

In the last chapter, we looked at FPGA resources and how to use them. We went into detail about RAM, DSP blocks, and PLLs. We also looked at how we can interface with external components using tri-state IO, I2C, and PWM.

In this chapter, we'll look at some ways that set FPGAs apart from microcontrollers and microprocessors. Microprocessors are custom-designed ASICs that can have very high performance when running at very high frequencies – up to 5 GHz as of writing this book. These processors are general-purpose, meaning they need to balance their operations for a wide variety of tasks. In contrast, the Artix 7 we are targeting can hit speeds of up to 300-400 MHz. Higher-end FPGAs can hit speeds of up to 800 MHz.

Looking at the raw numbers, you might question what would make an FPGA an attractive solution. We know they are costly and now that they run slower than a microprocessor. Unlike microprocessors, FPGAs can be targeted for a specific application. Because of this, we can utilize design techniques such as parallelism; that is, replicating logic in order to perform more tasks for a given clock cycle than a microprocessor can. We can also use pipelining to achieve a high throughput. Both of these techniques allow us to create designs that can perform better than a microprocessor solution.

In this chapter, we will look deeper at fixed-point numbers with regard to our temperature sensor. We'll also look at floating-point numbers and see why we might want to use one over the other. Then, we'll look at the limitations of using floating-point numbers in an FPGA (or even in general). We'll then explore parallelism and pipelined designs.

By the end of this chapter, you should have a good handle on fixed- and floating-point math. You'll understand **Advanced eXtensible Interface (AXI)** streaming and how you can connect multiple components together using it. This will demonstrate pipelining, one of the two ways of getting performance from an FPGA. We'll briefly discuss how FPGAs are used in parallel systems.

In this chapter, we are going to cover the following main topics:

- Introduction to fixed-point numbers
- Project 8 – Using fixed-point arithmetic in our temperature sensor
- Project 9 – Updating the temperature sensor project to a pipelined floating-point implementation
- Parallel designs

Let's get started!

Technical requirements

The technical requirements for this chapter are the same as those for *Chapter 2, FPGA Programming Languages and Tools*.

To follow along with the examples and projects in this chapter, take a look at the code files for this chapter by going to this book's GitHub repository: https://github.com/PacktPublishing/The-FPGA-Programming-Handbook-Second-Edition/tree/main/CH7.

Introduction to fixed-point numbers

We've worked extensively with binary and BCD numbers throughout this book. Binary is great for math because addition, subtraction, and multiplication are cheap and easy. Division isn't too bad, but it's time-consuming. We have only really used BCD numbers for displaying output, but sometimes we'll want to represent a number with a fractional component, such as in regard to the temperature sensor output.

In the previous chapter, we needed to introduce fixed-point numbers. Recall the temperature sensor format:

```
[15:7] Integer
[6:3] fraction * 0.0625
[2:0] Don't Care
```

If we look at mathematical operations, we know that adding two numbers increases the result size by 1 bit. We can see in *Figure 7.1* how we need to align the fraction point. The fractional portion doesn't increase in size, but the carry out will go into the integer portion, thus the fractional point of the result doesn't move. The result will be one bit larger for an addition, as we would expect, but in the integer portion.

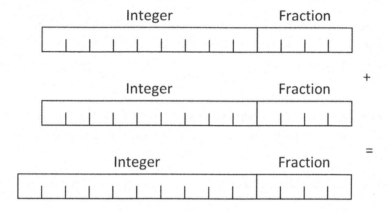

Figure 7.1: Sizing binary addition

To multiply two numbers, we need to add the sizes together. In this case, the fractional portion result will be the addition of the two input fractional portion sizes and the resultant integer portion is the sum of the size of the two integer portions. We can see this in *Figure 7.2*.

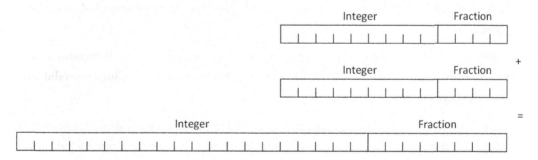

Figure 7.2: Sizing binary multiplication

The important thing to remember is that when you're adding two fixed-point numbers, the decimal point will remain in the same location. When multiplying, you add both the integer bit positions to get the resultant integer bits and the number of both fractional bits to get the resultant fractional bits. This can be seen in the preceding diagram. Here, we are multiplying two numbers of 9.4, which results in 18.8.

One of the important things to remember is that when you add, you must make sure the decimal points of both numbers are aligned. When you multiply, there is no such requirement.

The advantage of dealing with fixed-point numbers is that the same hardware logic is used for math operations in binary as fixed point. The only difference is maintaining where the decimal point is in your logic.

Now that we have learned how to utilize fixed-point arithmetic, we'll put it to work in our temperature sensor.

Project 8 – Using fixed-point arithmetic in our temperature sensor

Previously our temperature sensor output wasn't available for 16 seconds, the time it takes to fill the smoothing FIFO. This project will show us how we can get accurate outputs during those first 16 seconds.

Let's look at how we can optimize our temperature averaging to handle the 16 seconds where the temperature is incorrectly calculated. This happens because we are dividing an invalid temperature over the first 15 clock cycles.

There are cases where either a delay or inaccurate results can't occur. I was asked a job interview question regarding how to make sure that the output from this type of filter was valid during the bring-up time. This is a practical question that you may need to address someday.

Using fixed-point arithmetic to clean up the bring-up time

First, let's look at what a fixed-point scaling factor looks like. In the end, we want to scale to that of a single value from the sensor. To do this, we want to scale by a fraction. The following table shows the first 15 cycles, plus the steady state of the accumulator. I've populated the following table to show the fractions we need to calculate:

Cycle	Accumulator value	Multiply
1	T0+0+0+0+0+0+0+0+0+0+0+0+0+0+0+0	1
2	TO + T1+0+0+0+0+0+0+0+0+0+0+0+0+0+0	1/2
3	TO + T1 + T2 + 0+0+0+0+0+0+0+0+0+0+0+ 0	1/3
4	TO + T1 + T2+T3+0+0+0+0+0+0+0+0+0+0+0+	1/4
5	TO + T1 + T2 +T3+T4+0+0+0+0+0+0+0+0+0+0+0	1/5
6	TO + T1 + T2 + T3 + T4+T5+0+0+0+0+0+0+0+0+0+	1/6
7	TO + T1 + T2 + T3 + T4 + T5 +T6+0+0+0+0+0+0+0+0+ 0	1/7
8	TO + T1 + T2 + T3 + T4 + T5 + T6 +T7+0+0+0+0+0+0+0+0	1/8
9	TO + T1 + T2 + T3 + T4 + T5 + T6 + T7 + T8 +0+0+0+0+0+0+6	1/9
10	TO + T1 + T2 + T3 + T4 + T5 + T6 + T7 + T8 + T9+0+0+0+0+0+0	1/10
11	TO + T1 + T2 + T3 + T4 + T5 + T6 + T7 + T8 + T9 + T10+0+0+0+0+0	1/11
12	TO + T1 + T2 + T3 + T4 + T5 + T6 + T7 + T8 + T9 + T10 + T11 +0+0+0+ 0	1/12
13	TO + T1 + T2 + T3 + T4 - + T5 + T6 + T7 + T8 + T9 + T10 + T11 + T12 +0+0+0	1/13
14	TO + T1 + T2 + T3 + T4+ T5 + T6 + T7 + T8 + T9 + T10 + T11 + T12 + T13 +0+0	1/14
15	TO + T1 + T2 + T3 + T4 - T5 + T6 + T7 + T8 + T9 + T10 + T11 + T12 + T13 + T14	1/15
16+	TO + T1 + T2 + T3 + T4 + T5 + T6 + T7 + T8 + T9 + T10 + T11 + T12 + T13 + T14 + T15	1/16

Table 7.1: Fractions to be calculated

We'll need to multiply the accumulator by the fractional value and shift it to get the scaled result. If we do this, rather than see the temperature ramp up, we should see it stay consistent.

I recommend the following site for converting fractional values into a binary representation: `https://www.exploringbinary.com/binary-converter/`. By converting the fractions into a decimal fraction and using this website, I came up with the following conversion table in **SystemVerilog**:

```
divide[0]    = 17'b1_00000000_00000000; // 1
divide[1]    = 17'b0_10000000_00000000; // 1/2
divide[2]    = 17'b0_01010101_01010101; // 1/3
divide[3]    = 17'b0_01000000_00000000; // 1/4
divide[4]    = 17'b0_00110011_00110011; // 1/5
divide[5]    = 17'b0_00101010_10101010; // 1/6
divide[6]    = 17'b0_00100100_10010010; // 1/7
```

```
divide[7]    = 17'b0_00100000_00000000; // 1/8
divide[8]    = 17'b0_00011100_01110001; // 1/9
divide[9]    = 17'b0_00011001_10011001; // 1/10
divide[10]   = 17'b0_00010111_01000101; // 1/11
divide[11]   = 17'b0_00010101_01010101; // 1/12
divide[12]   = 17'b0_00010011_10110001; // 1/13
divide[13]   = 17'b0_00010010_01001001; // 1/14
divide[14]   = 17'b0_00010001_00010001; // 1/15
divide[15]   = 17'b0_00010000_00000000; // 1/16
```

Similarly, in **VHDL** it would look like this:

```
Divide(0)    <= "1_00000000_00000000"; -- 1
Divide(1)    <= "0_10000000_00000000"; -- 1/2
...
Divide(15)   <= "0_00010000_00000000"; -- 1/16
```

Remember from the previous chapter that we can create a ROM using an initial statement in SystemVerilog or as part of a signal declaration in either VHDL or SystemVerilog. The first thing we need to do is decide how many bits of precision we need. We first looked at the Xilinx DSP48 block in *Chapter 1, Introduction to FPGA Architectures*. A **DSP48** can handle an 18x25 2's complement multiplication. Because of this, I chose a 17-bit unsigned scaling factor. Making the factor larger could impact the number of multipliers used or the speed of operation; making it smaller won't make a difference in terms of resources needed, but could reduce the accuracy.

The preceding table is of the format 1.16 and is truncated and not rounded. You can consider rounding the values. Rounding a binary number is as simple as adding the uppermost bit you are going to truncate to the bits you are going to keep. This is shown in *Figure 7.3*, where the bit below the range we are keeping is added into the result.

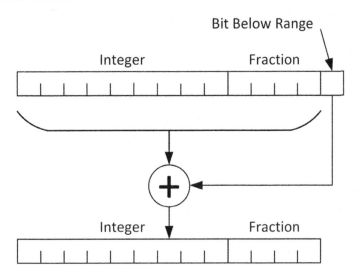

Figure 7.3: Rounding

`0.00000` rounding to 4 bits would be `0.0000`.

`0.00001` rounding to 4 bits would be `0.0001`.

`0.11111` rounding to 4 bits would be `1.0000`.

We've got our scaling factors, but how can we utilize them? I've modified the pipeline we created so that the accumulator now calculates on every input, the scaling factor is applied, and the data is displayed. Previously, we only output the data once 16 cycles of data had been accumulated.

SystemVerilog

```
always @(posedge clk) begin
  rden            <= '0;
  smooth_convert  <= '0;
  convert_pipe    <= convert_pipe << 1;
  if (convert) begin
    convert_pipe[0] <= '1;
    smooth_count    <= smooth_count + 1'b1;
    accumulator     <= accumulator + signed'(temp_data[15:3]);
  end else if (smooth_count == SMOOTHING + 1) begin
    rden            <= '1;
```

```
      smooth_count     <= smooth_count - 1'b1;
      accumulator      <= accumulator - signed'(dout);
    end else if (convert_pipe[2]) begin
      if (sample_count < SMOOTHING) sample_count <= sample_count + 1;
      smooth_data      <= accumulator * divide[sample_count];
    end else if (convert_pipe[3]) begin
      smooth_data      <= accumulator >>> SMOOTHING_SHIFT;
      smooth_convert <= ~SW;
    end
  end
```

VHDL

```
smooth : process(clk)
begin
  if rising_edge(clk) then
    rden          <= '0';
    smooth_convert <= '0';
    convert_pipe   <= convert_pipe(3 downto 0) & '0';
    if convert then
      convert_pipe(0) <= '1';
      smooth_count    <= smooth_count + 1;
      accumulator     <= accumulator + temp_data_u13_q4;
    elsif smooth_count = SMOOTHING + 1 then
      rden          <= '1';
      smooth_count <= smooth_count - 1;
      accumulator  <= accumulator - unsigned(dout);
    elsif convert_pipe(2) then
      if sample_count < SMOOTHING then
        sample_count <= sample_count + 1;
      end if;
      smooth_data <= resize(accumulator * unsigned(DIVIDE(sample_count)),
smooth_data'length);
    elsif convert_pipe(3) then
      smooth_convert <= not SW;
      smooth_data    <= shift_right(smooth_data, 16)(smooth_data'range);
    end if;
  end if;
end process;
```

The pipeline is now free running since it shifted `convert_pipe` freely. What we've changed is that we scale the accumulator value by the scaling factor we defined. Remember our discussion regarding multiplication. Here, we've added 16 bits of the fraction to our scaled value, so we need to remove that at the end. We can accomplish this by adding a stage, `convert_pipe[3]`.

We can run the simulation and see that the data is fairly constant. I've modified the testbench to input a constant 25 degrees Celsius, `0x19` in hex. Now, build the bitstream and try it on the board. Rather than 16 seconds of 0, you should see 1 second and then data being displayed. It should be fairly constant for the time the board is up.

From this project, you should notice that fixed-point arithmetic isn't costly and is very easy to implement. The pipeline only has four clock cycles of latency to calculate the smoothed-out temperature over the last 16 cycles.

 Latency means that the first value will take that many cycles, in this case 4, to be produced. Techniques such as pipelining can ensure that data flows continuously after that.

Temperature conversion using fixed-point arithmetic

Our temperature sensor project should be good enough for everyone. We can display the device temperature to 1/16 of a degree Celsius precision and we've added averaging, which means we can now bring it up cleanly. However, it is missing one thing. If you are outside the US, I'm sure you couldn't care less what the temperature is in anything except Celsius, but in the US, we stubbornly hold onto imperial measurements. Bear with me as I add Fahrenheit conversion so that I can tell what the temperature actually is.

First, let's take a look at the formula that's used to convert Celsius into Fahrenheit:

$$T_{Fahrenheit} = \left(T_{Celsius} \times \frac{9}{5}\right) + 32$$

As we can see, the formula is straightforward. We implement a divider and a multiplier, but since 9/5 is a constant, we can create a fixed-point representation of it and then multiply it by the constant. Recall how long it took for our divider and that we can perform multiplication in a single cycle. This highlights something important to bear in mind. Often, there are multiple ways of tackling a problem. The first or most obvious solution isn't always the best. Emphasis should be placed on reducing computational complexity while still achieving the desired result.

As is usually the case, we have a choice regarding where we can perform this operation. To keep things small and simple, I propose we do this once we scale down our intermediate result. This reduces the multiplier's size.

We'll also need a way to select Celsius or Fahrenheit, so we'll add SW[0] to control Celsius/Fahrenheit and LED[0] to indicate if we are displaying Fahrenheit.

I've modified our pipeline slightly so that we can apply the conversion:

SystemVerilog

```
end else if (convert_pipe[3]) begin
  smooth_data    <= accumulator >>> SMOOTHING_SHIFT;
  smooth_convert <= ~SW;
end else if (convert_pipe[4]) begin
  smooth_data              <= ((smooth_data * signed'(NINE_FIFTHS)) >>> 16)
+ signed'((unsigned'(32) << 4));
  smooth_convert           <= SW;
end
```

VHDL

```
elsif convert_pipe(3) then
    -- If SW is not set, output the temperature in degrees Celsius
    smooth_convert <= not SW;
    smooth_data    <= shift_right(smooth_data, 16)(smooth_data'range);
elsif convert_pipe(4) then
    -- If SW is set, output the temperature in degrees Farenheit
    -- °F = (°C * 9/5) + 32
    smooth_convert    <= SW;
    data_mult_u46_q20 := smooth_data * unsigned(NINE_FIFTHS);
    data_shift_u30_q4 := resize(shift_right(unsigned(data_mult_u46_q20),
16), data_mult_u46_q20'length - 16);
    data_add_u30_q4   := data_shift_u30_q4 + 32 * 16;
    smooth_data       <= resize(data_add_u30_q4, smooth_data'length);
end if;
```

The main change is that, in convert_pipe[3], we selectively send the Celsius data to the BCD conversion by using smooth_convert <= ~SW. convert_pipe[4] handles the heavy lifting of the Fahrenheit conversion. Note that in this case, we are taking advantage of more of the DSP 48 than we have in the past since we are performing multiplication and adding a single clock cycle. Build the design and verify the Fahrenheit display using the defaults:

This is a good example of how tool versions can positively or negatively affect a design. In the first version of this book, using Vivado 2020.1, the design met timing using the defaults. Using Vivado 2022.2, the design no longer meets timing, as shown below.

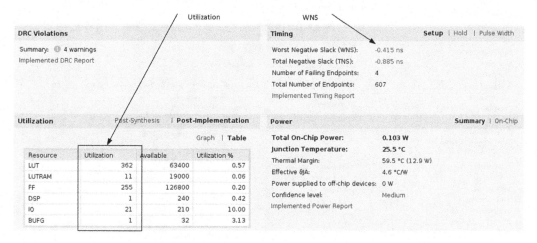

Figure 7.4: i2c_temp, fixed point with Fahrenheit conversion with defaults

In *Chapter 14, Advanced Topics*, we'll go into more detail about timing closure. Now we have some choices. We could use a PLL to generate a slower clock, or we could try some other build options. Let's quickly explore what we can do to select other build options.

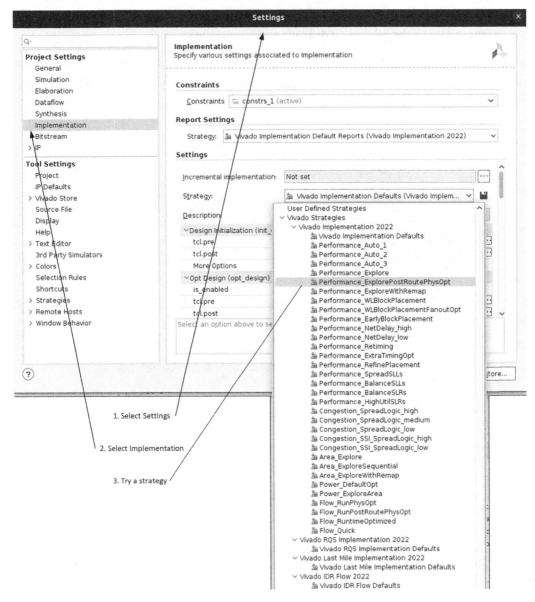

Figure 7.5: Implementation options

Typically, I like to try implementation strategies since I have had very good luck in the past. You can change the project settings and select **Performance_ExplorePostRoutePhysOpt**. You can also feel free to play around with any of these options or read more about them at https://docs.xilinx. com/r/en-US/ug904-vivado-implementation/Implementation-Strategy-Descriptions. Close the design and regenerate the bitstream.

There are multiple places in the flow where the design can be optimized by Vivado:

- Synthesis
- Placement
- Routing

These options are automated; however, the user has control over trying different options to meet the specific design goals.

When the build completes it is still failing timing, although it is very close to meeting timing.

Design Timing Summary

Setup		Hold		Pulse Width	
Worst Negative Slack (WNS):	-0.029 ns	Worst Hold Slack (WHS):	0.136 ns	Worst Pulse Width Slack (WPWS):	3.750 ns
Total Negative Slack (TNS):	-0.029 ns	Total Hold Slack (THS):	0.000 ns	Total Pulse Width Negative Slack (TPWS):	0.000 ns
Number of Failing Endpoints:	1	Number of Failing Endpoints:	0	Number of Failing Endpoints:	0
Total Number of Endpoints:	615	Total Number of Endpoints:	615	Total Number of Endpoints:	285

Timing constraints are not met.

Figure 7.6: Performance_ExplorePostRoutePhysOpt

We can also try to apply synthesis optimizations. You can see the predefined choices below.

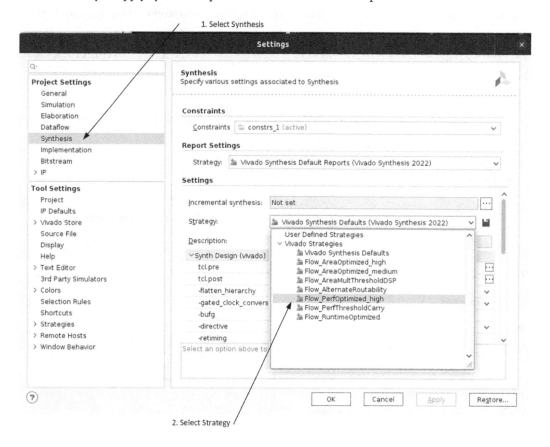

Figure 7.7: Synthesis options

Since we aren't meeting timing, we can try to use a performance optimization. Select **Flow_PerfOptimized_high** and regenerate the bitstream. You can see the definitions of the options here: https://docs.xilinx.com/r/en-US/ug901-vivado-synthesis/Vivado-Preconfigured-Strategies.

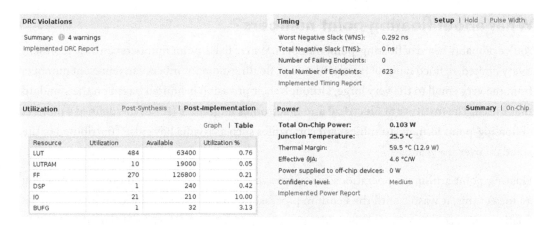

DRC Violations				Timing	Setup	Hold	Pulse Width

DRC Violations

Summary: ● 4 warnings
Implemented DRC Report

Timing   Setup | Hold | Pulse Width

Worst Negative Slack (WNS):   0.292 ns
Total Negative Slack (TNS):   0 ns
Number of Failing Endpoints: 0
Total Number of Endpoints: 623
Implemented Timing Report

Utilization   Post-Synthesis | **Post-Implementation**

Graph | **Table**

Resource	Utilization	Available	Utilization %
LUT	484	63400	0.76
LUTRAM	10	19000	0.05
FF	270	126800	0.21
DSP	1	240	0.42
IO	21	210	10.00
BUFG	1	32	3.13

Power   Summary | On-Chip

Total On-Chip Power: 0.103 W
Junction Temperature: 25.5 °C
Thermal Margin: 59.5 °C (12.9 W)
Effective θJA: 4.6 °C/W
Power supplied to off-chip devices: 0 W
Confidence level: Medium
Implemented Power Report

Figure 7.8: i2c_temp, fixed point with Fahrenheit conversion with optimizations

After applying both optimizations, we are now meeting timing requirements comfortably. I wanted to use this as an example of how to optimize your design and how things may change from one tool release to another. It's common for things to get better and, as we have seen, sometimes worse. We don't care much about power or area, but those options are available for designs that may need them.

Now let's take a look at the conversion pipeline in the simulation:

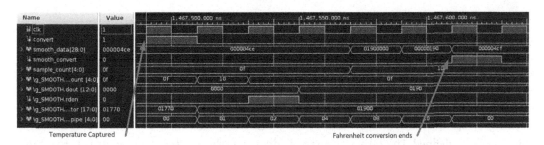

Figure 7.9: Fixed-point I2C simulation with Fahrenheit conversion

Here, you can see that the pipeline is short and performs the conversion with a small number of device resources when we use a fixed-point implementation.

Looking at our design, we didn't have to modify the I2C interface. In fact, we can make it a more general-purpose core that we could use to connect to other I2C devices. We'll address this in *Chapter 8, Introduction to AXI*.

What about floating-point numbers?

You've probably heard of floating-point numbers. Where fixed-point numbers can only represent a very limited, defined range of fractional values, floating-point numbers can represent numbers from the very small to the very large, although their precision is limited based on the standard that's used. The **Institute of Electrical and Electronics Engineers** (**IEEE**) has defined a number of floating-point formats. Graphics card companies such as Nvidia have also contributed to the standard over the years.

Floating-point arithmetic operations are expensive compared to fixed-point ones. To give you an idea of this, it wasn't until the Pentium processor that Intel standardized on integrating its floating-point coprocessor into the main microprocessor. Prior to the Pentium processor, every x86, from 8086 to the 80486, had a corresponding x87 processor (8087, 80287, and so on) that provided floating-point operations.

One of the reasons for Xilinx's choices in designing the DSP48 blocks in their designs was to better support floating points in FPGAs. Floating points are no longer as prohibitive to include as they were when I started FPGA design, though they are still generally slower and more complex than fixed points.

Let's take a look at the IEEE single and double-precision floating-point representations of numbers:

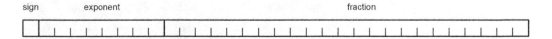

Figure 7.10: IEEE single precision floating-point representation

The sign bit is the same as a 2's complement number in that a 1 indicates a negative value and a 0 indicates a positive value. The fraction is an unsigned 24-bit number. You'll notice that only 23 bits have been defined. The 24th bit is an implied 1, where the number represented is 1.fraction. This is made possible since the value of 0 is represented by the 32-bit field being set to all 0s.

The exponent is biased from 127, so the actual exponent is -127 to give a value from -126 to +127. -127 and +128 are reserved.

What we can infer from this is that a floating point is an excellent choice when we have numbers that are relatively close together but have a large potential range of values. Floating points cover these cases but at the cost of resources and processing time. Math is more costly and slower than with a fixed point, but if in one set of calculations you are operating at a microscopic scale and, in another set, you are at a galactic scale, you can use a single format.

Double precision extends the exponent to 11 bits and the fraction to 52 bits.

In the past, if you wanted to design something using a floating point, you'd need to design your own floating-point operators. An example of a floating-point operator can be found in my GPLGPU project at `https://github.com/asicguy/gplgpu/tree/master/hdl/math`.

I'll discuss the main components here. For this analysis, I'll be focusing on the floating-point designs for the GPLGPU that were implemented in ASICs in 1998 and re-implemented in FPGAs in the early 2000s. Depending on the speed you are targeting, the pipelining may be more or less the same, but this is a good baseline and starting point for discussion.

Floating-point addition and subtraction

While multiplication is typically a slow operator for binary or fixed-point numbers, addition/subtraction can actually have more latency in terms of floating-point numbers. The reason for this is that we need to align our decimal point as if we were doing the calculations by hand. Remember that the fraction has an implied 1. This means that once the addition or subtraction is complete, we need to adjust the exponent so that the final fraction is of the form 1.x.

Floating-point multiplication

Floating-point multiplication is not as complex. We simply add the exponents and multiply the mantissa.

A simple example is 2*2 which we can look at as:

$2 * 2 = 4$, which is equivalent to $1*2^1 * 1*2^1 = (1*1)*2^{(1+1)} = 1*2^2 = 4$

Floating-point reciprocal

Here is where things get interesting. Integer division is a series of subtractions that are performed by restoring and non-restoring division. This gives us a precise answer, though for large integer values, it can take hundreds of clock cycles to complete.

Like our integer division algorithms, we'll need a similar algorithm for floating-point multiplication. What I've used in the past is the Newton-Raphson successive approximation method. It consists of an initial guess that's provided via a lookup table. This is precalculated. Then, successive approximations converge on a solution. You may remember (or have heard about) the Pentium division bug. This bug occurred due to bad table values in their division algorithm.

A more practical floating-point operation library

Fixed point is a more practical application for FPGAs, but floating point is certainly a viable option, which is why we are looking at it here. You are welcome to explore or use the functions in the GPLGPU. They are licensed under GPL v3. However, let's explore what Xilinx has to offer for floating-point libraries:

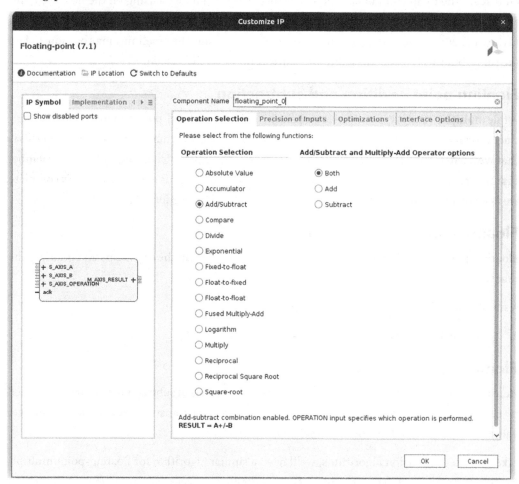

Figure 7.11: Xilinx floating point IP

We talked about the Xilinx IP catalog previously. Search for floating and you'll find the floating-point IP wizard. You will see that Xilinx provides a complete set of operators with Vivado.

Like much of Xilinx IP, it utilizes an AXI interface – specifically, the AXI streaming interface. Let's explore it in more detail.

A quick look at the AXI streaming interface

Xilinx IP along with IP from most FPGA vendors has almost universally migrated to using the AXI bus, which is a set of protocols defined by ARM. There are three AXI variants; we'll look at them in more detail in *Chapter 8, Introduction to AXI*. However, we will need to take a quick look at the AXI streaming interface in order to use the Xilinx floating-point IP.

When Xilinx started building **System-on-Chip (SOC)** FPGAs with integrated processors, they needed a data bus standard for their IP, as well as user-produced IP. Since ARM already had IP interfaces defined, Xilinx took its IP with native interfaces or older-style interfaces and ported them to AXI for compatibility with the ARM processors.

AXI streaming is point-to-point communication that's been optimized for data movement. It is the simplest of the AXI protocols in that it doesn't require address decoding, so it's used for a lot of IP work. First, let's take a look at how an AXI streaming interface works:

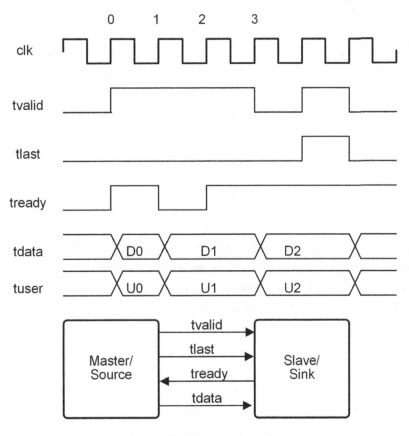

Figure 7.12: AXI stream example

Figure 7.12 shows the AXI interface signals and how a source/sink device would be connected together. The interface itself is straightforward. The data source drives a valid signal, along with data. A transfer is terminated when `tlast` is asserted. The slave can throttle the data using `tready`. You can see from the waveform that data is only transferred when `tread` and `tvalid` are asserted. If `tready` goes low, the source must hold `tlast`, `tdata`, and `tvalid` until `tready` goes high.

Now, let's examine what we need to add or change in the design to convert it into floating point.

Project 9 – Updating the temperature sensor project to a pipelined floating-point implementation

In Project 9, we'll be looking at how we can use floating points in our temperature sensor project. This will give us an idea of the cost of using floating points in a real-world application. First, let's put our proposed design into a diagram to determine what we need:

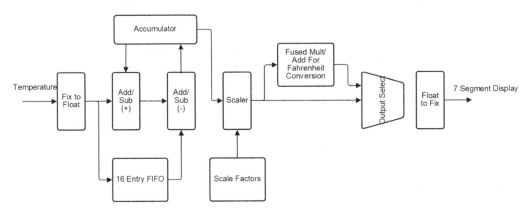

Figure 7.13: Floating-point conversion pipeline

The pipeline looks very similar to our previous temperature pipeline. The main difference is that we are now converting to/from floating point on the input and output. Internally, the old 4-5 stage pipeline is handled similarly. However, each stage is no longer a single clock cycle since floating-point operations take longer to process.

To convert our temperature sensor and Fahrenheit conversion, we will need the following floating-point operations, all of which we can generate from the Vivado IP catalog, as we'll see in the next section.

Fixed-to-floating-point conversion

Recall the temperature sensor outputs fixed point numbers. We'll need to convert this into a floating point for our design. We'll need to make a couple of modifications to customize the **fix_to_float** operator for our particular use case:

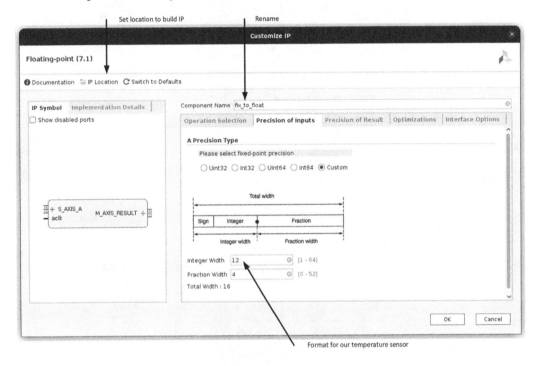

Figure 7.14: fix_to_float format configuration

Recall that the format of the temperature sensor is 4 bits of a fraction and 9 bits of an integer. Xilinx likes to make the streaming interface a multiple of 8 so, in *Figure 7.14*, I set the conversion to 12.4 (12 bits integer, 4 bits of fraction).

Figure 7.15: Changing the interface

In *Figure 7.15*, I show the interface options we'll be setting. We'll want to modify the flow control so that it's non-blocking. It's not strictly necessary for this design, but it will maximize our resource usage when pipelining it to give us an idea of the worst-case floating-point resources. This pane also gives you the option of adding some of the optional components of the AXI bus: the tlast and tuser signals. tlast is useful if you'll be passing large amounts of data and you need to determine when a grouping of data finishes. On the other hand, tuser allows you to pass information, along with data, so that you can use it in your design.

Floating-point math operations

If we construct our pipeline with a little extra control logic, we can share the addition and subtraction, as we did in our fixed-point case:

Figure 7.16: Add/Subtract

Make sure that you change the interface, as shown in *Figure 7.16*.

We'll need two additional components: a multiplier and a fused multiply-add. Make sure that you follow *Figure 7.16* when modifying the interfaces for both. When you generate the fused multiply-add, make sure you select only **Add**:

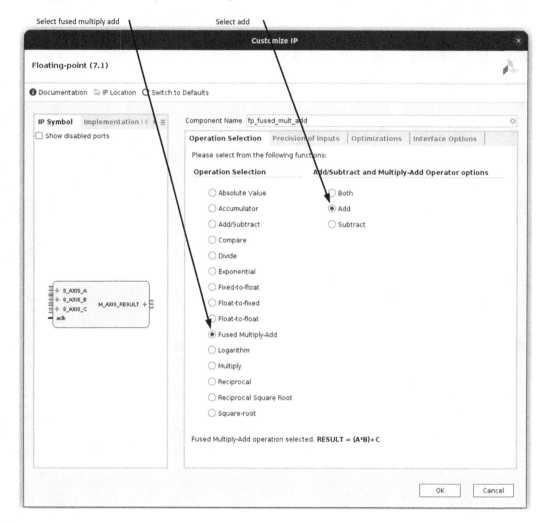

Figure 7.17: Fused Multiply-Add

Figure 7.17 shows the configuration for the fused multiply-add that we'll need to generate. Finally, we'll need to convert back to a fixed point for our seven-segment display.

Float-to-fixed-point conversion

Let's look at what we need to do to generate our fixed-point output:

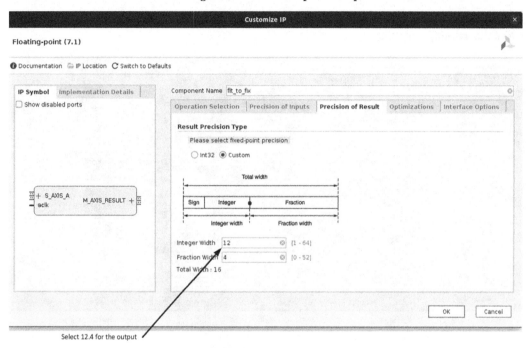

Figure 7.18: Customizing float to a fixed output

With that, we've got all the components of our pipeline so that we can take fixed point values in, operate entirely on the data as a floating point, and then write the data out as a fixed point. We can then compare the fixef-to-floating-point design differences to see the cost for the precision.

Let's take a look at our simulation to see what our latency looks like.

Simulation

If you take a look at the latency in the components, you'll see that each floating-point operation is adding quite a bit of latency over our fixed-point attempt. Our simulation can show us what the actual latency looks like.

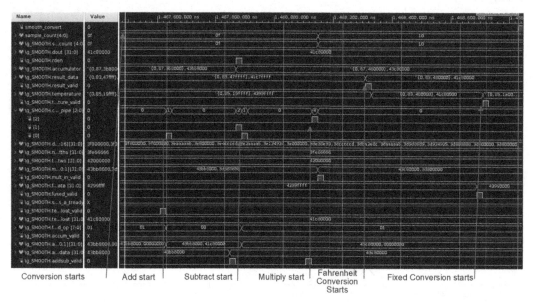

Figure 7.19: Floating-point temperature simulation

Figure 7.19 shows how much latency has been added. We've gone from 5 clocks to about 50, a 10x increase in delay to generate the data. We have plenty of time, so this isn't really a problem. See the section on parallelism for more explanation. Let's look at our resource usage:

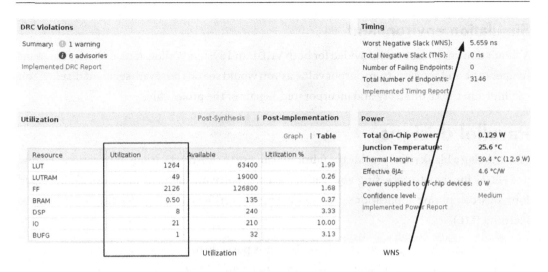

Figure 7.20: Floating-point temperature utilization

Let's compare the utilization of our fixed-point implementation to our floating-point implementation:

Resource	Fixed	Floating	change
LUT	433	1250	2.82x
LUTRAM	13	46	3.53x
FF	264	2133	8.07x
BRAM	0	0.5	0.5
DSP	1	8	8x

Table 7.2: Fixed versus floating point comparison

Even though the design is quite small, the difference is pretty remarkable in terms of latency and resource usage. In general fixed point is preferable since it is smaller and faster than floating point. If you need to handle a much larger dynamic range of values, then floating point can be considered.

This project should give you some insight into some of the advanced math options of using floating point, as well as how the AXI streaming interface can be used to connect multiple pieces of the IP together. You may have noticed that we didn't have to keep track of pipelining as we simply used the valid signals in and out of each core as our control signals.

Simulation environment

A simulation environment is provided for both VHDL and SystemVerilog. It reads back a constant temperature and converts to an output value as you would see on the seven-segment display. You can find it in the tb directory and incorporated as part of the project file.

Parallel designs

FPGAs, being a blank slate, provide the fabric we can use to construct various applications. People use FPGAs for signal-processing applications such as **software-defined radio** (**SDR**), high-performance computing applications, and, more recently, **artificial intelligence** (**AI**) and **machine learning** (**ML**).

FPGAs have an advantage over CPUs here since it is possible to implement hundreds and up to tens of thousands of individualized math operations on every clock cycle at speeds from 200-600 MHz, where a CPU may run at up to 5 GHz but can only operate on a few dozen (at most) math operations in parallel. Parallel designs are developed like any other FPGA design and can be tailored to a specific application.

ML and AI and massive parallelism

In recent years, ML and AI have boomed. Self-driving cars, deep fake generation and analysis, and market predictions are a few of the topics that these applications have been applied to.

It's easy to see why. The Artix part we are targeting has up to 240 DSP blocks. The largest Virtex Ultrascale+ that Xilinx makes has almost 4,000 DSP blocks and 9,000 logic cells. Xilinx advertises up to 38.3 TOP/s for INT8 operations in the VU13P.

It's beyond the scope of this book to provide an overall introduction, but I would certainly encourage investigating the resources available for parallel designs, such as **Parallel Programming for FPGAs** (https://kastner.ucsd.edu/hlsbook/).

Parallel design – a quick example

Let's look at a quick example that shows a massively parallel implementation. In this case, we want to create an adder tree that will output the sum of 256 inputs in 8 clock cycles.

Here, we need to discuss latency and throughput. Latency is the number of clock cycles (or time) it takes to produce a result. In the parallel example presented here, we have a latency of 8 clock cycles. Because the design is pipelined, we can produce a new result every clock cycle after the initial data, as long as new data is being fed in every clock cycle, as shown in *Figure 7.21*.

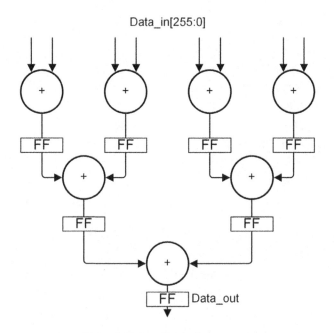

Figure 7.21: Parallel design example

Let's see how this can be implemented in SystemVerilog:

```systemverilog
always @(posedge clk) begin
  for (int i = 0; i < 128; i++)
    int_data0[i] <= in_data[i*2+0] + in_data[i*2+1];
  for (int i = 0; i < 64; i++)
    int_data1[i] <= int_data0[i*2+0] + int_data0[i*2+1];
  for (int i = 0; i < 32; i++)
    int_data2[i] <= int_data1[i*2+0] + int_data1[i*2+1];
  for (int i = 0; i < 16; i++)
    int_data3[i] <= int_data2[i*2+0] + int_data2[i*2+1];
  for (int i = 0; i < 8; i++)
    int_data4[i] <= int_data3[i*2+0] + int_data3[i*2+1];
  for (int i = 0; i < 4; i++)
    int_data5[i] <= int_data4[i*2+0] + int_data4[i*2+1];
  for (int i = 0; i < 2; i++)
    int_data6[i] <= int_data5[i*2+0] + int_data5[i*2+1];
  out_data  <= int_data6[0] + int_data6[1];
  int_valid <= int_valid << 1 | in_valid;
  out_valid <= int_valid[6];
end // always @ (posedge clk)
```

And using **VHDL**:

```vhdl
add : process(clk)
begin
  if rising_edge(clk) then
    for i in 0 to 127 loop
      int_data0(i) <= resize(signed(in_data(i * 2 + 0)), int_
data0(i)'length) + signed(in_data(i * 2 + 1));
    end loop;
    for i in 0 to 63 loop
      int_data1(i) <= resize(int_data0(i * 2 + 0), int_data1(i)'length) +
int_data0(i * 2 + 1);
    end loop;
    for i in 0 to 31 loop
      int_data2(i) <= resize(int_data1(i * 2 + 0), int_data2(i)'length) +
int_data1(i * 2 + 1);
    end loop;
    for i in 0 to 15 loop
      int_data3(i) <= resize(int_data2(i * 2 + 0), int_data3(i)'length) +
int_data2(i * 2 + 1);
    end loop;
    for i in 0 to 7 loop
      int_data4(i) <= resize(int_data3(i * 2 + 0), int_data4(i)'length) +
int_data3(i * 2 + 1);
    end loop;
    for i in 0 to 3 loop
      int_data5(i) <= resize(int_data4(i * 2 + 0), int_data5(i)'length) +
int_data4(i * 2 + 1);
    end loop;
    for i in 0 to 1 loop
      int_data6(i) <= resize(int_data5(i * 2 + 0), int_data6(i)'length) +
int_data5(i * 2 + 1);
    end loop;
    out_data  <= std_logic_vector(resize(int_data6(0), out_data'length) +
int_data6(1));
    int_valid <= int_valid(5 downto 0) & in_valid;
    out_valid <= int_valid(6);
  end if;
end process;
```

Both versions will create a tree of 255 adders. The operation is both parallel, in the sense that we are going to handle all the inputs simultaneously, and pipelined, in that new data can be fed into every clock cycle. As we mentioned previously, after 8 clock cycles, we'll have the first sum available for use. Every cycle after that, a new sum will be available.

There is an associated testbench that you can use to verify the operation since it cannot be implemented on the board because it has a very wide input bus.

 Care must be taken when pipelining to make sure control signals arrive along with the data and high fanout nets may need special consideration, although the tool does take care of high fanout nets behind the scenes.

Summary

In this chapter, we took our temperature sensor project and improved upon it using fixed-point math. In project 8, we removed our startup condition so that the temperature is output almost immediately and constantly filtered through the life of the design. We then looked at floating-point operations and converted the design into a floating-point pipeline in project 9. This led us to introduce AXI streaming, which will only become more important as we proceed throughout this book. Finally, we took a look at the concept of parallel designs.

In the next chapter, we are going to delve further into AXI interfaces, package up some of our IP into AXI format so that we can reuse it, and introduce the IP integrator and block design tool.

Questions

1. If we have a large dynamic range in our numbers, what are we better off using?

    a. Integers

    b. Fixed point

    c. Floating point

    d. Imaginary

2. Which order represents the number complexity from least complex to most complex?

    a. Fixed point, integers, floating point

    b. Integer, fixed point, floating point

    c. Floating point, fixed point, integer

    d. Integer, floating point, fixed point

3. The following code is an example of what kind of design?

    ```
    always @(posedge clk) begin
      if (stage[0]) out[0] <= fp_out[0];
      if (stage[1]) out[1] <= out[0] + fp_out[1];
      if (stage[2]) out[2] <= out[1] + out[0] + fp_out[2];
    end
    ```

    a. Pipelined

    b. Parallel

    c. State machine

4. The following code is an example of what kind of design?

    ```
    always @(posedge clk) begin
      for (int i = 0; i < 128; i++) dout[i] <= din[i*2] + din[i*2+1];
    end
    ```

    a. Pipelined

    b. Parallel

    c. State machine

5. Which of the following signals makes up an AXI streaming interface?

    a. tdata

    b. tvalid

    c. tready

    d. tlast

    e. tuser

    f. taddr

6. A 16.16 * 8.16 fixed-point multiplier would result in an output of what?

    a. 16.16

    b. 17.16

    c. 32.32

    d. 24.32

Answers

1. c) Floating point

2. a) Fixed point, integers, floating point

3. a) Pipelined

4. b) parallel

5. a, b, c, d, e

6. d) 24.32

Challenge

We are not using all of the seven-segment display. Earlier, we used an LED to indicate degrees Celsius or Fahrenheit. Can you modify the code so that it uses one (or two) of the seven segments to display C/F or °C/°F?

Could you further modify the design to produce Kelvin as well as Celsius and Fahrenheit?

Further reading

Please refer to the following links for more information regarding what was covered in this chapter:

- The Nexys A7 reference manual: `https://reference.digilentinc.com/reference/programmable-logic/nexys-a7/reference-manual`

- Temperature sensor specification: `https://www.analog.com/media/en/technical-documentation/data-sheets/adt7420.pdf`

- Xilinx DSP 48 users guide for 7-series parts (Artix-7): `https://www.xilinx.com/support/documentation/user_guides/ug479_7Series_DSP48E1.pdf`

Join our community on Discord

Join our community's Discord space for discussions with the authors and other readers:

`https://packt.link/embedded`

8

Introduction to AXI

In *Chapter 7, Math Parallelism and Pipelined Design*, we learned what sets FPGAs apart from microprocessors. We looked at fixed-point and floating-point numbers and how to use the Xilinx components utilizing AXI streaming interfaces. We added floating-point math to our temperature sensor and took a look at how FPGAs can operate in massively parallel designs. In this chapter, we'll take a look at the interface that FPGA vendors have standardized on, AXI.

As **FPGAs** became larger and more complex, vendors such as Xilinx began offering **Intellectual Property (IP)**, designed and tested to accelerate design implementation. The first IP often had simple interfaces, sometimes referred to as native interfaces. Xilinx offered early high-end parts with PowerPC cores and their own Microblaze cores, each of which had differing interfaces. When Xilinx adopted ARM processors as part of their Zynq family, they standardized the ARM processor interfaces, using the **Advanced eXtensible Interface (AXI)**. In order to best use Xilinx IP, we have already looked at the AXI streaming interface. There are two other interfaces that are commonly used: AXI-Lite and AXI Full.

By the end of this chapter, you'll have a good handle on the flavors of AXI and when to use them. You'll know how to create your own IP using AXI for easier integration with other IP. Finally, you'll have developed a temperature sensor using AXI and the IP Integrator.

In this chapter, we are going to cover the following main topics:

- AXI streaming interfaces
- Project 10 – Creating IP for Vivado using AXI streaming interfaces
- Introduction to the IP Integrator
- AXI4 interfaces (full and AXI-Lite)
- Developing IPs – AXI-Lite, full, and streaming

Technical requirements

The technical requirements for this chapter are the same as those for *Chapter 2, FPGA Programming Languages and Tools*.

To follow along with the examples and the project, you can find the code files for this chapter at the following repository on GitHub: `https://github.com/PacktPublishing/Learn-FPGA-Programming/tree/master/CH7`.

AXI streaming interfaces

We took a brief dip into AXI and the streaming interface in *Chapter 7, Math, Parallelism, and Pipelined Design*. AXI streaming is used primarily as a lightweight conduit to move data between two points, as shown in *Figure 7.1*. The essence of the bus is that data is presented from an upstream master interface via the `tdata` bus. `tvalid` signals when it is ready for the downstream device, the slave, to consume. When the slave asserts the `tready` signal, the `tdata` is accepted. There is an optional `tlast` signal to indicate when a burst is completed, useful for packet-style interfaces.

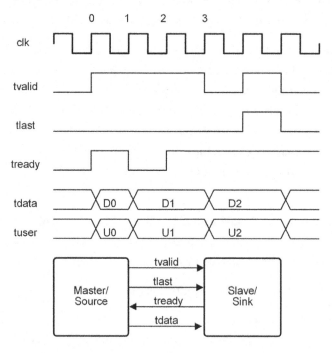

Figure 8.1: AXI streaming with an optional tuser signal

There is an optional sideband bus included for completeness, `tuser`, which can be passed along with the stream, but it's up to the source and sink to understand how to interpret it.

Before we dive into the other AXI types, let's break up our I2C temperature sensor into AXI streaming-based IPs.

Project 10 — Creating IP for Vivado using AXI streaming interfaces

In this project, we are going to take our I2C temperature sensor and split it into IP that we can use in the IP Integrator to reconstruct our project within the Xilinx **Block Design (BD)** tool.

Our initial design looked like this:

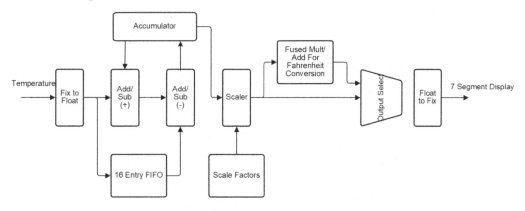

Figure 8.2: Original temperature sensor pipeline

Looking at the Xilinx floating-point IP, fix to float, float to fix, add/sub, scaler, and fused multiply/add are all IP blocks with streaming interfaces. What we need to address is the I2C interface that reads the temperature from the adt7420, the temperature pipeline itself, and the seven-segment display interface. Let's tackle the seven-segment display first.

Seven-segment display streaming interface

The first thing we need to do is create a directory to house our IP sources. This will make packaging easier. We'll do this by creating a directory under CH8/(VHDL | SystemVerilog)/ip_source/ seven_segment. Inside this directory, we have an hdl directory that contains the stripped-down seven-segment portion of our temperature sensor in both VHDL and SystemVerilog.

In this chapter, the user-generated IP is local to the language used since we will use either VHDL or SystemVerilog to generate the IP core. Any Xilinx IP will reside at the top level of the chapter.

If we abide by a few rules, it will be easier to create the IP. The complete manual can be found at https://docs.xilinx.com/r/en-US/ug1118-vivado-creating-packaging-custom-ip. We have already named our clock signal clk, which is one of the ways the tool can automatically identify clock signals. To create an AXI streaming bus that can be extracted automatically, we need to name our interface signals in a consistent way:

- `<interface name>_tdata (required)`
- `<interface name>_tvalid (required)`
- `<interface name>_tready`
- `<interface name>_tstrb`
- `<interface name>_tkeep`
- `<interface name>_tlast`
- `<interface name>_tid`
- `<interface name>_tdest`
- `<interface name>_tuser`

Our port list for the IP in **SystemVerilog** now looks like this:

```
module seven_segment
  #(
    parameter NUM_SEGMENTS = 8,
    parameter CLK_PER     = 10,  // Clock period in ns
    parameter REFR_RATE   = 1000 // Refresh rate in Hz
  )(
    input wire                        clk,
    input wire                        rst,
    input wire                        seven_segment_tvalid,
    input wire [NUM_SEGMENTS*4-1:0]   seven_segment_tdata,
    input wire [NUM_SEGMENTS-1:0]     seven_segment_tuser,
    output logic [NUM_SEGMENTS-1:0]   anode,
    output logic [7:0]                cathode
  );
```

Here's the equivalent in **VHDL**:

```vhdl
entity seven_segment is
  generic(
    NUM_SEGMENTS : integer := 8;
    CLK_PER      : integer := 10;      -- Clock period in ns
    REFR_RATE    : integer := 1000     -- Refresh rate in Hz
  );
  port(
    clk                  : in  std_logic;
    rst                  : in  std_logic;
    seven_segment_tvalid : in  std_logic;
    seven_segment_tdata  : in  std_logic_vector(NUM_SEGMENTS * 4 - 1
downto 0);
    seven_segment_tuser  : in  std_logic_vector(NUM_SEGMENTS - 1 downto
0);
    anode                : out std_logic_vector(NUM_SEGMENTS - 1 downto
0);
    cathode              : out std_logic_vector(7 downto 0)
  );
end entity seven_segment;
```

anode and cathode will become external interfaces on the board. We've named our AXI streaming interface seven_segment and clk should be recognized without any special handling.

> There is one extreme caveat for VHDL designs. VHDL-2008 is not supported **at all** in the IP as of Vivado 2022.2. It has been this way for several releases, so I would not anticipate a change anytime soon. So, if you do want to package VHDL IP, make sure to only use non-VHDL-2008 within the IP.

Let's look at packaging our IP:

1. First, let's create a project or open an existing project – the i2c_temp_flt_bd project since we need an open project to create and package IP.

2. The first step in this process would be to create IP:

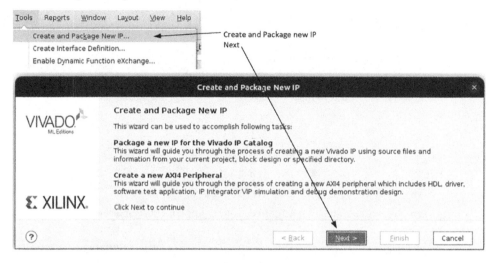

Figure 8.3: Creating and packaging the IP

3. The first dialog box simply summarizes what we are going to do. We've modified the code to encapsulate the IP.

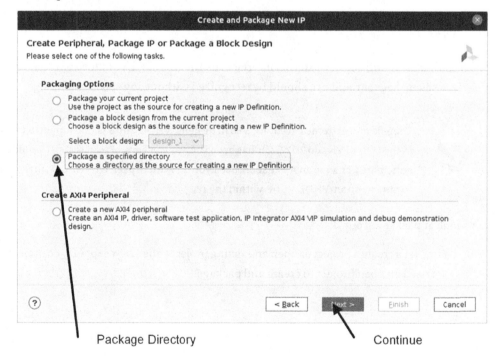

Figure 8.4: Packaging the directory

4. Make sure to select **Package a specified directory** and click **Next**.

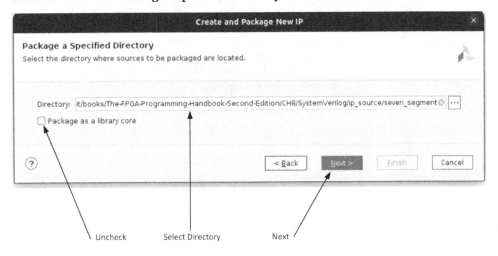

Figure 8.5: Specifying the source directory

5. Make sure that **Package as a library core** is unchecked. Select the seven_segment directory under **Create and Package New IP**.

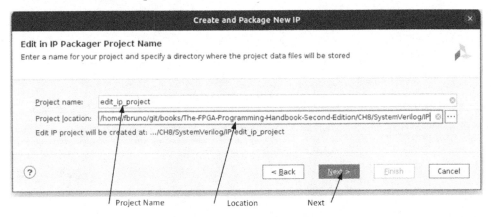

Figure 8.6: Destination directory

6. We need to specify the project name and the destination location. In this case, we'll create an IP directory within the SystemVerilog and VHDL directory. Then, select **Next**.

7. This will package the IP and open a new project pointing to the **IP** you have created. If the screen shown in *Figure 8.7* doesn't automatically open, select **Edit Packaged IP** so we can look at the options.

Figure 8.7: Edit Packaged IP

8. Now we can look at the **Identification** tab.

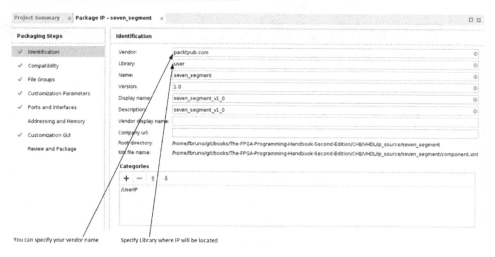

Figure 8.8: Identification settings

9. The **Identification** tab allows you to set up some options regarding the IP. I have specified packtpub.com as the vendor but left the library as user. It's also possible to specify the version of the IP.

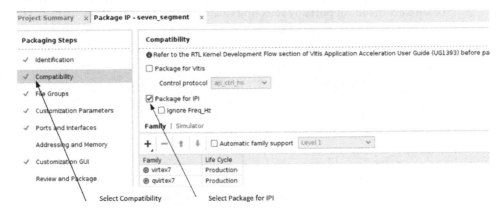

Figure 8.9: Compatibility settings

10. Be sure to select the **Package for IPI (IP Integrator)** option located within **Compatibility**. Now let's verify the ports and interfaces, as shown in the following figure:

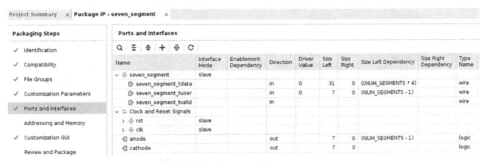

Figure 8.10: Verifying ports

11. We can see that the IP packager was able to find the clock port and the seven-segment AXI slave port automatically. The other two ports are simply brought out as is. You'll also notice that the port sizes are based on a parameter, NUM_SEGMENTS. We can look at the parameters the IP supports by selecting **Customization Parameters**.

Figure 8.11: Customization Parameters

12. Here, we see the parameters that can be overridden at the top level. If we change them, the IP will apply the new values. Now select **Review and Package**.

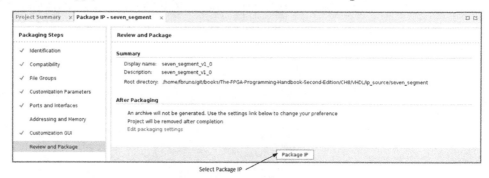

Figure 8.12: Review the IP

13. Finally, review the IP and then click **Package IP**.

At this point, the IP is ready to use. You will notice that I've added the optional tuser interface in this version of the streaming interface. I did this because we need a way of passing along the digit point for the display. Since there is no standard for using tuser, it's important that the master interface knows how to drive it and the slave knows how to interpret it.

Previously, in Project 7 – the temperature sensor, we introduced the I2C interface used on the adt7420. I've packaged that up for us so we can use it with the IP Integrator by providing IO for the board and a common AXI streaming interface for use in the Block Design tool.

I've also packaged up the floating point temperature sensor core we developed in Project 9 into an AXI streaming interface core. The reason I created the temperature sensor core itself is so that we can use the **Block Design (BD)** tool as an alternative to developing this version of the design. We could have kept our old top level and simply instantiated our two new cores. Typically, I prefer to work in an HDL directly, but there are times, such as when developing an FPGA **System on Chip (SOC)**, when you will need to use the **BD** tool for at least some of the design.

Let's take a quick look at the adt7420 code that makes up our new IP.

Developing the adt7420 IP

First, let's take a look at the new top-level module for our IP in **SystemVerilog**:

```
module adt7420_i2c
  #(
  parameter  INTERVAL    = 1000000000,
  parameter  CLK_PER     = 10
  )(
  input wire            clk, // 100Mhz clock
  input wire            rst, // synchronous, active high
  // Temperature Sensor Interface
  inout wire            TMP_SCL,
  inout wire            TMP_SDA,
  inout wire            TMP_INT,
  inout wire            TMP_CT,
  output logic          fix_temp_tvalid,
  output logic [15:0]   fix_temp_tdata
  );
```

VHDL:

```
entity adt7420_i2c is
  generic(
    INTERVAL : integer := 1000000000;
    CLK_PER  : integer := 10
  );
  port(
    clk             : in   std_logic;  -- 100 MHz clock
    rst             : in   std_logic;  -- synchronous, high-active
    -- Temperature Sensor Interface
```

```
    TMP_SCL              : inout std_logic;
    TMP_SDA              : inout std_logic;
    TMP_INT              : inout std_logic;   -- currently unused
    TMP_CT               : inout std_logic;   -- currently unused

    fix_temp_tvalid : out   std_logic;
    fix_temp_tdata  : out   std_logic_vector(15 downto 0)
  );
end entity adt7420_i2c;
```

We've got our clock, our I2C bus, and connections to the temperature-sensing chip.

This file contains the I2C state machine. Feel free to take a look. The difference is that the output of the temperature is now AXI streaming. The IP is already built, but if you want, you can build it again as an exercise.

 There seems to be a problem with Vivado 2022.2. Although we specify the IP directory as the output, it seems to generate the IP in place. This isn't a problem – just realize the final location of the IP will be ip_repo.

Finally, we can take a quick look at the core of the design where we perform the floating-point temperature smoothing, Fahrenheit conversion, and output to our seven-segment display IP.

Understanding the flt_temp core

The floating-point temperature sensor core is the most complex block in our design. It connects to our other two IP cores as well as the floating-point logic we previously generated. The core of the flt_temp module is unchanged from our previous design; however, we now have a new interface definition for the AXI streaming interfaces.

I encourage you to take a look at the **Hardware Description Language** (HDL). We'll see in the next section, as we build the BD, what the cores look like.

Introduction to the IP Integrator

Xilinx has made great strides in making FPGAs useable by more people besides hardcore engineers, and the IP Integrator is one of the tools they have created in order to accomplish this goal. In this section, we'll take the packaged cores that I've created and create a design using them.

Note that as of Vivado 2022.2, Vivado IP Integrator doesn't support VHDL-2008. The files can be added to the IP. However, when the IP is added to the design, it will fail in synthesis because all VHDL 2008 files will be loaded as VHDL. The VHDL is included and the IP files are built in the hopes that this is added in the future, but for now, it is recommended that you use SystemVerilog for this section or rewrite the VHDL 2008 as an exercise.

The IP Integrator provides a graphical user interface for hooking up IP cores using schematic capture with BD. We've gone through the preceding steps for our three IP cores. This procedure has added the cores to our project for use:

1. Our first step is to create our BD and add the cores:

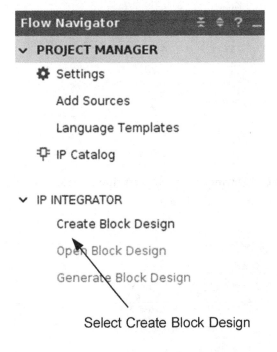

Figure 8.13: Create Block Design

2. Selecting **Create Block Design** will bring up the tool we'll be using in this section.

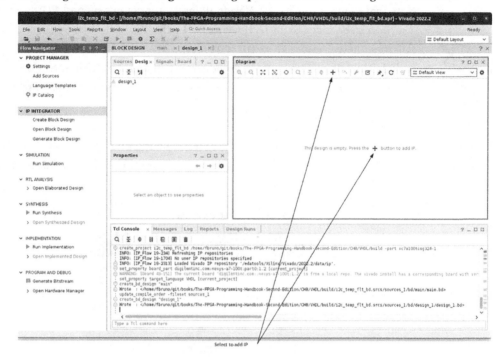

Figure 8.14: Adding an IP

3. With the main BD window up, the first thing to do is to add the IP. We'll start with our adt7420_i2c core IP and take a look at it.

Figure 8.15: Selecting our IP

4. Clicking + will display a popup to search for our IP. We can type in ad and find the interface we are looking for. Double-click to add to the design. Now we can take a look at what the core looks like when placed and the options we can set:

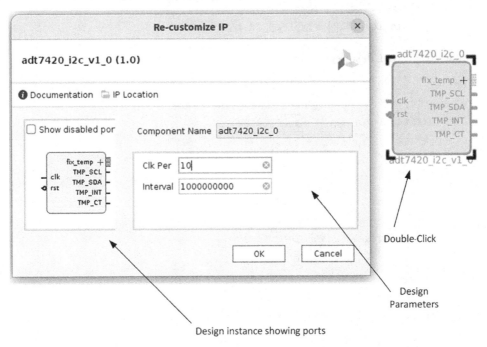

Figure 8.16: IP core configuration

If you recall from our original design, we specified two parameters for this core. Unless you modify them, they will appear as is within the core configuration when you double-click on the core instance in the block diagram:

```
module adt7420_i2c
  #(
  parameter  INTERVAL    = 1000000000,
  parameter  CLK_PER     = 10)
```

Since the parameters in our cores are already set to what we need for the Nexys A7 board, we don't need to change anything. Look at the design instance and you'll see our port list:

```
    input wire             clk, // 100Mhz clock
    input wire             rst, // synchronous, active high
    // Temperature Sensor Interface
    inout wire             TMP_SCL,
```

```
    inout wire            TMP_SDA,
    inout wire            TMP_INT,
    inout wire            TMP_CT,
    output logic          fix_temp_tvalid,
    output logic [15:0] fix_temp_tdata
```

Similarly, the **VHDL** design generics:

```
entity adt7420_i2c is
  generic(
    INTERVAL : integer := 1000000000;
    CLK_PER  : integer := 10
  );
  port(
    clk             : in    std_logic;   -- 100 MHz clock
    rst             : in    std_logic;   -- synchronous, high-active
    -- Temperature Sensor Interface
    TMP_SCL         : inout std_logic;
    TMP_SDA         : inout std_logic;
    TMP_INT         : inout std_logic;   -- currently unused
    TMP_CT          : inout std_logic;   -- currently unused

    fix_temp_tvalid : out   std_logic;
    fix_temp_tdata  : out   std_logic_vector(15 downto 0)
  );
end entity adt7420_i2c;
```

Because the streaming interface was identified when packaging the IP, it's collapsed in the diagram and marked as fix_temp. To expand the interface, you can double-click on the signal name in the BD. The clock port will be connected to our clock source and we'll hook up the TMP_* ports to external interfaces:

1. Let's continue and add all of the IPs we'll need for the design:

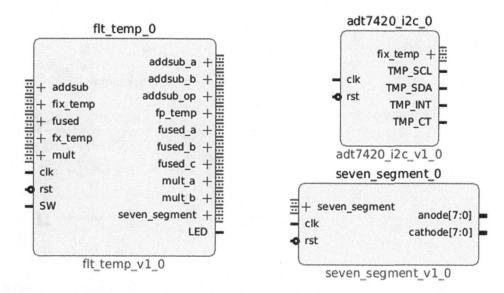

Figure 8.17: User IPs added to the design

We still have quite a few IPs to add to our design; we need all our floating-point cores. Take a look back at *Figure 8.2* if you need to, but our names should also give us a clue as to what's needed. All the floating-point cores are simply configurations of the floating-point IP, so search in the add IP popup for floating point. We'll need to do this step five times for all the IP:

- fixed_to_float
- float_to_fixed
- fp_addsub
- fp_fused_mult_add
- fp_mult

as shown in the next block diagram.

 We will be using a clock generator in the board design and as such we want to add a reset port to our blocks to make sure the design is held in reset until the clock generator stabilizes. Resets are optional in the Xilinx floating point IP so make sure to select the reset option when configuring.

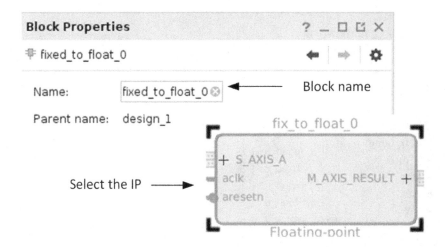

Figure 8.18: Block properties

The default name for the IP is simply the IP name with an incrementing number appended to it. We can rename our instances so they are more user-friendly. Select the IP after you configure it and then on the left side of the BD window, you'll see the **Block Properties** pane. This gives easy access to the configuration as well as the ability to change the instance name.

Let's continue with the rest of the floating-point IP.

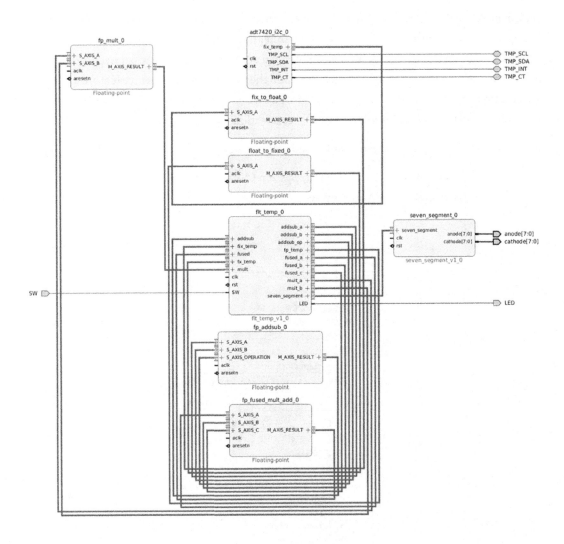

Figure 8.19: Full design

We can now look at the design. We'll need to hook up the streaming interfaces manually as I did in *Figure 8.19*. You'll also have noticed that a banner appeared at some point when adding the IP, telling you that the BD tool recognizes that it can automate some of the connections for you. Before we use the connection automation, let's add the System Clock. One nice feature of having a **Board Definition File (BDF)** that gets loaded when we define the board, which we did way back in *Chapter 2*, is that it contains all the external connections for the BD tool.

To automatically connect the system clock and reset:

1. Select the **Board** tab, right-click on the **System Clock**, then select **Auto Connect**. Similarly, select **Reset** then select **Auto Connect**.

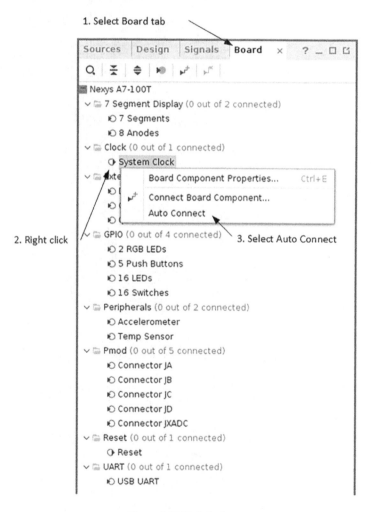

Figure 8.20: Full design

2. Now we can **Run Connection Automation**.

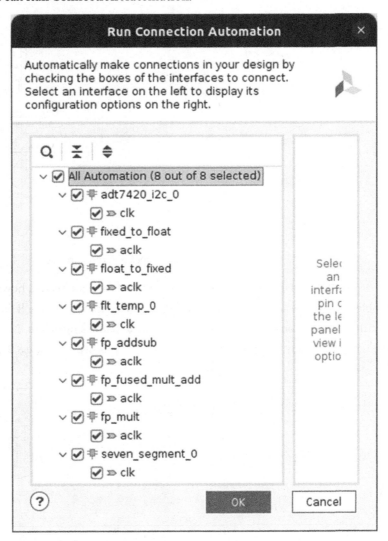

Figure 8.21: Connection automation

3. In this case, the tool will connect our clocks and system reset for us.

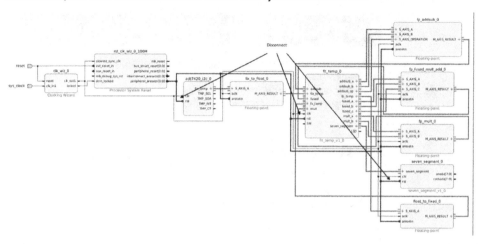

Figure 8.22: Automated clock and reset hookup

4. What you'll notice is that now the clocks and resets are connected, however, we have a problem. Our IP is active high reset. The Xilinx IP is active low. We'll fix that by disconnecting the resets on our IP by selecting the wire and pressing delete. Then we can rewire the resets manually to the rst_clk_wiz_0_100M, as shown in *Figure 8.23*.

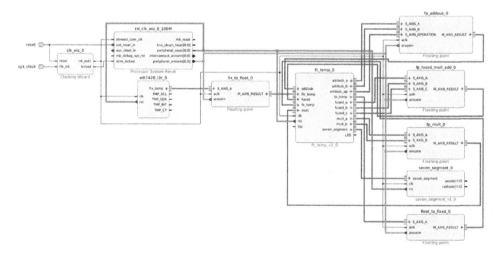

Figure 8.23: Final clock and reset hookup

5. Once that's complete, we can connect our external ports. In this case, we'll do it manually. This is accomplished by right-clicking on a port, for example, **TMP_SCL**, and selecting **Make External**. Verify that the port name created is identical to the name on the IP block to ensure that it matches the XDC file.

Generally, it may add a _0 on the end, like TMP_SCL_0. In this case, you can select the pin and remove the suffix of _0. Make sure to add the following external ports: TMP_SDA, TMP_SCL, SW, LED, anode, and cathode.

Note that resets are optional unless your design requires one, since FPGAs can be configured with power-up states defined. The SystemVerilog code is written without resets and the VHDL code is implemented using resets to show the differences.

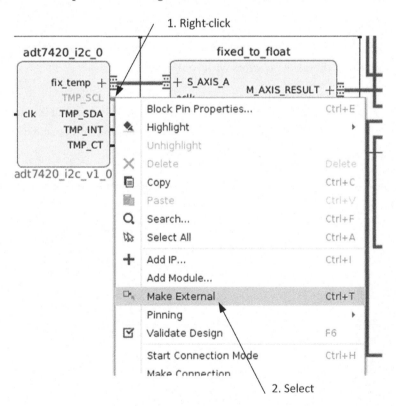

Figure 8.24: Connection automation

6. Now we must validate the design as shown in *Figure 8.23*.

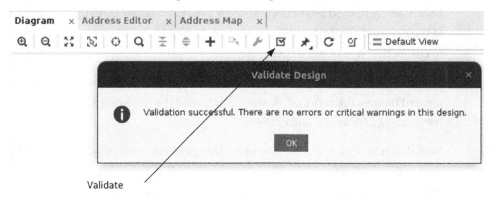

Validate

Figure 8.25: Validate Design

When you have completed your schematic, click the validate design button. This will ensure that there are no errors with your design.

 If you were building something with AXI-Lite or full interfaces, you would need to make sure the addressing was set up prior to building. We'll look at that in the next chapter.

7. The design has no errors, so we need to build the output products and then generate the bitstream:

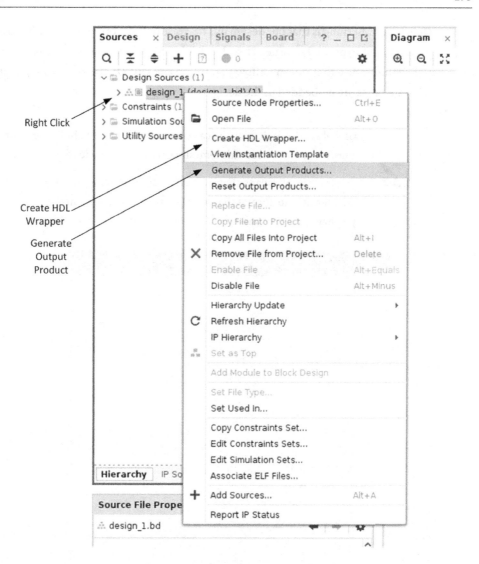

Figure 8.26: Generating output products

8. One important thing is that our design has tri-state buffers internally. In order to have the design function properly, we need to select **Global** for the synthesis options. This appears to be a limitation that doesn't allow you to use the **Out Of Context (OOC)** synthesis if tri-state ports are embedded in the design.

Global synthesis defines the case where the IPs will be built every time synthesis is run. We need this here since we have embedded tri-states.

OOC synthesis means that the individual IP will be synthesized once into an intermediate format that will then be read in later. This saves time when you have lots of IP and no embedded tri-states.

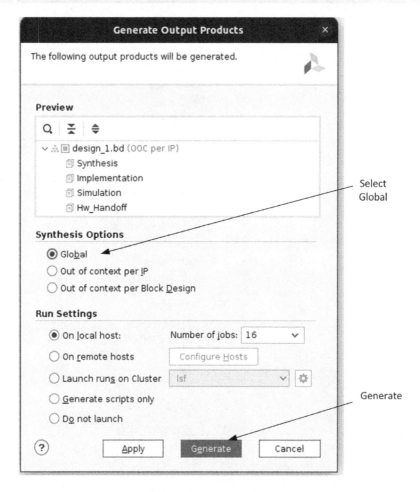

Figure 8.27: Global synthesis

9. Finally, we need to create the HDL wrapper, which will become the top level of our design (refer to *Figure 8.26*):

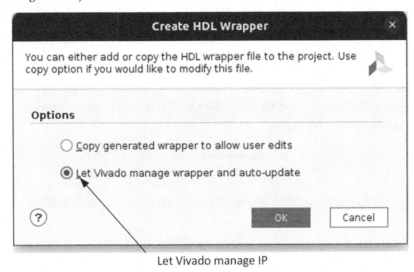

Let Vivado manage IP

Figure 8.28: Create HDL Wrapper

10. Be sure to add the xdc file located at the root of the CH8 directory to the design prior to building.

Let's look at the final design. Here, the schematic diagram is complete:

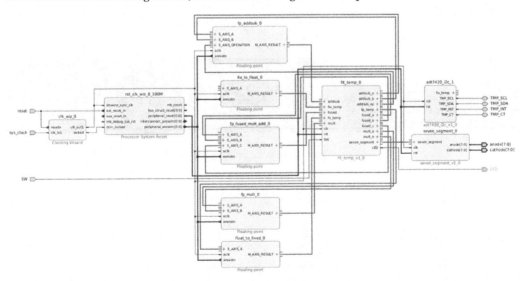

Figure 8.29: Completed BD

Functionally, this design will be equivalent to what we developed in *Chapter 7, Math, Parallelism, and Pipelined Design.* This is simply another way of jumpstarting your designs if you are using a lot of IPs. It is most useful when using processors and is practically required for **SOC** designs. In the end, you can embed your own IPs as we have done or actually package up your BD and include it in an HDL design.

Sometimes the BD tool can get very cluttered and hard to read. Although you can manually move things around to try to get a better view, you can also select the regenerate layout button to re-place the design for better visibility.

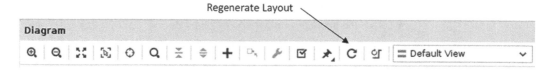

Figure 8.30: IPI toolbar

Let's look at debugging our design.

IP Integrator debugging

The IP Integrator makes it easy to debug your design. Simply right-click on any net or bus and select **Debug**. This is especially useful when used on AXI buses as the **Integrated Logic Analyzer (ILA)** understands the bus structure and the transaction protocol and will display information in a meaningful way:

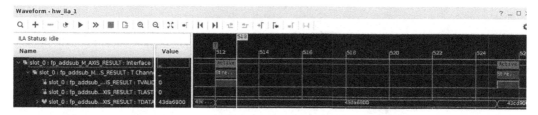

Figure 8.31: AXI Streaming ILA

Add a debug core by right-clicking on the `fp_addsub` master output. Generate the bitstream and set a trigger on the rising edge (R) of `tvalid`. You should trigger a pair of transactions. Try adding some other ILAs and watch the transactions. As the temperature sensor is running, you can trigger on the `tvalid` signals and watch as data propagates through the floating-point pipeline.

 Make sure that you run connection automation if necessary and check the design after adding the ILA. You may need to adjust the reset input to the currently instantiated reset pin.

Setting up a design as complex as this, we'd like an easy way to package it up. We have a couple of ways to do this.

Packaging the project

To easily store a project to easily load again, we have two choices.

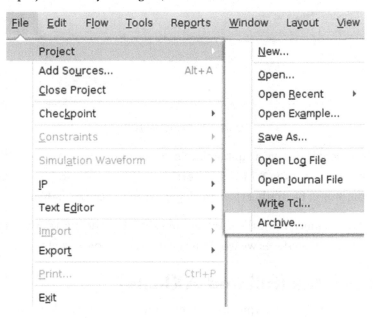

Figure 8.32: Completed BD

We can select **Write Tcl** to generate a Tcl script that we can execute to rebuild the design from the stored sources. It will also reconstruct the BD.

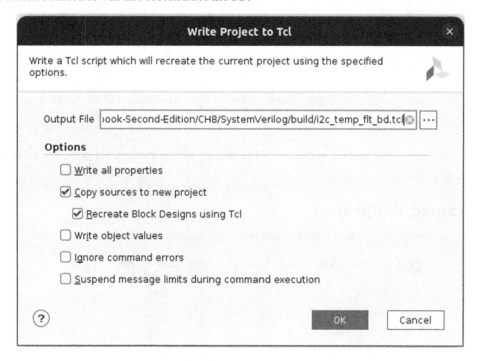

Figure 8.33: Completed BD

Also, we can use **Archive** to save a zip file that includes all the data to recreate the project. In general, I find it easier to use the Tcl script since it integrates more easily into source control and sits alongside the project files rather than archiving a specific version of them.

Now that we have examined using the IP integrator to build and debug a design, let's look at the other two flavors of AXI interfaces we will be using throughout the rest of the book.

AXI4 interfaces (full and AXI-Lite)

The AXI4 interface is a full-featured processor interface used by ARM to allow the easy connection of peripherals to their processors. Xilinx has adopted this interface to connect its hard and soft processors to other cores, whether AXI-Lite, full, or streaming. Because it is full-featured, it can be costly to implement and should only be considered when you need an addressable interface with high performance or bursting capability.

Hard IP refers to physical IP cores built into a Xilinx design. Examples of these would be PCIe interfaces, embedded ARM processors in a Xilinx Zynq FPGA, or hardened memory controllers. These are IP blocks that exist whether you use them or not.

Soft IP refers to IP that you create or Xilinx provides that is compiled in the FPGA fabric. It only exists in a design if you reference it.

There are five components to an AXI full or AXI-Lite interface. Read interfaces consist of an address component and a data component:

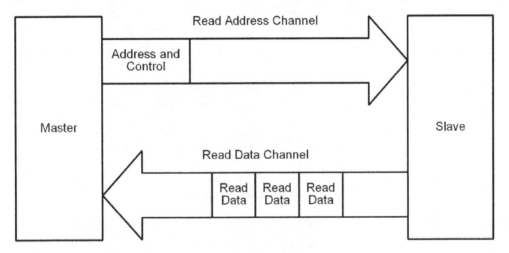

Figure 8.34: AXI read channel

The preceding figure conceptually shows how a read operation in AXI occurs. An address and a control bus signal the slave to perform a read. In an AXI-Lite interface, this is a single location; in a full interface, it can be for a burst of data. These types of reads are posted reads, meaning that if the interface supports it, multiple read requests can be made before data starts coming back.

When the slave interface is ready, it can start sending data back. If the master and slave support it, the slave can perform out-of-order reads, using the ID channel to signal which group the data is associated with. This can allow increased performance by not having to reorder data.

Write interfaces have three components: the write address, write data, and write response channels:

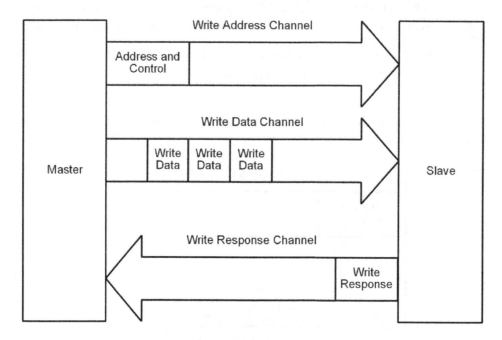

Figure 8.35: AXI write channel

The master will issue write commands via the write address channel, which is either preceded by data or followed by write data. The slave will respond via the write response channel, which will signal whether the write is completed successfully or with an error.

The main differentiators between full and AXI-Lite interfaces are bursting capabilities for full interfaces and single beat transfers for AXI-Lite interfaces. AXI-Lite interfaces have a few more restrictions, such as smaller bus width support and non-cacheable and normal non-locked accesses.

There are a variety of cores available for instantiating in BD or instantiating in your design:

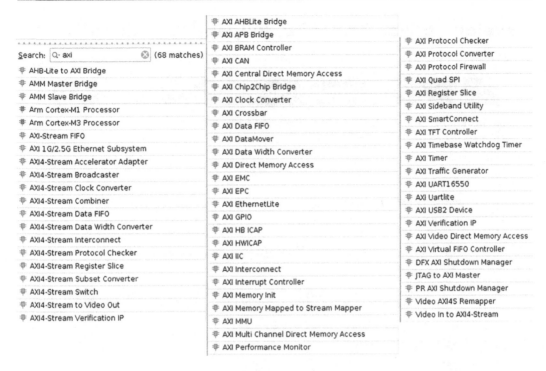

Search: Q· axi ⊗ (68 matches)

- AHB-Lite to AXI Bridge
- AMM Master Bridge
- AMM Slave Bridge
- Arm Cortex-M1 Processor
- Arm Cortex-M3 Processor
- AXI-Stream FIFO
- AXI 1G/2.5G Ethernet Subsystem
- AXI4-Stream Accelerator Adapter
- AXI4-Stream Broadcaster
- AXI4-Stream Clock Converter
- AXI4-Stream Combiner
- AXI4-Stream Data FIFO
- AXI4-Stream Data Width Converter
- AXI4-Stream Interconnect
- AXI4-Stream Protocol Checker
- AXI4-Stream Register Slice
- AXI4-Stream Subset Converter
- AXI4-Stream Switch
- AXI4-Stream to Video Out
- AXI4-Stream Verification IP

- AXI AHBLite Bridge
- AXI APB Bridge
- AXI BRAM Controller
- AXI CAN
- AXI Central Direct Memory Access
- AXI Chip2Chip Bridge
- AXI Clock Converter
- AXI Crossbar
- AXI Data FIFO
- AXI DataMover
- AXI Data Width Converter
- AXI Direct Memory Access
- AXI EMC
- AXI EPC
- AXI EthernetLite
- AXI GPIO
- AXI HB ICAP
- AXI HWICAP
- AXI IIC
- AXI Interconnect
- AXI Interrupt Controller
- AXI Memory Init
- AXI Memory Mapped to Stream Mapper
- AXI MMU
- AXI Multi Channel Direct Memory Access
- AXI Performance Monitor

- AXI Protocol Checker
- AXI Protocol Converter
- AXI Protocol Firewall
- AXI Quad SPI
- AXI Register Slice
- AXI Sideband Utility
- AXI SmartConnect
- AXI TFT Controller
- AXI Timebase Watchdog Timer
- AXI Timer
- AXI Traffic Generator
- AXI UART16550
- AXI Uartlite
- AXI USB2 Device
- AXI Verification IP
- AXI Video Direct Memory Access
- AXI Virtual FIFO Controller
- DFX AXI Shutdown Manager
- JTAG to AXI Master
- PR AXI Shutdown Manager
- Video AXI4S Remapper
- Video In to AXI4-Stream

Figure 8.36: Available AXI IPs

A typical design would consist of a processor, such as the ARM Cortex or Xilinx Microblaze, or your core logic and connected peripherals. The peripherals typically connect to an AXI interconnect block, which can become costly to implement depending on the number of active master interfaces, whether buffering is enabled, and whether it's a full crossbar or not.

 We will look at using a Microblaze in *Chapter 13, Embedded Microcontrollers using the Xilinx MicroBlaze*.

We'll take a quick look at an alternative way to package a core we have written as IP from scratch for easy reuse.

Developing IPs — AXI-Lite, full, and streaming

We'll look at how we can develop an IP through packaging it by defining the interfaces first:

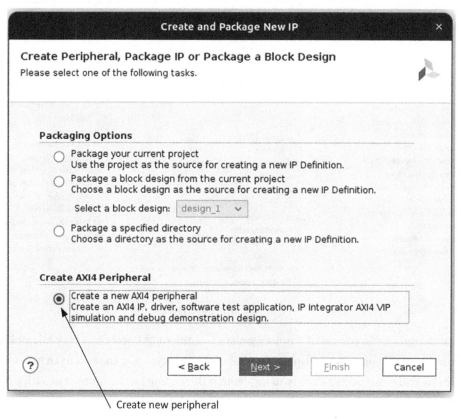

Figure 8.37: Creating a new AXI4 peripheral

This is a way of creating an IP by creating a wrapper first and then inserting your IP:

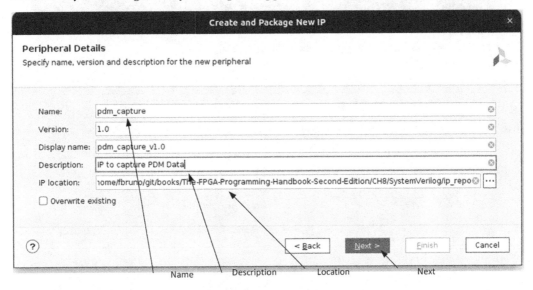

Figure 8.38: Defining the IP

We'll create a pdm_capture module that will have a register to trigger a read. We can then read back the same register to determine whether the read is completed. Data can then be read from a second register.

 Note that the same limitations regarding VHDL apply here in that VHDL-2008 is not supported.

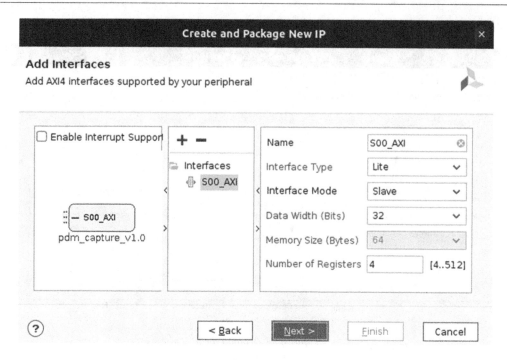

Figure 8.39: Default interface definition

The default interface definition is perfect for what we need. Select **Next** and make sure to select **Edit IP** to make sure that **Package for IPI** is selected under **Compatibility** as we did previously.

You can investigate the options and see that it is very easy to add any of the AXI interfaces we've discussed. If you explore the IP directory, you'll see the following files created under the HDL directory for Verilog:

- `pdm_capture_v1_0.v`: The top level of our IP. We'll add our interface to the microphone here.

- `pdm_capture_v1_0_S00_AXI.v`: The AXI portion of the design with registers.

You'll see in both generated modules places to put logic and ports:

```
module pdm_capture_v1_0_S00_AXI #
(
  // Users to add parameters here
  Place USER parameters here
  // User parameters ends
  // Do not modify the parameters beyond this line
```

Looking at the port list, you can see where to place the ports needed for the top level:

```
(
    // Users to add ports here
    Place USER ports here
    // User ports ends
    // Do not modify the ports beyond this line
```

Finally, within the design itself, there are bracketing comments on where to add your code:

```
// Add user logic here
    Place USER logic here
// User logic ends
```

For VHDL, the files are as follows:

- pdm_capture_v1_0.vhd: The top level of our IP. We'll add our interface to the microphone here.

- pdm_capture_v1_0_S00_AXI.vhd: The AXI portion of the design with registers.

The generated VHDL follows the same format as the Verilog version.

There is an additional way to add an IP in the IP integrator that doesn't involve explicitly creating an IP block; however, currently, it does require that the top level of the IP be a Verilog file and not SystemVerilog. Note the same VHDL limitation of no VHDL-2008 support is still in place as of 2022.2.

Adding an unpackaged IP to the IP Integrator

At https://github.com/PacktPublishing/The-FPGA-Programming-Handbook-Second-Edition/blob/main/CH8/SystemVerilog/build/i2c_temp_flt_unpkg.xpr or https://github.com/PacktPublishing/The-FPGA-Programming-Handbook-Second-Edition/blob/main/CH8/VHDL/build/scaffold/i2c_temp_flt_bd.xpr, there are two files for SystemVerilog, adt7420_i2c_mod.sv and adt7420_i2c_bd.v. and for VHDL: adt7420_i2c_bd.vhd. Now, adt7420_i2c_mod.sv is a copy of the adt7420_i2c.sv IP file that has been renamed so it doesn't cause problems with a naming conflict. adt7420_i2c_bd.v provides the Verilog wrapper. We don't need a wrapper for VHDL since all files must be VHDL 97.

Add an IP by doing the following:

1. Open https://github.com/PacktPublishing/The-FPGA-Programming-Handbook-Second-Edition/blob/main/CH8/SystemVerilog/build/i2c_temp_flt_bd.tcl.

2. Right-click on **Design Sources** and add the files as we have previously done.

3. Open the IP Integrator.

4. In the BD, right-click.

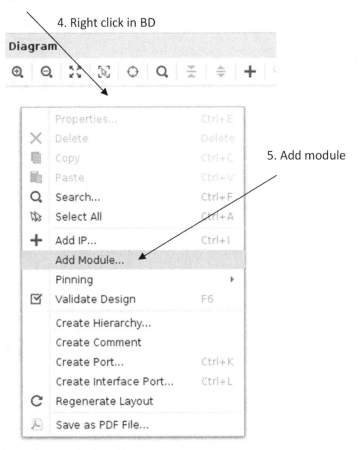

Figure 8.40: Default interface definition

5. Select **Add Module**.

Figure 8.41: Adding a module to the IP Integrator

6. Select **OK**.

Now we can compare the HDL module to the IP we created earlier:

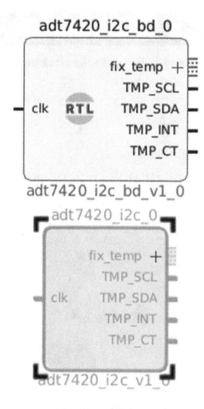

Figure 8.42: HDL module versus created IP

The RTL module acts just like an IP block created earlier in the chapter. You can modify the parameters and the interfaces are detected if named properly.

We'll be leaving the IP Integrator and will explore other FPGA features in the next few chapters.

Summary

We've seen how to generate IPs from an existing SystemVerilog file and used this to recreate our temperature sensor project using the IP Integrator. We looked at how we can easily debug using the IP Integrator and how the ILA is AXI-aware. We've also looked at how we can package IPs by using the IP packager to generate a wrapper with AXI interfaces that we can use to create our core designs.

We've gone from flashing LEDs in *Chapter 2, FPGA Programming Languages and Tools*, to using a seven-segment display to display information in *Chapter 4, Counting Button Presses*. In *Chapter 9, Lots of Data? MIG and DDR2*, we are going to look at developing a display controller using the **Video Graphics Array** (**VGA**) interface, which will give us much more capability in displaying the outputs from our temperature sensor, microphone, and calculator.

Questions

1. What are AXI streaming interfaces best for?

    a. Burst transactions to multiple memory addresses

    b. Point-to-point connections

    c. High-performance connections

    d. Both b and c

2. What is the IP Integrator?

    a. An easy way to create block-based designs using Xilinx or user-defined IP

    b. A context-sensitive editor for HDL designs

    c. Not very good at aiding design debuging

3. If you want to create an IP from an existing design, you would use **Create and package new IP**. True or false?

4. You cannot use **Create and package new IP** to generate a design wrapper with AXI interfaces to create your own designs. True or false?

5. When should full AXI interfaces be used?

    a. When you need a high-performance interface that can burst data to multiple memory addresses.

    b. When you only write a single register at a time infrequently.

    c. When you have lots of data to move between two cores where the destination is a FIFO-like interface.

    d. All the time. They are cheap to implement and can do everything.

Answers

1. d) Both b and c

2. a) An easy way to create block-based designs using Xilinx or user-defined IP

3. True

4. False

5. a) When you need a high-performance interface that can burst data to multiple memory
    addresses.

Completed designs

Building a design as complex as this from scratch can be difficult, and also, you likely would not
want to commit all of the output products in source control. As previously mentioned, you can
generate a Tcl file to rebuild the project. A copy of this Tcl file is stored under **build/completed**.
You can source the Tcl file from within Vivado instead of opening a project and it will rebuild the
design from scratch.

Further reading

For more information about what was covered in the chapter, please refer to the following:

*   `https://www.xilinx.com/content/dam/xilinx/support/documents/sw_manuals/`
    `xilinx2022_2/ug1119-vivado-creating-packaging-ip-tutorial.pdf`

*   `https://developer.arm.com/documentation/ihi0022/e/AMBA-AXI3-and-AXI4-`
    `Protocol-Specification`

*   AMBA AXI-Stream Protocol Specification, `https://developer.arm.com/documentation/`
    `ihi0051/latest/`

Join our community on Discord

Join our community's Discord space for discussions with the authors and other readers:

`https://packt.link/embedded`

9

Lots of Data? MIG and DDR2

We've been working our way up toward a more functional design that can gather information, do some useful work, and present it in a meaningful manner. In the previous chapters, we captured audio data and temperature data. We also looked at wrapping some of the interfaces so that we could use the IP integrator. The IP integrator also allowed for easily instancing floating-point operations. This has given us some functional designs, but we've been limited to using LEDs and then seven-segment displays, making it difficult to visualize information such as the **Pulse Densilty Modulation (PDM)** waveform data or even the temperature.

We have another option when it comes to displaying using our boards: the **Video Graphics Array (VGA)** connector. We will need access to quite a bit of memory to effectively use it. To display 640x480 8-bit color, we would need 300 kilobytes, and almost 1 megabyte for true color. We can certainly play some games to stretch out our memory, but alternatively, we can use the on-board **Double Data Rate, 2nd generation (DDR2)** as a frame buffer and draw what we want to be displayed on it.

By the end of this chapter, you'll have been introduced to external memory, generated a DDR2 controller, and tested it both in simulation and on the board. You'll be comfortable with how to use external memory in your designs.

In this chapter, we are going to cover the following main topics:

- Project 11 – Introducing external memory
- DDR memory basics
- Using the Xilinx **Memory Interface Generator (MIG)**
- A brief look at other memory types

Technical requirements

The technical requirements for this chapter are the same as those for *Chapter 2, FPGA Programming Languages and Tools*.

To follow along with the examples and the project, you can find the code files for this chapter in the following repository on GitHub: `https://github.com/PacktPublishing/The-FPGA-Programming-Handbook-Second-Edition/tree/main/CH9`.

Note on VHDL

This chapter is strictly about SystemVerilog and we will only be using SystemVerilog to generate the DDR2 IP. Generating the DDR2 IP for VHDL is limited to the Xilinx Native interface, which we will not be looking at. Once the IP is generated, it can be used within a VHDL design, as we will see in *Chapter 10*.

Project 11 – Introducing external memory

Up until now, we've been using internal **Block RAM (BRAM)** or distributed RAM. These types of memory are very fast. BRAM can be accessed in a single clock cycle up to the **maximum frequency (fmax)** of the device given certain constraints. **Lookup table memory (LUTRAM)** is a little more flexible in that it can be used asynchronously (i.e., as though it were combinational logic). Both types of memory are very convenient for small storage, lookup tables, fast memory for things such as caches, and if you have enough for a design, keeping board costs and complexity down.

Introduction to DDR2

BRAM/LUTRAM is **Static RAM (SRAM)**. SRAM takes a much larger area in silicon, up to four transistors (4T) per bit of storage, as shown in *Figure 9.1*.

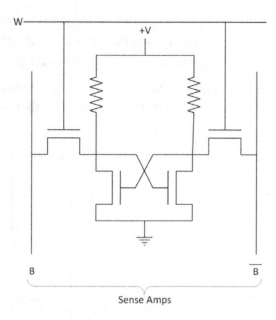

Figure 9.1: 4T SRAM cell

This results in a much smaller capacity and greater expense than dynamic memory, which, in contrast, is primarily a capacitor used to hold a charge with a transistor attached to it, which you can see in *Figure 9.2*.

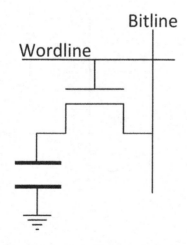

Figure 9.2: External DRAM performance

You can see the reduction in physical complexity from an SRAM cell to a DRAM cell. DRAM is also built on an optimized **Application-Specific Integrated Circuit (ASIC)** process to minimize the area of the chip. This allows for much higher densities, as we see in *Figure 9.3*.

There are many external memory types available for use in designs. Looking just at the **synchronous dynamic RAM (SDRAM)** that is still available, we can see how the performance has doubled with each generation:

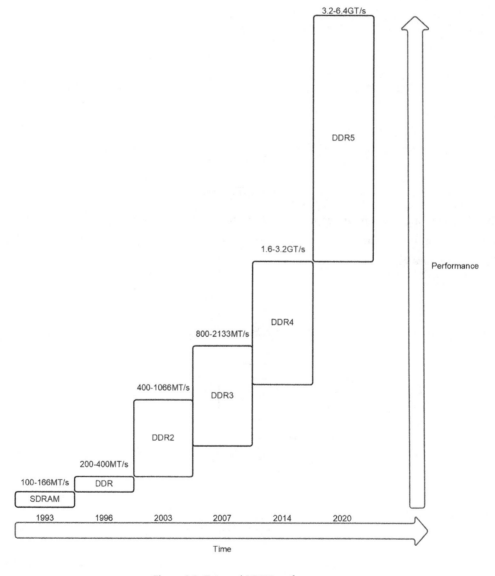

Figure 9.3: External DRAM performance

Looking at the preceding chart, the first question to ask would be what is the performance of the internal BRAM versus the external memory? What are the trade-offs? A single FPGA BRAM would be in the range of 300 MT/s. As we discussed previously, we can take advantage of parallelism and access many BRAMs in parallel, although effectively using all that memory would require a highly parallel structure.

The disadvantage of external memory and each passing generation is that latency, the time it takes from requesting data to getting it back, goes up. SDRAM can take five or so clocks at 100 MHz. DDR4 can take 80 clocks at 300 MHz. The logic to interface with the memories also gets very complex. You can write a DDR2 controller yourself; I have done it before. DDR4 controllers from Xilinx have embedded processors to handle initialization and periodic operations. When we generate our memory controller, we can look at the timing in a simulation.

We won't be tackling memory controller design using VHDL or SystemVerilog here. If you are interested, I would advise looking for SDRAM or DDR memory controllers online. There are many freely available.

Finally, as we mentioned previously, DRAM brings with it capacity. Newer FPGAs have optional **High-Bandwidth Memory (HBM)**, which provides internal DRAM with large capacities and very wide interfaces, which is how it gets the name high-bandwidth memory. For most FPGAs, the cost-effective solution is to use external memory when capacity is more important than bandwidth.

With our introduction out of the way, let's look at DDR2 specifically since that is what we have available to us on the Nexys A7.

Behind the scenes, there is a lot that the Xilinx memory controller handles for us. Dynamic memory is partitioned into **rows**, **columns**, and **banks**:

- A DRAM column indexes into a DRAM row when it's active. These are accessed via read or write commands to DRAM. These read or write commands can occur very rapidly.
- There are multiple rows within a bank, however, only one row can be activated at a time. This is accomplished via the `activate` command.
- There are multiple banks within DRAM. Each bank can have one active row, allowing for easy column access which allows for quicker access to large blocks of data.

When you want to switch rows within a bank, the open row must be precharged to close it before the new bank/row can be activated.

Finally, a refresh command must be issued periodically to DRAM, which requires all open banks to be precharged prior to the refresh. The refresh reads out a row and writes it back again to refresh the charges in the capacitors holding the data.

DDR/2/3/4/5 memories are all newer versions of DRAM that improve memory timing, access speed, and latency.

Luckily, most of that can be hidden from us by using the MIG, although at any point it is possible to expose more control or even write your own controller to interface with the DDR I/O.

With this background behind us, let's look at the steps for generating the memory.

Generating a DDR2 controller using the Xilinx MIG

The Nexys A7 shares the same pinout as the Nexys DDR and you can find a premade project on the website at https://reference.digilentinc.com/reference/programmable-logic/nexys-4-ddr/start?_ga=2.168036321.1345263114.1604794648-84804473.1599434198#additional_resources. We will, however, go through generating a component here so that you can see the options and how they relate to the underlying DDR2 architecture:

1. First, open `CH9/SystemVerilog/build/ddr2.xpr`. We need to use **IP catalog** to generate the MIG controller:

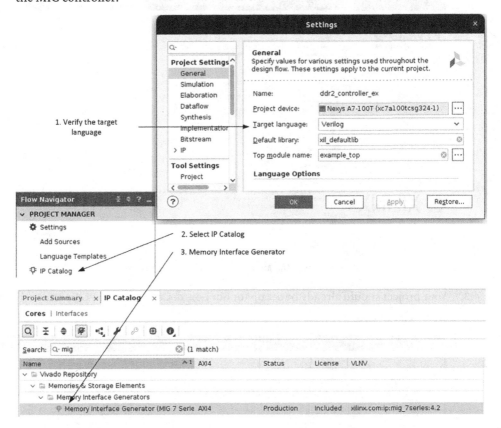

Figure 9.4: Start the MIG

2. Select **IP Catalog** and search for **MIG**. Then, double-click to start the MIG wizard.

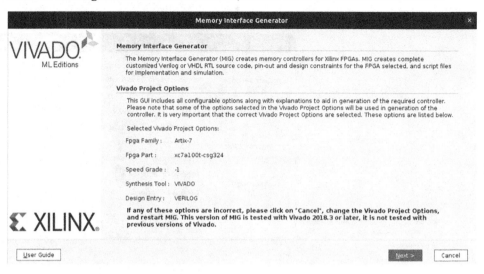

Figure 9.5: The Memory Interface Generator start screen

3. Your project should already be set up for our board. Confirm the FPGA part for the board, then select **Next**:

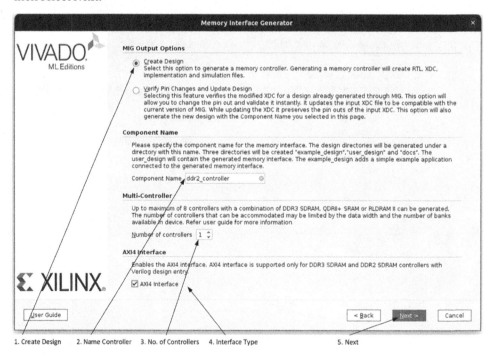

Figure 9.6: MIG options

4. Now, we need to select **Create Design** to generate our new MIG design. I've renamed the controller to something more meaningful. On our board, we only need one controller and I've chosen an **AXI4** interface as opposed to a native interface. Then, select **Next** so that we can look at pin compatibility:

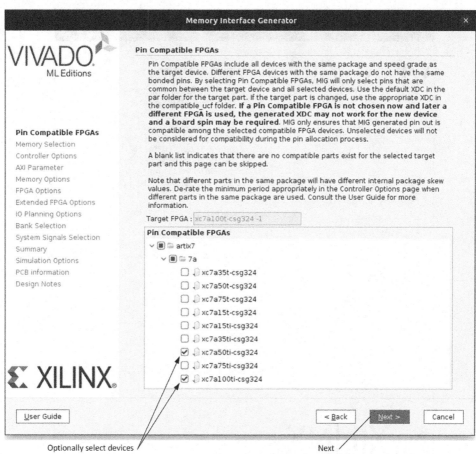

Figure 9.7: Pin compatibility

5. If you were generating a MIG controller for your own board, you may want to have the
    option of using a larger or smaller part. In this case, you could select multiple pin-com-
    patible FPGAs to make sure your MIG controller would work in any part you eventually
    put on your board. Select **Next** to choose the memory type:

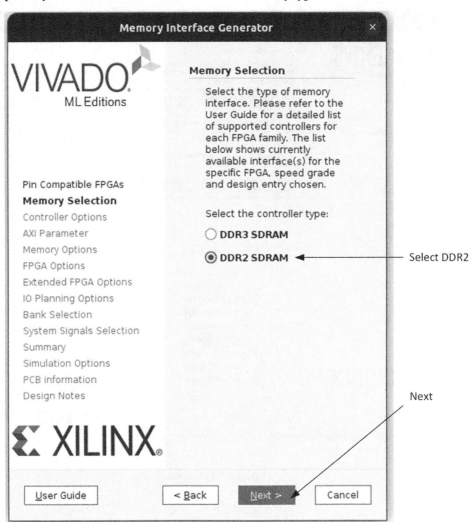

Figure 9.8: Memory selection

6. The Artix 7 supports DDR2 and 3 using the MIG. Our board has DDR2, so make sure to pick that one. Although all DDRs have similar names (i.e. DDR, DDR2, DDR3, etc.), they are not compatible with each other. Make sure you pick the correct memory type for your board. Select **Next** so that we can select the controller options:

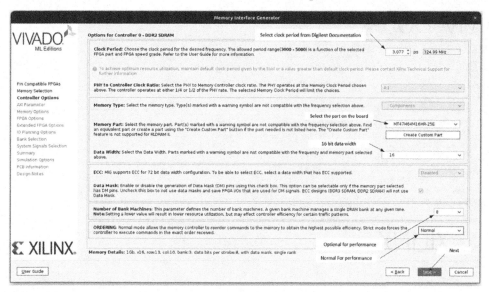

Figure 9.9: Controller options

Section 3.1 of the Nexys A7 documentation (link in *Further reading*) recommends the settings we will use in this section. Most importantly, we need to select the correct part. Digilent also recommends a slightly slower clock speed for easier implementation. Select a data width of 16. There are two more options that are more or less optional.

The first is the number of bank machines. Remember that the device has eight banks. To improve performance, we can implement multiple bank machines at the expense of the area in our design.

Finally, we can choose to maintain the strict ordering of requests or allow reordering. If we allow reordering, we can improve performance.

Next, we'll look at the AXI (Advanced eXtensible Interface) parameters.

Setting AXI parameters

There are a few parameter options that we have control over:

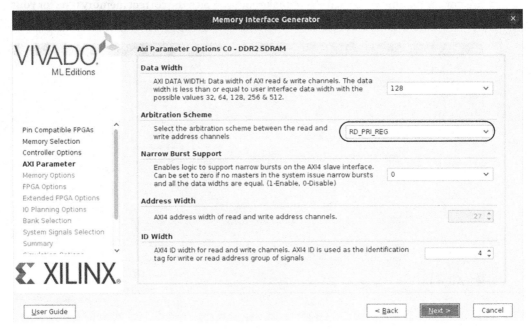

Figure 9.10: AXI parameters

The main thing we need to consider for AXI parameters is the arbitration scheme. Because a major aspect of the controller is to handle our display, we need to make sure we never starve our display controller. To do this, we specify a read priority for arbitration.

> The arbitration scheme allows us to change the way the memory controller will re-spond to AXI read and write requests. RD_PRI_REG gives the read port priority over the write port so that we are always able to supply data for the display. Writes will occur when the display output is inactive.

In the next section, we'll set the memory options.

Setting memory options

There are two options we need to set according to the Digilent documentation. These are shown in *Figure 9.11*. The first is the burst type, which can be sequential or interleaved. Throughout my time designing with external memory, I've never used interleaved; however, the option is there if you have a use for it:

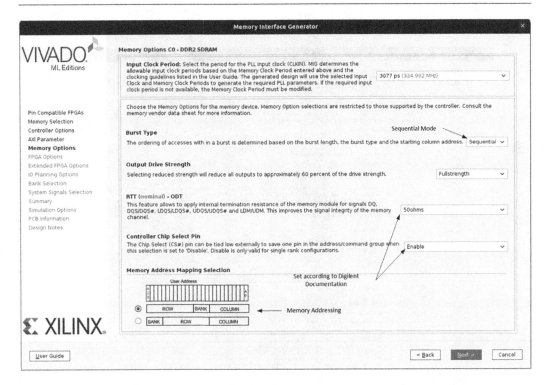

Figure 9.11: Memory options

We also have a choice of how we address the memory. There are three components to any address: the bank, the row, and the column. Remember that the memory can only open up one row per bank, but can have one active row for each of the eight banks. Ideally, we would analyze our usage pattern to maximize our performance. Often, this is done by analyzing a software (C) model of your system or through simulation. For now, I'm going to choose [**ROW, BANK, COLUMN**] so that we access multiple banks when we implement our VGA controller in a later chapter.

Next, we'll address the FPGA options for the controller.

Defining the FPGA options

There are several options available for the FPGA, some of which we need to change for the board we are using:

1. We'll be generating the clock internally, so we will specify both the system clock and the reference clock as **No Buffer**. I've also enabled the debug interface so that we can take a closer look inside the FPGA while it's running.

2. We can leave the rest of the settings as the default:

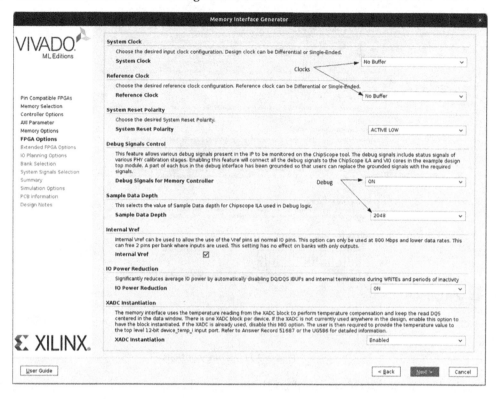

Figure 9.12: MIG FPGA options

3. On the next screen, we can leave everything as the default:

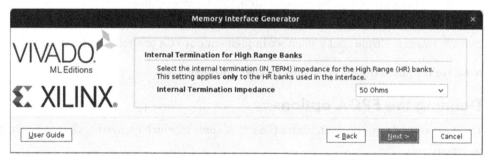

Figure 9.13: Extended FPGA options

4. For **Pin/Bank Selection Mode**, select **Fixed Pin Out**.

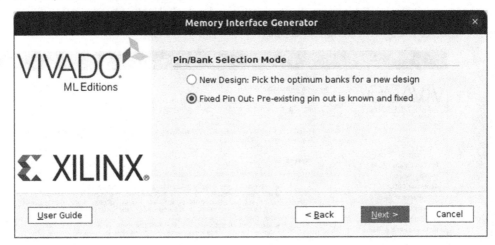

Figure 9.14: Extended FPGA options

5. On the next screen, we'll define the pins. Digilent has provided a `.ucf` file for the DDR constraints. It's included in CH9/xdc/Nexys4DDRmemorypinout.ucf:

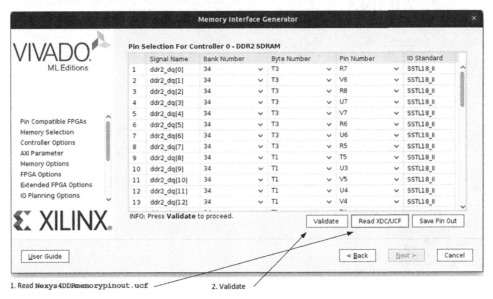

Figure 9.15: Pin selection

6. First, select **Read XDC/UCF** and read the `Nexys4DDRmemorypinout.ucf` file. Then, you must select **Validate** to verify the pinout and unlock the **Next** button. Now, we can move on to the system signals selection:

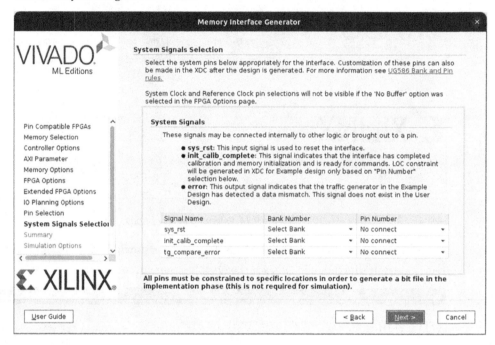

Figure 9.16: System signals selection

7. We have already selected internal signals for some connections. We will also use the others internally since they are not brought out on the board. Don't change anything on this screen and we'll look at the summary screen after hitting **Next**:

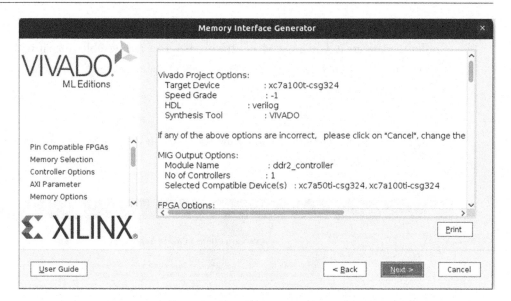

Figure 9.17: MIG summary

8. On this screen, you can review the summary of the DDR2 controller that we are going to generate. Verify that it matches the parameters we've selected and then hit **Next**:

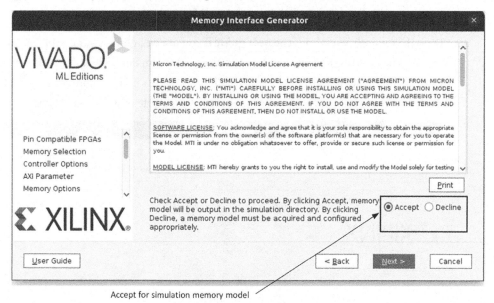

Figure 9.18: Simulation options

9. Xilinx provides a Micron DDR2 memory model for use with simulations of the DDR2 core. In order to generate it, you must accept the license. This is advisable since it will allow you to simulate the core against a real DDR2 model. Select **Accept** (recommended) or **Decline**, then select **Next**:

> If you decline the memory model, then you will not be able to simulate using the memory.

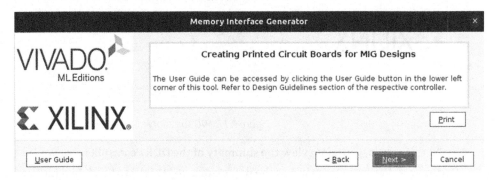

Figure 9.19: Printed circuit board (PCB) information

10. The MIG reminds you about the user guide if you are designing your own PCB. Since we can assume that Digilent has already handled this, it can be safely ignored. If you decide to design your own board in the future, Xilinx provides many resources and checklists that you should follow. Feel free to inspect the user guide or just select **Next**:

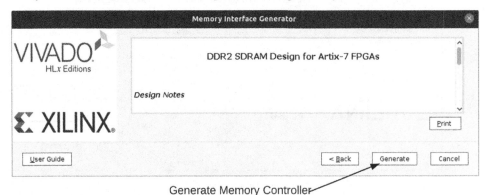

Generate Memory Controller

Figure 9.20: Generating the core

We've reached the end of the options and you can simply select **Generate**. One more window will pop up to generate **Object Oriented Concepts (OOC)** modules. Select **Generate** again.

11. Now, the core generation is complete. You'll see the core inside your design sources:

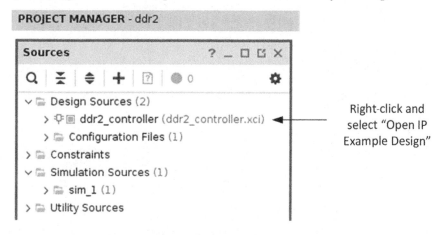

Figure 9.21: Creating the example design

One very nice thing about a lot of the Xilinx cores – the MIG cores in particular – is that you can generate an example design for simulation and sometimes implementation. As previously mentioned, when optimizing addressing, you will likely want to simulate the design to verify operation, and the example design can give you a jump start on this.

12. To generate the example design, right-click on the .xci file in the design sources and select **Open IP Example Design:**

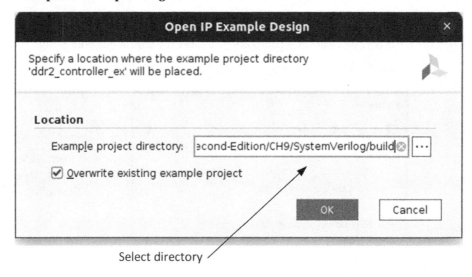

Figure 9.22: Open IP Example Design

13. Make sure you've selected a good subdirectory for your example design and select **OK:**

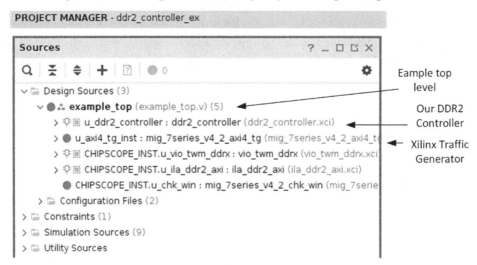

Figure 9.23: Viewing the example design

You can now see that we have the example design loaded, along with a simple testbench. We'll want to modify the top level so that we can run it on the board and look at it using the **Integrated Logic Analyzer (ILA).**

The ILA is a tool that is used to probe signals in a design. Xilinx provides the ability to use FPGA resources to integrate an ILA into a design. You can specify the signals to monitor and capture and then you can view them much like you would simulation waveforms.

Before we change anything, let's verify that the generated testbench runs without problems. This is a good engineering practice. There is nothing worse than modifying and running, then realizing that the original generated design didn't work properly in the first place.

To do this, select **Run Simulation** as we have done previously.

Notice that this simulation takes a lot longer than anything we've done so far. You can see from the timescale that the testbench is operating at very precise timing for the DDR simulation:

```
`timescale 1ps/100fs
```

We can also look at the simulation output to see just how long a simulation is. The initialization and calibration phase takes 100 microseconds. The actual test takes about half that time:

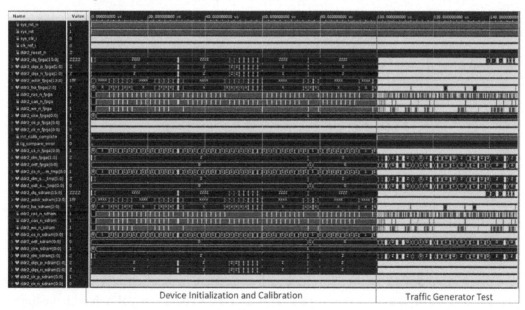

Figure 9.24: MIG simulation

If your simulation completes successfully, you should see finish highlighted in your simulation window:

```
548 ⊟        //********************************************************************
549          // Reporting the test case status
550          // Status reporting logic exists both in simulation test bench (sim_tb_top)
551          // and sim.do file for ModelSim. Any update in simulation run time or time out
552          // in this file need to be updated in sim.do file as well.
553 ⊟        //********************************************************************
554          initial
555          begin : Logging
556             fork
557                begin : calibration_done
558       O          wait (init_calib_complete);
559       O          $display("Calibration Done");
560       O          #50000000.0;
561       O          if (!tg_compare_error) begin
562       O              $display("TEST PASSED");
563                 end
564                 else begin
565       O              $display("TEST FAILED: DATA ERROR");
566                 end
567       O          disable calib_not_done;
568      O→            $finish;
569                end
570
571                begin : calib_not_done
572                   if (SIM_BYPASS_INIT_CAL == "SIM_INIT_CAL_FULL")
573                      #2500000000.0;
574                   else
575       O             #1000000000.0;
576       O          if (!init_calib_complete) begin
577       O              $display("TEST FAILED: INITIALIZATION DID NOT COMPLETE");
578                 end
579       O          disable calibration_done;
580       O             $finish;
581                end
582             join
583          end
```

Figure 9.25: Simulation completes successfully

If you did generate the VHDL version, then you'll notice that the testbench is still in Verilog.

Once we make our changes, the simulations will no longer work properly.

Now that we have proven out the Xilinx testbench using the Xilinx traffic generator module. Let's go ahead and modify our design so that we can run it on the board and look at it with the ILA.

Modifying the design for use on the board

For the following section, you can copy over the ddr2_controller_ex or apply the changes directly to the example design since you can always regenerate it.

Looking at the Xilinx implemented design, sys_clk_i is being generated at 325 MHz. The first thing we'll need to do is modify our top level for the board, which means we'll need to add a **Mixed Mode Clock Manager (MMCM)** to take our 100 MHz system clock and generate the 325 MHz clock. We'll also need to generate clk_ref_i. If we look at the testbench, we'll see that this clock should be 200 MHz:

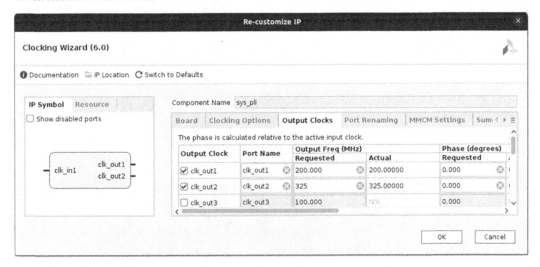

Figure 9.26: The sys_pll settings

Note that in the sys_pll clock output clock definitions, one interesting thing about the output clocks is that order matters. If you try to swap the clocks, that is, instead of clk_out1 being 200 MHz and clk_out2 being 325 MHz, they are 325/200 MHz, you'll find that the clocks are no longer precise. clk_out1 will always produce the most accurate clock, but it will affect the other clocks being generated as the internal PLL (Phase Locked Loops) frequency is based upon this.

We'll also remove the reset port so the clock is free running.

> clk_out1 provides the most precise clock, so if you have strict requirements, make sure to use clk_out0.
>
> Sometimes, you need to try different combinations of output clocks to get close to what you are targeting.

Next, we'll address our top level. I've provided an edited file under the SystemVerilog directory. It is recommended to make these changes yourself unless you are using Vivado 2022.2, in which case, the files may have changed and it may not work as expected.

SystemVerilog:

```systemverilog
//input          sys_clk_i, // remove
//input          clk_ref_i, // remove
input           ext_clk,   // add
output          tg_compare_error,
output          init_calib_complete,
input           sys_rst,
output          LED        // add
);
// Add the following to instantiate the PLL
wire clk_ref_i;
wire sys_clk_i;
assign LED = sys_rst;
sys_pll u_sys_pll
(.clk_out1       (clk_ref_i),
  .clk_out2      (sys_clk_i),

  .clk_in1       (ext_clk),
  .resetn        (sys_rst)
);
```

I've removed the two clocks, clk_ref_i and sys_clk_i, and made them internal. I've added an external clock, ext_clk, so that we can bring in 100 MHz from the crystal oscillator and use the PLL to generate the 200 and 325 MHz clocks that we need for the DDR2. I've also instantiated the PLL in the top-level design.

We'll also need to modify the testbench for the 100 MHz clock:

```systemverilog
parameter CLKIN_PERIOD          = 10000; //3077;
// Input Clock Period
```

The modified testbench can be found under the language TB directory. I've commented out the old clock period for 325 MHz and replaced it with a 100 MHz clock. Now, our PLL will generate the correct clocks and we can verify this in simulation. Notice the testbench no longer works and will need some changes to make it work again; for now, let's build our design for the Nexys A7. Be sure to add ddr.xdc from CH9/xdc.

Once you've downloaded the image to the board, you can bring up the ILA. The pattern generator and checker are running constantly, so you can trigger the ILA immediately to see activity on the DDR2 internal interfaces:

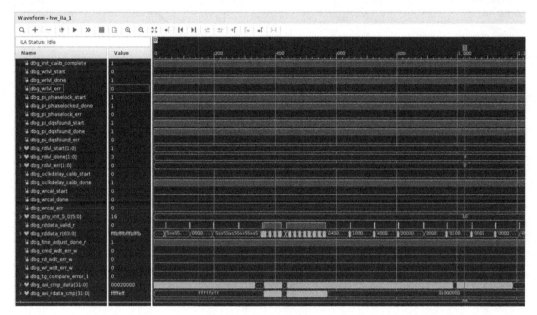

Figure 9.27: DDR2 ILA

Looking at the LED on the board should show no errors detected and the ILA will show the activity generated.

The DDR2 core, as we generated it, has one other trick up its sleeve. It also has the Vivado debug logic core **Virtual I/O (VIO)** interface. This interface can be used in your designs to provide input and output functionality from within Vivado to aid on-chip debugging. In the case of the DDR2 interface, it provides insight into what is going on in the core and allows changing configuration on the fly.

You can bring up the VIO by selecting the hw_vios tab:

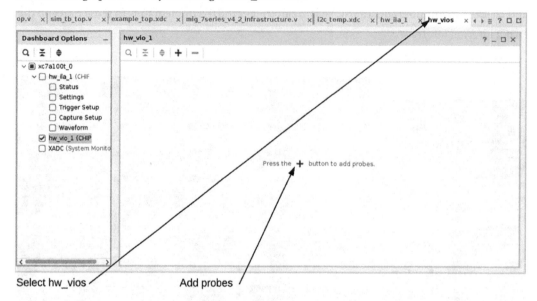

Figure 9.28: Adding hardware (HW) VIOs

You can click the + button to add probes. For now, simply add them all:

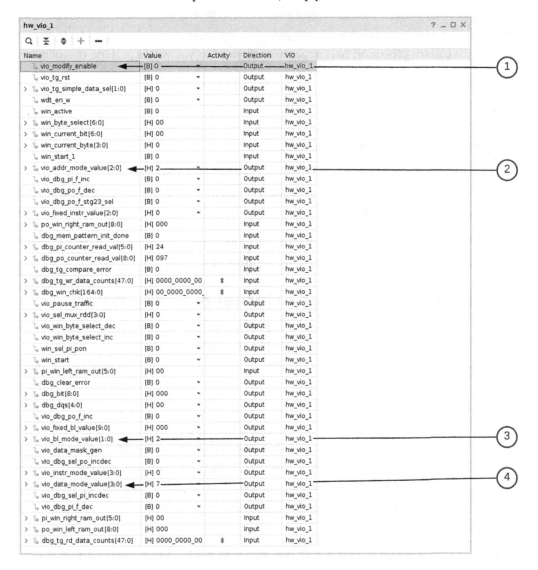

Figure 9.29: VIO signals

From *Figure 9.29*, you can see signals labeled Output and Input. The direction is relevant to the VIO core. You can monitor input signals and make changes to output signals that will be reflected in the pattern generator and checker. In the preceding figure, I have marked the order to apply a change to the pattern generator. To change the configuration, you would perform the following operations:

1. Set vio_modify_enable to 1.
2. Set vio_addr_mode_value to 1 = fixed address, 2 = **pseudorandom binary sequence** (**PRBS**) address, or sequential address.
3. Set vio_bl_mode_value to 1 = Fixed bl or 2 = PRBS bl.
4. Set vio_data_mode_value to 1 = fixed, 2 = DGEN_ADDR, 3 = DGEN_HAMMER, 4 = DGEN_NEIGHBOR, 5 = DGEN_WALKING1, and 6 = DGEN_WALKING0, DGEN_PRBS.

Now, we've looked at DDR2, in the next chapter, we'll be using it for our display controller. Briefly, we'll look at other external memory types that are used with FPGAs.

Introducing a few other external memory types

There are a variety of memory types, such as **Quad Data Rate** (**QDR**) SRAM, HyperRAM, and **Serial Peripheral Interface** (**SPI**) RAM, that have been introduced over the years and are or have become more common with FPGAs. I want to briefly touch on them as you might be interested in them for your own projects in the future.

QDR SRAM

QDR SRAM is commonly used in networking applications. Like DDR memory, data is transferred on both edges of the clock for performance. Unlike DDR, QDR has both read and write channels, so you can issue read and write commands simultaneously. Also, unlike DDR DRAM, this is SRAM, so there are no refresh cycles, and the latency for a read or write can be as low as about 13 clock cycles at 300 MHz.

QDR has a much larger capability than FPGA internal memory, but much less than DDR. It's also relatively expensive, meaning it is mostly used in networking applications.

Pros:

*   It can carry out simultaneous read and write operations.
*   It has more storage than typical internal FPGA RAM.
*   It behaves like SRAM with an initial latency.

Cons:

- It is very expensive.
- It is smaller than HBM or DDR memory.
- It has a lower clock speed than DRAM.

HyperRAM

HyperRAM is a type of self-refreshing DRAM designed for **Low Pin Count (LPC)** applications. It has performance and sizes similar to DDR (not later generations like DDR2, DDR3, etc.) memories, making it ideal for some applications, such as MicroBlaze-based systems. Compared to DDRx interfaces, a HyperRAM interface requires significantly fewer signals to connect to an FPGA, which reduces the number of IO pins required and makes the board design a lot easier. As the Xilinx Vivado tool currently does not come with a HyperRAM controller IP core, you'll typically have to purchase a commercial IP core in order to use that technology. There are also **Peripheral module Interface (PMOD)** boards available for HyperRAM.

Pros:

- It has a low pin count.

Cons:

- Older DDR technology.
- It has no Xilinx core support.

SPI RAM

There is a very **Low Pin Count (LPC)** RAM-utilizing SPI. These types of RAM have similar capabilities to DDR (not later generations like DDR2, DDR3, etc.) and fairly good performance using as few as eight pins. PMOD boards are available with these memories also.

Summary

In this chapter, we've looked at external memory, in particular, DDR2, as that is what we have readily available on the Nexys A7. We've looked at generating a core using the Xilinx MIG controller and how to generate the example design. We then ran the example design on the board and, using the ILA, saw it in operation. We've also taken a quick look at other external memory types.

Up until now, we've limited ourselves to LEDs and seven-segment displays for our output. In the next chapter, we are going to take the DDR controller and create a VGA controller. Dust off your CRT or LCD with a VGA connector and we'll work on displaying our temperature sensor data, our audio data, and calculator data using a real display.

Questions

1. Which of the following is true about internal versus external memory?

    a. DDR memory storage capacity is much smaller than BRAM.

    b. For the same memory data width, DDR has a much higher performance than BRAM.

    c. The latency to access data from BRAM and DDR is identical.

    d. You should always use LUTRAM first before using any other memory type.

2. To generate DDR2 memory for our project, we used the Xilinx:

    a. **Massive IP Goliath (MIG)**

    b. **Minimally Informative Google (MIG)**

    c. **Memory Interface Generator (MIG)**

3. We can use ILAs to examine data in the FPGA and VIOs to read and write data.

    a. True.

    b. False.

4. Artix 7 FPGAs can use which of the following memories from the MIG?

    a. DDR2.

    b. DDR3.

    c. DDR4.

    d. LPDDR2.

    e. QDR.

    f. DDR2 and DDR3.

5. It is possible to use HyperRAM, SPI RAM, and SDRAM if you are willing to write your own controllers.

    a. True.

    b. False.

Answers

1. b
2. c
3. a
4. f
5. a

Challenge

We've created the DDR2 using the MIG and we have the example design. We don't have a way of inserting errors. Can you utilize a button or switch on our board and use it to inject an error into the data either to or from the memory?

Hint: You can use an XOR gate to inject the error. When the bit coming from the pushbutton or switch is 0, then the output of the XOR will be unchanged. If you set the bit, it will invert the data passing through.

Further reading

For more information about what was covered in this chapter, please refer to the following:

- `https://www.micron.com/products/dram/ddr2-sdram/part-catalog/`
  `mt47h64m16hr-25`
- `https://reference.digilentinc.com/reference/programmable-logic/nexys-a7/`
  `reference-manual`

Join our community on Discord

Join our community's Discord space for discussions with the authors and other readers:

`https://packt.link/embedded`

10

A Better Way to Display – VGA

We've been on quite a journey so far. We have come across a lot, starting from understanding basic digital circuits to designing a calculator. We've interfaced with external components such as a temperature sensor and microphone. We've looked at computer math and even advanced math topics such as floating point operations, pipelined design, and parallelism. However, up until now, we've been limited to displaying information using LEDs, single color or RGB, as well as the seven-segment display. We are quite capable of performing operations and displaying limited information, as we have demonstrated with our temperature sensor and calculator. The Nexys A7 offers an additional output that can provide us with an almost unlimited method of displaying information, the **Video Graphics Array (VGA)** connector. The VGA connector on the Nexys A7 can display resolutions of up to 1600x1200, with up to 2^{12} or 4,096 colors. What allows us to unlock this capability is that we now know how to use our external memory, which will provide our framebuffer.

By the end of this chapter, we'll have created a method of displaying data on a **cathode ray tube (CRT)** or LCD monitor via the VGA connector. In *Chapter 11, Bringing It All Together*, we'll use this methodology to upgrade some of our projects to utilize the new display.

In this chapter, we are going to cover the following main topics using a project, **Introducing the VGA:**

- Defining registers
- Generating timing for the VGA
- Displaying text
- Testing the VGA controller
- Examining the constraints

Technical requirements

The technical requirements for this chapter are the same as those for *Chapter 2, FPGA Programming Languages and Tools*.

To follow along with the examples and the project, you can find the code files for this chapter in the following repository on GitHub: `https://github.com/PacktPublishing/The-FPGA-Programming-Handbook-Second-Edition/CH10`.

A VGA-capable monitor and cable are also required if you want to implement the project on the board.

Note

If you don't have access to a VGA-capable monitor, you can use a VGA to HDMI converter such as the BENFEI VGA to HDMI VGA to HDMI adapter with audio support and 1080 P resolution.

Project 12 – Introducing the VGA

The earliest professional computer displays were simple monochrome text displays. The earliest personal computers, such as the Apple 2, could display 280x192 pixels with a small number of colors. The Commodore 64 and IBM/PC could display 320x200 pixels, again with limited color palettes. The original IBM VGA was introduced in 1987 and it allowed for higher resolutions and standardized the connector going forward until digital displays such as LCDs became the norm.

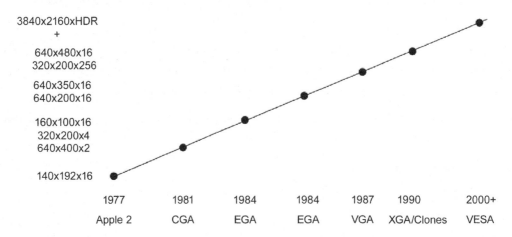

Figure 10.1: Displaying the VGA evolution

The first thing we'll need to look at is how the screen is drawn. Whether you are using a CRT display or a modern LCD, the timing is still supported to provide backward compatibility. Originally, the VGA output was designed to drive an electron gun to light up phosphors on a CRT. This meant timing spanned the entire display, plus time for the gun to shift from one side of the screen to the other, or from the bottom back to the top. *Figure 10.1* shows the various timing parameters and their relationship to what is displayed on the screen:

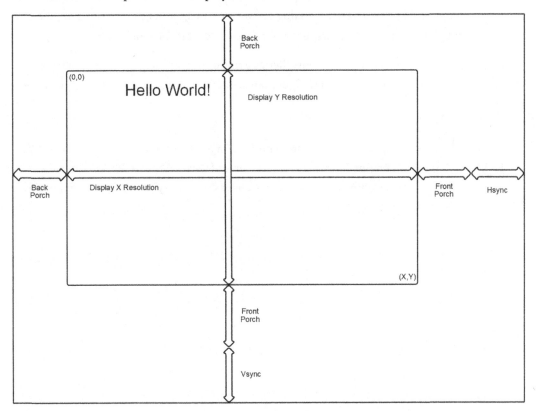

Figure 10.2: VGA screen timing information as displayed on the monitor

The main components of the output that we need to generate are as follows:

- **Hsync (horizontal synchronization signal):** This signal originally moved the electron gun of a CRT monitor from the right-hand side of the display to the left-hand side of the display. In current monitors, it simply resets the X counter to 0 and increments the Y counter to set up to display the next pixel.

- **Vsync (vertical synchronization signal)**: This signal originally moved the electron gun of a CRT monitor from the lower left-hand corner to the upper right-hand corner of the display. In current monitors, it simply resets the X and Y counters to 0 to set up to display the next pixel.

- **Red [3:0], Green[3:0], Blue[3:0]**: – **RGB** color values. In a real display, these would be 8 bits per color (24 **bits per pixel (bpp)**). However, Digilent opted to create a resistor array implementation of a **digital-to-analog converter (DAC)** rather than a true DAC, thereby limiting the bpp colors to 4 bits red, 4 bits green and 4 bits blue or 12bpp.

We're going to want to make the VGA controller as generic as possible. To do this, we'll create a register-based interface, so we'll need to figure out what the values we'll need for a given resolution are.

The following timing list is comprehensive for a 4:3 aspect ratio display (older CRT/TV). Depending on the display you use, some of these will not work. We'll default to 640x480 pixels @ 60 Hz since this is the base VGA display and should be supported by everything.

We can look at a list of **Video Electronics Standards Association (VESA)** standards to get an idea of what we want to display:

Resolution	Refr rate	Horiz total	Vert total	Clock	FP	tHS	Pol	BP	FP	tVS	Pol	BP
640x480	60	800	525	25.18	16	96	-	48	10	2	-	33
640x480	72	832	520	31.5	16	40	-	128	9	3	-	28
640x480	75	840	500	31.5	16	64	-	120	1	3	-	16
640x480	85	832	509	36	56	56	-	80	1	3	-	25
800x600	60	1056	628	40	40	128	+	88	1	4	+	23
800x600	72	1040	666	50	56	120	+	64	37	6	+	23
800x600	75	1056	625	49.5	16	80	+	160	1	3	+	21
800x600	85	1048	631	56.25	32	64	+	152	1	3	+	27
1024x768	60	1344	806	65	24	136	-	160	3	6	-	29
1024x768	70	1328	806	75	24	136	-	144	3	6	-	29
1024x768	75	1312	800	78.75	16	96	+	176	1	3	+	28
1024x768	85	1376	808	94.5	48	96	+	208	1	3	+	36
1280x1024	60	1688	1066	108	48	112	+	248	1	3	+	38
1280x1024	75	1688	1066	135	16	144	+	248	1	3	+	38
1280x1024	85	1728	1072	157.5	64	160	+	224	1	3	+	44
1600x1200	60	2160	1250	162	64	192	+	304	1	3	+	46
1920x1200	60	2616	1242	195	96	200	+	400	3	3	+	36

Figure 10.3: VESA modes

The preceding table contains the timing for the possible modes our display will support. The first thing to note is that the clock frequency that we'll need varies quite a bit from 25.18 MHz to 195 MHz. We'll address this by introducing clock reconfiguration, which is available in the Clocking Wizard. We can also make use of registers for storing the various parameters we'll need, so we'll use an AXI-Lite interface for our registers.

Now, let's take the relevant numbers from the preceding table and put them into a timing diagram so that we can visualize the actual signals going to the display:

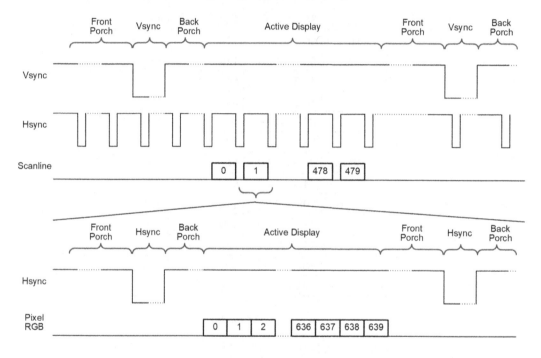

Figure 10.4: Video timing diagram

In *Figure 10.2*, we can see how the timing works. The timing is broken up into two sections. The first is the frame time, which can be looked at as the Vsync timing, which is the time it takes to draw the whole display based on the number of scanlines. The second is the actual time it takes to draw a scanline, which is composed of the Hsync plus data.

To keep things simple, we'll assume that data is stored as 1-bit values. Typically, VGA and VESA modes would have 8-, 16-, or 32-bit colors. 8-bit values would be used as an index into a palette of 256 colors out of 16 million colors. 16-bit colors would typically have 565 or 555 (RGB) values, and 32-bit colors were actually 888 RGB values capable of displaying 16 million colors. For our purposes, and since we are tackling quite a bit, I'll limit us to storing 1-bit colors. A pixel will be on or off.

Note

When dealing with colors, we'll reference them by the number of bits used to represent them (8, 16, 24, or 32) and the number of bits per color channel (565, 555, or 888), where each digit represents the number of bits used for each color: red, green, and blue.

Defining registers

The first step we'll need for our VGA controller is to define a set of registers we can use to solve our problem. The idea of using registers is to provide us with an easy and reusable interface that allows us to generate whatever timing we need. We know the timing parameters from *Figure 10.1* and the associated table. From this, we can derive some parameters. For our VGA, we propose the following set:

- **Horizontal display start**: The number of horizontal pixels before the display starts, equivalent to the horizontal back porch minus one.

- **Horizontal display width**: The width of the display.

- **Horizontal sync width**: Hsync width.

- **Horizontal display total width**: The total width of the display and non-display portions.

- **Vertical display start**: The number of display lines before the display starts, equivalent to the vertical back porch minus one.

- **Vertical display height**: The height of the visible display.

- **Vertical sync width**: Vsync height in scan lines.

- **Vertical display total height**: The total height of the display and non-display portions.

- **VGA format**: The pixel depth for a given screen.

- **Display address**: The display address to read from. This can be written at any time, but will not take effect until the beginning of the next frame to prevent tearing.

- **Horizontal and vertical polarity selections**: Because different modes have active high or low polarities for the sync pulses, we need to provide a way of selecting between them.

- **Display pitch**: We need to know how many display pages to read for a given scanline as well as how many to count for each subsequent scanline.

- **Load mode**: Typically, in complex designs, we may have multiple registers that make up a complete set of values necessary for a given function. We must provide a way to update them all simultaneously once updating is complete.

Because this is an infrequently used interface, performance isn't really a concern. Therefore, our registers will be accessible via an AXI-Lite interface.

Coding a simple AXI-Lite interface

The write side of the AXI interface involves three components: the address bus, the data bus, and the response bus. We can see the address interface in the core interface definition:

```
input wire              reg_awvalid,
output logic            reg_awready,
input wire [11:0]       reg_awaddr,
input wire              reg_wvalid,
output logic            reg_wready,
input wire [31:0]       reg_wdata,
input wire [3:0]        reg_wstrb,
input wire              reg_bready,
output logic            reg_bvalid,
output logic [1:0]      reg_bresp,
```

The slave device must be able to handle the address and data buses independently. In our design, we'll write both at the same time, but it's possible that a master device may provide either an address or data before the other. We'll address this in our register state machine:

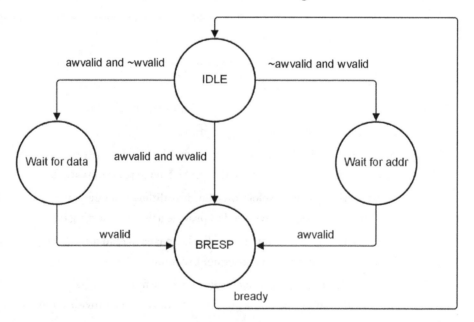

Figure 10.5: AXI Lite state machine

Figure 10.5 shows the basic state machine. If `awvalid` and `wvalid` are both high, then we can generate the response. If we are missing one of the components of a full transfer, either `awvalid` or `wvalid`, we proceed to a wait state and then to the `BRESP` state where we wait for the downstream interface to acknowledge the write.

 A lot of IPs will actually simply wait for the `awvalid` and `wvalid` to be high together. The state machine could be simplified to do this, however, this way of doing things is more accurate to how the bus may behave.

Finally, in the `BRESP` state, as soon as we see `bready`, we generate a success response and transition back to idle.

Now, let's examine the actual timing generation.

Generating timing for the VGA

We'll need two **Phase-Locked Loops (PLLs)** or **Mixed Mode Clock Managers (MMCMs)** for our design. The first PLL will be a duplicate of the one we created in *Chapter 9, Lots of Data? MIG and DDR2*, to generate clocks for the DDR2 memory controller and also our internal clocks. We will generate the second PLL so that we can change the timing parameters. By default, when the design powers up, it will display a VGA resolution of 640x480 @ 60 Hz. The main difference in our configuration is selecting **Dynamic Reconfig**:

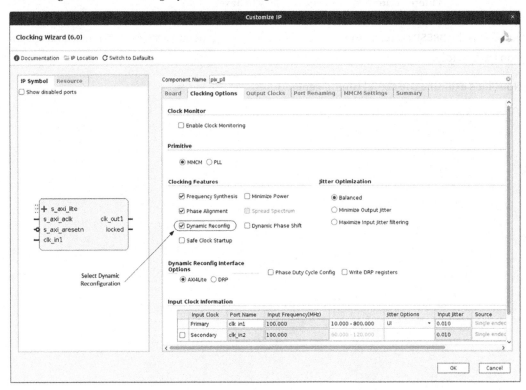

Figure 10.6: Dynamic Reconfig

Adding dynamic reconfiguration exposes an AXI-Lite interface in the Clocking Wizard that we can use to reconfigure the PLL on the fly. This allows us to change the video timing information on the fly and to achieve the different resolutions we might want. The registers we need to focus on can be found in the Clocking Wizard 6.0 guide at `https://www.xilinx.com/support/documentation/ip_documentation/clk_wiz/v6_0/pg065-clk-wiz.pdf`. We'll only be reconfiguring `clk0`. In the following screenshot, I've extracted the information we need from the **Clocking Wizard**. In *Figure 10.7*, you can see how to extract these numbers yourself:

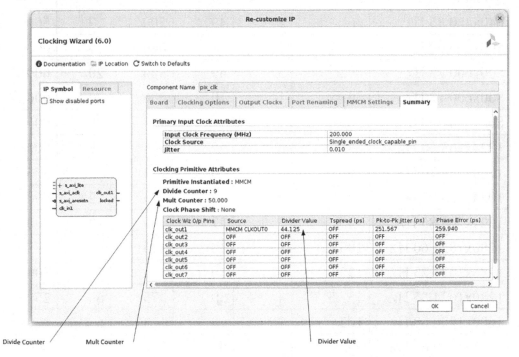

Figure 10.7: Extracting reconfiguration parameters

The parameters we need (based on a 200 MHz input clock) are as follows:

- **Divide Counter:** In *Figure 10.7*, for 25.18 MHz, this is 9.

- **Clock feedback multiplier (Mult Counter) integer:** For 25.18 MHz, this is 50.

- **Clock feedback multiplier (Mult Counter) fraction:** For 25.18 MHz, this is 000.

- **Clock feedback divider value integer:** For 25.18 MHz, this is 44.

- **Clock feedback divider value fraction:** For 25.18 MHz, this is 125.

The values can be calculated, but you need to be careful to make sure you don't exceed the maximum PLL frequency. The following figure shows the values we need for all our VGA frequencies:

Resolution	VGA clk	0x200			0x208	
		[7:0]	[15:8]	[25:16]	[7:0]	[17:8]
640x480 60 Hz	25.18	3	21	625	28	625
640x480 72/75 Hz	31.5	4	39	375	31	250
640x480 85 Hz	36	5	49	500	27	500
800x600 60 Hz	40	1	10	000	25	000
800x600 75 Hz	49.5	5	49	500	20	000
800x600 72 Hz	50	1	10	000	20	000
800x600 85 Hz	56.25	1	10	125	18	000
1024x768 60 Hz	65	5	50	375	15	500
1024x768 70 Hz	75	4	40	125	13	375
1024x768 75 Hz	78.75	4	39	375	12	500
1024x768 85 Hz	94.5	5	47	500	10	000
1280x1024 60 Hz	108	1	10	125	9	375
1280x1024 75 Hz	135	1	10	125	7	500
1280x1024 85 Hz	157.5	4	39	375	6	250
1600x1200 60 Hz	162	1	10	125	6	250
1920x1200 60 Hz	195	1	9	750	5	000

Figure 10.8: Dynamic reconfiguration values for the PLL

We can use the preceding table to create code to load our pixel PLL. We also need to load the register values for the resolution we need. Let's set that table up first.

First, we'll define a structure type to hold the table we'll use to set up the PLL and VGA controller for each of the 17 resolutions that we'll support. We'll create a simple AXI-Lite state machine that can configure the desired resolution, but in the future, we could use a microcontroller in the system:

```
typedef struct packed {
    logic [7:0 ] divide_count;
    logic [15:8] mult_integer;
```

```
    logic [25:16] mult_fraction;
    logic [7:0]   divide_integer;
    logic [17:0]  divide_fraction;
    logic [11:0]  horiz_display_start;
    logic [11:0]  horiz_display_width;
    logic [11:0]  horiz_sync_width;
    logic [11:0]  horiz_total_width;
    logic [11:0]  vert_display_start;
    logic [11:0]  vert_display_width;
    logic [11:0]  vert_sync_width;
    logic [11:0]  vert_total_width;
    logic         hpol;
    logic         vpol;
} resolution_t;
```

The structure encapsulates all the necessary parameters. We can define a variable and initialize it in an initial block to use as a constant:

```
resolution_t resolution[17];
initial begin
  // 640x480 @ 60Hz
  resolution[0].divide_count       = 8'd9;
  resolution[0].mult_integer       = 8'd50;
  resolution[0].mult_fraction      = 10'd000;
  resolution[0].divide_integer     = 8'd44;
  resolution[0].divide_fraction    = 10'd125;
  resolution[0].horiz_display_start = 12'd47;
  resolution[0].horiz_display_width = 12'd640;
  resolution[0].horiz_sync_width    = 12'd96;
  resolution[0].horiz_total_width   = 12'd799;
  resolution[0].vert_display_start  = 12'd32;
  resolution[0].vert_display_width  = 12'd480;
  resolution[0].vert_sync_width     = 12'd2;
  resolution[0].vert_total_width    = 12'd524;
  resolution[0].hpol               = '0;
  resolution[0].vpol               = '0;
```

In **VHDL**:

```vhdl
type resolution_t is record
  divide_count        : unsigned(7 downto 0);
  mult_integer        : unsigned(15 downto 8);
  mult_fraction       : unsigned(25 downto 16);
  divide_integer      : unsigned(7 downto 0);
  divide_fraction     : unsigned(17 downto 0);
  horiz_display_start : unsigned(11 downto 0);
  horiz_display_width : unsigned(11 downto 0);
  horiz_sync_width    : unsigned(11 downto 0);
  horiz_total_width   : unsigned(11 downto 0);
  vert_display_start  : unsigned(11 downto 0);
  vert_display_width  : unsigned(11 downto 0);
  vert_sync_width     : unsigned(11 downto 0);
  vert_total_width    : unsigned(11 downto 0);
  hpol                : std_logic;
  vpol                : std_logic;
end record;
type resolution_array is array (natural range <>) of resolution_t;
constant RESOLUTION : resolution_array(0 to 17) := (
  0  => (
    -- 25.18 MHz 640x480 @ 60Hz
    divide_count        => 8d"9",
    mult_integer        => 8d"50",
    mult_fraction       => 10d"000",
    divide_integer      => 8d"44",
    divide_fraction     => 18d"125",
    horiz_display_start => 12d"47",    -- BP - 1
    horiz_display_width => 12d"640",
    horiz_sync_width    => 12d"96",
    horiz_total_width   => 12d"799",   -- 800 - 1
    vert_display_start  => 12d"32",    -- 33 - 1
    vert_display_width  => 12d"480",
    vert_sync_width     => 12d"2",
    vert_total_width    => 12d"524",   -- 525 - 1
    hpol                => '0',
    vpol                => '0'
```

```
    ),
    1  => (
      -- 31.5Mhz 640x480 @ 72 Hz...
```

We will define all 17 modes in our code. Only the first/default mode is shown here. With this, we can now create our state machine to load the VGA and PLL.

The state machine is divided into two sections: CFG_WR0-2 loads the **MMCM** with our clock configuration settings, while CFG_WR3-5 loads the resolution for the VGA controller. The state machine operates as follows:

1. It detects a button press and starts loading MMCM parameters.

2. CFG_WR0 checks which valid signals are active. In the event that only wvalid or awvalid is active, we have two substates, CFG_WR1 and CFG_WR2, to await the missing valid signal.

3. Once both valid signals are active, we wait for the BRESP, then advance the register write state. We must write all 24 registers in the MMCM before we move on to the VGA.

4. After the MMCM is written, we wait for the PLL to re-lock then program the VGA controller.

5. The VGA portion of the state machine operates similarly to the MMCM portion and we advance through the VGA parameters. Once complete, we go back to idle.

6. The VGA core handles the monitor timing and the display output.

Depending on your monitor type, you may not be able to display all resolutions. Some monitors are also more forgiving of timing problems than others. My particular monitor could go to 1280x1024 @ 85 Hz but no higher. Due to timing constraints, I would recommend not going higher than 1280x1024 @ 75 Hz.

Let's now take a deeper dive into the timing generator.

The VGA monitor timing generator

To handle sync generation, we'll need two counters. The first counter, horiz_count, will generate the timing and pixel output for each scanline. The second counter, vert_count, counts the number of scanlines to determine when to start displaying pixels and generate the Vsync:

SystemVerilog

```
  if (horiz_count_v >= horiz_total_width) begin
    horiz_count_v = '0;
    if (vert_count_v >= vert_total_width) vert_count_v <= '0;
```

```
  else vert_count_v = vert_count_v + 1'b1;
  // Start reading from memory address 0x0, increment by pitch value at
  // the start of each active scan line.
  if (vert_count_v <= vert_display_start + 1) begin
    mc_addr <= '0;
  end else if (vert_count_v <= vert_display_start + vert_display_width)
begin
    mc_addr <= mc_addr + pitch;
  end

  // Issue a memory read request at the beginning of each active scan line
  if ((vert_count_v > vert_display_start) &&
      (vert_count_v <= (vert_display_start + vert_display_width))) begin
    mc_req   <= ~mc_req;
    mc_words <= pitch[$high(pitch):4]; // in units of 16-byte words
  end
  if (vert_count_v == vert_display_start) begin
    vga_sync_toggle <= ~vga_sync_toggle;
  end
  if (vert_count_v == vert_display_start) vga_sync_toggle <= ~vga_sync_
toggle;
end else
  horiz_count_v <= horiz_count_v + 1'b1;
horiz_count <= horiz_count_v;
vert_count  <= vert_count_v;
```

VHDL

```
if horiz_count_v >= horiz_total_width then
  horiz_count_v := (others => '0');
  if vert_count_v >= vert_total_width then
    vert_count_v := (others => '0');
  else
    vert_count_v := vert_count_v + 1;
  end if;
  -- Start reading from memory address 0x0, increment by pitch value at
the start of
  -- each active scan line.
```

```
   if vert_count_v <= vert_display_start + 1 then
      mc_addr <= (others => '0');
   elsif vert_count_v <= vert_display_start + vert_display_width then
      mc_addr <= mc_addr + pitch;
   end if;
   -- Issue a memory read request at the beginning of each active scan line
   if vert_count_v > vert_display_start and vert_count_v <= vert_display_
start + vert_display_width then
      mc_req   <= not mc_req;
      mc_words <= pitch(pitch'high downto 4); -- in units of 16-byte words
   end if;
   if vert_count_v = vert_display_start then
      vga_sync_toggle <= not vga_sync_toggle;
   end if;
else
   horiz_count_v := horiz_count_v + 1;
end if;
horiz_count <= horiz_count_v;
vert_count  <= vert_count_v;
```

The preceding code zeroes out the horiz_count signal when we reach the end of a scanline. You'll notice that the comparison is greater than or equal to a horiz_total_width signal. The way we update counters doesn't stop or restart the timing generation. This will ensure that if we were to accidentally put something out of range, the counts will recover by resetting back to 0. Similarly, we do the same with the vertical count.

This block also generates a few other parameters we need for displaying pixels. The first is the scanline information. This calculates the scanline currently being operated on. Scanline zero would be the first displayable scanline.

We also register the address for the current scanline and the pitch, which is also the number of 16-byte words to be read for each scanline. Note that this number can be greater than or equal to the number of bytes we need.

It helps when you are using slower parts or trying to achieve a higher clock speed to look for opportunities to precalculate mathematical operations when you can. In the following code, I'm calculating the address we need:

```
mc_addr   <= scanline + pitch;
```

This is because you'll see in the code where we read from memory that we need to make sure we don't violate AXI rules:

```
vga_hblank <= not ((horiz_count_v ?> horiz_display_start) and (horiz_
count_v ?<= (horiz_display_start + horiz_display_width)));
vga_hsync  <= polarity(1) xor not (horiz_count_v ?> (horiz_total_width -
horiz_sync_width));
vga_vblank <= not ((vert_count_v ?> vert_display_start) and (vert_count_v
?<= (vert_display_start + vert_display_width)));
vga_vsync  <= polarity(0) xor not (vert_count_v ?> (vert_total_width -
vert_sync_width));
```

You'll see that we are generating the Hsync and Vsync as shown in *Figure 9.1* at the end of the scanline and the display window. We calculate the time to generate this by creating the sync from the horizontal or vertical total minus the sync width. We also need to use our polarity registers to generate the correct sync polarity. Exclusive-OR gates can be used as programmable inverters.

We also generate the blank signals. These aren't technically necessary unless you are using a real DAC, as those signals are used to zero out the pixel output, although you could use the blanks to 0 out the pixel data during that time. I've included them since, in simulation, it can assist in ascertaining when data is expected to be output.

In this section of code, we also generate a toggle `mc_req` signal for requesting data to be displayed:

```
if (vga_hblank && ~last_hblank && ~vga_vblank)
   mc_req <= ~mc_req;
last_hblank   <= vga_hblank;
```

We are taking advantage of the *dead time* of the display to prefetch the next scanline of data. When `hblank` goes away, in other words, the rising edge of `hblank`, we'll generate a request as long as we are not in the vertical blanking period.

Now that we have an operational display, we need something interesting to display on it.

Displaying text

A text character in its oldest and simplest form is a bitmap. Modern operating systems may use things such as TrueType, which can scale cleanly and easily at different resolutions. However, the oldest form of displaying text was to store a pattern in memory and then copy it to the screen. In this section, we'll introduce a character generator, which will allow us to easily display text on the screen.

I've included a file called `text_rom.sv`. It is essentially a lookup table:

```
module text_rom
  (input              clock, // Clock
   input [7:0]        index, // Character Index
   input [2:0]        sub_index, // Y position in character
   output logic [7:0] bitmap_out);
```

Functionally, we can view the `text_rom` in the following diagram:

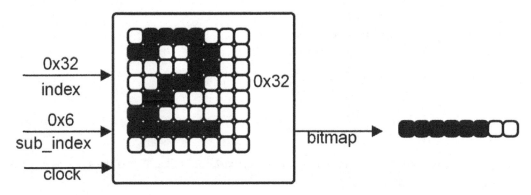

Figure 10.9: text_rom

Every clock cycle, a character is looked up using the index and the subindex references the scanline of the character. In *Figure 10.9*, you can see an example where we are requesting the 0x32 character, which is the **American Standard Code for Information Interchange (ASCII)** for the number 2. We are asking for the seventh scanline of the character (note that the first scanline is `sub_index = 0`). This returns the value `0xFC` on the next cycle, which represents the pixels from the sixth scanline of the number 2.

 ASCII code is one of the major standards for encoding text. One nice thing about ASCII is that the numbers 0-9 are encoded from 0x30-0x39.

text_rom.sv contains all the ASIC uppercase and lowercase characters and numbers as well as a few fill characters. ASCII is normally represented by an 8-bit value, so there is plenty of room to add new characters to display:

```
always @(posedge clock)
  case ({index, sub_index})
    ...
    // 2
    {8'h32, 3'h0}: bitmap <= 8'h78;
    {8'h32, 3'h1}: bitmap <= 8'hCC;
    {8'h32, 3'h2}: bitmap <= 8'h0C;
    {8'h32, 3'h3}: bitmap <= 8'h38;
    {8'h32, 3'h4}: bitmap <= 8'h60;
    {8'h32, 3'h5}: bitmap <= 8'hC0;
    {8'h32, 3'h6}: bitmap <= 8'hFC;
    {8'h32, 3'h7}: bitmap <= 8'h00;
```

Here, we can see what the lookup for the number 2, 0x32, looks like. This is the same as what is represented in *Figure 10.9*.

One thing about the way data is stored is that in the application I developed, we'll need to flip the data coming out. I've added the following code:

```
always @* begin
  for (int i = 0; i < 8; i++) begin
    bitmap_out[i] = bitmap[7-i];
  end
end
```

This code flips the bits. Without it, the text will appear reversed. You may or may not need this for your own applications, so it's good to know it exists in the event that you need it or need to remove it.

Back to our top-level VGA. We'll add a string of text with each resolution setting so that when the display is set, we can print out what we have set it to:

```
res_text[0]                        = "  zH06 @ 084x046";
```

Notice that the text is written backward as a string. This is because we are starting from bit 0 of character 0 and building it up to character 15, bit 7.

Requesting memory

For our display, we need to take our memory request signal and synchronize it to the memory controller clock. We'll also use this opportunity to reset the pixel First In **First Out (FIFO)**. Note that we are toggling the request signal at the end of the line, so this provides a couple of key features for our design:

- We won't be displaying anything, so we can simply reset the FIFO.
- We should have quite a bit of time to reset the FIFO and start getting data back for displaying.

We can construct a state machine to handle our memory accesses as shown in the following code block:

SystemVerilog

```
MEM_IDLE: begin
  mem_arvalid <= '0;
  if (^mc_req_sync[2:1]) begin
    mc_addr_reg  <= mc_addr;
    mc_words_reg <= mc_words;
    fifo_rst     <= '1;
    mem_cs       <= MEM_W4RSTH;
  end
end
MEM_W4RSTH: begin
  mc_addr_high <= mc_addr_high_comb;
  len_diff  <= (AXI4_PAGE_SIZE - mc_addr_reg[11:0]);
  if (wr_rst_busy) begin
    fifo_rst <= '0;
    mem_cs   <= MEM_W4RSTL;
  end
end
```

VHDL

```
when MEM_IDLE =>
  if xor(mc_req_sync(2 downto 1)) then
    mc_addr_reg  <= mc_addr;  -- assuming mc_addr is stable an can be
safely registered into mem_clk domain here
```

```
      mc_words_reg <= mc_words; -- assuming mc_words is stable an can be
  safely registered into mem_clk domain here
      fifo_rst      <= '1';
      mem_cs        <= MEM_W4RSTH;
    end if;


  when MEM_W4RSTH =>
    mc_addr_high := mc_addr_high_comb(mc_addr_high'high downto 12);
    len_diff      <= resize(AXI4_PAGE_SIZE - (mc_addr_reg mod AXI4_PAGE_
  SIZE), 13); -- max. value : 4096
    --
    if wr_rst_busy then
      fifo_rst <= '0';
      mem_cs   <= MEM_W4RSTL;
    end if;
```

When we synchronize and detect an edge on the request, we reset the FIFO. The FIFOs provide an output to indicate when they are busy during a reset, so, in the second state, we wait for the reset to go high, then release the reset, and enter the state to wait for it to go low again. We can take advantage of our wait time to calculate the next address and see how many scanlines there are before we reach the 2K (2,048) byte boundary.

Note that we are also capturing the data, address, and word count in the destination clock domain. This is not strictly necessary, however, it does keep it clear when we use the variables that they are on the correct clock domain.

 To be fully compatible with AXI4, when making a burst request over AXI, you cannot cross a 4.096-byte boundary. We must take this into account and break up bursts that might possibly violate this rule.

We'll use these parameters to test for a boundary crossing in the following code block:

SystemVerilog

```
MEM_W4RSTL: begin
  if (~wr_rst_busy) begin
    mem_arid    <= '0;
    mem_araddr  <= mc_addr_reg;
    mem_arsize  <= 3'b100; // 16 bytes
```

```
       mem_arburst <= 2'b01; // incrementing
       mem_arlock  <= '0;
       mem_arvalid <= '1;
       if (mc_addr_high[31:12] != mc_addr_reg[31:12]) begin
         // Look if we are going to cross 4K boundary
         next_addr <= mc_addr_reg  + {len_diff, 4'h0};
         len_diff  <= mc_words_reg - ((len_diff >> 4) + |len_diff[3:0]);
         mem_arlen <= (len_diff >> 4) + |len_diff[3:0] - 1;
         mem_cs <= MEM_W4RDY1;
       end else begin
         mem_arlen   <= mc_words_reg - 1;
         mem_cs <= MEM_W4RDY0;
       end // else: !if(next_addr[12])
     end
   end // case: MEM_W4RSTH
```

VHDL

```
when MEM_W4RSTL =>
  if not wr_rst_busy then
    mem_arid    <= (others => '0');
    mem_araddr  <= std_logic_vector(mc_addr_reg);
    mem_arsize  <= "100";      -- 16 bytes
    mem_arburst <= "01";       -- incrementing
    mem_arlock  <= '0';
    mem_arvalid <= '1';
    --
    if mc_addr_high(mc_addr_high'high downto 12) /= mc_addr_reg(mc_addr_
reg'high downto 12) then
      -- Burst is crossing a 4 KiB address boundary.
      assert len_diff mod BYTES_PER_PAGE = 0 severity failure;
      assert len_diff < 256 * BYTES_PER_PAGE report "burst length out of
range" severity failure;
      mem_arlen <= std_logic_vector(resize((len_diff / BYTES_PER_PAGE) -
1, 8));
      next_addr <= mc_addr_reg + resize(len_diff * BYTES_PER_PAGE, mc_
addr_reg'length);
      len_diff  <= resize(mc_words_reg * BYTES_PER_PAGE - len_diff, len_
diff'length);
```

```
      mem_cs    <= MEM_W4RDY1;
    else
      -- Burst is not crossing a 4 KiB address boundary.
      assert mc_words_reg <= 256 report "burst length out of range"
severity failure;
      mem_arlen <= std_logic_vector(resize(mc_words_reg - 1, 8));
      mem_cs    <= MEM_W4RDY0;
    end if;
  end if;
```

When the reset is released, we can make a request to the memory controller. We have already calculated the next address, so we can test the upper bits to see whether the next address falls into the next 2,048-byte page. Based on the test, we'll either make a single request or a request for the last part of the current 2,048-byte page. In either case, we can move directly to the second request or back to IDLE if the awready signal is high, otherwise, we need to move to a state to wait for awready.

We'll also pre-calculate the address and length of the second request in the event we need it:

SystemVerilog

```
MEM_REQ: begin
  mem_arid    <= '0;
  mem_araddr  <= next_addr;
  mem_arsize  <= 3'b100; // 16 bytes
  mem_arburst <= 2'b01; // incrementing
  mem_arlock  <= '0;
  mem_arvalid <= '1;
  mem_arlen   <= len_diff;
  mem_cs      <= MEM_W4RDY0;
end // case: MEM_W4RSTH
```

VHDL

```
when MEM_REQ =>
  mem_arid    <= (others => '0');
  mem_araddr  <= std_logic_vector(next_addr);
  mem_arsize  <= "100";        -- 16 bytes
  mem_arburst <= "01";         -- incrementing
  mem_arlock  <= '0';
```

```
mem_arvalid <= '1';
mem_arlen   <= std_logic_vector(len_diff(7 downto 0));
mem_cs      <= MEM_W4RDY2;
```

The final state handles the remainder of the scanline if it crosses the 2,048-byte boundary.

To handle the data coming back, we'll use a Xilinx async, xpm_fifo, as shown in the following code block (SystemVerilog instance is shown in the following):

```
// Pixel FIFO
// Large enough for one scanline at 1920x32bpp (480 bytes)
xpm_fifo_async
  #(.FIFO_WRITE_DEPTH      (512),
    .WRITE_DATA_WIDTH      (128),
    .READ_MODE             ("fwft"))
u_xpm_fifo_async
  (.rst                    (fifo_rst),
   .wr_clk                 (mem_clk),
   .wr_en                  (mem_rvalid),
   .din                    (mem_rdata),
   .wr_rst_busy            (wr_rst_busy),
   .rd_clk                 (vga_clk),
   .rd_en                  (vga_pop),
   .dout                   (vga_data),
   .empty                  (vga_empty),
   .rd_rst_busy            (rd_rst_busy));
```

The main thing to observe regarding the FIFO is that we are writing on the memory clock and reading on the VGA pixel clock. In this design, I haven't taken any precautions to make sure the data is loaded for a scanline or to handle exceptions. This results in the memory reads being *fire and forget*, meaning we don't need to wait for and check a response. We have a state machine that makes the request and the data is pushed back into a FIFO to be read out.

The FIFO is configured as **first-word fall-through (FWFT)**, which means the data is ready on the output for immediate use. This also means that the data can be used and the pop signal advances to the next location. In a traditional FIFO, you'd have to pop (the head of the queue) the data and it would be ready on the next cycle. A traditional FIFO has a little better timing, however, a FWFT can be easier to use.

Finally, we need to read from the FIFO and display the output on the screen:

SystemVerilog

```systemverilog
initial begin
    scan_cs = SCAN_IDLE;
  end
always @(posedge vga_clk) begin
  vga_pop <= '0;
  case (scan_cs)
    SCAN_IDLE: begin
      if (horiz_count == horiz_display_start) begin
        if (vga_data[0]) vga_rgb <= ~vga_empty;
        else vga_rgb <= '0;
        scan_cs   <= SCAN_OUT;
        pix_count <= '0;
      end
    end
    SCAN_OUT: begin
      pix_count <= pix_count + 1'b1;
      // Right now just do single bit per pixel
      if (pix_count == 126) begin
        vga_pop <= ~vga_empty;
      end
      if (vga_data[pix_count]) vga_rgb <= '1;
      else vga_rgb <= '0;
      if (rd_rst_busy) scan_cs <= SCAN_IDLE;
    end
  endcase // case (scan_cs)
end
```

VHDL

```vhdl
if rising_edge(vga_clk) then
  if vga_rst or rd_rst_busy then
    scan_cs   <= SCAN_IDLE;
    vga_pop   <= '0';
```

```
        vga_rgb    <= (others => '0');
        pix_count := 0;
    else
      vga_pop <= '0';
      case scan_cs is
        when SCAN_IDLE =>
          if horiz_count = horiz_display_start then
            pix_count := 0;
            if vga_data(pix_count) and not vga_empty then
              vga_rgb <= (others => '1');
            else
              vga_rgb <= (others => '0');
            end if;
            scan_cs    <= SCAN_OUT;
            pix_count := pix_count + 1;
          end if;

        when SCAN_OUT =>
          if vga_data(pix_count) then
            vga_rgb <= (others => '1');
          else
            vga_rgb <= (others => '0');
          end if;
          if pix_count = 126 then
            vga_pop <= not vga_empty;
          end if;
          pix_count := pix_count + 1 when pix_count < 127 else 0;
      end case;
    end if;
  end if;
```

The display state machine is pretty simple. We wait until we reach the first scanline and then, based on the pixel format, we can display it on the screen. This version of the code only supports 1 bpp.

At this point, we can run on the board and we should see VGA output. We've initialized the core to run at 640x480 @ 60 Hz. You may notice some garbage on the screen. This is because it is displaying uninitialized memory.

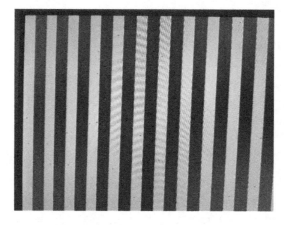

Figure 10.10: First VGA screen attempt

I've fixed this problem in the code you are running. Without a startup clearing of the memory, we are at the mercy of old data or data from the memory controller initialization being displayed:

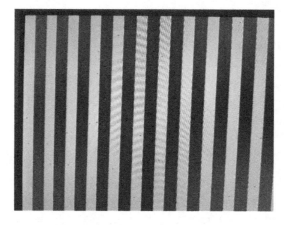

Figure 10.11: Sample resolutions

When you first bring up the project, it will clear the screen and display 640x480 pixels @ 60 Hz. This is accomplished by one state that is only executed when powering on:

SystemVerilog

```
CFG_IDLE0: begin
  update_text   <= ~update_text;
  cfg_state     <= CFG_IDLE1;
end
```

VHDL

```
when CFG_IDLE0 =>
  update_text    <= not update_text;
  cfg_state      <= CFG_IDLE1;
```

We've now completed a simple, yet useful, VGA controller. I hope when looking at this that you can see that writing useful hardware isn't out of reach. Certainly, there is a lot of work that goes on behind the scenes in order to make sure it works for what you want. Take a look at *Figure 10.11* for some example resolutions you might see. In the next section, we'll look at actually testing the VGA controller.

Testing the VGA controller

Most of the testing was done on the board. The turnaround time for a compile is short. The simulation time for a full frame is very long using the Vivado Simulator due to the PLLs and the memory controller simulation. It is, however, a good way to check the first few scanlines of a display to make sure they look okay and that the timing works.

The two main pieces that we need for simulating are the clock generator, which provides the timing for our simulation, and the register load, which initializes the registers in the design:

```
initial clk = '0;
always begin
  clk = #5 ~clk;
end
...
initial begin
  SW        <= 8;
  button_c <= '1;
  repeat (1000) @(posedge clk);
  while (~u_vga.init_calib_complete) @(posedge clk);
  $display("DDR calibration complete");
  while (~u_vga.locked) @(posedge clk);
  button_c <= '1;
  repeat (100) @(posedge clk);
  button_c <= '0;
  repeat (10000) @(posedge clk);
end
```

A more complete testbench could contain tasks for saving video frames, but given the speed, you are better off running on the board. To run on the board, we need to examine the constraints necessary.

Examining the constraints

In the VGA, we have quite a bit of clock domain crossing to handle. The FIFO handles the data, but we have data going from our AXI interface to our memory controller clock and then to the VGA display clock. On top of this, we have a variable frequency VGA clock from the programmable MMCM.

When you implement an MMCM or PLL, Vivado will automatically create a generated clock on the output. Since we will reprogram the PLL during operation, we'll need to override this with the maximum clock we expect to see during operation:

```
create_clock -period 7.41 -name vga_clk -add [get_pins u_clk/clk_out1]
```

Experimenting a bit, I was able to discover that we could reliably run up to about 135 MHz, so I provided this as a clock on the PLL output.

Now, we need to add constraints for our synchronizer inputs. Since these are single signal toggle synchronizers, we'll false-path the input to the first stage of the synchronizer flip flops:

```
set_false_path -from u_vga_core/load_mode_reg*/C -to */load_mode_sync_
reg[0]/D
set_false_path -from u_vga_core/mc_req_reg*/C -to */mc_req_sync_reg[0]/D
set_false_path -from update_text_reg/C -to update_text_sync_reg[0]/D
```

We'll also add in max_delay constraints to make sure to properly constrain the registers between clock domains and not push the tool to meet unreasonable timing requirements. We do this as follows:

```
set_max_delay -datapath_only -from */horiz_display_start_reg* [expr 1.5 *
$vga_clk_period]
set_max_delay -datapath_only -from */horiz_display_width_reg* [expr 1.5 *
$vga_clk_period]
...
set_max_delay -datapath_only -from *sw_capt_reg*/C [expr 1.5 * $clkui_
period]
```

set_max_delay allows us to set the amount of time from any point to any other point. -datapath_only tells the timing engine to not consider clock delays in computing the delays.

Synthesis for the VHDL version and Verilog version differs. A superset of the constraints is in the XDC file. Unused constraints will cause a warning, but not an error. I've done it in this project to keep things common, but for your own projects, you should make sure the constraints do not generate warnings.

With this, we have implemented our design on the board and met timing requirements. In the next chapter, we'll add a keyboard and use the VGA as a capstone project where we can use it to display data from our previous projects.

Summary

In this chapter, we've introduced a better way of displaying data by creating a VGA controller and a character generator. Previously, we were limited to the physical outputs: a row of 16 LEDs, 2 tricolor LEDs, and the 7-segment display. We made good use of them for the simple testing of logic functions, our traffic light controller, and our simple calculator. We've used ROM to display text. We've introduced a programmable PLL and used the DDR2 controller we created in *Chapter 9, Lots of Data? MIG and DDR2*. We're now ready to tackle our capstone project.

In the next chapter, we'll wrap up the book by putting everything together. We can use our VGA to display the output from our temperature sensor, calculator, and microphone. We'll also introduce the PS/2 keyboard interface to provide an easier way to control the system.

Questions

1. You can use an XOR gate as which of the following?

    a. A way to add two bits

    b. A way to multiply two bits

    c. A programmable inverter

2. 2. What resolution are we limited to when generating a VGA controller?

    a. 640x480 @ 60 Hz

    b. 1280x1024 @ 85 Hz

    c. 1920x1200 @ 60 Hz

    d. A resolution our monitor can handle and a pixel clock that we can reliably meet timing for in our design

3. Building a VGA controller in an FPGA is impractical.

    a. True

    b. False

4. How many colors can we represent with 888 or 24 bpp?

    a. 2 colors

    b. 16 colors

    c. 64 K colors

    d. True color, or 16 million colors

5. An AXI-Lite write interface consists of which of the following?

    a. A write address

    b. Write data

    c. A write response

    d. All of the above

6. An AXI-Lite read interface consists of which of the following?

    a. A read address

    b. Read data

    c. A read response

    d. All of the above

    e. (a) and (b)

Answer

1. c) A programmable inverter

2. d) A resolution our monitor can handle and a pixel clock that we can reliably meet timing for in our design

3. b) False

4. d) True color, or 16 million colors

5. d) All of the above

6. d) All of the above

Challenge

The current VGA design only displays black and white. Can you change the design to display two different colors? Can you modify it to use some switches on the board to select these colors?

Further reading

For more information about what was covered in this chapter, please refer to the following links:

- `https://www.xilinx.com/support/documentation/ip_documentation/clk_wiz/v6_0/pg065-clk-wiz.pdf`
- `https://glenwing.github.io/docs/VESA-DMT-1.13.pdf`

Join our community on Discord

Join our community's Discord space for discussions with the authors and other readers:

`https://packt.link/embedded`

11

Bringing It All Together

Take a deep breath and reflect on what you've accomplished in getting to this point in the book. You started the journey with little or no HDL coding knowledge and were unaware of how to build hardware in an FPGA or build a simple testbench. Over the course of this book, you've gone from simple logic functions utilizing switches to light LEDs to writing text out on a VGA screen.

In this chapter, we'll investigate the **Personal System/2 (PS/2)** interface, which, although antiquated, is a way of communicating with a keyboard or mouse that Digilent has chosen to use. We'll then be taking our VGA from *Chapter 10, A Better Way to Display – VGA*, and adapting it to display more data than the resolution we currently have selected. We'll use it to output scan codes from the keyboard so that you can see how it operates. We'll also adapt our temperature sensor to display on the VGA. Finally, we'll take the audio captured by the PDM microphone and display it as a waveform on the screen.

By the end of this chapter, you'll have an interactive piece of hardware that displays keyboard scancodes, temperature in Fahrenheit or Celsius (selectable via the keyboard), and audio data as a waveform.

In this chapter, we are going to cover the following main topics:

- Investigating the keyboard interface
- Project 13 – Handling the keyboard
- Project 14 – Bringing it all together

Technical requirements

The technical requirements for this chapter are the same as those for *Chapter 2, FPGA Programming Languages and Tools*.

To follow along with the examples and the project, you can find the code files for this chapter at the following repository on GitHub: `https://github.com/PacktPublishing/The-FPGA-Programming-Handbook-Second-Edition/tree/master/CH11`.

If you want to implement the project on the board, you'll require a VGA-capable monitor, cable, and USB keyboard.

The Nexys A7 only supports a USB keyboard capable of supporting PS/2 BIOS modes. While writing this chapter, I was only able to find one older keyboard that worked 100%. This is a limitation of the Digilent board. The board uses a **Programmable Interrupt Controllers (PIC)** microcontroller, which handles the complexity of USB and converts the signaling to PS/2, which is a much older and simpler keyboard-and-mouse interface. The PIC source code for interfacing the USB to PS/2 is a closed source. If you can't find a compatible keyboard or don't want to buy one, you can still view the PS/2 output in the **Integrated Logic Analyzer (ILA)**. Here is one keyboard that is known to work: `https://www.amazon.ca/gp/product/B07THJFXJN/ref=ppx_yo_dt_b_search_asin_title?ie=UTF8&psc=1&fpw=alm`. Modern gaming-type keyboards do not appear to work reliably.

Now, let's look at the keyboard interface on the Digilent boards.

Investigating the keyboard interface

I'm sure you are familiar with computer keyboards as a user, but perhaps you don't know how keyboards are physically implemented.

Keyboards consist of a matrix of switches. When you depress a key, you close a circuit. A keyboard controller activates one line at a time and checks to see which lines are connected, which will identify a unique key (assuming only one key is pressed). It will also detect when a key is released:

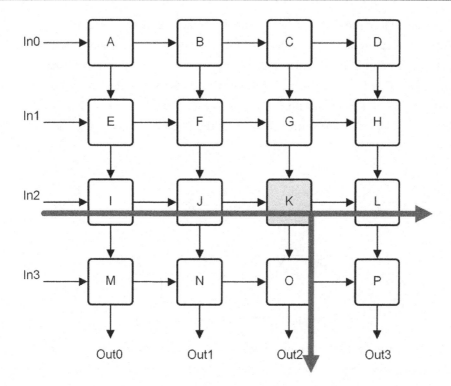

Figure 11.1: Keyboard matrix

The keyboard controller will apply a voltage across each input one at a time in our preceding example: in0, in1, in2, in3, and so on. With the voltage applied, it will monitor the outputs one at a time, out0, out1, out2, out3, and so on, to identify whether any key is pressed. In *Figure 11.1*, when the controller scans input 2, and the *K* key is depressed, output 2 will be active high.

 Modern keyboards are a bit more complex than this, especially gaming keyboards that can monitor for multiple simultaneous keypresses.

When IBM introduced the PS/2 computer, they introduced a new keyboard-and-mouse standard. The keyboard integrated the matrix decoder into the keyboard itself, which simplified the connection to the computer into two wires. The protocol consists of 11-bit transfers that consist of a start bit, data byte, odd parity, and stop bit. The data is transmitted from the **Least Significant Bit (LSB)** to the **Most Significant Bit (MSB)**. On Digilent boards, the keyboard is connected to a USB interface and a PIC microcontroller converts the USB interface to a PS/2 device to simplify FPGA development. The FPGA acts as the host:

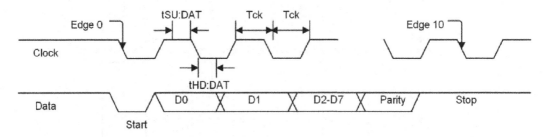

Figure 11.2: PS/2 device-to-host timing

Figure 11.2 shows the waveform of how a device communicates with the host. The device is always responsible for generating the clock to the host. There are two modes of operation: device-to-host (i.e., a keypress) and host-to-device (i.e., setting the state of the caps lock light on the keyboard). We can look at how this protocol works by examining the PS/2 state machine:

SystemVerilog

```
IDLE: begin
  if (counter_30us != COUNT_30us) begin
    counter_30us <= counter_30us + 1'b1;
    xmit_ready      <= '0;
  end else begin
    xmit_ready      <= '1;
  end
  data_counter    <= '0;
  if (~ps2_clk_clean && ps2_clk_clean_last) begin
    counter_30us <= '0;
    state <= CLK_FALL0;
  end else if (~tx_ready && xmit_ready) begin
    counter_30us <= '0;
    tx_data_out    <= {1'b1, ~^tx_data,tx_data, 1'b0};
```

```
    state          <= XMIT0;
  end else if (send_set && xmit_ready) begin
    clr_set        <= '1;
    counter_30us <= '0;
    tx_data_out    <= {1'b1, ~^send_data, send_data, 1'b0};
    state          <= XMIT0;
  end
end
```

In the idle state, we watch for a falling edge of ps2_clock: ~ps2_clk_clean && ps2_clk_clean_last, we receive an external request to send data, or we send the initialization data:

```
CLK_FALL0: begin
  // capture data
  data_capture <= {ps2_data_clean, data_capture[10:1]};
  data_counter <= data_counter + 1'b1;
  state        <= CLK_FALL1;
end
CLK_FALL1: begin
  // Clock has gone low, wait for it to go high
  if (ps2_clk_clean) state <= CLK_HIGH;
end
CLK_HIGH: begin
  if (data_counter == 11) begin
    counter_30us <= '0;
    done         <= '1;
    err          <= ~^data_capture[9:1];
    state        <= IDLE;
    end else if (~ps2_clk_clean) state <= CLK_FALL0;
end
```

The VHDL version can be found under CH11/VHDL/hdl. It follows the same structure.

The next three states handle capturing the data from the device:

1. Capture the data when the clock goes low in CLK_FALL0.

2. Wait for the clock to go high in CLK_FALL1.

3. In CLK_HIGH, if we receive 11 data bits, go back to idle, or wait for the clock to fall and return to CLK_FALL0.

You can see from the FPGA perspective that the receive protocol is very straightforward. We package up the data for use by the instantiating design using the following code:

```
initial begin
  out_state = OUT_IDLE;
  rx_data   = '0;
  rx_user   = '0;
  rx_valid  = '0;
end
always @(posedge clk) begin
  case (out_state)
    OUT_IDLE: begin
      if (done) begin
        rx_data   <= data_capture[8:1];
        rx_user   <= err; // Error indicator
        rx_valid  <= '1;
        out_state <= OUT_WAIT;
      end
    end
    OUT_WAIT: begin
      if (rx_ready) begin
        rx_valid  <= '0;
        out_state <= OUT_IDLE;
      end
    end
  endcase
  if (reset) out_state <= OUT_IDLE;
end
```

This creates an AXI streaming interface out of the ps2_host module.

The PIC microcontroller that acts as the USB to PS/2 interface is essentially a black box into which we have no visibility. This causes a problem if the keyboards are not behaving as expected. As I debugged the problem of finding a keyboard that worked with the Nexys A7, I developed a complete host interface and generated a startup sequence similar to the ones I found online captured by people during startup. The startup sequence is shown in *Figure 11.4*.

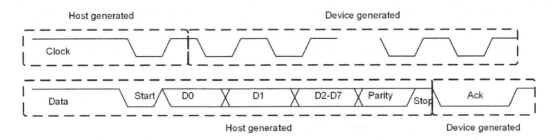

Host generated   Device generated

Clock

Data Start D0 D1 D2-D7 Parity Stop Ack

Host generated   Device generated

Figure 11.3: PS/2 host-to-device timing

When using a PS/2 mouse, host-to-device communication is required. For keyboards, it's not strictly necessary, although to set the keyboard lights, such as caps lock or num lock, the host controls this by issuing commands. *Figure 11.3* shows how this communication occurs. The protocol operates as per the write portion of the following state machine:

```
XMIT0: begin
    // Drop the clock to signal to device and hold low 30us
end
XMIT1: begin
    // put out the data and release the clock to device
    // Wait 20us
end
XMIT2: begin
    // Every clock negedge advance the data
end
XMIT3: begin
    // Wait for clock to drop
end
XMIT4: begin
    // Wait for ACK
end
XMIT5: begin
    // Wait for data to go high
end
XMIT6: begin
    // Wait for clock to rise then go back to idle
end
```

A mouse or keyboard can be connected at any one time, but not both. The project only supports a keyboard. As part of my debugging efforts, I generated the entire initialization represented in the following start_state state machine:

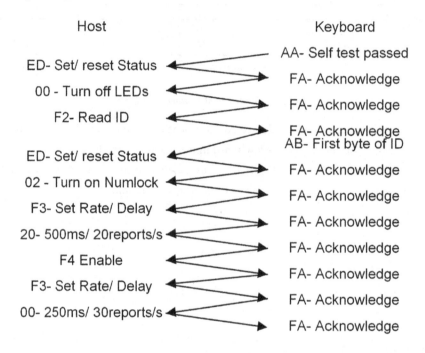

Figure 11.4: PS/2 initialization

The state machine sends and receives the sequence before bringing up the device. If you experience problems with the keyboard you are trying to use, you can use the **ILA** that we introduced in *Chapter 4, Counting Button Presses*, to determine whether the sequence has been followed properly.

In *Figure 11.5*, you can see the keyboard scancodes for each key. Here, we discuss how scancodes are sent from the keyboard to the host. During normal operation, once the keyboard is initialized, scancodes are generated for every keypress:

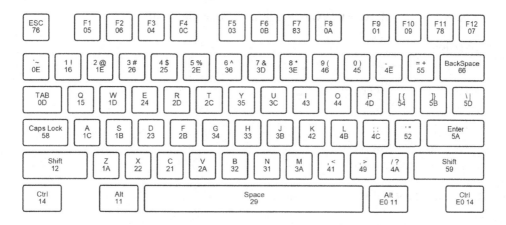

Figure 11.5: PS/2 keyboard scan codes

On the Digilent board, when a key is pressed on the keyboard, the PIC will convert the USB proto-col to PS/2 and generate a scancode representing the keypress to the FPGA. *Figure 11.5* shows the scancodes for most keys. If a key is shifted, a shift modifier code is sent before the key's scancode. If a key is held down, the key will be repeatedly sent every 100 ms. When a key is released, an F0 scancode is sent along with the keycode. Finally, there are some extended keys that will have an E0 code sent prior to the scancode. When this type of key is released, an 0xE0 and 0xF0 value will be sent to represent a keyup event. The FPGA can also communicate with the keyboard for setting the caps lock or num lock LEDs.

Now, let's look at developing a project where we can test the capabilities of the keyboard.

Project 13 — Handling the keyboard

We've looked at what the PS/2 protocol looks like. Let's now put together a simple interface so that we can test our knowledge before we move on to our design integration. The first step is that we need to debounce our PS/2 signals. I've put together a debounce circuit and testbench so we can verify it. This cannot be built as is, but let's look at it. Open up https://github.com/PacktPublishing/The-FPGA-Programming-Handbook-Second-Edition/blob/main/CH11/SystemVerilog/build/debounce.xpr. This version of the code will act as a reusable core. We want to make sure that we only change state after we've seen the CYCLES number of the same value. This will act as our debouncing circuit.

The interface is straightforward, as we can see in the following code:

SystemVerilog

```
module debounce
  #(parameter   CYCLES = 16)
  (input wire   clk,
   input wire   reset,
   input wire   sig_in,
   output logic sig_out);
```

Here we can see the VHDL version.

VHDL

```
entity debounce is
  generic(CYCLES : integer := 16);
  port(clk    : in  std_logic;
       reset  : in  std_logic;
       sig_in : in  std_logic;
       sig_out : out std_logic);
end entity debounce;
```

The actual debouncing is handled by checking to see whether we have maintained the same state for the CYCLES period. Notice that we double-clock the sig_in signal to make sure we don't have metastability problems:

SystemVerilog

```
always @(posedge clk) begin
  sig_in_sync <= sig_in_sync << 1 | sig_in;
  if (sig_in_sync[1] != current_state) begin
    current_state            <= sig_in_sync[1];
    cycle_count              <= '0;
  end else if (cycle_count == CYCLES) begin
    cycle_count              <= '0;
    sig_out                  <= current_state;
  end else begin
    cycle_count              <= cycle_count + 1'b1;
  end
  if (reset) begin
    current_state <= '0;
    cycle_count   <= '0;
```

```
      sig_out          <= '0;
   end
end
```

VHDL

```
if rising_edge(clk) then
   sig_in_sync <= sig_in_sync(0) & sig_in;
   if sig_in_sync(1) /= current_state then
      current_state            <= sig_in_sync(1);
      cycle_count              <= 0;
   elsif cycle_count = CYCLES then
      cycle_count              <= 0;
      sig_out_r                <= current_state;
   else
      cycle_count              <= cycle_count + 1;
   end if;
   if reset then
      current_state <= '0';
      cycle_count   <= 0;
      sig_out_r     <= '0';
   end if;
end if;
```

The nice thing about a small design like this is that it's easy to test exhaustively, as can be seen in the following testbench for SystemVerilog:

```
initial begin
   sig_in    = '0;
   // Test that we don't switch states too soon
   for (int i = 0; i < CYCLES; i++) begin
      sig_in    = '1;
      repeat (i) @(posedge clk);
      sig_in    = '0;
      repeat (CYCLES-i) @(posedge clk);
   end
   sig_in    = '1;
   repeat (100)  @(posedge clk);
   for (int i = 0; i < CYCLES; i++) begin
```

```
    sig_in    = '0;
    repeat (i) @(posedge clk);
    sig_in    = '1;
    repeat (CYCLES-i) @(posedge clk);
  end
  sig_in    = '0;
  repeat (100) @(posedge clk);
  $display("Test Finished!");
  $finish;
end // initial begin
```

The VHDL testbench is very similar. The main difference is a clocked procedure that acts like the repeat () @(posedge clk) of SystemVerilog:

```
procedure wait_nclk(signal clk: std_ulogic; n: positive) is
begin
  for i in 1 to n loop
    wait until rising_edge(clk);
  end loop;
end procedure wait_nclk;
...
  -- Test that we don't switch states too soon
  for i in 0 to CYCLES loop
    sig_in    <= '1';
    wait_nclk(clk, i);
    sig_in    <= '0';
    wait_nclk(clk, CYCLES-i);
  end loop;
  sig_in    <= '1';
  wait_nclk(clk, 100);
  for i in 0 to CYCLES loop
    sig_in    <= '0';
    wait_nclk(clk, i);
    sig_in    <= '1';
    wait_nclk(clk, CYCLES-i);
  end loop;
  sig_in    <= '0';
  wait_nclk(clk, 100);
```

```
    report "Test Finished!";
    finish;
```

The first loop incrementally changes the number of cycles and, the signal is high until we reach the CYCLES threshold and the debounced output switches. Similarly, the second loop does the opposite to change from high to low. *Figure 11.6* shows the simulation output:

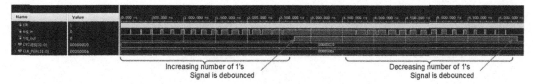

Figure 11.6: Debounce simulation

We have a good debounce circuit, so we can move on to our PS/2 code. We'll make our keyboard handler use AXI streaming to more easily integrate into other designs. The interface to our core will be designed as follows:

SystemVerilog

```
module ps2_host
  #(parameter         CLK_PER = 10,
    parameter         CYCLES  = 16)
  (input wire         clk,
   input wire         reset,
   inout              ps2_clk,
   inout              ps2_data,
   // Transmit data to the keyboard from the FPGA
   input wire         tx_valid,
   input wire [7:0]   tx_data,
   output logic       tx_ready,
   // Data from the device to the FPGA
   output logic [7:0] rx_data,
   output logic       rx_user, // Error indicator
   output logic       rx_valid = '0,
   input wire         rx_ready
   );
```

VHDL

```vhdl
entity ps2_host is
  generic(CLK_PER : integer := 10;
          CYCLES  : integer := 16);
  port(clk     : in std_logic;
       reset   : in std_logic;

       ps2_clk  : inout std_logic;
       ps2_data : inout std_logic;

       -- Transmit data to the keyboard from the FPGA
       tx_valid : in    std_logic;
       tx_data  : in    std_logic_vector(7 downto 0);
       tx_ready : out   std_logic := '1';

       -- Data from the device to the FPGA
       rx_data  : out   std_logic_vector(7 downto 0);
       rx_user  : out   std_logic;
       rx_valid : out   std_logic;
       rx_ready : in    std_logic);
  end entity ps2_host;
```

We have our two tristate signals, ps2_clk and ps2_data. We have a transmit interface that is currently undeveloped. This interface could be used to set the caps lock, repeat rate, or other parameters the keyboard can receive. There is a second bus that reports data received from the keyboard.

Parity is a method of detecting single-bit errors. There are two types of parity, even and odd. Even refers to setting the parity value such that the number of ones in a string of bits is even, and odd refers to setting the parity value such that the number of ones in a string of bits is odd.

Odd parity example:

8'b01010101 parity = 1'b1 would be correct. There is an odd number of ones including parity.

8'b01010101 parity = 1'b0 would be an error. There is an even number of ones including parity.

We do have a user signal, which we'll use to report a parity error if detected.

SystemVerilog

```systemverilog
// Clean up the signals coming in
debounce
  #(.CYCLES    (CYCLES))
u_debounce[2]
  (.clk       (clk),
   .reset     (reset),
   .sig_in    ({ps2_clk,       ps2_data}),
   .sig_out   ({ps2_clk_clean, ps2_data_clean})
   );
```

VHDL

```vhdl
    u_debounce0 : debounce
      generic map(CYCLES    => CYCLES)
      port map   (clk       => clk,
                  reset     => reset,
                  sig_in    => to_x01(ps2_clk),
                  sig_out   => ps2_clk_clean);

    u_debounce1 : debounce
      generic map(CYCLES    => CYCLES)
      port map   (clk       => clk,
                  reset     => reset,
                  sig_in    => to_x01(ps2_data),
                  sig_out   => ps2_data_clean);
```

The first step will be to instantiate two debouncing circuits on the ps2 data lines. In SystemVerilog, this can be done using an array of instances, an example of which is what I used in the preceding code. In SystemVerilog or VHDL, you could use a generate, but then it would require creating arrays of I/Os to index, so I chose two separate instances for VHDL.

There is one new function here that is very important for simulation with VHDL modules. Because VHDL carries the drive strength of a signal, an "H," which is a pull-up value, is not equivalent to a "1." We need to use a resolution function to_x01, which will convert the multiple drive strengths of a VHDL signal to simply an "X," "0," or "1." This allows the VHDL code to properly use the data on ps2_clk and ps2_data.

Now, we need to generate our tristate data:

SystemVerilog

```systemverilog
// Enable drives a 0 out on the clock or data lines
assign ps2_clk  = ps2_clk_en  ? '0 : 'z;
assign ps2_data = ps2_data_en ? '0 : 'z;
```

VHDL

```vhdl
ps2_clk  <= '0' when ps2_clk_en else  'Z';
ps2_data <= '0' when ps2_data_en else 'Z';
```

 VHDL is case insensitive; however, Vivado would not accept a lowercase "z" as valid for the tristate value. I'm not sure if this is a Vivado-specific problem, but it's corrected by using upper case.

We'll need the tristate on data because it can be driven by the host or keyboard. The tristate on the clock is needed for the master implementation. Note that when enable is asserted, we drive a low signal. We tristate the output when driving a one on the enable, relying on the external pullup resistor to raise the logic level high.

With the keyboard interface designed, let's look at how we might test this.

Testing the PS/2

Now that we've got our PS/2 keyboard state machine, we can write a quick testbench.

 Because of the testbench complexity, we'll use the SystemVerilog testbench for both the VHDL and SystemVerilog implementations. This is an advantage of modern tools that support both languages. Of course, it is possible to test it completely with VHDL, but that is an exercise for the user.

Open https://github.com/PacktPublishing/The-FPGA-Programming-Handbook-Second-Edition/blob/main/CH11/SystemVerilog/build/ps2.xpr or https://github.com/PacktPublishing/The-FPGA-Programming-Handbook-Second-Edition/blob/main/CH11/VHDL/build/ps2.xpr. We have a test that can be used to verify that scancodes from the keyboard can be received properly. The main component of the state machine is the send_key task. This task takes in a scancode and converts it to a PS/2 interface:

```
task send_key;
  input [7:0] keycode;
```

```
   input        error;
   begin
     // Generate the PS/2 timing to send the keycode and use
     // error to generate good/ bad parity
   end
endtask // send_key
```

A SystemVerilog task is used to encapsulate a series of events. It also, unlike functions, supports timing constructs. In this case, we are generating the PS/2 data stream for the host.

We'll also add another task to handle the keyboard receive:

```
task rx_key;
   input [7:0] exp_data;
   begin
     // Wait for ED
     edge_count = '0;
     // Wait for first falling edge, then rising edge
     @(negedge ps2_clk);
     @(posedge ps2_clk);
     while (edge_count < 10) begin
       repeat (100) @(posedge clk);
       ps2_clk0 = '1;
       repeat (100) @(posedge clk);
       if (edge_count == 10) ps2_data0 = '1;
       data_capt[edge_count++] <= ps2_data;
       ps2_clk0 = '0;
     end
     repeat (100) @(posedge clk);
     ps2_data0 = '1;
     repeat (100) @(posedge clk);
     ps2_clk0 = '1;
     repeat (100) @(posedge clk);
     ps2_data0 = '0;
     ps2_clk0 = '0;
     repeat (100) @(posedge clk);
     $display("Captured data: %h", data_capt[8:1]);
     if (data_capt[7:0] != exp_data) begin
       $error("Data miscompared! Expected %h != Received %h",
              exp_data, data_capt[8:1]);
     end
```

```
    end
endtask // rx_key
```

This task, or a similar block in the testbench, is required since there is handshaking between the testbench (device) and the host, and the device is responsible for generating the clock. One thing to note about the rx_key task is that it doesn't maintain proper timing. I chose to go down this route as the host only detects edges and this will speed up the simulation. In general, however, it's good practice to match your simulations to what the actual signals look like as this can uncover obscure problems you may otherwise miss.

We'll also want to implement a self-checking function. In order to do this, we'll introduce a construct that allows parallel operation, the fork…join function. *Figure 11.7* shows conceptually what we are trying to accomplish by running the stimulus in one process and checking logic in another process so they can run in parallel:

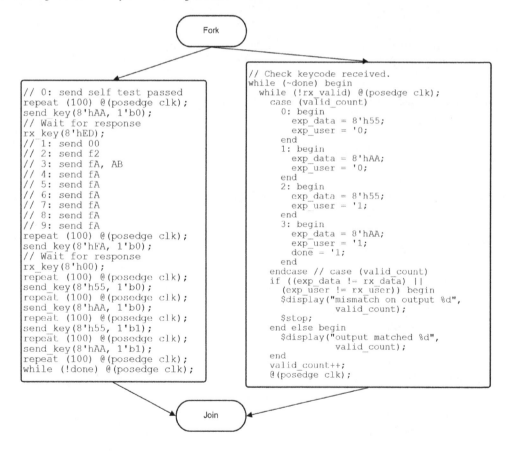

Figure 11.7: Fork join conceptually used in the testbench

The left and right blocks after the fork represent begin...end blocks. Since they are within the fork... join keywords, the two begin...end blocks will run in parallel to one another. The left side generates the stimulus and responses, while the right side checks the last four send key combinations. We can run this in the simulator:

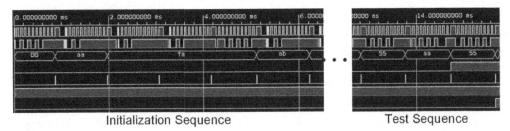

Initialization Sequence   Test Sequence

Figure 11.8: PS/2 test sequence

Figure 11.8 shows the waves from simulating the PS/2 testbench. The initialization sequence represents the keyboard self-test passed through the boot sequence of a computer. The test sequence contains two sets of good data and two sets of errored data. It is good practice to test failure conditions as well as passing conditions. The testbench is self-checking so it will verify both cases.

Now, we've got a better way of getting data into the FPGA via the keyboard and we'll use it in our final project, bringing it all together.

Project 14 — Bringing it all together

You should take a moment to consider the path you've taken over the course of the book. In the beginning, you toggled some switches and lit some lights. You've built some simple designs, such as a calculator and a traffic light controller. You've captured and converted temperature sensor information, captured audio data, and displayed data on a VGA monitor.

Now, we'll look back on these projects to gather a few of them and combine them into a final design. The base will be the VGA we created in *Chapter 10, A Better Way to Display – VGA*. This will allow us to easily display text or graphics. In the previous section, we simulated the PS/2. However, we haven't seen it in operation. Luckily, every keypress generates at least 3 bytes – 1 byte for keydown and 2 bytes for keyup for most keys. We can come up with a clever way of displaying this to the screen. Finally, we can look at the audio data.

> This project is contained within https://github.com/PacktPublishing/
> The-FPGA-Programming-Handbook-Second-Edition/blob/master/CH11/
> SystemVerilog/build/final_project.xpr or https://github.com/
> PacktPublishing/The-FPGA-Programming-Handbook-Second-Edition/blob/
> master/CH11/VHDL/build/final_project.xpr.

We can see the data in the ILA, but what if we could view the waveform on the screen? In the next section, we will show how we can do that using the VGA we developed.

Displaying PS/2 keycodes on the VGA screen

Our PS/2 host interface block provides a convenient way of capturing information via the streaming interface. This interface provides one byte at a time, which we receive from the keyboard. Let's look at how we might capture and display the information on the screen.

To display the VGA mode information, we created a 16-byte (128-bit) array to store the information. This fits nicely into our DDR2 interface implementation, so we'll maintain similar arrays for the PS/2 characters. Since every byte from the PS/2 takes two bytes in our character array, we can define our storage as follows:

SystemVerilog

```systemverilog
typedef struct packed
               {logic [7:0] data;
                logic       error;
                } ps2_t;
localparam PS2_DEPTH = 8;
ps2_t                     ps2_data_capt;
logic [PS2_DEPTH*2-1:0][7:0] ps2_data_store;
logic                     ps2_toggle;
(* async_reg = "TRUE" *) logic [2:0] ps2_sync;
logic                     update_ps2;
logic                     clear_ps2;
logic pix_clk_locked_clk200;
logic pix_clk_locked_clk200_old = '0;
```

VHDL

```vhdl
type ps2_t is record
  data  : std_logic_vector(7 downto 0);
  error : std_logic;
end record;

signal ps2_data_capt      : ps2_t;
signal ps2_data_store     : res_text_capt_t(PS2_DEPTH*2-1 downto 0)
                            := (others => ' ');
signal ps2_toggle         : std_logic := '0';
signal ps2_sync           : std_logic_vector(2 downto 0):= "000";
```

```
attribute ASYNC_REG of ps2_sync : signal is "TRUE";
signal update_ps2           : std_logic:= '0';
signal clear_ps2            : std_logic:= '0';
```

We'll run the PS/2 interface on the 200 MHz clock. Luckily, we made our design clock frequency independent and we can let it know how fast we'll run it by specifying the clock period. The interface from the PS/2 to the VGA will be asynchronous, so we do have to consider clock domain crossing.

Since we'll also be using the keyboard to choose between Fahrenheit and Celsius, we'll need to detect when the *C* or *F* key is pressed and keep track of the state:

SystemVerilog

```
// toggle sync and capture the data
always @(posedge clk200) begin
  if (ps2_rx_valid) begin
    ps2_toggle     <= ~ps2_toggle;
    ps2_data_capt <= '{data: ps2_rx_data, error: ps2_rx_err};
    case (ps2_rx_data)
      8'h2B: ftemp <= '1; // F = fahrenheit
      8'h21: ftemp <= '0; // C = celsius
    endcase
  end
end
```

VHDL

```
process (clk200)
begin
  if rising_edge(clk200) then
    if ps2_rx_valid then
      ps2_toggle     <=  not ps2_toggle;
      ps2_data_capt <= (data => ps2_rx_data, error => ps2_rx_err);
      case ps2_rx_data is
        when x"2B" =>
          ftemp <= '1'; -- F = fahrenheit
        when x"21" =>
          ftemp <= '0'; -- C = celsius
        when others =>
      end case;
    end if;
```

```
    end if;
  end process;
```

If you recall the AXI streaming interface, we'll get a valid signal along with the data. When ps2_rx_valid goes high, we'll toggle a signal that we can capture on the ui_clk signal, the user interface clock, which is the clock used to communicate with the DDR controller. We'll store the data in the structure alongside the signal. Finally, we'll look for the scancode for *F* and *C*, 0x2B and 0x21, respectively. We'll keep track of whether we want Fahrenheit or Celsius by using an ftemp signal.

On the ui_clk domain, we'll look for an edge on the synchronized toggle signal. We'll create a shift register, as shown in *Figure 11.9*. PS/2 scancodes will get the hexadecimal number converted to ASCII characters, they will be pushed into location 0, and each character position will be pushed along the pipeline:

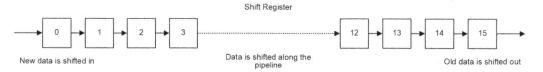

Figure 11.9: Shift register

Shift registers are a common design component, so much so that the slices in the Xilinx FPGAs have special modes to more optimally use them as shift registers. For the most part, this is handled behind the scenes by the tools, although it is possible to force implementations if desired.

We can see how this is coded in the final project:

SystemVerilog

```
  if (^ps2_sync[2:1]) begin
    update_ps2 <= '1;
    for (int i = PS2_DEPTH-1; i >= 0; i--) begin
      if (i == 0) begin
        for (int j = 1; j >= 0; j--) begin
          // Convert nibble into a character
        end
      end else begin
        ps2_data_store[i*2+:2] <= ps2_data_store[(i-1)*2+:2];
      end
    end
  end
```

VHDL

```vhdl
if xor(ps2_sync(2 downto 1)) then
  update_ps2 <= '1';
  for i in PS2_DEPTH-1 downto 0 loop
    if i = 0 then
      for j in 1 downto 0 loop
        // Convert nibble into a character
      end loop;
    else
      ps2_data_store(i*2+1 downto i*2) <= ps2_data_store((i-1)*2+1 downto
(i-1)*2);
    end if;
  end loop;
end if;
```

The outer loop works from the uppermost character, copying the next lower character into it until it reaches character 0, when we convert each nibble into an ASCII character.

Once the register is loaded, we signal the text state machine to update the screen:

SystemVerilog

```systemverilog
end else if (update_ps2) begin // if (^update_text_sync[2:1])
  // We'll start the PS2 output on Line 8
  y_offset     <= 10 * real_pitch;
  clear_ps2    <= '1;
  char_index   <= ps2_data_store[0];
  capt_text    <= ps2_data_store;
  s_ddr_awvalid <= '0;
  s_ddr_wvalid <= '0;
  text_sm      <= TEXT_WRITE0;
```

VHDL

```vhdl
elsif update_ps2 then
  -- We'll start the PS2 output on Line 10
  y_offset     <= 10 * to_integer(unsigned(real_pitch));
  clear_ps2    <= '1';
  char_index   <= char_ps2;
```

```
capt_text      <= ps2_data_store;
s_ddr_awvalid  <= '0';
s_ddr_wvalid   <= '0';
text_sm        <= TEXT_WRITE0;
```

We are reusing the same interface we had with the VGA, modified slightly so that we can pass in the char_index signal, which is used to reference the character we want to display from the ROM lookup table, but also the capt_text signal that we'll use to hold the string we want to display on the screen. We'll expand upon this for the temperature sensor and audio data. When we run this in the final project, you'll see the scancodes' output on the display, as shown in *Figure 11.10*:

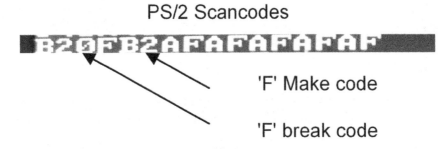

Figure 11.10: Displaying scancodes as keys are pressed

Each keystroke pushes one or more bytes into the shift register from the left to the right. This is why the third byte, B2, which is actually 0x2B in hex, is the make code of the *F* key, F0 is the break code, and B2 is the *F* key. These three bytes represent pressing and releasing the *F* key. You'll also notice a string of AF values, again 0xFA, since it is nibble swapped, which represents the keyboard acknowledgment if you examine the initialization routine in *Figure 11.4*.

With this code, we now can display 8 bytes of PS/2 data on the screen. Let's now look at adding the temperature sensor.

Displaying the temperature sensor data

Previously in *Chapter 7, Math, Parallelism, and Pipelined Design*, we developed the floating-point temperature sensor module. We now need to take the data that would be displayed to the seven-segment display, convert it to ASCII, and display it on the VGA screen. To accomplish this, I've created a wrapper, i2c_wrapper. This module encapsulates the i2c_temp_flt module we developed previously to receive the data from the adt7420, calculate the temperature in Fahrenheit or Celsius, and create the output string, again adhering to the 16 characters we defined previously.

Recall that `temp_valid` and `encoded` are the outputs from the temperature sensor core. The encoded value is a decimal representation, with the decimal point always at position 4. We also have the ability to select Fahrenheit or Celsius, so we'll want to add an *F* or *C* to the output to differentiate the mode we are in:

CH11/SystemVerilog/hdl/i2c_wrapper.sv

SystemVerilog

```
always @(posedge clk) begin
  if (temp_valid) begin
    update_temp               <= ~update_temp;
    capt_temp                 <= "    F 0000.0000";
    capt_temp[9]              <= 8'h0C; // Degree symbol
    if (ftemp) capt_temp[10] <= "F";
    else       capt_temp[10] <= "C";
    for (int i = 7; i >= 0; i--) begin
      if (i > 3) begin
        capt_temp[7-i] <= 8'h30+encoded[i];
      end else begin
        capt_temp[8-i] <= 8'h30+encoded[i];
      end
    end
  end
end // always @ (posedge clk)
```

VHDL

```
process (clk)
begin
  if rising_edge(clk) then
    if temp_valid then
      update_temp               <= not update_temp;
      capt_temp_r(9)            <= x"0C"; -- Degree symbol
      if ftemp then
        capt_temp_r(10) <= x"46"; -- F
      else
        capt_temp_r(10) <= x"43"; -- C
      end if;
```

```
      for i in 7 downto 0 loop
        if i > 3 then
          capt_temp_r(7-i) <= x"3" & encoded(i);
        else
          capt_temp_r(8-i) <= x"3" & encoded(i);
        end if;
      end loop;
    end if;
  end if;
end process;
```

The key point is the update_temp toggle signal since we are running on the 200 MHz clock domain and need to have a clean way of signaling to our display function that new data is available. We define the format of capt_temp and override the F/C based on the ftemp signal.

We can use a trick so that the ASCII for 0-9 is 0x30-0x39. The loop spaces the digits around the decimal point, and we add the integer value to 0x30 to give us the ASCII character to display.

To display the string, we'll use the same function in the text state machine:

SystemVerilog

```
end else if (update_temp_capt) begin
  // We'll start the temperature output on line 16
  y_offset        <= 18 * real_pitch;
  update_temp_capt <= '0;
  char_index      <= capt_temp[0];
  capt_text       <= capt_temp;
  s_ddr_awvalid   <= '0;
  s_ddr_wvalid    <= '0;
  text_sm         <= TEXT_WRITE0;
```

VHDL

```
elsif update_temp_capt then
  -- We'll start the temperature output on line 18
  y_offset         <= 18 * to_integer(unsigned(real_pitch));
  update_temp_capt <= '0';
  char_index       <= capt_temp(0);
  for i in 0 to 15 loop
    capt_text(i)   <= character'val(to_integer(unsigned(capt_temp(i))));
```

```
    end loop;
    s_ddr_awvalid    <= '0';
    s_ddr_wvalid     <= '0';
    text_sm          <= TEXT_WRITE0;
```

When the synchronized update is captured and we are not working on another text update, we'll pass along the captured temperature string and output to the display. One additional enhancement we can make is to create a custom character to represent the degrees symbol.

Adding a custom character to the text ROM

One addition we made is to add the degrees symbol to the ROM characters. You can see where we set this:

```
    capt_temp[9]             <= 8'h0C; // Degree symbol
```

I've selected the first empty location, 0x0C, in the text ROM and created a representation for the degrees symbol. In *Figure 11.11*, you can see how a character is constructed:

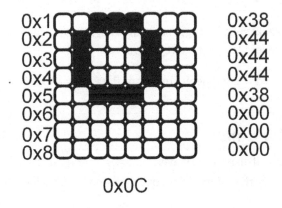

Figure 11.11: Constructing the degrees symbol

There are eight scanlines for every character. Each scanline represents the bits to display. To calculate the bytes, every lit pixel in each nibble needs to be added together. By doing this, we can construct the lookup for the symbol:

SystemVerilog

```
// Degree Symbol
{8'h0C, 3'h0}: bitmap <= 8'h38; // 8'h00111000
{8'h0C, 3'h1}: bitmap <= 8'h44; // 8'h01000100
{8'h0C, 3'h2}: bitmap <= 8'h44; // 8'h01000100
```

```
{8'h0C, 3'h3}: bitmap <= 8'h44; // 8'h01000100
{8'h0C, 3'h4}: bitmap <= 8'h38; // 8'h00111000
{8'h0C, 3'h5}: bitmap <= 8'h00; // 8'h00000000
{8'h0C, 3'h6}: bitmap <= 8'h00; // 8'h00000000
{8'h0C, 3'h7}: bitmap <= 8'h00; // 8'h00000000
```

VHDL

```
-- Degree Symbol
when x"0C" & "000" => bitmap <= x"38"; -- 8b"00111000"
when x"0C" & "001" => bitmap <= x"44"; -- 8b"01001000"
when x"0C" & "010" => bitmap <= x"44"; -- 8b"01001000"
when x"0C" & "011" => bitmap <= x"44"; -- 8b"01001000"
when x"0C" & "100" => bitmap <= x"38"; -- 8b"00111000"
when x"0C" & "101" => bitmap <= x"00"; -- 8b"00000000"
when x"0C" & "110" => bitmap <= x"00"; -- 8b"00000000"
when x"0C" & "111" => bitmap <= x"00"; -- 8b"00000000"
```

https://github.com/PacktPublishing/The-FPGA-Programming-Handbook-Second-Edition/
blob/main/CH11/SystemVerilog/hdl/text_rom.sv

Now that we've completed the temperature sensor data, let's look at how we can display the audio data.

Displaying audio data

The final display section will display the waveform as a raw graphic. There are a couple of choices in terms of how we display the information, but in the end, we'll want to show the amplitude of the wave.

Normally, these types of waveforms are displayed across a screen from left to right, as in *Figure 11.12*:

Figure 11.12: Typical sine wave representation

This type of implementation cannot be done easily and efficiently at the hardware level. For the purposes of the final project, I propose that we display the output vertically. Because the VGA scans pixels horizontally, it would be easier to represent the time axis vertically and the amplitude axis horizontally.

Recall the `pdm_input` module. It captures a 7-bit audio sample that can natively be represented as a dot on a 128-bit scanline segment.

Since we created a reusable design where we can specify the clock frequency, we can use the `pdm_inputs` core as we created it. We will need to add some external logic to buffer the data. Since we'll be displaying vertically, we are limited to fewer than 480 scan lines. We'll limit our display area to 256 scanlines of audio. Since we'll be plotting data and capturing samples in parallel, we'll need a simple dual-port RAM – one read port and one write port:

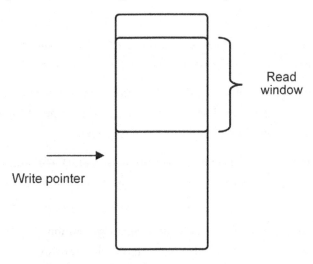

Figure 11.13: Buffering audio data for display

We'll create a storage buffer of 1,024 samples, although 512 would be more than enough. The reason for not using only 256 samples is that there is a possibility of overwriting data before it's read. This will ensure that the 256 samples plotted are consecutive:

SystemVerilog

```
always @(posedge clk200) begin
  if (amplitude_valid) begin
    amplitude_store[amp_wr] <= amplitude;
    amp_wr                  <= amp_wr + 1'b1;
  end
```

```
    amp_data <= amplitude_store[amp_rd];
  end
```

VHDL

```
process (clk200)
begin
  if rising_edge(clk200) then
    if amplitude_valid then
      amplitude_store(amp_wr) <= std_logic_vector(amplitude);
      amp_wr                  <= amp_wr + 1;
    end if;
    amp_data <= amplitude_store(amp_rd);
  end if;
end process;
```

The storage is inferred as we discussed back in *Chapter 6, FPGA Resources and How to Use The*m, the only difference being that the amp_wr pointer is incremented on every sample.

Finally, we create a signal that will update the display on every VSync. This required a modification to the VGA to generate a toggle signal on every VSync. I decided to put the logic in the vga_core module, as VGA sync polarity changes for different resolutions.

To pass the data to the text state machine, I decided to use a FIFO. This allows us to easily cross clock domains, and we can pass the vertical location as well as the scanline segment we want to display.

I create a state machine, wave_sm, that handles the scanline generation. The VHDL closely matches the SystemVerilog, so it's not reproduced here, but it is in the repository:

```
case (wave_sm)
  WAVE_IDLE: begin
    if (^vga_sync_toggle_sync[2:1]) begin
      // get the amplitude data from behind the write pointer
      // by 256 samples
      amp_rd    <= amp_wr - 256;
      rd_count <= '0;
      wave_sm  <= WAVE_READ0;
    end
  end
  WAVE_READ0: begin
    // address to ram valid this cycle
```

```
      amp_rd    <= amp_rd + 1'b1;
      rd_count <= rd_count + 1'b1;
      wave_sm  <= WAVE_READ1;
    end
    WAVE_READ1: begin
      // address to ram valid this cycle
      amp_rd              <= amp_rd + 1'b1;
      rd_count            <= rd_count + 1'b1;
      pdm_push            <= '1;
      pdm_din.address     <= 31 + rd_count;
      pdm_din.data        <= 1'b1 << amp_data;
      if (rd_count[8]) wave_sm <= WAVE_IDLE;
    end
  endcase // case (wave_sm)
```

When vga_sync toggles, we look back by rewinding 256 samples and then read out and push the display segments for 256 scanlines. On the text state side, we will write one scanline at a time:

SystemVerilog

```
end else if (!pdm_empty) begin
  pdm_pop             <= '1;
  char_y              <= '1; // Force only one line to be written
  // update_temp_capt <= '0;
  s_ddr_awvalid       <= '1;
  s_ddr_awaddr        <= pdm_dout.address * real_pitch;
  s_ddr_wvalid        <= '1;
  s_ddr_wdata         <= pdm_dout.data;
  text_sm             <= TEXT_WRITE2;
```

VHDL

```
elsif not pdm_empty then
  pdm_pop             <= '1';
  char_y              <= 7; -- Force only one line to be written
  --update_temp_capt <= '0';
  s_ddr_awvalid       <= '1';
  s_ddr_awaddr        <= "00000" & (pdm_dout.address * real_pitch);
  s_ddr_wvalid        <= '1';
  s_ddr_wdata         <= pdm_dout.data;
  text_sm             <= TEXT_WRITE2;
```

We handle this by setting the char_y count to 7, so we'll only write one scanline for every FIFO pop. We'll also trigger the write here since we don't need to loop over multiple scanlines.

At this point, you should build the project and see what it looks like on the board. Once you download the bitstream, you'll be greeted with a display as seen in *Figure 11.14*:

Figure 11.14: Initial bringup

I would recommend playing some audio or downloading a tone generator to get a more interesting output, as shown in *Figure 11.15*:

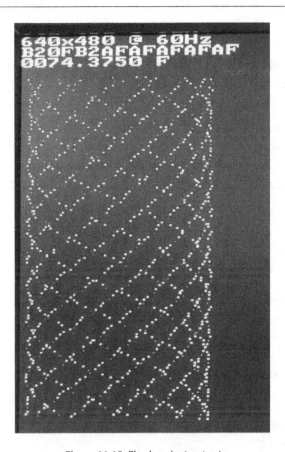

Figure 11.15: Final project output

This screenshot was taken of the final project capturing a tone from a cell phone tone generator application. You can see all the components represented here:

- Resolution
- Scancodes
- Temperature sensor in Fahrenheit
- The audio capture

You've now completed the capstone project of the book. You've brought together some reusable components and created a useful application from them. No longer restricted by a few LEDs, you've created a graphical display and added output text and graphics to it.

Summary

In this chapter, we've explored the PS/2 keyboard interface by creating an interface that can write to and receive data from the keyboard. With the PS/2 ready to use, we've then taken pieces from the last few chapters: the VGA to display our data, the temperature sensor to provide some numerical output, and the PDM interface so we can add something more graphics oriented. You've now completed the journey from basic logic gates to coding something that can display text and graphics on the screen. It's possible to go much further with writing pure SystemVerilog, but first, we will explore some more external interfaces using PMODs and then implement a Xilinx NIOS processor.

Questions

1. PS/2 keyboards use a two-wire interface consisting of:

    a. Keyup/keydown

    b. Clock/data

    c. Data in/data out

2. A scancode is generated whenever a key is:

    a. Pressed

    b. Released

    c. Held down

    d. All of the above

3. To display the scancodes on the VGA, we used:

    a. A hex-to-ASCII converter

    b. A shift register

    c. A BCD encoder

    d. (a) and (b)

4. To display audio data, how was the text state machine modified?

    a. It takes in 128 bits of graphical data and writes that to the correct address for that scan line using text_sm.

    b. The graphics are mapped to characters and we reuse the text_sm state variable.

    c. We created a new graphics state machine.

5. To trigger an audio update, we:

    a. Update on every sample captured

    b. Update every second

    c. Update on every vertical sync

    d. Update whenever nothing else is going on

Answers

1. b
2. d
3. d
4. c
5. c

Challenge

Usually, audio data is displayed horizontally. Can you modify the code to create a horizontal display? This is a challenging problem and could take a little while to get right. Here are a couple of hints:

- You may want to clear the area and then simply plot the dots that need to be set.
- You may want to buffer up 128 bits of each scanline and use the existing FIFO interface to display the data.

There are a bunch of ways to accomplish this, but you should be able to find one that works.

Further reading

For more information about what was covered in this chapter, please refer to the following link:

- `https://www.avrfreaks.net/sites/default/files/PS2%20Keyboard.pdf`

Join our community on Discord

Join our community's Discord space for discussions with the authors and other readers:

`https://packt.link/embedded`

12

Using the PMOD Connectors – SPI and UART

In the previous chapter, we focused on putting together everything we learned throughout the book. We took our temperature sensor, which relied on math and pipelining, our VGA controller, which had multiple clock domains and state machines, and our character generator. We modified our state machines to display the waveform from our microphone and made a simple project to bring it all together. Now we'll take a look at what to do if we have external devices to connect.

Up until now, we've focused on the resources that are built into the FPGA and on the board. You have probably noticed that the Nexys A7 board has five black connectors, two on the left-hand side, and three on the right-hand side of the board. These are Digilent **Peripheral MODule** connectors or **PMODs**.

PMOD connectors allow system designers to purchase pre-made daughter cards or to design their own cards to interface with the FPGA on the board. PMOD connectors in general follow a specification; however, if you are designing your own boards, you can deviate. The specification can be found at https://digilent.com/reference/pmod/start.

By the end of this chapter, we will have created AXI reusable components for a **Universal Asynchronous Receiver-Transmitter (UART)** and a **Serial Peripheral Interface (SPI)** bus.

In this chapter, we are going to cover the following main topics:

- Understanding **Peripheral Modules (PMODs)**
- Introduction to **Universal Asynchronous Receiver-Transmitter (UART)**
- Understanding **Serial Peripheral Interface (SPI)**

Technical requirements

The technical requirements for this chapter are the same as those for *Chapter 2, FPGA Programming Languages and Tools*.

To follow along with the examples and the project, you can find the code files for this chapter at the following repository on GitHub: `https://github.com/PacktPublishing/The-FPGA-Programming-Handbook-Second-Edition/tree/main/CH12`.

If you wish to use the PMODs that are used in this section, they can be found on Digilent's website: `https://digilent.com/shop/fpga-boards/accessories/pmod-expansion-modules/`

UART PMOD

The UART PMOD can be found at `https://digilent.com/shop/pmod-usbuart-usb-to-uart-interface/`. Alternatively, you can use the UART on the board by using the pins defined in the XDC file if you don't wish to use the PMOD.

ACL2 PMOD

The ACL2 PMOD can be found at `https://digilent.com/shop/pmod-acl2-3-axis-mems-accelerometer/`. Alternatively, the Nexys A7 includes the same part on the board and you can simply use the pins for the SPI bus defined in the XDC file for the Nexys A7.

If you do decide to use the built-in components, feel free to skip over the PMOD connector sections below and skip to the UART directly.

Understanding Peripheral Modules (PMODs)

Digilent introduced the PMOD connector as a way to provide a standardized interface for its development boards. The goal of the PMOD specification is to allow the development of lower-speed daughter cards, such as I2C, SPI, UART, and **General-Purpose Input/Output (GPIO)** peripherals. The standard is open and has been adopted by multiple companies both for their development boards and to provide different PMODs for developers.

> PMOD connectors primarily provide low-speed connections of a predefined type. In practice, the power connections are the only pins that are constant, and the others could be used for any signaling up to about 100MHz operation, even though this would technically be beyond the original spec.

From the Nexys A7 perspective, four of the PMODs connect to GPIO and the fifth is dual-purpose analog/digital.

Pin	PMOD JA	PMOD JB	PMOD JC	PMOD JD	PMOD XADC
1	C17	D14	K1	H4	AD3P – A13
2	D18	F16	F6	H1	AD10P – A15
3	E18	G16	J2	G1	AD2P – B16
4	G17	H14	G6	G3	AD11P – B18
7	D17	E16	E7	H2	AD3N – A14
8	E17	F13	J3	G4	AD10N – A16
9	F18	G13	J4	G2	AD2N – B17
10	G18	H16	E6	F3	AD11N – A18

Table 12.1: Nexys A7-100T PMOD pinouts

On the Nexys A7, all the pins use 3.3v logic, so inputs to the device should not exceed this value. If you need to connect to something other than 3.3v logic, you will need to investigate using level shifters. *Figure 12.1* shows a PMOD connector and the signal numbering on it. You can see from the connector that there are 8 user pins that we'll discuss based on the PMOD type, plus power and ground signals.

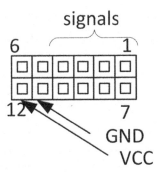

Figure 12.1: PMOD pinout

One thing that we haven't touched on yet is that the 7 series and later devices from Xilinx all have a multiport **Xilinx Analog-to-Digital Converter (XADC)**. The XADC PMOD can be used as a 1-megasample-per-second ADC. We will not be using this functionality, but more information can be found at https://docs.xilinx.com/r/en-US/ug480_7Series_XADC.

Note that the PMOD connectors on the board have 12 pins. The PMOD specification defines a 12-pin version and the 12 pins can be split into two 6-pin PMODs, pins 1-6 and 7-12, as we'll see in the following tables. You'll see that most PMOD types have a six-pin variant, such as Type 1, and a 12-pin variant, such as Type 1A.

There are several standard interface types defined by Digilent.

PMOD Type 1 and 1A

The PMOD Type 1 and 1A are defined for GPIO pins from the FPGA. This allows 4 or 8 GPIOs to be defined for a daughter card. Examples of these kinds of cards are a button array, a seven-segment display, and a user-defined board.

An example of the type 1 PMOD is the Digilent CON1 (`https://digilent.com/shop/pmod-con1-wire-terminal-connectors/`).

Pin #	Signal	Direction	Alternate Signal	Alternate Direction	Type 1	Type 1A
1	IO1	I/O	-	-	X	X
2	IO2	I/O	PWM	OUT	X	X
3	IO3	I/O	-	-	X	X
4	IO4	I/O	-	-	X	X
5	GND	-	-	-	X	X
6	VCC	-	-	-	X	X
7	IO5	I/O	-	-		X
8	IO6	I/O	PWM	OUT		X
9	IO7	I/O	-	-		X
10	IO8	I/O	-	-		X
11	GND	-	-	-		X
12	VCC	-	-	-		X

Table 12.2: PMOD Type 1 and 1A pinout

Note that the direction is user-defined based upon the daughter card installed. Now we can look at some of the standard bus-based types.

PMOD Type 2 and 2A

The PMOD Type 2 and 2A are defined for SPI and extended SPI ports, which are discussed in the SPI section later in this chapter. It's possible on some SPI interfaces that not all pins are necessary and some might be left unconnected. Also, for Type 2A, expanded SPI, any additional pins required for the interface would show up on the GPIO pins and can be seen as alternate pins.

An example of a PMOD Type 2A interface is Digilent's PMODRF2. `https://www.mouser.com/datasheet/2/690/pmodrf2_rm-845761.pdf`

Pin #	Signal	Direction	Alternate Signal	Alternate Direction	Type 2	Type 2A
1	CS – Chip select	OUT	-	-	X	X
2	MOSI – Master output serial input	OUT	-	-	X	X
3	MISO – Master input, serial output	IN	-	-	X	X
4	SCK – Serial clock	OUT	-	-	X	X
5	GND	-	-	-	X	X
6	VCC	-	-	-	X	X
7	GPIO – General Purpose IO	I/O	INT	IN		X
8	GPIO – General Purpose IO	I/O	RESET	OUT		X
9	GPIO – General Purpose IO	I/O	CS2	OUT		X
10	GPIO – General Purpose IO	I/O	CS3	OUT		X
11	GND	-	-	-		X
12	VCC	-	-	-		X

Table 12.3: PMOD Type 2 and 2A pinout

 CS is usually defined as active low.

PMOD Type 3 and 3A

The PMOD Type 3 and 3A are defined for UART and extended UART ports. Like the SPI port, un-used pins may be used as GPIO ports. We will discuss the UART signaling later in this chapter.

An example of a PMOD Type 3 is the RS232 interface: `https://digilent.com/shop/pmod-rs232-serial-converter-and-interface-standard/`.

An example of a PMOD Type 3A is the Low Power Bluetooth® Pmod™ Board: `https://www.renesas.com/us/en/products/wireless-connectivity/bluetooth-low-energy/us159-da14531evz-low-power-bluetooth-pmod-board-renesas-quick-connect-iot`.

Pin #	Signal	Direction	Alternate Signal	Alternate Direction	Type 3	Type 3A
1	CTS – Clear to send	IN	GPIO	I/O	X	X
2	TXD – Transmit Data	OUT	-	-	X	X
3	RXD – Receive Data	IN	-	-	X	X
4	RTS – Request to send	OUT	GPIO	I/O	X	X
5	GND	-	-	-	X	X
6	VCC	-	-	-	X	X
7	GPIO – General Purpose IO	I/O	INT	IN		X
8	GPIO – General Purpose IO	I/O	RESET	OUT		X
9	GPIO – General Purpose IO	I/O	-	-		X
10	GPIO – General Purpose IO	I/O	-	-		X
11	GND	-	-	-		X
12	VCC	-	-	-		X

Table 12.4: PMOD Type 3 and 3A pinout

PMOD Type 4, 5, and 5A

PMOD type 4, 5, and 5A are used for controlling one or more H-bridges. These are for motor control and speed measurement. For further information, see the Digilent PMOD specifications.

PMOD Type 6 and 6A

These PMOD types are used for I2C busses. Like the other busses, they cover expanded versions of the bus as well.

An example of a PMOD Type 6A is the Air Quality Sensor ZMOD4510: https://community. element14.com/challenges-projects/design-challenges/low-power-iot/b/blog/posts/ smart-air-quality-monitor-3---exploring-air-quality-sensor-zmod4510-and-pmod-type-6a-extended-i2c.

Pin #	Signal	Direction	Alternate Signal	Alternate Direction	Type 6	Type 6A
1	NC	-	INT	IN	X	X
2	NC	-	RESET	IN	X	X
3	SCL	I/O	-	-	X	X
4	SDA	I/O	-	-	X	X
5	GND	-	-	-	X	X
6	VCC	-	-	-	X	X
7	GPIO	I/O	INT	IN		X
8	GPIO	I/O	RESET	OUT		X
9	GPIO	I/O	-	-		X
10	GPIO	I/O	-	-		X
11	GND	-	-	-		X
12	VCC	-	-	-		X

Table 12.5: PMOD Type 6 and 6A pinout

Finally let's look at the I2S version of the interface.

PMOD Type 7 and 7A

I2S is a bus used for audio data and is beyond the scope of this book. Digilent does sell I2S PMODs, namely the PMODI2S and PMODI2S2, if you wanted to explore this further.

Pin #	Signal	Direction	Alternate Signal	Alternate Direction	Type 6	Type 6A
1	LRCLK	OUT	-	-	X	X
2	DAC DATA	OUT	-	-	X	X
3	ADC DATA	IN	-	-	X	X
4	BCLK	OUT	-	-	X	X
5	GND	-	-	-	X	X
6	VCC	-	-	-	X	X
7	GPIO	I/O	-	-		X
8	GPIO	I/O	-	-		X
9	GPIO	I/O	MCLK	OUT		X
10	GPIO	I/O	-	-		X

| 11 | GND | - | - | - | | X |
| 12 | VCC | - | - | - | | X |

Table 12.6: PMOD Type 7 and 7A pinout

The above tables outline the connections for the different types.

Now let's focus on UART.

Introduction to Universal Asynchronous Receiver-Transmitter (UART)

The UART interface is one of the oldest interfaces still active and in use. It was developed in the 1960s by Digital Equipment Corporation for its PDP-1 minicomputer.

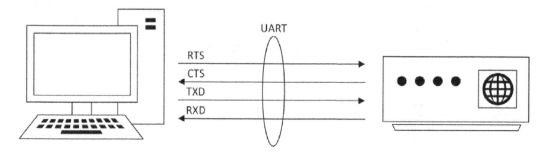

Figure 12.2: Serial connection between a computer and test equipment

Today it is used as a debug port from televisions to test equipment. It's commonly used to communicate with embedded processors like the Microblaze that we will use in *Chapter 13, Embedded Microcontrollers using the Xilinx MicroBlaze*.

Let's take a look at the physical connections of the UART bus.

Bus interface

The UART interface is a slow speed compared to modern-day interfaces. Current serial interfaces such as USB or PCIe lanes can be multiple gigabits per second. UART is a serial interface that can be run in full duplex where data is sent and received simultaneously, or half duplex where RX and TX do not run at the same time. In the design we will develop here it will max out around 75 Kbps.

As we saw from the PMOD definition, the physical interface consists of a required signal a **Receive Line (RXD)** and a **Transmit Line (TXD)**. There are also two optional flow control signals, **Clear to Send (CTS)** and **Request to Send (RTS)**. The RXD and TXD signals consist of serialized data of 7 or 8 bits, a start bit, an optional parity followed by 1 or 2 stop bits. An example of the data format can be seen in *Figure 12.2*. In order for two UARTS to connect, they must agree on a baud rate.

> Baud rate refers to the speed that the interface will run at. Examples of common baud rates are 300 **bits per second (bps)**, 1200 bps, 9600 bps, 14400 bps, 56kbps, and 112kbps. There are many options, however both UARTs must agree on the rate.

Once we have selected a rate to operate at, we can then generate a clock frequency to generate or capture data. Lower-speed UARTs run too slowly to generate a reliable clock using just a PLL and even if you try to match a baud rate, there will be a tiny error between the RX and TX since they both generate clocks independently. This is where oversampling comes into play. Typically, a clock faster than the baud rate is generated and the incoming data is sampled at a multiple of the baud rate. 8x or 16x is typical. The design we will develop will use 7x oversampling. Oversampling gives us a much larger margin of error for mismatched rates. In the event the rates are too mismatched for even oversampling to overcome, we can use parity checking to catch errors and abort the connection.

Now let's see what the UART looks like on the wire.

Waveform

Here we can see what the RXD or TXD looks like using just a clock. *Figure 12.3* shows a serial stream with 8 data bits, parity, and two stop bits.

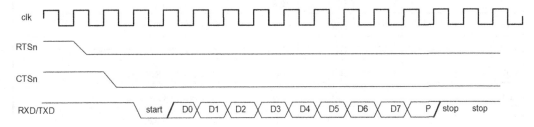

Figure 12.3: UART waveform

The clock shown is for reference and is aligned to the data simply for convenience. The clock is not part of the interface itself. As we mentioned, the UART needs to be set to match the other side and we will discuss sampling shortly to show why we don't actually need the clock as shown. When the UART is idle, the bus is held high. When it is pulled low for a one-bit period, it signifies a start. The **RTSn** and **CTSn** are optional and reflect whether the receiver and transmitter are ready. This is an example of hardware handshaking. There is also a mechanism for software handshaking; however, we will not be discussing that here.

Register interface

When we develop **Intellectual Property (IP)** that has an equivalent closed source implementation or we are trying to reimplement an older piece of IP, it's often a good idea to keep the register interface the same. In the case of a UART, one of the most common UARTs is the 16550 so we will model our interface on this. This has the advantage of allowing us to reuse drivers or at least give us a starting point of open source software.

A standard 16550 UART register map looks as follows.

Address	DLAB	R/W	Reset	Register	Definition
000	0	R	0x0	RBR	Receive Buffer Register
000	0	W	0x0	THR	Transmit Holding Register
000	1	R/W	0xF7	DLL	Divisor Register LSB
001	0	R/W	0x0	IER	Interrupt Enable Register
001	1	R/W	0x0	DLM	Divisor Register MSB
010	x	R	0x1	ISR	Interrupt Status Register
010	X	W	0x0	FCR	FIFO Control Register
011	X	R/W	0x0	LCR	Line Control Register
100	X	R/W	0x0	MCR	Modem Control Register
101	X	R	0x0	LSR	Line Status Register
110	X	R	0x0	MSR	Modem Status Register
111	X	R/W	0x0	SPR	Scratch Pad Register

Table 12.7: 16550 UART Register definition

The register interface looks a little convoluted and limited. Understand that this is really a holdover from the original UARTs developed for personal computers with limited address space. It fits snugly in I/O space for an IBM PC. Let's now look at the registers and how they are used.

RBR — Receive Buffer Register

Reading this register provides the data received by the device. When a FIFO is used in the UART, this will be the oldest data received by the UART. It's important for the processor to keep up with the UART data or some may be lost. In our later project, data from the PC will show up here.

THR — Transmit Holding Register

Data written to this register will be pushed into the FIFO when used or shifted out when not used. The processor should check the THR empty flag before writing the register to ensure the UART is ready for data.

IER — Interrupt Enable Register

This register provides the mechanism for enabling the interrupts that the UART can generate for the processor.

7	6	5	4	3	2	1	0
Reserved	Reserved	Reserved	Reserved	Modem Status Register (MSR) change	Line Status Register (LSR) change	Transmit Hold Register (THR) empty	RX data available

Table 12.8: Interrupt Enable Register

ISR — Interrupt Status Register

The Interrupt Status Register provides feedback to the processor on what caused an interrupt to fire. The register is cleared when read.

Bit 0 signals an interrupt is pending when set to 0x0.

The interrupt is defined by the following table.

Bit 3	Bit 2	Bit 1	Meaning	To clear
0	0	0	MSR change	MSR Read
0	0	1	THR change	IIR Read or THR Write
0	1	0	RX data available	RBR Read
0	1	1	LSR change	LSR Read
1	1	0	Character timeout	RBR Read

Table 12.9: Interrupt Status Register

FCR – FIFO Control Register

The FIFO Control Register controls the UART FIFO behavior.

Bit	Field	Definition
0	FIFO Enable	0 = Disable, 1 = Enable
1	Clear RX FIFO	Write 0x1 to clear the RX FIFO
2	Clear TX FIFO	Write 0x1 to clear the TX FIFO
3	DMA Mode	The UART doesn't currently support it, but it could be added
4	Reserved	Reserved
5	Reserved	Reserved
7:6	FIFO Depth	0x00 – 1 byte 0x01 – 4 bytes 0x10 – 8 bytes 0x11 – 16 bytes

Table 12.10: FIFO Control Register

Note that the current implementation doesn't support **Direct Memory Access (DMA)**, which would allow the UART to write data directly into system memory instead of waiting for data to become ready and then read it, however we could add that in the future. As we are converting to AXI, this would likely require additional control or external logic to implement.

LCR – Line Control Register

The LCR defines how receive and transmitted characters are formatted.

Bit	Field	Definition
1:0	Word Length	0x00 – 5 bits 0x01 – 6 bits 0x10 – 7 bits 0x11 – 8 bits (We currently only support 8 bits)
2	Stop Bits	0x0 – 1 stop bit (We currently only support 1 stop bit) 0x1 – 1.5 stop bits for 5-bit character/2 stop bits for all others
5:3	Parity	0xxx0 – No parity 0x001 – Odd parity 0x011 – Even parity 0x101 – High parity 0x111 – Low parity

6	Set Break	Send a break character – currently unsupported
7	DLAB	Used to select Frequency Registers

Table 12.11: Line Control Register

MCR – Modem Control Register

The MCR handles control outputs as well as loopback mode.

Bit	Field	Definition
0	DTR	Controls DTR – 0x0 sets dtr_n to 0x1, i.e., not ready. 0x1 sets dtr_n to 0x0, i.e., ready
1	RTS	Controls RTS – 0x0 sets rts_n to 0x1, i.e., not ready. 0x1 sets rts_n to 0x0, i.e., ready
3:2	Reserved	Reserved
4	Loopback	Sets loopback mode, i.e., internally connects TX to RX for testing
5	Auto Flow	Set auto flow control
7:6	Reserved	0x0

Table 12.12: Modem Control Register

LSR – Line Status Register

The LSR register gives us status on the receive and transmitters of the UART. It must be read prior to reading the data from the RHR register.

Bit	Field	Definition
0	Data Ready	The RX FIFO has data available
1	Overrun Error	We have received data but the RX FIFO was full
2	Parity Error	Parity error detected
3	Framing Error	Invalid stop bit detected
4	Break Interrupt	Not currently implemented
5	THR Empty	Shows when TX Register is available for data
6	TX Empty	When the TX FIFO and THR are empty, this is set
7	FIFO Data Err	Signals errored data in the FIFO

Table 12.13: Line Status Register

MSR – Modem Status Register

The UART we will implement has a subset of these bits defined; only the CTS status and change.

Bit	Field	Definition
0	CTS Change	The CTS has changed since the last time this register has been changed
1	DSR Change	The DSR has changed since the last time this register has been changed
2	Ring Indicator	Trailing edge of Ring Indicator set
3	CD Change	Carrier detect has changed
4	CTS	Status of CTS
5	DSR	Status of DSR
6	RI	Status of Ring Indicator
7	CD	Status of Carrier Detect

Table 12.14: Modem Status Register

SCRATCH – Scratch Pad Register

This provides a space in memory for the CPU to store a byte of information. It is generally kept for compatibility.

DLL, DLM – Divisor Register LSB and MSB

Table 12.15 shows the register settings necessary to run the UART at different baud rates depending on the clock being used. It also provides the error rate of the generated clock to the ideal clock.

Baud Rate	DLM	DLL	% Error
300	0x89	0xFF	0.006382%
1200	0x2E	0x7F	0.006325%
2400	0x17	0x3F	0.00625%
4800	0x0B	0x9F	0.0061%
9600	0x05	0xCF	0.0058%
14400	0x03	0xDF	0.0055%
19200	0x02	0xE7	0.0052%
28800	0x01	0x0EF	0.0046%
38400	0x01	0x73	0.004%
57600	0x00	0xF7	0.0028%

Table 12.15: Divisor Register Settings

Having gone through the register interface, let's take a look at implementation.

UART Implementation

There are a variety of ways that we can design our UART. We need to consider the existing implementations, which we have done in copying the existing 16550 register map. We also want to consider our usage, which will be for lower speed communication with the host PC. As such, we don't really need a DMA implementation. This design will rely on polling. Also, I've limited us to a subset of the UART capabilities with 8-bit data and 1 stop bit.

First, let's look at the CPU interface.

CPU Interface

As we have seen, sticking to a standard bus like AXI is useful for reusability. We'll use an AXI lite interface for the UART since we have no need for bursting and the data traveling through the UART is slow enough that we don't need fast access to registers. Also, AXI lite allows quick connection to a processor or using standalone as we have done previously with the VGA.

The RX Interface consists of:

- RX Data from the receive state machine.
- RX Break detects (not currently implemented).
- RX Parity and Framing error.
- RX FIFO status out to the RX state machine.
- The TX interface consists of the TX FIFO signals to the TX state machine.

The uart_cpu.sv and uart_cpu.vhd files contain the CPU interface as well as the RX and TX FIFOs. It is instantiated under the top level of the UART.

UART Core

The UART itself contains the clock enable generation, voting logic, and state machines for RX and TX data handling.

Clock enable generation

On the TX side, we have a free-running counter. We don't need to worry about adjusting to align the receiver with the transmitter because they are independent. From the **SystemVerilog** code:

```
always @(posedge sys_clk) begin
  tx_baudclk_en <= '0;
  if (tx_clken_count == {1'b0, baud_terminal_count[15:1]}) begin
```

```
      tx_baudclk_en <= '1;
      tx_clken_count <= '0;
    end else
      tx_clken_count <= tx_clken_count + 1'b1;
    if (~sys_rstn | baud_reset) begin
      tx_clken_count <= '0;
      tx_baudclk_en  <= '0;
    end
  end
end
```

In **VHDL**:

```
if rising_edge(sys_clk) then
  tx_baudclk_en <= '0';
  rx_baudclk_en <= '0';
  if tx_clken_count = to_integer(unsigned('0' & baud_terminal_count(15
downto 1))) then
    tx_baudclk_en  <= '1';
    tx_clken_count <= 0;
  else
    tx_clken_count <= tx_clken_count + 1;
  end if;
  if not sys_rstn or baud_reset then
    tx_clken_count <= 0;
    tx_baudclk_en  <= '0';
  end if;
end if;
```

The RX side operates on 7x oversampling of the data:

```
always @(posedge sys_clk) begin
  rx_baudclk_en <= '0;
  if (rx_clken_count == {2'b0,baud_terminal_count[15:2]}) begin
    rx_baudclk_en <= '1;
    rx_clken_count <= rx_clken_count + 1'b1;
  end else if (rx_clken_count == {1'b0, baud_terminal_count[15:1]}) begin
    rx_clken_count <= 16'h0;
  end else
    rx_clken_count <= rx_clken_count + 1'b1;
```

```
    if (~sys_rstn | baud_reset | rx_baud_reset) begin
      rx_clken_count <= '0;
      rx_baudclk_en  <= '0;
    end
  end // always @ (posedge sys_clk)
```

In **VHDL:**

```
if rising_edge(sys_clk) then
  rx_baudclk_en <= '0';
  if rx_clken_count = to_integer(unsigned('0' & baud_terminal_count(15
downto 2))) then
    rx_baudclk_en  <= '1';
    rx_clken_count <= rx_clken_count + 1;
  elsif rx_clken_count = to_integer(unsigned('0' & baud_terminal_count(15
downto 1))) then
    rx_clken_count <= 0;
  else
    rx_clken_count <= rx_clken_count + 1;
  end if;
  if not sys_rstn or baud_reset or rx_baud_reset then
    rx_clken_count <= 0;
    rx_baudclk_en  <= '0';
  end if;
end if;
```

We monitor the three center samples to determine the value of the current bit.

Voting logic

We can look at the voting logic here in **SystemVerilog:**

```
always @* begin
  case (rx_data_shift[4:2])
    3'b000: vote_bit = '0;
    3'b001: vote_bit = '0;
    3'b010: vote_bit = '0; // Bad sample, framing error?
    3'b011: vote_bit = '1;
    3'b100: vote_bit = '0;
    3'b101: vote_bit = '1; // Bad sample, framing error?
    3'b110: vote_bit = '1;
```

```
    3'b111: vote_bit = '1;
  endcase // case (rx_data_shift[4:2])
end // always @ *
```

And here in **VHDL**:

```
process (all) begin
  case rx_data_shift(4 downto 2) is
    when "000" => vote_bit <= '0';
    when "001" => vote_bit <= '0';
    when "010" => vote_bit <= '0';
    when "011" => vote_bit <= '1';
    when "100" => vote_bit <= '0';
    when "101" => vote_bit <= '1';
    when "110" => vote_bit <= '1';
    when "111" => vote_bit <= '1';
  end case; -- case (rx_data_shift[4:2])
end process;
```

Looking at the three center samples, we can determine whether we are in or transitioning to a 0 or 1 state. We should be running with a very low error rate, so we should not really see a non-all 0 or 1 condition.

I would encourage you to look over the source code to understand its function.

My UART origins

The UART here is a slightly enhanced version of a take-home project I wrote for my interview at SpaceX. The original version was set up to handle an odd-sized data width greater than 8 bits. Often companies such as SpaceX, Facebook, Microsoft, etc., will want to see how your coding looks. They often put a twist on a common problem and ask for a demonstration of your capabilities at handling it. I put a lot of research into UARTs at the time and spent about 8 or so hours coding this up along with the testbench, which we will discuss below.

Testing

The testing of the UART consists of two parts, a SystemVerilog-based simulation and on-board testing. Both of these are described in the following sections.

Simulation

The easiest way to verify something this complex is a good testbench and simulation. It also allows us to try different configurations easily.

To test the UART, I took a different approach than we have in the book so far. This is set up to run the Vivado simulator from the command line. We haven't done this yet, but it is possible to run xsim from the command line on the source code or a project. In this case, we'll look at how to compile for SystemVerilog simulation and mixed mode with VHDL.

```
xvlog -sv ../../tb/*.sv ../hdl/*.sv
```

xvlog compiles Verilog or SystemVerilog code. Similarly, there is an .xvhdl for compiling VHDL code.

```
xvhdl --2008 ../hdl/uart_cpu.vhd ../hdl/uart.vhd
```

xelab elaborates the code in the design for simulation.

```
xelab tb_uart -debug typical
xsim tb_uart -R -log verilog.log
```

Finally, we can run **xsim** with the xsim command. In this case, we are only running a command line. It is also possible to run with the GUI for waveform debugging.

 Note that due to the testbench complexity, I've used the SystemVerilog testbench to validate both the VHDL and SystemVerilog code. This testbench is located at the root of the CH12 directory since it is shared by both languages.

The actual simulation tests are iterated by using the shell script, runsim, as detailed below.

Runsim

runsim is a shell script that copies a test included in the testbench, compiles the design, runs the simulation, and checks the results. It tracks the tests in two files: passed and failed. At the end of the tests, there should be one expected failure.

The usage is:

- runsim -a to run all the tests
- runsim -f test_name to copy and run a single test

The tests cover a variety of conditions, including rate mismatches, internal and external loopback, and flow control. It also measures the % error in the baud rate from what is configured due to PLL mismatches.

Since runsim is a shell script, if you are running under Windows you may need to either explore using something like **Cygwin** or **Windows Subsystem for Linux (WSL)** that allow you to run Unix shell scripts under Windows. Alternatively, you can manually copy the tests to the the_test.h file and execute all the commands within Vivado to build and run the tests.

Debugging

In the event that a test fails, you can run the test standalone by using the -gui switch with **xsim**. This allows you to use the waveform viewer to run the simulation interactively.

For complicated designs or real-world IP that must be robust, this kind of environment, or even something more advanced like UVM or OSVVM, are good choices for thorough testing.

Additionally, we want to make sure that we can communicate with the PC using the board.

On-board testing

We've created a uart_top module that contains the UART and the seven-segment display. Using CuteCom under Ubuntu we tested sending raw characters to the UART and having them displayed on the seven-segment display.

To run on the board, you'll need terminal software like PuTTY or CuteCom. I am using CuteCom because it allows you to send raw hex data rather than ASCII.

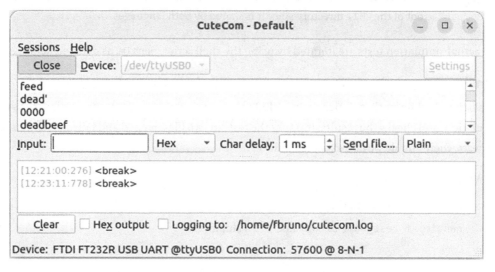

Figure 12.4: CuteCom to send deadbeef to the board

Make sure to set the session to use 57600, 8-N-1. Then type something in – in our case, deadbeef. You'll see the data displayed on the seven-segment display. Note that if you send raw hexadecimal, it will display the digits as it is. If you send ASCII codes, you will see the ASCII code for the text, not the actual text.

Figure 12.5: deadbeef displayed on the board

We've looked at the UART and created a simple UART from scratch. The UART here is missing a few pieces but could be fleshed out with a little work. With the basic UART out of the way, let's look at the last interface in common use for hobbyists that we'll address, the SPI.

Understanding Serial Peripheral Interface (SPI)

Like I2C, the SPI bus is a simple bus for low speed communications. It operates faster than I2C since it uses chip selects rather than passing addresses that need to be decoded, wasting valuable bandwidth. It also utilizes a separate receive and transmit bus, so that it can operate bidirectionally at the same time. It is a four-wire interface that has bidirectional data, a clock, and chip select.

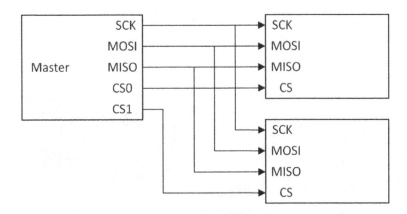

Figure 12.6: deadbeef displayed on the board

It's used in places where you may want to have easy read and write access with optional bursti-ness – typically used on things like ADCs, DACs, and other sensors that typically do not operate with high performance. It's also a common interface for **Erasable Programmable Read-Only Memory (EPROM)** or low-speed access to Flash or SD cards.

Let's look at the Digilent ACL2 PMOD, a 3-axis MEMS accelerometer.

ACL2 PMOD

The ACL2 PMOD from Digilent is based on an **Analog Devices (ADI)** 3-axis **micro-electrome-chanical system (MEMS)**, the ADXL362. This device can return a 12-bit signed value of physical acceleration for each of the three axes (X, Y, and Z).

Figure 12.7: SPI write waveform

We'll be using a subset of features of the SPI bus for simplicity.

Generic SPI

To develop the SPI, we'll need to look at the actual physical and protocol interface. First, we'll look at the physical interface.

SPI physical interface

A SPI bus physical interface consists of four wires:

Signal	Direction	Definition
CSn	Output	Chip Select (Active low)
SCLK	Output	Clock
MOSI	Output	Data (Master Output, Slave Input)
MISO	Input	Data (Master Input, Slave Output)

Table 12.16: SPI bus physical interface

The physical interface is standard, but the protocol can vary a bit amongst devices. In the case of the ACL2 PMOD, which uses the ADI ADXL362, there are three commands, Read (0x0A), Write (0x0B), and Read FIFO (0x0D).

 SPI specifies the physical interface and many devices will follow the same timing diagram. As we will see in developing the SPI for the ADXL362, there is a nonstandard way of reading back data from the FIFO, although it is optional.

Now let's look at the SPI protocol.

SPI protocol interface

SPI typically consists of an instruction, an address, and then the data to be written over the MOSI bus or read from the MISO bus. These are not always standard, so it's important to verify the operation by reading the documentation for the device we'll be interfacing with. In this case, we'll use the ADXL362, the documentation for which can be found here: https://www.analog.com/media/en/technical-documentation/data-sheets/ADXL362.pdf.

Read and write are standard, but there is a third instruction for reading data from the FIFO, which we'll show here but not implement in the design.

SPI register write

The register write is defined in the following diagram.

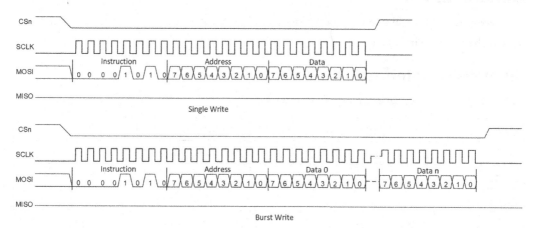

Figure 12.8: SPI write waveform

There are three distinct phases: the instruction, which is 0x0A; the address, which corresponds to the ADXL362 specification; and for the ACL PMOD, we'll need to do some writes to set up the device, which we'll discuss in the coding section.

The implementation I've developed only supports single writes; however, you can see from the diagrams, as long as the chip select is applied and a clock is generated, data can be continuously written to consecutive memory locations.

Now let's look at reading the data.

SPI register read

The register reads are defined in the following diagram.

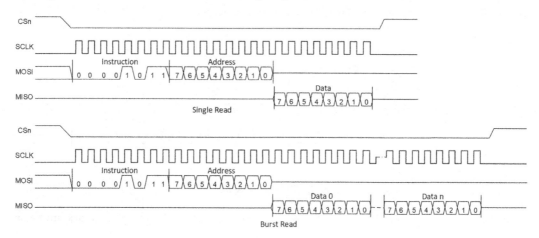

Figure 12.9: SPI read waveform

Like the writes, if the chip select is low and the clock is generated, data will be read from consecutive memory locations. To keep things generic, I've only implemented single reads.

There is one other SPI function I'll go over even though I'm not utilizing it.

SPI FIFO read

This is a specific instruction for the ADXL362 that allows you to read all the ACL data in a single burst from the head of the FIFO. The timing diagram is below.

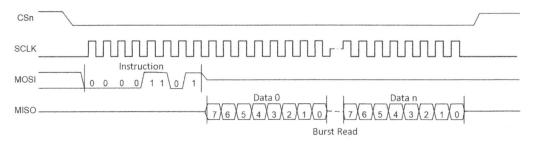

Figure 12.10: SPI read waveform

Now that we know the timing we need to implement the SPI, let's take a look at our assumptions.

Constructing the SPI

First, we can treat this as a low-speed interface and we don't really need to support bursting. Second, the ADXL362 offers two ways of reading the data, one that consists of two reads and yields a 12-bit value, and the other that is a single read containing only the upper 8 bits of data.

Given this, we can simplify the design by using an AXI lite bus for the interface. Note that if we wanted to read the 12-bit data or support the FIFO mode, we would need to add those features in and possibly use a full AXI interface to handle the bursting.

The heart of the SPI interface is the state machine.

SPI state machine

The state machine primarily handles the AXI lite interface. The actual SPI signal generation and data capture are handled by shift registers and counters. By this point in the book, you should be able to look at the provided VHDL or Verilog code and identify the sections of code and what they are doing. The state machine should look familiar, as the basic structure is the same as other AXI lite state machines in the book. The major differences are:

- Lowering CSn when entering the REG_INIT state
- Enabling SCLK in REG_INIT and REG_ADDR
- Clocking out MOSI in REG_ADDR and capturing read data in REG_ADDR
- Terminating the transaction in REG_CSDISABLE by raising CSn

We set up the MOSI signal, which will be the reg_addr bus when a read or write to the AXI bus occurs. We do this by creating a shift register.

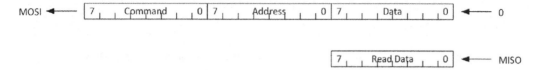

Figure 12.11: Shift register implementation

Above we can see the shift register implementations for MOSI and MISO. Data is transmitted and received from upper to lower bits.

SPI write command

SystemVerilog:

```
reg_addr    <= {8'h0A, 2'b0, reg_awaddr};
wr_data     <= {reg_addr, reg_din};
```

VHDL:

```
reg_addr    <= x"0A" & "00" & reg_awaddr;
wr_data     <= reg_addr & reg_din;
```

SPI read command

SystemVerilog:

```
reg_addr    <= 8'h0B, 2'b0, reg_awaddr};
wr_data     <= {reg_addr, 8'h0};
```

VHDL:

```
reg_addr    <= x"0B" & "00" & reg_awaddr;
wr_data     <= reg_addr & x"00";
```

Additionally, for the SPI read command, we need to capture the data on the correct data cycles.

SystemVerilog:

```
if ((bit_cnt > 15) && (clk_cnt[4:0] == 6'h1)) reg_rdata <= reg_rdata << 1
| MISO;
```

VHDL:

```vhdl
if (bit_cnt > 15) and (clk_cnt = 1) then
  reg_rdata <= reg_rdata(6 downto 0) & MISO;
end if;
```

You can see the similarities in the code, and looking through the full source, they line up very closely. The majority of the SPI code resides in the CPU interface state machine. It serializes the data out and captures at the appropriate point.

The top level of the design initializes the ADI ADXL362 and then goes into a loop where it constantly reads the X, Y, and Z axes' 8-bit registers and displays them on the seven-segment display. Once the design is loaded, tilt the board in various directions. You'll notice the numbers will change as the board orientation changes. Currently, we are reading the registers very quickly. This can be changed by adding a delay using the counter we set up to wait after the last measurement is taken. This is left as an exercise for the reader.

Figure 12.12: Demonstration of displaying the X, Y, and Z axes on the board

If you pick up the board and rotate it around the three axes, you'll see the data change. The data is signed and so will be from -128 to 127, 80 to 7F. In *Figure 12.12*, you can see the values of -1, -3 and 67.

Summary

In this chapter, we've looked at two more serial interfaces commonly used among hobbyists and in industry, namely the UART and SPI. We've developed IP, simulated the UART, and tested both IPs on the board. We've also looked at the PMOD interface, and hopefully, you've checked out the Digilent website and come up with different ideas for projects using readily available components and IP.

Although we'll use a Xilinx IP, the UART will become an important interface for us when we look at the Microblaze in the next chapter.

Questions

1. The UART and SPI are examples of:

    a. Serial interfaces

    b. High-speed interfaces like PCIe

    c. Low-speed, lightweight interfaces

    d. a and c

2. UART interfaces are commonly used for:

    a. CPU terminal connections

    b. Graphical displays

    c. Multi-chip busses

3. MISO, MOSI, CSn, and SCLK are all part of the _____ bus:

    a. I2C

    b. SPI

    c. UART

    d. DDR2

4. Which signals are part of the UART interface? (Choose all that apply)

    a. CSn

    b. RXD

    c. TXD

    d. SCLK

5. Which bus uses oversampling of data?

    a. UART

    b. I2C

    c. SPI

Answers

1. a) Serial interfaces

2. a) CPU terminal connections

3. b) SPI

4. b) RXD and c) TXD

5. a) UART

Further reading

For more information about what was covered in this chapter, please refer to the following link:

*   https://www.avrfreaks.net/sites/default/files/PS2%20Keyboard.pdf

Join our community on Discord

Join our community's Discord space for discussions with the authors and other readers:

https://packt.link/embedded

13

Embedded Microcontrollers Using the Xilinx MicroBlaze

In the previous chapter, we learned about the Digilent PMODs and interfacing with SPI and UART devices. As we've progressed through the book, we've covered many topics – the Xilinx MIG, complex state machines, and driving a display, to name a few. As our skills developed, we turned to packaging our IPs, so that we could use them in new designs with minimal effort. We have mentioned microcontrollers and microprocessors, and in this chapter, we will introduce the Xilinx MicroBlaze processor, learning how to implement one using Vivado and how to develop software for it using Vitis.

In this chapter, we are going to cover the following main topics:

- Understanding embedded microcontrollers
- Introduction to Xilinx MicroBlaze
- Implementing a MicroBlaze for the Nexys A7 using Vivado
- Writing a simple "Hello World" program and loading it using Vitis

Technical requirements

The technical requirements for this chapter are the same as those for *Chapter 2, FPGA Programming Languages and Tools*. We'll also need to make sure that Vitis is installed for programming the software.

To follow along with the examples and the project, you can find the code files for this chapter in the following repository on GitHub: https://github.com/PacktPublishing/The-FPGA-Programming-Handbook-Second-Edition/tree/master/CH13.

Understanding Embedded Microcontrollers

Microcontrollers are processors that are useful for small tasks that can be reconfigured fairly easily. They aren't able to play Crysis or have high benchmark scores; in fact, they likely won't support floating points. But they do allow us to run small, lightweight tasks without the time and complexity of developing hardware. In fact, if you were to look at some of the more advanced Xilinx cores, like the DDR4 controller, they use a MicroBlaze processor to handle the state machine aspects of the memory initialization process.

The Xilinx MicroBlaze processor is a configurable 32-bit processor that can be instanced as a simple microcontroller all the way to a full-blown processor capable of running Linux. In this chapter, we will be looking at the embedded aspects of it.

That said, FPGAs truly shine when you implement custom logic. This allows parallelization, pipelining, and custom interfaces to application-specific devices on your board. However, hardware development is time-consuming, and the design and verification time for larger, more complex designs can be prohibitive. Software can be much faster as compile times are short and you can debug and run through implementations much faster. Also, some applications just make more sense to run on a processor or would be too complex to completely implement in hardware.

Now let's briefly discuss soft and hard processor systems.

Soft vs hard processors

FPGAs from the 7 series onward offer the option to have a hard ARM processor subsystem included on the FPGA die. This started with the Zynq product family. All the latest Xilinx Versal FPGAs include an ARM processor complex. The advantage of hard processor systems is that they are much smaller than soft processor systems, and consume little or no FPGA resources when configured. They can provide high-speed processing of data, allowing the programmable logic to do what it is good at and the processor to handle what it's good at, a concept known as heterogeneous computing.

We don't have a hard option in the Artix family, but there are a number of soft IP cores available online, including free implementations of older architectures, such as the Z80, 6502, 60000, or x86. The Xilinx IP library has a number of processors, such as the ARM M1 or M3, but they also have a full-featured, configurable processor, which we will focus on in this chapter, the MicroBlaze. This processor is quite capable and fully supported by the Xilinx Vitis tool for developing software.

Let's look at generating a MicroBlaze project.

Creating the MicroBlaze project

Make sure that you have Vitis installed as you will need this for the software portion of the chapter. Open the hello_world project that has been set up for you or follow the steps in *Chapter 2*, *FPGA Programming Languages and Tools*, to create a project from scratch.

For our MicroBlaze project, we'll need to create the **Block Design (BD)**, instance any peripherals we want to connect, and then export the design so that we can craft our Hello World program.

Block Design

Once you have the project open, you'll need to create the block design.

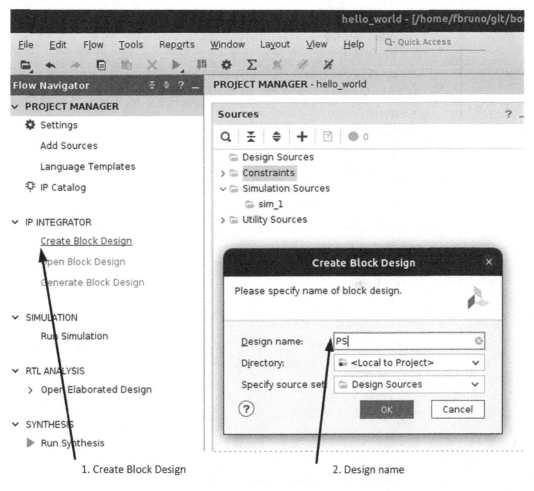

Figure 13.1: Create Block Design

To keep consistent with Xilinx naming, since the Zynq family of FPGAs was introduced, I've named the block design PS, short for processor system.

Next, we need to decide if we want to use the DDR on the board or not. This decision is best made upfront as if we use the DDR controller, we might want to use the clocks generated by it for the MicroBlaze. For the project, we don't really need to use the DDR, but we will use it regardless.

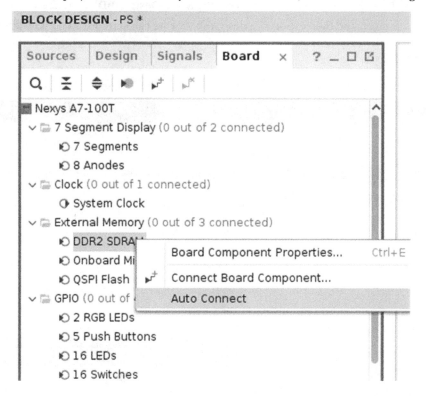

Figure 13.2: Connect the DDR2

Previously, we created the DDR2 controller outside of the **Block Design** tool. Since we have a board configuration file loaded for the Nexys A7, the easiest way to add the DDR2 is to select the **Board** tab. Right-click on the **DDR2 SDRAM** and select **Auto Connect**, as shown in *Figure 13.2*.

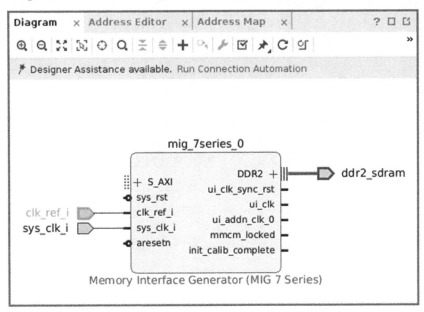

Figure 13.3: Fix clock connection

As we can see in *Figure 13.3*, the default connection hooks up an external pin for the clk_ref_i. ui_addn_clk_i should be set to 200 MHz. We can use this to drive clk_ref_i. To do this, select clk_ref_i and either right-click to delete or use the *Delete* key. Once that is done, hook up clk_ref_i to ui_addn_clk_0. To keep the naming consistent with what we've used in the book, change sys_clk_i to ext_clk.

Make sure to add the board .xdc file, ddr2.xdc, at this point.

Finally, run connection automation to bring out the reset pin. This completes the DDR2 subsystem. Now we can add the MicroBlaze.

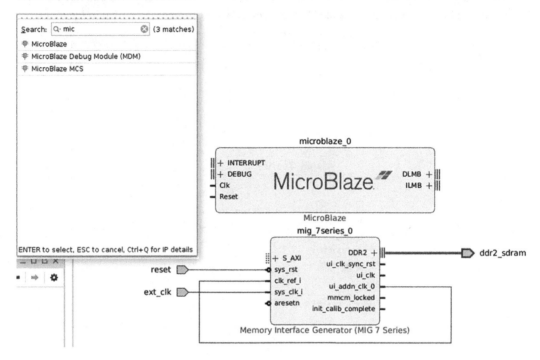

Figure 13.4: Add the MicroBlaze

Add the **MicroBlaze**, as shown in *Figure 13.4*, and then run the block automation. From here, we need to configure the processor.

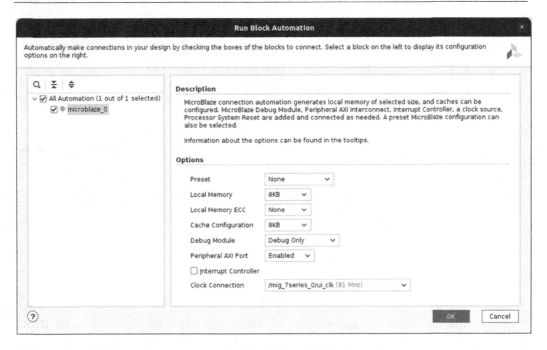

Figure 13.5: MicroBlaze configuration

The implementation we are generating has DDR so we do not need much of the local memory. The ECC option is for high-reliability applications where we need to have error checking and correction. Our design is simple, so 8 KB of cache memory is good. There are multiple debug configurations, but for now, we'll use debug only. We will want the peripheral AXI port so we can connect the IP to the MicroBlaze.

We aren't doing anything that requires speed, so to make timing closure easier, we'll use the DDR UI clk, which is 81 MHz. *Figure 13.6* shows the implementation of the MicroBlaze design.

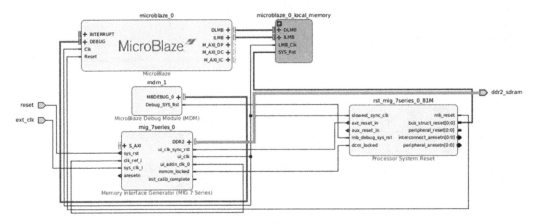

Figure 13.6: MicroBlaze design

We can see the MicroBlaze instance with our local memory and the MIG instance for the DDR2. Now we need to run connection automation to connect the DDR interface to the MicroBlaze, as shown in *Figure 13.7*.

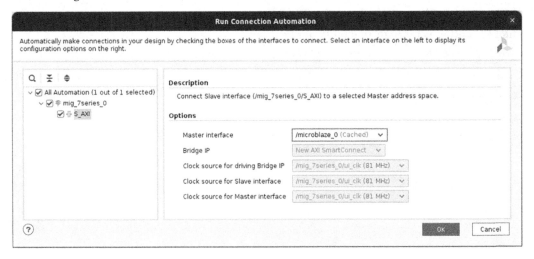

Figure 13.7: Connect DDR2 to MicroBlaze design

Figure 13.8 shows the completed system. You'll see that all the necessary signals have been connected and an AXI crossbar has been instanced, providing us with a place to add additional peripherals to the design. At this point, we have a completed system, but no way of getting data in and nothing to send data out.

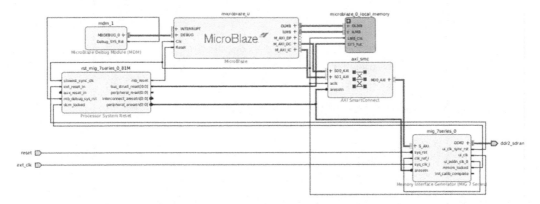

Figure 13.8: MicroBlaze design with DDR

Now that we have the heart of the design set up, we need to add the MicroBlaze peripherals.

MicroBlaze Peripherals

As the MicroBlaze uses AXI, we are at liberty to use any AXI components of our own design or the Xilinx IP included with Vivado. In *Chapter 8, Introduction to AXI*, we saw a list of Xilinx IPs, which was extensive. We've used some of them, such as the floating point and the MIG. We can now add some for our MicroBlaze.

When we look at the board connections in Vivado, we can see the connections predefined for the board.

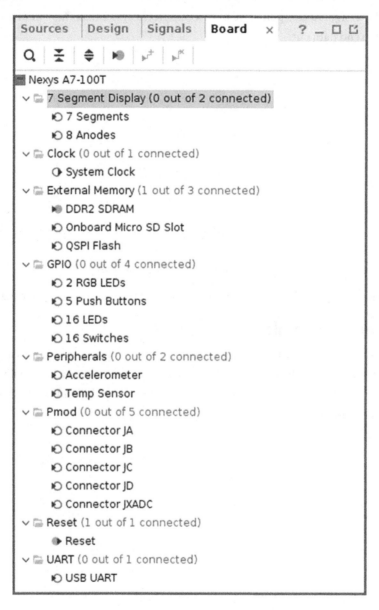

Figure 13.9: Predefined board connections

Looking at the list, some things jump out. We can see not only the push buttons, LEDs, and switches but also the built-in accelerometer, temperature sensor, and UART. First, let's connect a UART so we can use it to display output from the MicroBlaze. We can do this by right-clicking on it and selecting **AXI Uartlite**.

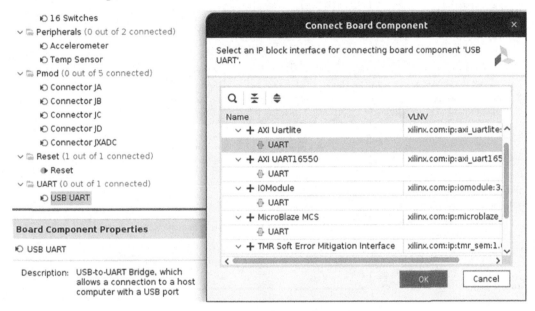

Figure 13.10: Add the UART

While we're at it, let's add the push buttons, LEDs, and switches. We will do this by using the AXI GPIOs provided by the Xilinx. Here I am adding one for the push buttons.

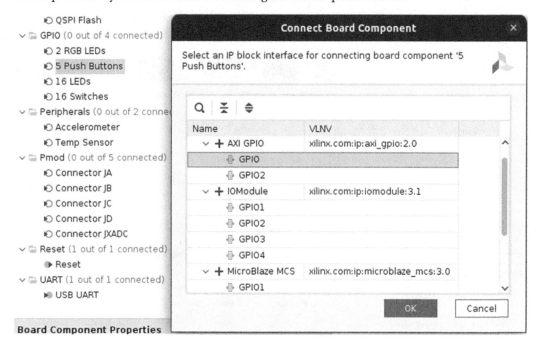

Figure 13.11: AXI GPIO

I chose to add a new GPIO component for each interface, the push button, LED, and switches. Each AXI GPIO can actually support up to two sets of GPIOs, but for simplicity, we'll only use one. Once we have completed adding the GPIOs, we can change the peripheral names to more accurately represent what they are driving. Also, make sure to change the signal names to match the .xdc file, then run the connection automation and you should see something like the following.

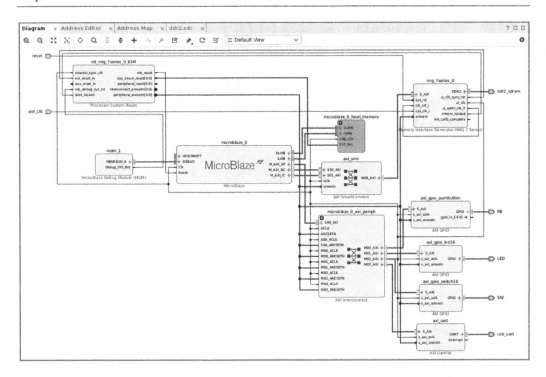

Figure 13.12: Completed MicroBlaze system

With the design completed, run the check design. You may see the following warnings since we changed the names in the .xdc and the block design. They are simply informing us of some behind-the-scenes renaming that the tool has done and can be safely ignored.

```
validate_bd_design -force
INFO: [xilinx.com:ip:smartconnect:1.0-1] PS_axi_smc_1: SmartConnect PS_
axi_smc_1 is in High-performance Mode.
WARNING: [filemgmt 56-443] The ECC Algorithm string is empty. Setting the
Memory Map to default ECC value to ECC_NONE.
INFO: [xilinx.com:ip:microblaze:11.0-16] /microblaze_0: Setting D-cache
cacheable area base address C_DCACHE_BASEADDR to 0x80000000 and high
address C_DCACHE_HIGHADDR to 0x87FFFFFF.
```

```
INFO: [xilinx.com:ip:microblaze:11.0-16] /microblaze_0: Setting I-cache
cacheable area base address C_ICACHE_BASEADDR to 0x80000000 and high
address C_ICACHE_HIGHADDR to 0x87FFFFFF.
WARNING: [BD 41-1771] Block interface /axi_gpio_led16/GPIO has associated
board param 'GPIO_BOARD_INTERFACE', which is set to board part interface
'led_16bits'. This interface is connected to an external interface /
LED, whose name 'LED' does not match with the board interface name
'led_16bits'.
This is a visual-only issue - this interface /axi_gpio_led16/GPIO will be
connected to board interface 'led_16bits'. If desired, please change the
name of this port /LED manually.
WARNING: [BD 41-1771] Block interface /axi_gpio_pushbutton/GPIO has
associated board param 'GPIO_BOARD_INTERFACE', which is set to board part
interface 'push_buttons_5bits'. This interface is connected to an external
interface /PB, whose name 'PB' does not match with the board interface
name 'push_buttons_5bits'.
This is a visual-only issue - this interface /axi_gpio_pushbutton/GPIO
will be connected to board interface 'push_buttons_5bits'. If desired,
please change the name of this port /PB manually.
WARNING: [BD 41-1771] Block interface /axi_gpio_switch16/GPIO has
associated board param 'GPIO_BOARD_INTERFACE', which is set to board
part interface 'dip_switches_16bits'. This interface is connected to an
external interface /SW, whose name 'SW' does not match with the board
interface name 'dip_switches_16bits'.
This is a visual-only issue - this interface /axi_gpio_switch16/GPIO will
be connected to board interface 'dip_switches_16bits'. If desired, please
change the name of this port /SW manually.
```

Since we have changed the names, we can safely ignore these warnings.

There are two final panes you can take a look at. These are the address editor and the address map. The address editor allows you to change the address locations and sizes of AXI peripherals. Vivado usually does a good job at mapping, but if you run into a problem, you can change them here.

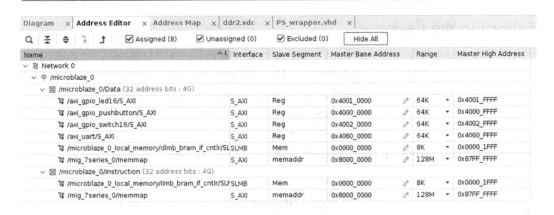

Figure 13.13: Address Editor

Figure 13.13 shows the address editor and *Figure 13.14* shows the address map in graph form.

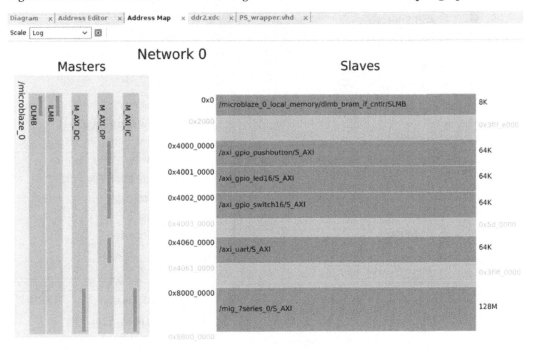

Figure 13.14: Address Map

Now we've developed the system, so let's create the HDL wrapper in VHDL or Verilog and compile the bitstream as described in previous chapters.

Exporting the design

With the hardware design for the MicroBlaze processor and peripherals complete, we must turn our attention to the software we will run on it. Up until now, we've designed hardware so everything was hard coded. A design would come up and function, or be reset and function. Now our MicroBlaze will simply sit and do nothing unless we tell it what to do, and for that, we'll need to write a little software. For this, we'll use Vitis, which can take the results from Vivado and, using the **Integrated Development Environment (IDE)**, we can write, test, and deploy our software.

In order to develop the software using Vitis, we need to export the hardware design, a step that we haven't done before. Select **File->Export->Export Hardware...**, as shown in *Figure 13.15*:

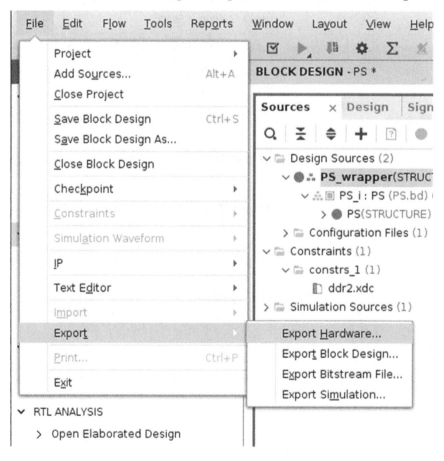

Figure 13.15: Export Hardware… option

If the window to generate output products pops up, select **Generate output products**. The next popup explains the process. Click **Next**.

Figure 13.16: Export Hardware Platform window

The next popup gives you the option of including the bitstream. Select **Include bitstream**.

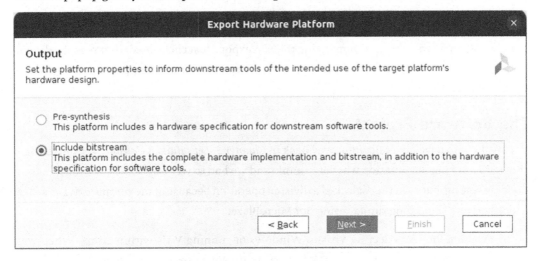

Figure 13.17: Include bitstream

Next, we'll get a window to name the **Xilinx Shell Architecture (XSA)** project and give a location to save it.

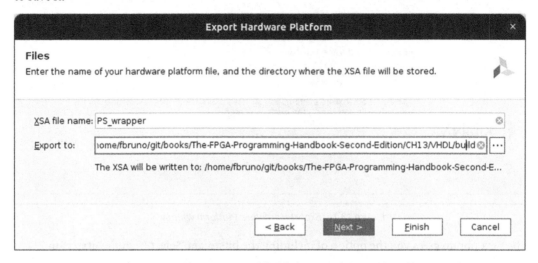

Figure 13.18: XSA name and location

Finally, a window will pop up summarizing the XSA export. Just click **Finish** to export the design for Vitis. Now that we've exported our hardware, we can run Vitis and import the hardware to write software.

The Software Project

We saw how to develop a calculator way back in *Chapter 5*, *Let's Build a Calculator*. Even though that hardware implementation was very simple and we had to write up some state machines to do some testing, but even then it lacked a division operation because of the complexity. Let's take a look at doing something similar using our MicroBlaze:

1. Launch Vitis by selecting **Vitis** in Windows or running **Vitis** within Linux. When you launch **Vitis**, it will first ask you for a workspace. Vitis uses this directory to store project files and software you will develop.

Figure 13.19: Vitis workspace

2. Once the workspace is open, you will be presented with the welcome screen.

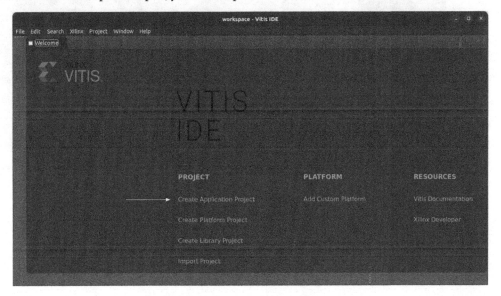

Figure 13.20: Vitis Workspace

3. From the welcome screen, select **Create Application Project**. This is what we'll use to set up the project for our design. The next screen will outline the process of creating the new application project.

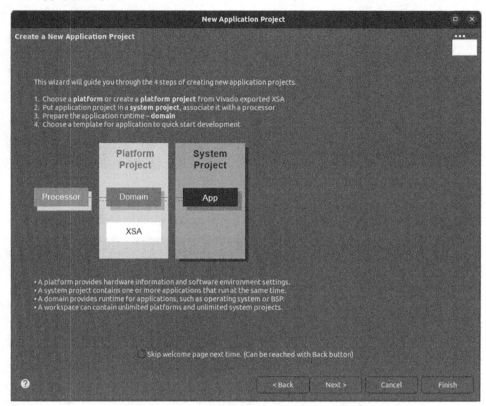

Figure 13.21: Create a new application overview

4. Click **Next** on the next screen. Specify the XSA file by selecting **Create a new platform from hardware (XSA)** and specifying the XSA file we generated.

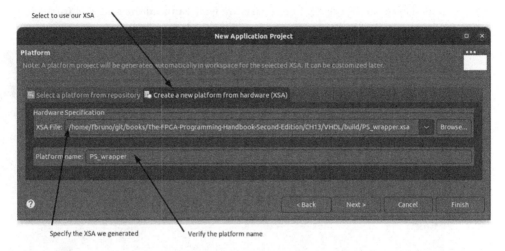

Figure 13.22: Create a new platform

5. Next, we'll name the application project, as shown in *Figure 13.23*.

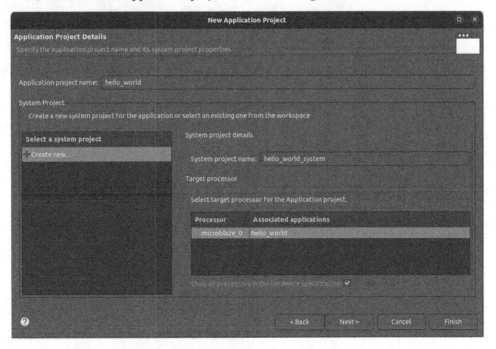

Figure 13.23: Application Project Details

6.   On the next screen, we specify the application details. Here you can select the operating system type – Linux, **Real-Time Operating System (RTOS)**, or standalone (bare metal) – and also the architecture. In our case, we want **standalone** and **32-bit** (the only architecture option).

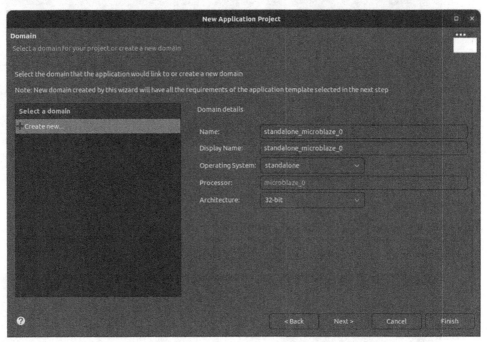

Figure 13.24: Domain details

7.   Next, we can select from a list of templates for our software. Choose **Hello World** and then click **Finish**.

Now we have our application loaded in Vitis.

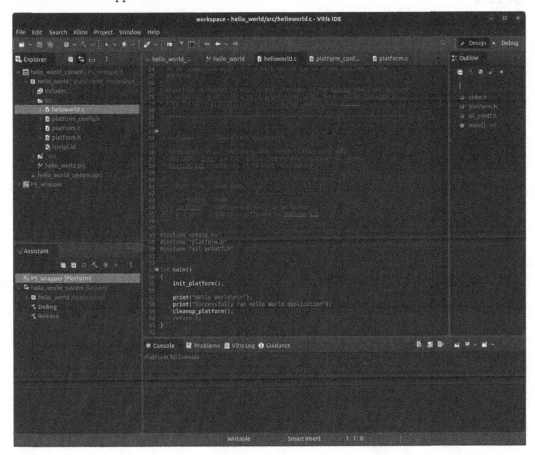

Figure 13.25: Vitis IDE

GPIOs

Remember that we have set up three sets of GPIOs: one for the LEDs, one for the switches, and one for the buttons. We can find the information about these in the project by looking at the MicroBlaze **Board Support Package (BSP)** header file, xparameters.h, which defines the memory location and parameters that the software can use to access the GPIO. All of this is done over the AXI bus and all peripherals will have similar parameters for use in developing software applications:

```
/* Definitions for driver GPIO */
#define XPAR_XGPIO_NUM_INSTANCES 3


/* Definitions for peripheral AXI_GPIO_LED16 */
#define XPAR_AXI_GPIO_LED16_BASEADDR 0x40010000
#define XPAR_AXI_GPIO_LED16_HIGHADDR 0x4001FFFF
#define XPAR_AXI_GPIO_LED16_DEVICE_ID 0
#define XPAR_AXI_GPIO_LED16_INTERRUPT_PRESENT 0
#define XPAR_AXI_GPIO_LED16_IS_DUAL 0



/* Definitions for peripheral AXI_GPIO_PUSHBUTTON */
#define XPAR_AXI_GPIO_PUSHBUTTON_BASEADDR 0x40000000
#define XPAR_AXI_GPIO_PUSHBUTTON_HIGHADDR 0x4000FFFF
#define XPAR_AXI_GPIO_PUSHBUTTON_DEVICE_ID 1
#define XPAR_AXI_GPIO_PUSHBUTTON_INTERRUPT_PRESENT 0
#define XPAR_AXI_GPIO_PUSHBUTTON_IS_DUAL 0



/* Definitions for peripheral AXI_GPIO_SWITCH16 */
#define XPAR_AXI_GPIO_SWITCH16_BASEADDR 0x40020000
#define XPAR_AXI_GPIO_SWITCH16_HIGHADDR 0x4002FFFF
#define XPAR_AXI_GPIO_SWITCH16_DEVICE_ID 2
#define XPAR_AXI_GPIO_SWITCH16_INTERRUPT_PRESENT 0
#define XPAR_AXI_GPIO_SWITCH16_IS_DUAL 0
```

Our Software Application

Let's consider the calculator we wrote back in *Chapter 5*. It's fairly simple in concept: set some switches, push some buttons, and calculate a response. All of this was hard-coded in hardware. Now let's see if we can do the same using C code compiled to run on the MicroBlaze.

First, we'll need to specify the header files we'll need in the project. Below are the few header files introduced here.

Includes

We'll need the following for our project. Adding #include in our C code will tell the C compiler to include the libraries we'll need for our software to work:

```
#include <stdio.h>
#include "platform.h"
#include "xparameters.h"
#include "xil_printf.h"
#include "xgpio.h"
#include "xil_types.h"
```

platform.h and xparameters.h are generated for the platform as part of the XSA.

stdio.h and xil_printf are used to write to the UART.

xgpio.h provides the functionality for enumerating and accessing the GPIOs in a more user-friendly manner.

Finally, we have xil_types for Xilinx-defined types we will use in the code.

Next, we'll create some defines to make things more readable.

Defines

We'll create some shortened names for easier readability and also masks for the switches, LEDs, and buttons, as well as enumerate the buttons for readability. These defines are constants, which makes the code easier to read and aids reusability:

```
#define BTN_ID XPAR_AXI_GPIO_PUSHBUTTON_DEVICE_ID
#define LED_ID XPAR_AXI_GPIO_LED16_DEVICE_ID
#define SW_ID XPAR_AXI_GPIO_SWITCH16_DEVICE_ID
#define BTN_CHANNEL 1
#define LED_CHANNEL 1
#define SW_CHANNEL 1
#define BTN_MASK 0b11111
#define LED_MASK 0b1111111111111111
#define SW_MASK 0b1111111111111111
#define btnc 1 << 0
#define btnu 1 << 1
```

```
#define btnl 1 << 2
#define btnr 1 << 3
#define btnd 1 << 4
```

Now let's look at the code initialization.

Main

Here we start the main block of our code. We define a configuration pointer, a unique variable type in C whose purpose is to point to a physical memory location, which we'll use to determine the devices automatically, and these device addresses will be stored in the XGpio types. We'll also create our accumulator and some registers we'll need for the current values in the GPIOS:

```
XGpio_Config *cfg_ptr;
XGpio led_device, btn_device, sw_device;
u32 btn_data, sw_data, last_data;
u32 accumulator = 0;
```

The init_platform function sets up the processor and the UART:

```
init_platform();
```

I've left in the initial print to the UART simply so we know when the code starts running:

```
print("Hello World\n\r");
```

Next, we'll initialize the GPIOs:

```
// Initialize LED Device
cfg_ptr = XGpio_LookupConfig(LED_ID);
XGpio_CfgInitialize(&led_device, cfg_ptr, cfg_ptr->BaseAddress);

// Initialize Button Device
cfg_ptr = XGpio_LookupConfig(BTN_ID);
XGpio_CfgInitialize(&btn_device, cfg_ptr, cfg_ptr->BaseAddress);

// Initialize Switch Device
cfg_ptr = XGpio_LookupConfig(SW_ID);
XGpio_CfgInitialize(&sw_device, cfg_ptr, cfg_ptr->BaseAddress);

// Set Button Tristate
XGpio_SetDataDirection(&btn_device, BTN_CHANNEL, BTN_MASK);
```

```
// Set Led Tristate
XGpio_SetDataDirection(&led_device, LED_CHANNEL, 0);

// Set Switch Tristate
XGpio_SetDataDirection(&sw_device, LED_CHANNEL, 0);
```

We now have pointers to our GPIOs and have initialized them.

Main Loop

The heart of our software will monitor the push buttons, look for a rising edge on one of them and performing a computation. The main loop is where anything that needs to be run repeatedly should go:

```
while (1) {
    btn_data = XGpio_DiscreteRead(&btn_device, BTN_CHANNEL);
    btn_data &= BTN_MASK;
    sw_data  = XGpio_DiscreteRead(&sw_device, SW_CHANNEL);

    switch (btn_data & ~last_data) {
        case btnu :
            accumulator *= sw_data;
            xil_printf("SW: %d\n", sw_data);
            xil_printf("Multiply Accumulator = %d\n", accumulator);
            break;
        case btnl :
            accumulator += sw_data;
            xil_printf("SW: %d\n", sw_data);
            xil_printf("Add Accumulator = %d\n", accumulator);
            break;
        case btnr :
            accumulator -= sw_data;
            xil_printf("SW: %d\n", sw_data);
            xil_printf("Subtract Accumulator = %d\n", accumulator);
            break;
    }
    last_data = btn_data;
    XGpio_DiscreteWrite(&led_device, LED_CHANNEL, accumulator);
}
```

We set up an infinite loop, `while (1)`. We then monitor the `btn_data` compared to the last button data to determine if a bit has changed. We use our `btn` constants as the case to select the `multiply`, `add`, or `subtract`.

Although we display the accumulator on the LEDs, we also print to the terminal through the UART.

Now we can start a terminal. As I mentioned in the last chapter regarding the UART, I'm using CuteCom. You can use any terminal program. You may need to hunt around to find the proper UART port. Under Linux, it will be one of the ports: `/dev/ttyUSB0`, `/dev/ttyUSB1`... `/dev/ttyUSB(n)`. In Windows, you can use the device manager to locate the com ports. Note that multiple ports are instanced for the board, so you may need to try different ones to find the correct one.

We are now ready to build and run the design.

Build and Debug

Either select **Project->Build Project** or select the hammer icon to build the design, as shown in *Figure 13.27*.

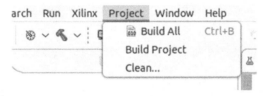

Figure 13.26: Build design

Once compiled, we can either run it directly or run it in the debugger. This chapter only goes through the process of running code on the MicroBlaze and is only meant as an introduction.

Figure 13.27: Debug/run design

Now let's run the design.

Running the design

One thing to note is I snuck in a division operation. In *Chapter 5, Let's Build a Calculator*, we saw the complexity of the division operation. These types of processes are things that a microprocessor like the MicroBlaze can handle using its **Arithmetic Logic Unit (ALU)** very well. So, rather than a complex state machine to implement the division, we can just use the division operator.

```
case btnd :
    accumulator /= sw_data;
    xil_printf("SW: %d\n", sw_data);
    xil_printf("Divide Accumulator = %d\n", accumulator);
    break;
```

We can look at the output of the terminal and test the calculator.

```
[19:18:23:778] <break>
[19:32:46:097] Hello World
[19:32:46:097] SW: 1
[19:32:56:465] Add Accumulator = 1
[19:32:58:689] SW: 1
[19:32:58:689] Add Accumulator = 2
[19:32:58:865] SW: 1
[19:32:58:865] Add Accumulator = 3
[19:32:59:809] SW: 1
[19:32:59:809] Add Accumulator = 4
[19:32:59:905] SW: 1
[19:32:59:905] Add Accumulator = 5
[19:33:00:609] SW: 1
[19:33:00:609] Add Accumulator = 6
[19:33:02:017] SW: 1
[19:33:02:017] Add Accumulator = 7
[19:33:03:281] SW: 1
[19:33:03:297] Multiply Accumulator = 7
[19:33:08:145] SW: 3
[19:33:08:161] Multiply Accumulator = 21
[19:33:08:289] SW: 3
[19:33:08:305] Multiply Accumulator = 63
[19:33:11:153] SW: 3
[19:33:11:153] Divide Accumulator = 21
[19:33:11:281] SW: 3
[19:33:11:281] Divide Accumulator = 7
```

There are a lot of things that you can do with the microprocessor in your application, and Vitis is a very complete and capable platform. I would encourage you to investigate Vitis further, as well as the many open-source and free projects and libraries that might help your design.

Summary

In this chapter, we've implemented a MicroBlaze processing system and developed a simple application to replace the calculator we developed in *Chapter 5, Let's Build a Calculator*. We saw how with a little code we could easily reproduce the state machines we wrote as well as implement the division operation. We saw how to add peripherals and how easy it was to build a system around the MicroBlaze. We exported the design from Vivado and read it into Vitis where we could run the design, interact with the board, and see the output using the LEDs and the terminal through the AXI Uartlite.

Questions

1. A MicroBlaze processor is a:

    a. Microprocessor

    b. Microcontroller

    c. Microcontroller or a microprocessor at design time

2. We use _____ to develop an FPGA with a built-in ARM processor or MicroBlaze:

    a. Vivado

    b. Vitis

    c. Vivado and Vitis

    d. All of the above

3. MicroBlaze applications can be developed to run under (multiple answers):

    a. Linux

    b. RTOS

    c. Bare metal

    d. All of the above

4. A MicroBlaze is a highly parallel, high-performance processor that, when implemented in an FPGA, negates the need for all other custom logic. True or false?

Answers

1. b) Microcontroller

2. c) Vivado and Vitis

3. d) All of the above

4. False

Challenge

We've developed other IPs through the course of this book, like the VGA controller and the seven-segment display. Can you add one or more of these IP blocks to create a more robust design?

Join our community on Discord

Join our community's Discord space for discussions with the authors and other readers:

https://packt.link/embedded

14

Advanced Topics

Over the course of the book, you've had the opportunity to try your hand at a few different projects. We learned about combinational and sequential logic. We implemented state machines and designed, simulated, and built a calculator. We learned about clock domain crossing and timing. We discussed FPGA resources and implemented **Random Access Memories (RAMs)** and FIFO queues. We interfaced with an external temperature sensor and microphone and looked at viewing data using the ILA. We then looked at using floating point and fixed point representations for the temperature conversion as well as adding a smoothing function.

We also looked at packaging IP. We instantiated a Xilinx memory controller and implemented a simple VGA controller so we could see our work on a monitor. We added keyboard functionality and showed how we can use it to control our design by switching between Fahrenheit and Celsius as well as displaying the keycodes so we can see what happens when a key is pressed and released. We also looked at the PMODs on the board and designed a UART as well as an SPI interface to enhance our knowledge. Finally, we looked at implementing and programming a Xilinx Microblaze processor.

To get you started quickly, we limited some of the syntax. This chapter will introduce a few new SystemVerilog and VHDL constructs that you may find useful for synthesis and verification. I'll also introduce some things to watch out for.

By the end of this chapter, you'll have been exposed to almost all the useful SystemVerilog and VHDL constructs for designing and testing FPGAs.

In this chapter, we are going to cover the following main topics:

- Exploring more advanced SystemVerilog constructs
- Exploring some more advanced verification constructs
- Other gotchas and how to avoid them

Technical requirements

The technical requirements for this chapter are the same as those for *Chapter 2, FPGA Programming Languages and Tools.*

To follow along with the examples and the project, you can find the code files for this chapter at the following repository on GitHub: `https://github.com/PacktPublishing/The-FPGA-Programming-Handbook-Second-Edition/tree/main/CH14`.

Exploring more advanced SystemVerilog constructs

We've used many basic constructs in our designs. The syntax we've used is enough to construct anything you would like to design. There are some other design constructs, that can be useful, so I'd like to at least introduce them with an example of how to use them. The most useful construct is the interface.

Interfacing components using the interface construct

SystemVerilog interfaces can be thought of as modules that extend across other modules. An interface in its simplest form is a bundle of wires, very much like a structure. However, unlike a structure, the direction of each individual signal is independent, meaning that you can have both inputs and outputs defined within the interface.

I've created a project to show our PS/2 Host interface, `ps2_host`, implemented using an interface: `https://github.com/PacktPublishing/The-FPGA-Programming-Handbook-Second-Edition/blob/main/CH14/SystemVerilog/build/ps2_host.xpr`.

Interfaces also have the added advantage that you can encapsulate functions, tasks, and assertions that are related to the given interface signals. This improves design reusability and improves design development. Most of the designs we have worked with so far have only had a few levels of nested modules. Large designs can have signals that can delve many times deeper. By encapsulating an interface, adding, removing, or resizing a signal becomes as easy as modifying the interface definition.

We can look at modifying the ps2_host module to use an interface. Remember that our original version back in *Chapter 11, Bringing It All Together*, had an interface that looked as shown in the following code:

```
// Transmit data to the keyboard from the FPGA
input wire          tx_valid,
input wire [7:0]    tx_data,
output logic         tx_ready,
// Data from the device to the FPGA
output logic [7:0]  rx_data,
output logic         rx_user, // Error indicator
output logic         rx_valid,
input wire          rx_ready
```

This type of design is a good example of implementing an interface. It's a good idea to maintain a constant naming convention. What I typically do is name an interface <interface_name>_intf and save each interface in its own .sv file.

Interfaces can contain parameters and a port list like a module. In ps2_intf, we won't need these; however, we will take advantage of the function encapsulation:

```
interface ps2_intf;
    // Interfaces can contain parameter lists like a module
    // Interfaces can contain IO like a module
    logic           tx_valid;
    logic [7:0]     tx_data;
    logic           tx_ready;
    logic [7:0]     rx_data;
    logic           rx_user;
    logic           rx_valid;
    logic           rx_ready;
```

The first part of the interface defines the signals within the interface itself. These are the signals that will be used for inter-module communication. The second section contains modports. An example is shown in *Figure 14.1*.

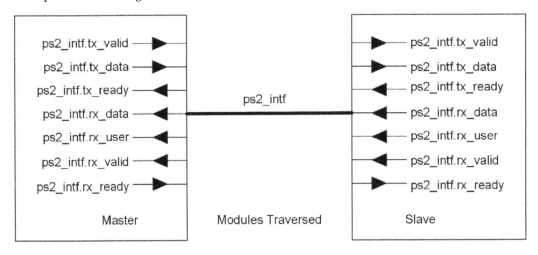

Figure 14.1: Interface signals and modports

Since interfaces only bundle the signals, much like a structure. Modports allow us to define the direction of signals where the interface is used. In *Figure 14.1*, you can see that the master and slave devices have opposite views of the direction of a signal. For example, tx_ready tells the master when the slave is ready to accept data. Therefore it's an output from the slave and an input to the master. If a modport is not used, the signal is considered bidirectional:

```
modport master
   (output tx_valid,
    output tx_data,
    input  tx_ready,
    input  rx_data,
    input  rx_user,
    input  rx_valid,
    output rx_ready);
modport slave
   (input  tx_valid,
    input  tx_data,
    output tx_ready,
    output rx_data,
    output rx_user,
```

```
    output rx_valid,
    input  rx_ready,
    import parity_gen,
    import parity_check);
```

The things to notice here are the import keywords on the slave modport. These allow the functions to be used within the slave interface. This allows us to limit the visibility of functions or internal signals to only authorized modports. This allows related functions such as the parity functions in the following code to be used by the instantiating module:

```
function parity_gen(input [7:0] din);
  begin
    return ~^din;
  end
endfunction // parity_gen
function parity_check(input [8:0] din);
  begin
    return ~^din;
  end
endfunction // parity_check
```

By encapsulating the functions within the interface, we keep everything needed to generate a PS/2 command or check the incoming scancode. This will help reusability in the future:

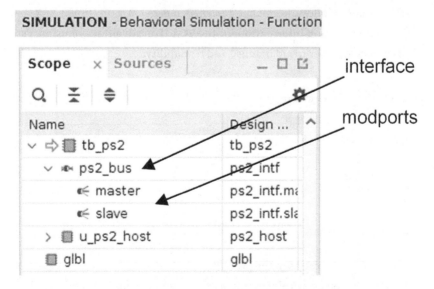

Figure 14.2: Interface signals in the Vivado simulator

You can see from *Figure 14.3* that the interface shows up separately in the signal list almost like a module. You can also see the modports show up when expanded. If you add the signals to the wave viewer, they look the same as any other signal:

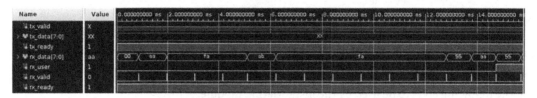

Figure 14.3: Simulation waveform for interfaces

The test included in this project will pass when run. We'll look a little closer at the testbench when we discuss queues. Interfaces are completely optional to use. Some people find them very useful, while others don't like to use them. If they work for you, they can really come in handy.

There are some Vivado limitations currently, however. The top-level module cannot use interfaces as ports. **Block Design** (**BD**) subdesigns cannot use interfaces either. If you limit the connections within a design using SystemVerilog, you will be fine.

Now let's look at structures in a little more detail.

Using structures

Throughout the book, we've used structures. They provide a convenient way to package data and make your design easier to follow. Recall in *Chapter 10, A Better Way to Display – VGA*, we used a structure to hold our resolution information for the VGA. The advantage of using a structure is to keep related signals together to aid in reuse and readability.

```
typedef struct packed {
  logic [7:0 ]  divide_count;
  logic [15:8]  mult_integer;
  logic [25:16] mult_fraction;
  ...
  logic         hpol;
  logic         vpol;
  logic [12:0]  pitch;
} resolution_t;
```

Creating a typedef of a structure as in the preceding code effectively creates a new type. You can create packed and unpacked arrays of structures or use them as you would for any other type. An example of this is creating our table of resolutions:

```
resolution_t resolution[18];
```

We have a couple of ways of assigning to. The first is assigning by component, which we used in *Chapter 10, A Better Way to Display – VGA*:

```
// 25.18 Mhz 640x480 @ 60Hz
resolution[0].divide_count        = 8'd9;
resolution[0].mult_integer        = 8'd50;
resolution[0].mult_fraction       = 10'd000;
...
resolution[0].hpol                = '0;
resolution[0].vpol                = '0;
resolution[0].pitch               = 13'd5*16; // 5 rows at 1bpp
```

Another way is to assign by name:

```
// 25.18 Mhz 640x480 @ 60Hz
resolution[0] = '{default:        '0,
                  divide_count:   8'd9,
                  mult_integer:   8'd50,
                  mult_fraction:  10'd000,
                  ...
                  Pitch:          13'd5*16}; // 5 rows at 1bpp
```

When assigning in this way, you can use the default keyword to assign values to anything not specified. The preceding two snippets of code are equivalent.

Another readability and coding for correctness construct is using block labels.

Block labels

Any begin...end block can be labeled. I've created an example project to show this: https://github.com/PacktPublishing/The-FPGA-Programming-Handbook-Second-Edition/blob/main/CH14/SystemVerilog/build/labels.xpr.

This is highly recommended for generate statements as this will be a requirement in future versions of SystemVerilog. This can help with readability. Block labels can also be useful if using disable, as we'll see. In the following code, we'll look at an example of how block labels can help catch coding errors:

```
always_ff @(posedge clk) begin
  // mismatched block label
```

```
    if (subtraction) begin : l_addition_op
      dout <= in0 - in1;
    end : l_subtraction_op
    // reusing a label
    if (addition) begin : l_addition_op
      dout <= in0 + in1;
    end : l_addition_op
  end
```

Labeling can also help to keep track of which block a section of code is in. Labels cannot be reused. Also, errors will result if the start and end labels are not the same. Running the preceding code through the Vivado simulator yields the following:

```
ERROR: [VRFC 10-3516] mismatch in closing label 'l_subtraction_op';
expected 'l_addition_op' [/home/fbruno/git/books/Learn-FPGA-Programming/
CH11/hdl/labels.sv:12]
ERROR: [VRFC 10-2934] 'l_addition_op' is already declared [/home/fbruno/
git/books/Learn-FPGA-Programming/CH11/hdl/labels.sv:16]
ERROR: [VRFC 10-3516] mismatch in closing label 'l_addition_op'; expected
'<unnamed>' [/home/fbruno/git/books/Learn-FPGA-Programming/CH11/hdl/
labels.sv:16]
ERROR: [VRFC 10-2865] module 'labels' ignored due to previous errors [/
home/fbruno/git/books/Learn-FPGA-Programming/CH11/hdl/labels.sv:1]
```

Labeling is optional but can be worthwhile if you practice it. Now let's look at looping constructs.

Looping using for loops

We have been using for loops throughout the book. In every case, we have defined the loop variables within the for loop and this is highly desirable. for loops also allow multiple loop variables, although only one test is allowed for ending the loop. Here's an example:

```
for (int i = 0, j = 0; i *j < 256; i++, j+=8) begin
```

The preceding example is perfectly fine for synthesis and implementation.

Looping using do...while

We have seen while loops, particularly in our PS/2 testing in *Chapter 11, Bringing It All Together*. do...while and while loops are synthesizable.

We can see two implementations of a `last_ones` function using both types of loops:

```
always_comb begin
  done = '0;
  i = 0;
  while (!done) begin
    if (vector[i] || (i==15)) done = '1;
    else i += 1;
  end
  last_ones = i;
end
```

Another way of coding this would be to use a do...while loop as shown in the following code. do... while loops are particularly useful when you want the loop to execute at least once:

```
always_comb begin
  done = '0;
  i = 0;
  do
    if (vector[i] || (i==15)) done = '1;
    else i += 1;
  while (!done);
  last_ones = i;
end
```

These could both be used to detect the smallest bit position set. As mentioned when we were looking at for loops, as long as you can unroll the loop, it's synthesizable.

We have looked at simple loops, but what if you have a more complex operation involving nested loops?

Exiting a loop using disable

We have used break in a for loop to exit when finding a bit set. What can we do if we have nested loops? The `disable` statement allows you to disable a named block. This is synthesizable, much like the break statement is synthesizable:

```
always_comb begin
  first_ones = '0;
  for (int i = 0; i < 4; i++) begin : outer_loop
    for (int j = 0; j < 8; j++) begin : inner_loop
```

```
      if (din[i][j]) begin
        first_ones = 6'(i*8 + j);
        disable outer_loop;
      end
    end : inner_loop
  end : outer_loop
end // always_comb begin
```

In the preceding code, we are searching a two-dimensional array, din, for the first one detected. Once found, we want to capture its position in the array, 6'(i*8 + j), and stop the search.

In addition to break and disable, SystemVerilog also supports continue.

Skipping code using continue

SystemVerilog includes a continue keyword that can be used in a loop. The continue allows us to test for a condition and skip to the end of the current loop.

Back in *Chapter 5, Let's Build a Calculator*, we developed a leading 1s indicator. When we are using loops, we can recode it to use continue:

```
always_comb begin
  LED = '0;
  for (int i = $low(SW); i <= $high(SW); i++) begin
    if (~SW[i]) continue;
    LED = i + 1;
  end
end
```

As an alternative to breaking a loop, we might want to skip over something in the loop if we should encounter it. The preceding loop shows how we can skip all 0s in a vector, only capturing the position of the final 1 detected.

Using constants

Constants provide a way of letting the tool know something cannot be changed during execution:

```
// do not allow changing this during execution
const int bus_width = 8;
```

If bus_width is used on the left-hand side of an equation in the design, the tool will produce an error.

In this section, we had a look at a few constructs for design. You may find some of them worthy of further investigation and use, but they are certainly optional, so use or ignore them as you see fit.

Next, let's look at convenient ways of packing and unpacking data.

Packing operators

Previously we have looked at index into arrays for packing and unpacking data. One operation we glossed over was the +: operation.

Indexed part select, +:, -:

We can index multiple bits of an array using the indexed part select. Most of the time if you are grabbing a byte from an array, you might use something like [7:0]. What happens if you want to break apart a 32-bit bus into bytes? You could create four index operations: [31:24], [23:16], [15:8], and [7:0]. We can also use the index part select as follows:

```
for (int i = 0; i < 4; i++) dout[i*8+:8]…
```

This will evaluate to the same 4 index values. Alternatively, there is the -: operation, which could also be used for a similar effect.

We can also use the streaming operator as discussed next.

Streaming operators

SystemVerilog provides operators that allow the easy packing and unpacking of data. These are the streaming operators, >> and <<. These operators are useful for both simulation and design, as we'll see in the following sections.

>>

The left-to-right stream fills data from low to high, as can be seen below. The format of both operators are {<<n{packed_array_out}}, where *n* defaults to a single bit but can be any integer. It represents the number of bits to move at a time from the source to the destination.

```
Packed data set to 76543210
…
Packing arrays into bytes
  packed byte        0: 10
  packed byte        1: 32
  packed byte        2: 54
  packed byte        3: 76
```

```
unpacked byte          0: 76
unpacked byte          1: 54
unpacked byte          2: 32
unpacked byte          3: 10
Packed data set to 76543210
Packed data set to 76543210
```

In this example, we create a packed array of 32'h76543210. We then use the left-to-right streaming operator to move data on 8-bit boundaries into a packed and unpacked array. You'll notice that when defining an unpacked array, loading it is the opposite. This is because when using the format

```
logic [7:0] unpacked_array_out[4];
```

it's equivalent to

```
logic [7:0] unpacked_array_out[0:3];
```

You can see streaming the packed and unpacked arrays back into the packed vector yields the initial results.

<<

The right-to-left stream effectively reverses the data, as can be seen below. We can see the operation of the << operator by unpacking and packing some data in simulation. See streaming.sv for the example.

```
Packed data set to 76543210
Packing arrays into bytes
   packed byte          0: 76
   packed byte          1: 54
   packed byte          2: 32
   packed byte          3: 10
unpacked byte          0: 10
unpacked byte          1: 32
unpacked byte          2: 54
unpacked byte          3: 76
Packed data set to 76543210
Packed data set to 76543210
```

Now let's look at some constructs for improving the simulation of your designs.

Exploring some more advanced verification constructs

The testing we have done thus far has been pretty simple, even when we used self-checking. There is one construct that I have found very useful over the years. The queue is easy to use and understand.

Introducing SystemVerilog queues

Often, you need to generate an input in a design that will produce an expected output sometime later. Examples of this are parsing engines, data processing engines, and, as we saw in *Chapter 10, A Better Way to Display – VGA*, the PS/2 interface.

When I modified the ps2_host module, I decided to upgrade the testbench for it using queues. I had to create a structure to define what I wanted to store in the queue:

```
typedef struct packed
  {
   logic [7:0] data;
   logic       parity;
  } ps2_rx_data_t;
```

This structure will store our expected data as we generate data in the ps2_host for testing.

A queue is defined as follows:

```
  ps2_rx_data_t ps2_rx_data[$];
```

It looks much like an unpacked array, except the size is defined as [$], which defines it as a queue that can be manipulated in tests. We can access the queue by pushing to the front or back and popping from the back or front. These functions, along with the size() operator, are the most useful for simulating. There are other functions for inserting or deleting, and I recommend further research if you think it might be useful for your application.

The following diagram shows the queue conceptually. Typically, you will push into one side and pop from the other. The choice is arbitrary. You will note that it's possible to push or pop from both sides, which can come in handy if you need to test the value on one side and possibly write it back to the same location:

Figure 14.4: SystemVerilog queue structure

This becomes useful in a testbench by storing what you expect to see. To do this for the ps2 testbench, I added the following to the send_key task. Since we know what we are sending into the PS/2 interface, we can store the expected output:

```
task send_key;
  input [7:0] keycode;
  input       error;
  ps2_rx_data_t local_data;
  begin
    local_data.data = keycode;
    local_data.parity = error;
    ps2_rx_data.push_front(local_data);
```

When the send_key task is called, we build the structure that represents the expected data and push it into the queue. I've replaced the checking function with the queue:

```
while (~done) begin
  while (!rx_valid) @(posedge clk);
  popped_data = ps2_rx_data.pop_back();
  exp_data    = popped_data.data;
  exp_user    = popped_data.parity;
  if ((exp_data != rx_data) ||
      (exp_user != rx_user)) begin
    $display("mismatch on output %d", valid_count);
    $display("exp_data = %h, exp_par = %b", exp_data, exp_user);
    $display("act_data = %h, act_par = %b", rx_data, rx_user);
    $stop;
  end else begin
    $display("output matched %d: %p", valid_count, popped_data);
  end
  valid_count++;
```

```
    @(posedge clk);
    if (valid_count == 16) done = '1;
end
```

Whenever there is an rx_valid signal, which indicates that RX data is available, the queue is popped and the data from the queue is compared to the data from the design. This is a good way of identifying errors in a design. In this testbench, we are checking a certain number of expected outputs. In other operations, you may use the size function to determine if there is data available:

```
if (popped_data.size() != 0)
```

Next, let's take a look at some improvements to the display system function.

Display formatting enhancements

We've used $display in our simulations. This system task is originally from SystemVerilog and it supported a way of displaying the basic types:

- %h, %H – Hexadecimal value
- %d, %D – Decimal value
- %b, %B – Binary value
- %m, %M – Hierarchical name
- %s, %S – String
- %t, %T – Time
- %f, %F – Real number in decimal format
- %e, %E – Real number in exponential format

If you use these as is, the display will pad data to fit the output. Here's an example:

```
int a, b;
$display("a=%h  b=%h", a, b);
// example output
A=00000001 b=0000FFFF
```

SystemVerilog offers a few enhancements. You can use %0h to completely remove leading 0s or %(number)h to limit the output to a certain number of digits. Also, %x can be used in the place of %h:

```
int a, b;
$display("a=%0x  b=%4x", a, b);
// example output
A=1 b=FFFF
```

%p allows you to print structures in a formatted fashion. I've modified tb_ps2.sv to use %p to print passing values:

```
$display("output matched %d: %p", valid_count, popped_data);
output matched        12: '{data:85,parity:1'b0}
output matched        13: '{data:170,parity:1'b0}
output matched        14: '{data:85,parity:1'b1}
output matched        15: '{data:170,parity:1'b1}
```

You can also display the name of an enumerated type by using .name:

```
enum bit {TRUE = 1'b1, FALSE = 1'b0} my_bool;
$display("The state of my_bool is %s", mybool.name);
```

SystemVerilog also adds $sformats, which is like $display, but it returns a string that you can pass into $display or a log.

I want to at least introduce you to assertions in SystemVerilog at a very high level. Assertions could take up a book all to themselves as verification is a topic unto itself.

A quick introduction to assertions

Assertions are a way of adding self-checking into your code. Assertions are generally ignored by synthesis, and they can be stored in separate files and bound to design modules. I won't go into assertions in depth here, but I encourage you to look into them via the link in the *Further reading* section. I would, however, like to introduce a few other assertions for displaying information. They behave like $display, but they have severity levels attached to them. These are as follows:

- $info
- $warning
- $error
- $fatal

These severity levels allow messages in a simulation to be filtered more easily. For example, you may want to mask $info messages or even $warning messages during long runs when the design is being regressed. There is another interesting use for $error or $fatal.

Using $error or $fatal in synthesis

Often, you may have a reusable module that will only work with certain combinations of parameters. You can use $error or $fatal to test for these conditions and cause synthesis to abort if they occur.

When using these tasks in this way, the evaluation needs to be static, such as testing a parameter setting. The test cannot be on something that can change such as signals to be synthesizable. For example, if we look back at *Chapter 4, Counting Button Presses*, and our seven-segment encoder, we might want to limit it to four or eight segments:

```
module seven_segment #(parameter NUM_SEGMENTS = 8, …
initial begin
  if (NUM_SEGMENTS != 4 || NUM_SEGMENTS != 8)
    $fatal("Number of segments must be set to 4 or 8");
end
```

In the preceding code snippet, if the number of segments is not 4 or 8, Vivado will fail the synthesis and record the user-defined error message.

Finally, let's take a look at some gotchas and things to watch out for.

Other gotchas and how to avoid them

As we near the end of our journey, there are a few more things that we should look at, along with how we can detect them or avoid them altogether: inferring single-bit wires, bit-width mismatches, upgrading or downgrading Vivado messages, and handling timing closure.

Inferring single-bit wires

Since the advent of Verilog, it has always been legal to use a wire without defining it. This can happen if it is a port on an instantiate module. There is an example project: https://github.com/PacktPublishing/The-FPGA-Programming-Handbook-Second-Edition/blob/main/CH14/SystemVerilog/build/inferred_wire.xpr.

You can see that I've created a variable-width adder module and connected three of them up:

```
adder #(4) u_add0 (.in0(SW[3:0]),   .in1(SW[7:4]),
                   .out(add0_out));
adder #(4) u_add1 (.in0(SW[11:8]), .in1(SW[15:12]),
                   .out(add1_out));
adder #(5) u_add2 (.in0(add0_out), .in1(add1_out),
                   .out(LED[5:0]));
```

There is no testbench, but if you try to simulate, you will get the following warnings:

```
WARNING: [VRFC 10-3091] actual bit length 1 differs from formal bit length
5 for port 'out' [/home/fbruno/git/books/The-FPGA-Programming-Handbook-
```

```
Second-Edition/CH14/SystemVerilog/hdl/inferred_wire.sv:16]
WARNING: [VRFC 10-3091] actual bit length 1 differs from formal bit length
5 for port 'out' [/home/fbruno/git/books/The-FPGA-Programming-Handbook-
Second-Edition/CH14/SystemVerilog/hdl/inferred_wire.sv:17]
WARNING: [VRFC 10-3091] actual bit length 1 differs from formal bit length
5 for port 'in0' [/home/fbruno/git/books/The-FPGA-Programming-Handbook-
Second-Edition/CH14/SystemVerilog/hdl/inferred_wire.sv:19]
```

You can see that single bit wires were inferred. To avoid these problems, uncomment the first and last lines of the file. `default_nettype allows us to define what happens with inferred wires. By specifying none, we tell the synthesis and simulation it's an error if we don't define the nettype of a signal. Now if we run it, you should see this:

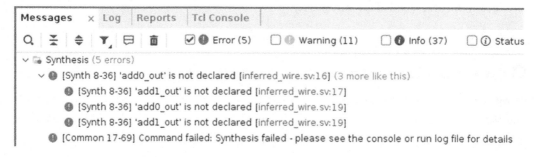

Figure 14.5: Synthesis errors with default_nettype none

It is best practice to always use default_nettype set to none at the top of a module and default_ nettype set to wire at the end. The latter is useful in the case of a legacy IP that may have inferred wires that you don't have the ability to change. Bit-width problems should not be overlooked.

Bit-width mismatches

Since it's only a warning, they can easily be overlooked; however, as the design is being developed, you should take care to watch for these issues.

We've talked about latches previously in *Chapter 3*, *Combinational Logic*, mentioning them in the *Creating combinational logic* section and warning about latches in the *Bringing it all together* section. We can use a feature of Vivado to upgrade warning messages to make latch inference an error.

Upgrading or downgrading Vivado messages

Vivado will display many messages during the design flow. As we discussed previously, latches should be considered an error if they are inferred.

I've created a project to illustrate this: https://github.com/PacktPublishing/The-FPGA-Programming-Handbook-Second-Edition/blob/main/CH14/SystemVerilog/build/latch_error.xpr.

Without tcl.pre in the project that I set up as specified in *Figure 14.5*, we would encounter the following warning. However, the design would generate a bitstream. If this is missed on something critical, such as a state machine, the design is destined to fail at some point:

```
WARNING: [Synth 8-327] inferring latch for variable 'LED_reg' [/home/
fbruno/git/books/The-FPGA-Programming-Handbook-Second-Edition/CH14/hdl/
latch_error.sv:9]
```

We can change the severity of any message in the flow by creating a tcl file, which is read in prior to synthesis:

```
set_msg_config -id {[Synth 8-327]} -new_severity ERROR
```

We will then specify to use this file prior to synthesis by changing an option in the synthesis settings:

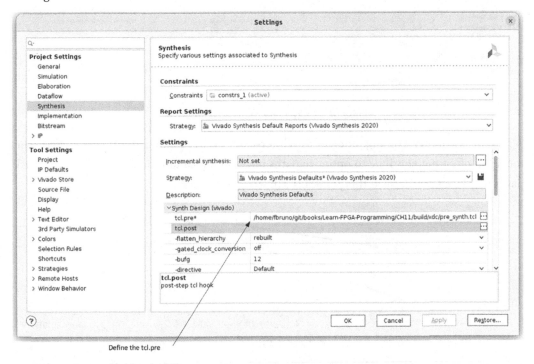

Figure 14.6: Setting up tcl.pre

Now, if you try to generate a bitstream, you will encounter the following:

```
ERROR: [Synth 8-327] inferring latch for variable 'LED_reg' [/home/fbruno/
git/books/The-FPGA-Programming-Handbook-Second-Edition/CH14/hdl/latch_
error.sv:9]
```

This same methodology can be used to promote or demote any message.

Finally, let's look at timing closure.

Handling timing closure

One of the biggest problems you will run into as a new design engineer is meeting the timing requirements in your designs. There are multiple sets of problems that you will encounter, as we have seen throughout the book. The first type of problem is missing a clock domain crossing. I've removed one of the constraints from the final project to demonstrate this failure:

Figure 14.7: Clock domain crossing problem

When you encounter a timing problem with inter-clock path violations, address them first. The tools will often not continue to optimize paths once timing cannot be met, so the intra-clock paths may be a false alarm at this point. Let's investigate the paths:

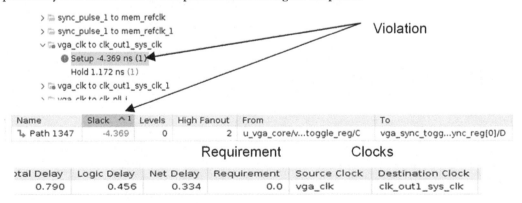

Figure 14.8: Timing violation report

Looking at the report we notice a couple of things. The first is the clock domains. We know we are crossing between two domains: vga_clk to clk_out1_sys_clk. The second is the requirement. When you see a requirement of 0, or sometimes a very small fraction of the clock period, you should realize that it's a clock domain problem. In this case, it is properly synchronized; I just removed the constraint.

The second type of failure is simply not having enough time in a clock period to do the operation as designed. This can be caused by any of the following:

- **Placement**: You can use pblock constraints to try to guide placement. This is hit or miss and is beyond the scope of this book.

- **Routing**: If you have a very high utilization, routing can become congested. Trying to redesign some paths to ease timing may help.

- **Too much logic in a path**: This can be resolved by adding pipelining or breaking up long paths if possible.

- **Lack of DSP pipelining**: This falls under the previous bullet of too much logic. If you are trying to do more than the DSP can handle without using some of the internal resources, you may need to evaluate adding pipeline stages.

If you are unable to fix the timing, the last possibility is to run the clock slower if possible.

We'll take a deeper look at addressing too much logic in the following section.

How to pipeline a design

We've seen that too much logic in a path can cause timing closure problems. This can be addressed in a few ways:

- Using aggressive optimizations
- Pipelining logic
- Pipelining DSP elements

Open up https://github.com/PacktPublishing/The-FPGA-Programming-Handbook-Second-Edition/blob/main/CH14/SystemVerilog/build/pipeline.xpr. This design implements a 32x64 bit multiplier, resulting in a 96-bit output:

```
always @(posedge clk) begin
  for (int i = 0; i <= PIPELINE; i++) begin
    if (i == 0) result[0] <= mult_a * mult_b;
    else        result[i] <= result[i-1];
  end
```

```
    if (button_1) result_rotate <= result[PIPELINE];
    else result_rotate <= {result_rotate[79:0],
                          result_rotate[95:80]};
  end
```

The core of the design is the multiplier. I've defined a PIPELINE parameter to enable the pipelining of the multiplier in the event if we cannot make timing. The way PIPELINE works is to add register stages after the multiplier, as we can see in *Figure 14.9*:

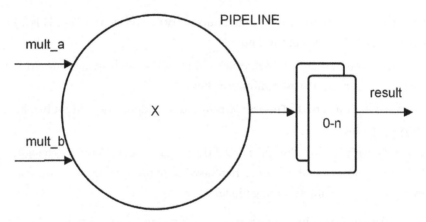

Figure 14.9: Pipeline before retiming

We are trying to do this in one clock cycle. I've set the clock frequency to 200 MHz to challenge the tool. This results in a timing failure, as shown in *Figure 14.9*:

Timing	Setup	Hold	Pulse Width
Worst Negative Slack (WNS):	-2.454 ns		
Total Negative Slack (TNS):	-257.8 ns		
Number of Failing Endpoints:	125		
Total Number of Endpoints:	535		
Implemented Timing Report			

Figure 14.10: 32x64-bit multiplier timing failure

As a first step, we can try adjusting the synthesis and implementation settings:

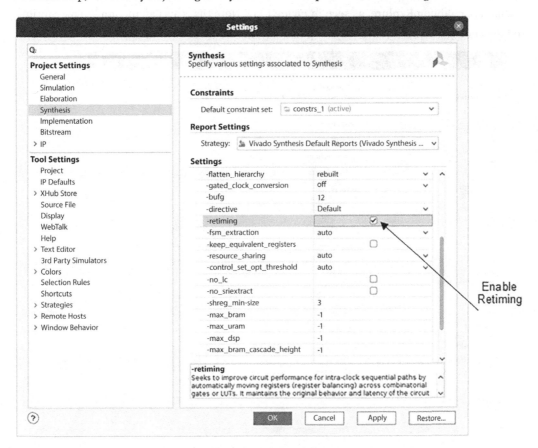

Figure 14.11: Synthesis options

We also want to enable opt_design and phys_opt_design, as well as play with some of the options, in this case enabling **Explore**, as seen in *Figure 14.12*. Note that this can incur a longer runtime, and depending on how achievable your goals are, it could incur a runtime penalty.

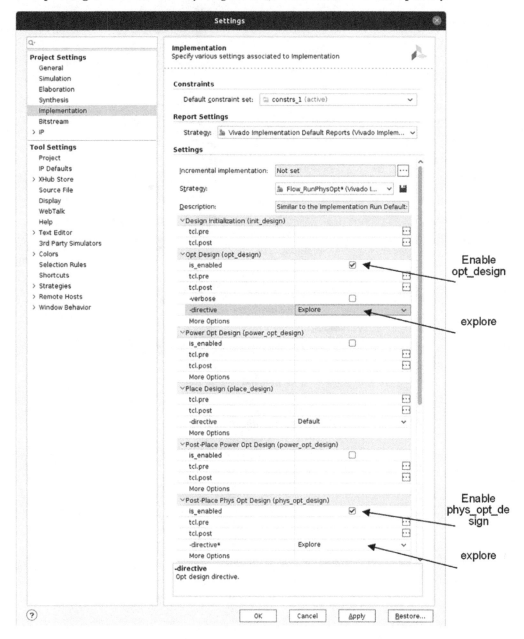

Figure 14.12: Implementation options

With these implementation options set, we can try another attempt at meeting timing. We are now met with a slightly smaller timing violation:

Timing	Setup	Hold	Pulse Width
Worst Negative Slack (WNS):	-2.376 ns		
Total Negative Slack (TNS):	-250.84 ns		
Number of Failing Endpoints:	125		
Total Number of Endpoints:	535		
Implemented Timing Report			

Figure 14.13: Advanced settings timing report

This is obviously not enough to significantly change the results, but it did buy us a little time. Now we can try to add some pipelining. I've made the design such that we can insert pipelining after the math operation. Retiming can move these registers into the design to break up long timing paths. This can be done on logic, DSP elements, and BRAMs. Let's initially try setting PIPELINE = 1 in the **General** settings tab:

Timing	Setup	Hold	Pulse Width
Worst Negative Slack (WNS):	-1.139 ns		
Total Negative Slack (TNS):	-101.029 ns		
Number of Failing Endpoints:	97		
Total Number of Endpoints:	631		
Implemented Timing Report			

Figure 14.14: PIPELINE=1 timing report

This setting actually uses the inserted registers to break up some of the external timing paths, leaving the DSP block intact. You can see this by looking at the schematic in Vivado and searching for the result registers.

Finally, if we set PIPELINE = 2 in the general settings and rerun, we'll see that retiming will push our design over the edge into positive slack:

Timing	Setup	Hold	Pulse Width
Worst Negative Slack (WNS):	0.444 ns		
Total Negative Slack (TNS):	0 ns		
Number of Failing Endpoints:	0		
Total Number of Endpoints:	617		
Implemented Timing Report			

Figure 14.15: PIPELINE=2 timing report

We gain this positive slack by the retiming engine pushing one set of registers into the multiplier. Conceptually, this would look like *Figure 14.16*:

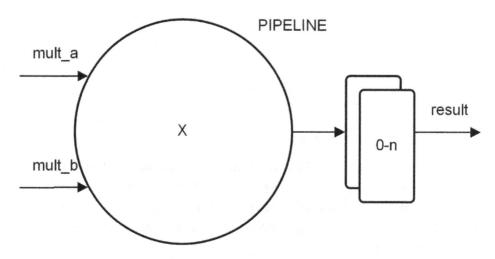

Figure 14.16: PIPELINE=2 Conceptual

This section should have given you some ideas about addressing timing problems. Sometimes, you do need to go a little deeper and rewrite the code. For example, the 32*64 multiplier could be broken into two 32*32 multipliers plus an adder, which I'll leave as an exercise for you.

Hopefully, this chapter has provided some additional resources and things to watch out for as you design your own projects.

Summary

In this chapter, we looked at some more advanced and lesser-used SystemVerilog constructs. The main one is interfaces, which allow better design reuse and encapsulation. We investigated some more advanced looping, structures, and labels.

We also looked at some more advanced verification constructs. These will help you as your designs grow and get more complex.

Finally, we looked at some gotchas, how to avoid them, and some basics of timing closure.

You've now completed the book and should be able to tackle some tasks on your own. As I mentioned at the beginning, there are many community efforts, such as the Mister Project, that could use some people with FPGA knowledge. There are also projects you can try to tackle on your own to land a job. Whatever you choose, I hope that you find it as fun and rewarding as I do.

Questions

1. Interfaces are useful for:

    a. Encapsulating signals belonging together

    b. Encapsulating functions, tasks, and assertions associated with the interface

    c. Changing a design deeply embedded within other designs

    d. All of the above

2. Structures can be assigned by:

    a. Component

    b. Name

    c. Interface

    d. (a) and (b)

3. Block labels allow the easier matching of begin...end blocks.

    a. True

    b. False

4. If we want to exit a loop, we can use:

    a. break on any loop

    b. disable on any loop label

    c. break on an outer loop or disable on any loop label

5. Continue can be used to skip the rest of a loop.

    a. True

    b. False

6. Queues are useful for:

    a. Creating a flexible FIFO for use in verification

    b. Creating a flexible FIFO for use in design and verification

    c. Nothing

7. What does the following code snippet do?

```
initial begin
  if (NUM_SEGMENTS != 4 || NUM_SEGMENTS != 8)
    $fatal("This design only supports 4 or 8 segments");
  end
end
```

    a. Cause a fatal error in simulation that means the design can only support 4 or 8 segments

    b. Cause a fatal error in synthesis that means the design can only support 4 or 8 segments

    c. All of the above

8. Things to watch out for in designs are:

    a. Accidently inferring single-bit wires

    b. Mismatched bit widths

    c. Latch inference

    d. Clock domain crossing issues

    e. All of the above

9. We have seen that we can use retiming to implement a 32x64 multiplier. In that section, I mentioned that you can implement this as two 32x32 multipliers and an adder. Write the SystemVerilog to implement this. Bonus: Does your implementation need to change if you implement signed multiplication?

Answers

1. d

2. d

3. a

4. c

5. a

6. a

7. c

8. e

Further reading

For more information about what was covered in the chapter, please refer to the following:

- `https://www.doulos.com/knowhow/systemverilog/systemverilog-tutorials/systemverilog-assertions-tutorial/`

Join our community on Discord

Join our community's Discord space for discussions with the authors and other readers:

`https://packt.link/embedded`

`packt.com`

Subscribe to our online digital library for full access to over 7,000 books and videos, as well as industry leading tools to help you plan your personal development and advance your career. For more information, please visit our website.

Why subscribe?

- Spend less time learning and more time coding with practical eBooks and Videos from over 4,000 industry professionals
- Improve your learning with Skill Plans built especially for you
- Get a free eBook or video every month
- Fully searchable for easy access to vital information
- Copy and paste, print, and bookmark content

At www.packt.com, you can also read a collection of free technical articles, sign up for a range of free newsletters, and receive exclusive discounts and offers on Packt books and eBooks.

Other Books You May Enjoy

If you enjoyed this book, you may be interested in these other books by Packt:

Developing IoT Projects with ESP32 – Second Edition

Vedat Ozan Oner

ISBN: 978-1-80323-768-8

- Explore ESP32 with IDE and debugging tools for effective IoT creation
- Drive GPIO, I2C, multimedia, and storage for seamless integration of external devices
- Utilize handy IoT libraries to enhance your ESP32 projects
- Manage WiFi like a pro with STA & AP modes, provisioning, and ESP Rainmaker framework features
- Ensure robust IoT security with secure boot and OTA firmware updates

- Harness AWS IoT for data handling and achieve stunning visualization using Grafana
- Enhance your projects with voice capabilities using ESP AFE and Speech Recognition
- Innovate with tinyML on ESP32-S3 and the Edge Impulse platform

Solutions Architect's Handbook – Third Edition

Saurabh Shrivastava

Neelanjali Srivastav

ISBN: 978-1-83508-423-6

- Explore various roles of a solutions architect in the enterprise
- Apply design principles for high-performance, cost-effective solutions
- Choose the best strategies to secure your architectures and boost availability
- Develop a DevOps and CloudOps mindset for collaboration, operational efficiency, and streamlined production
- Apply machine learning, data engineering, LLMs, and generative AI for improved security and performance
- Modernize legacy systems into cloud-native architectures with proven real-world strategies
- Master key solutions architect soft skills

Packt is searching for authors like you

If you're interested in becoming an author for Packt, please visit `authors.packtpub.com` and apply today. We have worked with thousands of developers and tech professionals, just like you, to help them share their insight with the global tech community. You can make a general application, apply for a specific hot topic that we are recruiting an author for, or submit your own idea.

Share your thoughts

Now you've finished *The FPGA Programming Handbook - Second Edition*, we'd love to hear your thoughts! Scan the QR code below to go straight to the Amazon review page for this book and share your feedback or leave a review on the site that you purchased it from.

https://packt.link/r/1805125591

Your review is important to us and the tech community and will help us make sure we're delivering excellent quality content.

Index

Download a free PDF copy of this book

Thanks for purchasing this book!

Do you like to read on the go but are unable to carry your print books everywhere?

Is your eBook purchase not compatible with the device of your choice?

Don't worry, now with every Packt book you get a DRM-free PDF version of that book at no cost.

Read anywhere, any place, on any device. Search, copy, and paste code from your favorite technical books directly into your application.

The perks don't stop there, you can get exclusive access to discounts, newsletters, and great free content in your inbox daily.

Follow these simple steps to get the benefits:

1. Scan the QR code or visit the link below:

https://packt.link/free-ebook/9781805125594

2. Submit your proof of purchase.
3. That's it! We'll send your free PDF and other benefits to your email directly.